Discovering Qualitative Methods

Field Research, Interviews, and Analysis

SECOND EDITION

Carol A. B. Warren
UNIVERSITY OF KANSAS

Tracy Xavia Karner
UNIVERSITY OF HOUSTON

New York   Oxford
OXFORD UNIVERSITY PRESS
2010

Oxford University Press, Inc., publishes works that further Oxford University's
objective of excellence in research, scholarship, and education.

Oxford   New York
Auckland   Cape Town   Dar es Salaam   Hong Kong   Karachi
Kuala Lumpur   Madrid   Melbourne   Mexico City   Nairobi
New Delhi   Shanghai   Taipei   Toronto

With offices in
Argentina   Austria   Brazil   Chile   Czech Republic   France   Greece
Guatemala   Hungary   Italy   Japan   Poland   Portugal   Singapore
South Korea   Switzerland   Thailand   Turkey   Ukraine   Vietnam

Copyright © 2010 by Oxford University Press, Inc.

Published by Oxford University Press, Inc.
198 Madison Avenue, New York, New York 10016
http://www.oup.com

Oxford is a registered trademark of Oxford University Press

Library of Congress Cataloging-in-Publication Data

Warren, Carol A. B., 1944–
Discovering qualitative methods : field research, interviews, and
analysis / Carol A. B. Warren.—2nd ed.
p. cm.
Includes bibliographical references and index.
ISBN 978-0-19-538429-1 (alk. paper)
1. Social sciences—Research—Methodology. I. Title.
H62.W2833 2009
001.4'3—dc22
2008050498

Printed in the United States of America
on acid-free paper

To the many people who have shared their lives with us, both personally and sociologically.

Contents

PART III

Preface

Welcome to the Study of Qualitative Methods

This book is for students who want to learn about, and perhaps do, research using qualitative methods—field research or ethnography, interviewing, and the use of documents, images, and the internet in social research. Although it is primarily based on our experience teaching sociology undergraduates, it will also be a useful reference text for graduate students, or students in fields such as anthropology that use qualitative approaches. Qualitative methods have a rich and lengthy history in anthropology, but a shorter one in other social science disciplines. It wasn't until the early twentieth century that our sociology colleagues began to fully acknowledge the utility and insight of qualitative inquiry. During the last few decades, qualitative methods have also become more commonplace in fields as diverse as business, education, and communication studies.

The past few decades have also seen increasing interest in interdisciplinary research and teaching. Researchers who use qualitative methods often have research interests that overlap with other disciplines, including the humanities as well as the other social sciences. Although the main focus of this book is social science research, we are also concerned to some extent with cultural studies, feminist theory, postmodernism, journalism, visual studies, and other interdisciplinary areas. Although many of the examples we use to illustrate our points are from qualitative sociological research, we also draw examples from these other fields from time to time.

All research is embedded in a particular society at a particular time and place, and reflects that society's ethical, political, economic, scholarly, and practical concerns. Field research and interviewing are specific methods of social research that have been used at least since the early nineteenth century in America and other countries, but the ways in which they were conceptualized and used were different in the 1920s than they are today. The use of documents and images was common in 1920s social research, but the internet as a source of documents and images is new.

Today, we are living in a global and globalizing society. Students who want to understand the impact of American industrialism and media on other economies and cultures can use qualitative methods locally to further this understanding. Many qualitative studies focus on the global through the lens of the local; within the United States, you could study Hispanic immigrant groups in California, Vietnamese workers in meat processing plants in Kansas, or Laotian churches in rural Missouri.

Whatever your research setting, there are many interesting issues in qualitative research to explore and discuss. We have prepared instructional materials, to complement this text, that provide further examples and exercises for increasing your qualitative research knowledge. There is also a website at the University of Houston (www.researchroom.uh.edu), developed by Karner, that you might find helpful. It provides a good overview of both qualitative and quantitative social science research methods, and is linked to this text.

Throughout the book, we will focus on just what qualitative research *is* and what unique insights and opportunities the qualitative approach offers the investigator. A qualitative approach to research seeks to explore the social construction of reality—how groups and individuals define situations and give meaning to their experiences and surroundings. Qualitative researchers recognize that research "findings" are not independent of the methods used to produce those findings, or of the standpoints and perspectives of the researcher.

Although all qualitative research methods are focused on understanding the social construction of reality, there are differences between field research, interviewing, and the use of documents, both epistemologically and in the conduct of the research. Ethnographic research focuses on behavior and interaction as well as talk, in the present, while interviews focus on talk, or accounts, that may include the past or future as well as the present. Both, however, focus on the lived experience of individuals and their meaning worlds. As anthropologist Ruth Behar notes:

> I came to ethnography because I wanted to be a storyteller who told stories about real people in real places. I was seduced by the notion of fieldwork, the idea of going some place to find a story I wasn't looking for.... The beauty and mystery of the ethnographer's quest is to find

the unexpected stories, the stories that challenge our theories. Isn't that the reason why we still go to the field? ... We go to find the stories we didn't know we were looking for in the first place. (Behar 2003, 16)

As you have undoubtedly experienced in other classes and in your everyday life, documents and images from libraries and from the internet can also be the source of the stories described by Behar.

Like stories themselves, the qualitative research process follows a certain sequence: research question(s); conceptualizing the study; designing the study; preparations, human subjects, and Institutional Review Board (IRB) issues; beginning the study; recording data; completing the interviewing or leaving the field; and, eventually, finalizing the study by writing a research report, article, or book. Unlike the stages of quantitative research, however, the steps we take in qualitative studies are not discrete; rather, they overlap and flow together as research discoveries are made.

Plan of the Book

Part I of *Discovering Qualitative Methods* introduces the logic, purpose, and history of the methods, and the politics and ethics associated with using them. Chapter 1 examines the epistemology—knowledge foundations—of qualitative methods, and the various approaches to field research and interviewing. In this chapter we discuss the history of qualitative methods in anthropology and sociology, from the Chicago School of the early 1900s to the current debates over postmodernism. The outcomes and purposes of qualitative research are also presented in this chapter, from the student papers written by undergraduates in sociology classes to the final reports provided by applied researchers who have obtained federal grant money to conduct their research.

Among the most important issues in doing qualitative research discussed in Chapter 2 are the politics and ethics of dealing with human subjects. When researchers conduct qualitative field research and interviewing, they interact with, talk to, and perhaps develop relationships of various kinds with people, individually and in groups. This interactive basis of qualitative research brings with it a good deal of personal and social responsibility, as well as various bureaucratic and legal issues. In the process of conducting qualitative research, both students and professionals are functioning not only as researchers, but also as concerned citizens and individuals, and as representatives of the colleges or universities sponsoring the research.

Part II, which focuses on doing qualitative research, begins with Chapter 3 on settings for and entrée to field research. In this chapter we talk about the kinds of settings that might be useful and interesting for both individual and team student researchers in terms of feasibility, cost, and IRB issues.

The various advantages and disadvantages of being a member or not being a member of the setting, and of being open or secretive about one's research purposes (overt versus covert research), are discussed in this chapter. Issues of entrée into different kinds of settings by different individuals, and the relevancies of gender, age, social status, and other researcher characteristics, are also covered.

As fieldwork continues over time, roles and relationships are offered, formed, and re-formed; this is the topic of Chapter 4. A researcher may intend to take on a particular kind of role within the setting, but the people in the setting may incorporate the researcher in a way that reflects their own interests and relevancies. Research over time often involves research bargains between the setting members and the field researchers, including emotional, practical, and financial involvements. Since field research is based on personal knowing, various kinds of relationships may be formed in the field, including at times the emotional and the sexual. Usually, in the end, the researcher must leave the field.

The central task of writing fieldnotes is discussed in Chapter 5. In field research, fieldnotes are the data—what has been recorded about the interaction and talk within the setting. The writing of fieldnotes must be consistent and systematic, so a commitment to this part of the task is vital. We urge student researchers to use computers for their research, because of the flexibility of this particular technology. Student researchers' fieldnotes will probably be supervised by instructors and may be read by fellow students; themes for analysis in these fieldnotes can come from both the readers and the writers. Fieldnotes must be read and reread thoroughly in order to form the basis for qualitative analysis.

In Chapter 6, the first steps toward interview research are discussed. Qualitative research involves a particular type of interview, known by various names; the one we have chosen is qualitative interview. The qualitative interview involves an interviewer (or perhaps more than one), an interviewee (or perhaps more than one), and a topic. This chapter begins with a consideration of the interview topic, since it is with a topic in mind that students generally begin to think of interview research. Armed with a subject matter that is of interest to the researcher and, it is hoped, to the interview respondents, too, the researcher develops specific interview questions and begins the process of locating and selecting respondents.

Chapter 7 discusses the interview as social interaction, talk, and process. An interview has elements similar to any other social interaction, including greeting and leaving rituals and question-and-answer sequences. It also takes place in a particular language, evoking specific linguistic meanings for respondent and interviewer. Qualitative interviews are typically recorded for audio, and may also be video recorded. After the interview, the recorded interview should be transcribed in its entirety either by the researcher or by someone else involved in the research. In this chapter we also consider what kinds of data are produced by interviews.

In Chapter 8, we turn our attention to qualitative research using texts, images, or documents. One contemporary data source is the internet, particularly those websites where individuals interact textually, such as chat rooms and support groups. Another source of both contemporary and historical materials can be found in the mass media. In this chapter, we discuss the analysis of magazines and advertisements in qualitative research on gender, both by social scientists and scholars involved in cultural studies. We also explore visual sociology, and the various uses of photographic, video, and other imagery in the field. The chapter includes a discussion of the use of historical documents as sources of data: voices from the past and present brought alive by the sociological researcher.

The focus of Part III is on the analysis, presentation, and writing up of qualitative data. At this point in the process, all your data from fieldwork, interviews, and documents are in the form of text as fieldnotes, interview transcripts, and copies or summaries of visual or textual material. All along, you—the researcher—will have been reading and rereading, thinking and rethinking these materials, beginning to identify analytic themes and patterns in your data. Once you have left the field or completed the interviews, it is time to focus fully on the analysis of qualitative data, which is discussed in Chapter 9. We outline the various stages and processes that one goes through in developing a full and thickly analytic description. Analysis is a time-consuming yet vital part of producing compelling qualitative research.

In Chapter 10, we talk about writing up qualitative studies, which—unless you are an ethnographic documentary filmmaker—is the most common endpoint of qualitative research. We discuss various potential audiences for your written paper, report, or book (probably limited to your instructor at this point), and how to write the paper. The various sections of the paper are discussed in this chapter, using examples from published qualitative research papers. The finished paper includes an abstract, introduction, background material, review of the substantive literature, review of the theoretical or conceptual literature, a methods section, findings from the data, and a discussion or conclusions.

Throughout the book we rely heavily on our own work for examples, especially when using fieldnotes and interview transcripts or examining the construction of published papers and visual and historical analysis. This reliance on our own work is not because we regard it as more exemplary than others'. Rather, we use fieldnote and interview examples from our own work, such as Warren's fieldnotes in Chapter 5, because we know them—how they were inscribed, stored, analyzed, used—and because in sociology, fieldnotes are often private documents. We use interview transcripts that we have worked with extensively, because we are deeply familiar with the material in them. We also use examples from qualitative work that describes methods in detail, such as Gary Alan Fine's (1996) observations of restaurant kitchens. And we use our own published work to discuss analysis and writing, because we know how we did it.

We hope that you will enjoy this book, and that it will be helpful to you as you begin to conduct qualitative research. You are at the beginning of a journey that may be short—one or two academic quarters; a semester—or long, the beginning of a career that involves using qualitative methods. Whichever it is, we wish you luck, success, and the joy of immersing yourself in the meaning worlds of others, in finding the unexpected stories you did not know you were looking for, and of learning, doing, and being as you take this journey. Welcome to the study of qualitative research.

Acknowledgments

First, both of us are thankful to have had each other in this endeavor, together with the support of Sherith Pankratz, Whitney Laemmli, and Miriam Sicilia of Oxford University Press. We are grateful especially to Bob Emerson, Anne Vittoria, and the many anonymous reviewers who read all or part of this manuscript and generously provided insights and enthusiasm for our efforts. Thanks also to those qualitative researchers whose important contributions we have used extensively, including Jack Katz, Jay Gubrium, Jim Holstein, Gary Fine, Mitchell Duneier, Patti and Peter Adler, Barrie Thorne, Cathy Greenblat, Doug Harper, Eric Margolis, Jerome Krase, D. Angus Vail, Viktoria Gotting, Michael Ball, Jerome Crowder, Caroline Knowles, Steven Gold, Sarah N. Gatson, Amanda Zweerink, Jane Adams, and Anita Wilson. We relied on the work of many other gifted qualitative researchers—far too numerous to mention—without which this book (and our own research) would certainly be impoverished.

We could not have done this without the invaluable assistance of Kathi Kirigin with computer and life matters (on Carol's end), and the supportive friendship of Carey Shuart, Ed Hill, Suzanne Bloom, Sara Clark, Heather Hales, and Jerome Crowder (on Tracy's end). We have both been lucky to have had the support of our colleagues (Carol's at the University of Kansas and Tracy's at the University of Houston), without which a project such as this might never have come to fruition. Tracy adds a note of gratitude to her International Visual Sociology Association (IVSA) colleagues for their friendship, inspiring work, and willingness to venture beyond the expected.

Considerable time has passed since Tracy first sat in Carol's Field Methods class at the University of Kansas back in the fall of 1989. This was an intellectual turning point for Tracy, the beginnings of a collaborative friendship, and an introduction to the methods that continue to inform her research to this day. Carol began her qualitative journey in Jack Douglas's PhD seminars at the University of California in 1970, following her general methodological training at San Diego State University. Thus, we both come out of the "California School," though once removed on Tracy's part, and we are especially thankful to the teachers and colleagues we have had the pleasure to know and learn from over the years. This includes our students, from whom we have had the opportunity to learn our methods anew each semester.

Coming from an interactionist perspective, we are acutely aware of the importance of others in our intellectual development, and in sharing the enchantment of the qualitative approach to understanding social life. And so, it is to all those colleagues and scholars who have gone before us, and to all the social scientists to come, that we dedicate this work. A labor of love and delight, this book is our challenge to readers to "get into the field" and use these methods to see and learn about your social world.

Go forth and do good (qualitative) work.

Carol A. B. Warren
Coronado, CA

Tracy Xavia Karner
Woodland Heights, TX

PART I

Chapter 1

Introduction to Qualitative Methods

Think about happiness. Imagine someone asking you, "Are you happy?" You might start to answer, but then you would probably stop and say to yourself, What does this question mean: am I happy now, or in general? What IS happiness, anyway? What if I'm happy at work, but not at school? How can I answer a general question truthfully? Then, suppose the questioner wants you to give a number to your happiness: 5—very happy, 4—somewhat happy, 3—neither happy nor unhappy, 2—somewhat unhappy, 1—very unhappy. Then what would you say?

Now, think about the relationship of education to income. You are in school working towards your degree. Your Aunt Harriet did not finish high school, but she started her own business and last year made two million dollars. Does this mean that the less educated you are the more you are likely to earn? Obviously not.

Happiness is a qualitative matter, to be studied qualitatively; the relationship between education and income is quantitative, to be studied quantitatively. Putting our two topics together, you could study the relationship between education and income quantitatively, then you could try to find out, qualitatively, how happy people are with the match between their education and their income. There are specific quantitative methods and procedures for the first question, and specific qualitative methods and procedures for the second—which is the purpose of this book.

Not only do quality and quantity require different methods, they also have a different underlying logic: a logic sometimes referred to as *epistemology*. It is important to understand this foundation before you go on to learn, and put into practice, the specific methods of qualitative research. Qualitative methods also have a history, which is important both in itself and to the extent that it shapes the present. And qualitative methods have a variety of purposes that range from the wish to change some aspect of society to the desire to capture it on film. This chapter is a discussion of the logic, history, purposes, and specific methods of qualitative inquiry, including field research, interviewing, and the analysis of documents and images.

Although field research and interviewing are described in detail in Chapters 3 through 7, a brief definition of these methods is in order here. Both methods involve, ideally, face-to-face interaction with respondents, although some qualitative researchers use the telephone or internet for interviewing when issues of cost or distance make this advisable. Both methods, since they involve people interacting, are heavily dependent on the social characteristics of the people involved—both researchers and respondents—and thus are "experience near" processes (Geertz [1973] 2000, [1983] 2000).

Field research or *ethnography* (sometimes referred to as participant observation or naturalistic observation) involves present-time face-to-face interaction in a setting, which can be anything from a bus stop to a casino to a small town. The field researcher enters and spends a certain amount of time interacting and observing in the setting—more time in a larger and more complex setting such as the small town, less time in a smaller and less complex setting such as the bus stop (the casino lies somewhere in between; one might go there at least once a week for a few months). The fieldworker takes extensive fieldnotes (see Chapter 5) as soon as possible after leaving the field; these fieldnotes then become the basis for ethnographic analysis.

Qualitative interviewing involves present-time face-to-face interaction, telephone contact, or mediated communication through the internet. The topic of the interview may be related to the past or future as well as to the present. The most common format of the interview is a dyad (one interviewer and one respondent), but there may be triadic interviews (one researcher and two respondents; for example, a married couple) or focus group interviews (one or two researchers and a group of respondents). Prior to the actual interviews, the researcher has developed—from general research questions—ten to fifteen actual interview questions, which are intended to address the topic of specific interest, whether this topic is the experience of HIV/AIDS, working-class graduate students, or motherhood. These questions form the basis for eliciting narrative stories from respondents, which are recorded and then transcribed to serve as the data for analysis.

Although field research and interviewing have been the major qualitative methods, visual and documentary materials can also be studied from a social constructionist perspective. With these methods, instead of "hanging around" a setting or asking questions, the researcher may be limited to what can be found (as with historical data), or may be unable to verify through observation claims such as age and gender (as with internet data). Gold mines of material in visual and textual form still await qualitative researchers, as we shall see in later chapters.

Qualitative and quantitative social research display similarities and differences. Both kinds of research involve a commitment to understanding others, and some dedication to learning or being trained in the specific methods. But quantitative methods are more programmatic (see Box 1.1), beginning with existing social theory and proceeding to the generation of hypotheses from that theory. Data collection consists of devising instruments and measures to transmute social interactions, behaviors, or attitudes into numbers. Analysis is accomplished by means of statistics, with the researcher designing and interpreting the statistical findings to either disprove or support the hypotheses. Contrast the approach of qualitative research in Box 1.2 with the quantitative procedure in Box 1.1. In qualitative research, you—or you

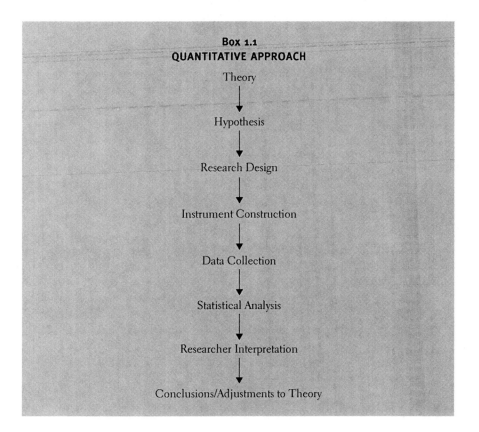

Box 1.1
QUANTITATIVE APPROACH

Theory

↓

Hypothesis

↓

Research Design

↓

Instrument Construction

↓

Data Collection

↓

Statistical Analysis

↓

Researcher Interpretation

↓

Conclusions/Adjustments to Theory

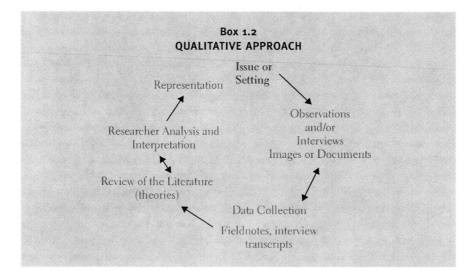

Box 1.2
QUALITATIVE APPROACH

Issue or
Setting

Representation

Observations
and/or
Interviews
Images or Documents

Researcher Analysis and
Interpretation

Review of the Literature
(theories)

Data Collection
Fieldnotes, interview
transcripts

In her recent work *Alive with Alzheimer's*, Cathy Stein Greenblat (2004) visually documents many of the social meanings of sleep found in care facilities. Here one resident is "dozing off" in the day room. *Copyright © 2004 by Cathy Greenblat. Excerpted from Alive with Alzheimer's. All rights reserved. Used with permission.*

and your team—are responsible for all stages of the research enterprise. Additionally, qualitative research is "experience near" (Geertz [1973] 2000, [1983] 2000)—close to other people and social settings—while quantitative research generates "experience distant" numerical summaries of social life.

The value of qualitative research in sociology has been discussed and debated for decades. While quantitative research can capture important statistical relationships—such as the relationship between gender and income—it is not well adapted to interpretive or social constructionist understandings. Statistics may record relationships between income and gender, but the meaning of being a single mother with a low income, raising small children with little help from an ex-husband, relatives, or the state, can be captured sociologically only by using qualitative methods. Both the statistical and the qualitative are significant components of understanding gender, class, and income in the United States. However, many aspects of social life can only be illuminated using qualitative approaches.

As an example, consider the meaning of sleep. We all know, individually, what sleep is—we get a good night's sleep, we toss and turn, we count sheep, we have insomnia. But in Jaber Gubrium's wonderful ethnography *Living and Dying at Murray Manor* (1975), the social meanings of sleep are illuminated. In this study of a nursing home, Gubrium explored what he called the different "social worlds" of elderly residents, lower-level staff, and upper-level staff. The residents "passed time" in various ways at Murray Manor, one of which was sleeping. Gubrium describes some of the shared social meanings of sleep (1975, 179–180):

> Where one sleeps to pass time makes a difference in how the sleeping is evaluated by others. Sleeping in bed most of the day is judged negatively, but spending nearly as much time sleeping in the Manor's lobby or lounges is considered just a matter of dozing off. The former is believed to be a deliberate plan to *just* sleep, whereas the latter is treated as one of those things that "happens" when it gets warm and quiet. Dozing off is defined as an event that "happens," even though for some patients and residents it happens fairly systematically.

Judgments about sleeping are made not only by the lower-level staff, but by the residents themselves, feeding into the patients' hierarchical status system. Patients may "boast that they 'don't sleep around all day like some others in this place do'" (1975, 179), thus laying claim to a more "normal adult" status than other more "deteriorated" residents.

The Logic of Qualitative Inquiry

The logic or epistemology of qualitative inquiry is referred to in a number of ways by qualitative methodologists; our chosen term among these alternatives is *social constructionism* (another common term is naturalism). Social constructionism takes the position that sociologists' knowledge about social life (or any other knowledge about anything, for that matter) involves both understanding the meaning that interaction has for the participants and realizing that any analysis of society is made from some standpoint or perspective that informs the analysis. Let us look at these assumptions in turn.

As you probably know from introductory and other sociology courses, sociology seeks to explore both the macro level of social structure and the micro level of social interaction. From the first assumption of social constructionism, it is clear that analysis is directed toward the micro level. Social constructionists use qualitative methods to try to understand the meanings that people bring to the social worlds they inhabit and construct—their relationships, groups, organizations, communities, or subcultures. And they use the methods to analyze documents and images generated by sources ranging from thirteenth-century self-help books to the internet.

To understand the second assumption of social constructionism, it is necessary to make some contrasts between constructionism and positivism (the logic of quantitative methods) as epistemologies. *Positivism* involves a "camera" theory of knowledge, in which it is assumed that if you have a good camera (research design) and film (methods), you can achieve an objective "photo" of whatever aspect of society you are studying. Any cameraperson trained to use the research design and methods (camera and film) correctly would "take the same picture" as any other cameraperson. Of course, we now realize that photographs are constructed, sometimes through direct manipulation with Photoshop, and always through the photographer's point of view. The choices of lens, setting, and where to point the camera all influence the resulting image. In spite of this, though, photographs are still treated as evidentiary in many cases—as accurate, objective documents of something that has occurred.

This "objective" conception of knowing is often compared with "subjective" knowing based on individual feeling or intuition and social constructionism is often wrongly described as subjective. Social constructionism proposes that sociological knowledge of the social world is neither objective nor subjective, but intersubjective—based on the shared meanings and understandings of the people being studied, and the shared meanings and understandings of the disciplinary community (qualitative sociologists) doing the studying.

While social constructionism and qualitative methods do not always go together, they often do, since field research and interviewing are ideally suited for exploring members' meanings and understandings. Similarly, although positivism and quantitative methods do not always go together, they, too, are ideally suited to one another. Quantitative methods seek to render social life in numerical patterns, whether by surveys related to the macro level of society or numerical scales related to the micro level.

GENERALIZABILITY, VALIDITY, AND RELIABILITY

Those of you familiar with any of social science's general methods texts are aware that there are inherent fundamental concerns: among these are generalizability, validity, and reliability. The purpose of positivist, often quantitative research is to *generalize* from the sample you are studying to the population from which the sample is drawn; for example, from your survey data of a random sample of five hundred people to the population of Wichita, Kansas. This generalizability is made possible by various random-sampling procedures, just as random assignment to experimental and control groups ensures generalizability in experimental research. Qualitative epistemology is based on the premise that social actors create emergent social worlds specific to time and place. Thus, the notion of generalizability for qualitative inquiry is concerned with social processes (such as power structures, insiders versus outsiders, or gender relations) that might be relevant in more than a single setting or interaction. So, when a qualitative researcher uses the term "generalizability" (and they seldom do), the reference is not to the statistical relation of the sample to the greater population, but to common patterns in social interaction and social life.

Qualitative researchers generate thickly descriptive analysis to persuade the reader that the interpretation is plausible, and might or might not be found in other places and at other times. One such example comes from ethnographies of bars, which have been done off and on during the past twenty years in various parts of the United States. Obviously, many types of bars exist in many kinds of areas—rural bars with a farm clientele, urban "leather" gay bars, hotel bars serving wealthy travelers, and so on. There are clear differences. But there are also similarities among these bars, such as distinctions between regulars and strangers; the fact that social behavior is loosened by alcohol; a workplace culture with typifications of customers; and often gendered and perhaps sexualized behavior seen among patrons. Although these are not statistical generalizations, anyone familiar with bars in the United States during the past twenty years can recognize these standard elements. In Simmel's (1950) terms, the content of social life (as in a bar) is quite varied, but its form is often discernibly similar.

In positivist, quantitative sociology, several types of *validity* are proposed in the context of scientific objectivity; most qualitative sociologists, however, do not claim scientific objectivity, or seek to test hypotheses. We (for we include ourselves among this group) seek not proof or some sort of statistical correlation, but thick description: is the interpretation provided by the researcher convincing to the reader—does it seem believable? The field researcher "wants to provide an account that communicates with the reader the truth about the setting and situation, as the ethnographer has come to know it" (Altheide and Johnson 1994, 496). A qualitative scholar's implied definition of validity is, often, his or her loyalty and commitment to representing as fully as possible the people and settings being studied.

In quantitative research, *reliability* refers to different researchers' coming to the same conclusions when examining the same data; the presumption behind reliability is that there is an objective reality to be found by quantitative methods. Qualitative researchers often work alone—without anyone else to examine the data—and are in search of interpretive analysis rather than the presumptively objective world. Angrosino (2007, 124), an anthropologist, defines reliability as "the degree to which there is consistency in the research process."

Qualitative researchers may attempt to assess validity or reliability through "member validations" of research findings or by triangulation—the use of different kinds of data and method to "capture" the analysis (see also Chapter 10). However, while an ethnographic depiction may "ring true" to outsiders or strangers to a given social world, it may not to those who have been written about (see Ellis 1995a). Ethnographers have come to believe that this may be because social life is composed not only of interactions but also of intentions; many of our interactions in life fall short of our intentions, and we may not have put our best foot forward. Ethnographers capture the observed experience, rather than the social fictions, of our everyday lives.

An example of the difference between observed interactions and social fictions about those interactions comes from Tamara Sniezek's (2002) research on wedding planning. In interviews with prospective brides and grooms, Sniezek found that both participants claimed that they were equally involved in the wedding planning. Her field observations, however, told her otherwise. While grooms often made suggestions and comments, agreeing or vetoing, it was the brides and their female relatives who did the legwork, actually finding the stationers, caterers, church, florists, photographers, and clothiers who eventually came to constitute the wedding event. This example also underlines the differences between qualitative interviewing and ethnography as methods. Although both are social constructionist, interviewing is more amenable to the presentation and preservation of social fictions than is ethnography.

In the camera theory of knowledge, validity may also be seen as compromised by bias—holding the camera or pointing it in such a way that the picture is skewed toward the researcher's own values or beliefs. In social constructionist research, the term "bias" is used in a commonsense way to refer to strong beliefs or feelings that people might have about certain aspects of the social world. For example, a student who sets out to study an abortion clinic and is pro-life has a different bias than a student who is pro-choice. It is quite possible that either, both, or neither of these students would be able to conduct an effective ethnography of this clinic; personal biases alone do not guarantee either well-done or badly done qualitative research. However, the awareness that all human activity, including research, is accomplished from a specific standpoint requires qualitative researchers to state the perspectives from which they write their accounts. Thus, in providing a thick description, qualitative researchers include themselves and how they came to acquire their knowledge as key elements in their representation of people or settings.

RESEARCH DESIGN, THEORY, AND REPRESENTATION

The relationship of theory to method is different in qualitative than in quantitative research. Most quantitative sociological research is *deductive* in the sense that researchers begin with theory (functionalist, conflict, Marxist, or feminist, for example), and derive one or more hypotheses from this theory (see Box 1.1). In a quantitative research design, the researcher decides what kind of samples and statistical methods to use in order to test these hypotheses.

In contrast, most qualitative research is *inductive*, with concepts derived from the data gathered; qualitative findings are then, often, linked to the symbolic interactionist, feminist, or other theories mentioned below. Although in this text we describe various steps that are taken in doing qualitative research, data gathering and analysis occur in a back-and-forth manner (see Box 1.2), making it difficult for qualitative researchers—especially ethnographers—to produce proscriptive research designs with the step-by-step precision produced by quantitative researchers (Ragin, Nagel, and White 2004).

Although it is not necessary—and it may not be possible—to set up research designs for ethnographic work, this step may be required if funding for the research is sought. Funded evaluation research and applied qualitative research in fields such as criminology, education, and gerontology, generally proceed from research questions to research designs that include hypotheses. Some researchers (e.g., Morse 2007) have suggested that this research design requirement is one of the political factors that keep qualitative research marginalized in social policy and in academia.

Since interview and focus group research involves specific questions—and decisions concerning number and type of respondent—an interview research design is required. Such a design moves from research questions to actual interview questions, then lays out the number and type (age, gender, and other relevant variables) of respondents required (see Chapters 6 and 7).

Qualitative analyses, as we discuss at greater length in Chapters 9 and 10, are often framed within sets of concepts developed during the early part of the century by anthropologists and sociologists, and later developed within various other disciplines. European influences entered the stream of qualitative analysis during the latter part of the twentieth century, when translations of German, French, and other works became more commonplace. The work of the American sociologist Erving Goffman on everyday life (1959, 1961, 1963a, 1963b), based on the conceptual work of European sociologist Georg Simmel (1950), is still of theoretical interest. In Warren's work on *Identity and Community in the Gay World* (1972), for example, she analyzed a male homosexual community using Simmel's concept of secrecy and Goffman's concept of stigma. Today, qualitative sociologists who study homosexual communities are unlikely to use either of these concepts (Warren 2003).

Some qualitative researchers link their data to theoretical systems; examples include symbolic interactionism and (especially for gender studies) feminism. Symbolic interactionism, which theorizes the relationship between self and society (Cooley 1922; Mead 1934; Blumer 1969), is an important component of qualitative sociology today, as is the work of Erving Goffman from the 1950s to the 1980s on everyday life (Goffman 1959, 1961, 1963a, 1963b, 1967, 1979). Feminist theory has been used by qualitative researchers in numerous disciplines—from cultural studies to anthropology—supplementing social science's historical interest in social class with a focus on gender. In sociology, both symbolic interactionists and feminists have their own societies and journals: the Society for the Study of Symbolic Interaction, and Sociologists for the Study of Women in Society.

Anthropologists—who have historically studied non-Western societies—have always focused on issues of race, ethnicity, nationality, globalization, and migration as well as gender and hierarchy. Nugent (2007), who studies photographic representations of Amazonian Indians, notes that these representations have, for the past century, coalesced around ethnic and racial tropes such as the "forest Indian," despite the historical reality of other Amazonian Indian lives, such as Jewish settlements and rubber factories.

In sociology and the other social sciences, race, immigration, and globalization have been the focus of qualitative research at the University of Chicago and in other urban centers since the early twentieth century, by white researchers (Duneier 1999; Wacquant 2004) as well as by African-American (Anderson 2004) and other minority (Venkatesh 2008) researchers. Black scholars also have their specialized organizations within academia, such as the Association of Black Sociologists.

Qualitative methods and theory change over time. One significant change in the epistemology of methods and theory has been the consideration, in interdisciplinary work from the 1970s onward, of the issue of *representation*. This term refers to the ways in which the interactions and talk of a given social group or individual are represented in fieldnotes, interview transcripts, visual images, and published reports. Representational concerns are wide ranging; they include a consideration of the rhetoric and metaphors of research (Gusfield 1976), the relative power of researcher and researched (Clifford and Marcus 1986; Nugent 2007), and the ways in which the researcher shapes the "voices"—or faces—of respondents (Holstein and Gubrium 1995; Nugent 2007). Postmodern and feminist theorists in particular have grappled with issues of representation. The significance of these various aspects of representation when doing your own qualitative research is likely to vary according to your instructor's focus. But the general issue of representation has been established in qualitative methods as central to any discussion of epistemology, despite occasional critiques of it as—once more—navel-gazing.

What is central is this: the qualitative researcher produces a visual record and/or an oral report and/or written representation of the social world he or she is studying, which is itself based on prior representations of the field in the form of images, fieldnotes or interview transcripts. The researcher then develops the analytic focus of the presentation and the parts of the fieldnotes, images, or transcripts that will be used to illustrate the analytic points made. Clearly, the representation of *reality* that ensues will have elements of "the field" or others' lived experience as part of it, and reflections of the analytic concerns and writing choices made by the qualitative researcher. As such, ethnographies and other studies based on qualitative data are intersubjective representations rather than objective portrayals of the social world, involving the researcher's interpretations and choices as well as the lived world of the respondents.

This intersubjectivity is not seen by qualitative sociologists as a flaw, as positivists see bias; representation is an inevitable part of the process of qualitative research. This does not mean that validity is abandoned, because the researcher strives to examine the world "out there" as closely and systematically as possible. It does mean that research findings are always from some point of view; they are not unmediated "snapshots" of an objective reality. When you become a qualitative researcher, you strive to become a good writer, but you also strive to become an attentive researcher. The foundation of qualitative research is still in research: that close-up immersion in and examination of lived worlds, first recommended in American anthropology and sociology in the nineteenth and early twentieth centuries.

Nineteenth Century Anthropology, the Chicago School, and the Development of Qualitative Methods

Like any other social phenomenon, the current status of qualitative methods has been shaped by its history. Qualitative methodologists may trace the history of qualitative methods as far back as Herodotus (called by some the father of the discipline of sociology as well as history), or to the travelers of the Middle Ages or the missionaries of the nineteenth century. But nineteenth- to early twentieth-century anthropology and the Chicago School of sociology formed the foundation of modern qualitative research (Bulmer 1984; Fine 1995; Emerson 2001).

British and American anthropologists of the nineteenth century studied the bodies, artifacts, and language of what they called "primitive people"; in America, these were often Native Americans. The Bureau of American Ethnology was founded in 1879 with the aim of developing "enlightened policies" towards Indians (Emerson 2001, 4). Franz Boas, who moved from Germany to the United States in the late nineteenth century, was the most important anthropologist working in America from his hiring at Columbia University in 1896 until World War II. Other anthropological stars in the developing twentieth-century firmament of qualitative methods were Bronislaw Malinowski, Ruth Benedict, and Margaret Mead. In sociology, the Chicago School was responsible for several key features of contemporary qualitative methods, including the use of documents (see Chapter 8), field-work (Chapters 3–5), and interviewing (Chapters 6 and 7).

With its interdisciplinary links between sociology, philosophy, social welfare, and other schools, the Chicago School flourished in the early part of the twentieth century. The methods used by Chicago researchers revolved around the "case study," a compilation of qualitative and quantitative approaches that highlighted the nature of a given social "case." The collection of documents was a central aspect of many Chicago School case studies, including the assemblage of Polish immigrants' letters analyzed in Thomas and Znaniecki's five-volume *The Polish Peasant in Europe and America (1918–1920)*.

Researchers of the Chicago School regarded the city as an urban laboratory, an ecological system amenable to a sociological analysis based on class and race. These researchers were often activist or reformist, using the case study to understand and solve social problems, locate "social pathology," and point out where reforms were needed. The social problems and "pathologies" studied by professors and students of the Chicago School included inner-city poverty and decay, racism, delinquency, gangs, riding the rails (hobos), and "deviant" sexualities such as homosexuality and prostitution. The tone of some of this research is captured in an unpublished "Glossary of Homosexual Terms" compiled by students at the University of Chicago during the 1930s:

> Older homosexual men were referred to as "Auntie" or "Ella."... Those who "practice[d] fellatio on men" were designated "goop gobblers," "fruiters," and "flute-players."... The terms "trade" and "hustler" were used to designate an otherwise "normal" man who was willing to "permit

[a] homosexual to have sex relations with him, usually for money."
(Heap 2003, 474)

Many of these "pathology and deviance" topics were the subject of ethnographies by the sociologists of the second Chicago School (Fine 1995) and a subsequent California School. The second Chicago School consisted of scholars who had been trained at the University of Chicago but were not necessarily teaching there. This cohort of qualitative sociologists included David Matza and Howard Becker (see http://home.earthlink.net/~hsbecker/), who were influential in the 1960s and 1970s "appreciative" (rather than reformist) studies of "deviant subcultures," a term that came to encompass a wide variety of topics ranging from marijuana smoking among jazz musicians to mental hospitals and juvenile delinquents. The California School, with centers in Berkeley, Los Angeles, and San Diego, continued the study of deviance throughout the 1970s and 1980s, again with a wide range of "deviance" topics, from nude beaches and homosexuality to drug dealers and topless bars. Some of the studies produced by qualitative scholars in California, including Warren's (1972) study of a Southern California male gay community, used interview as well as ethnographic methods.

Qualitative interviewing, like fieldwork, can be traced both to anthropologists' field questioning and to the early twentieth-century case study approach. Chicago researchers interviewed immigrants, delinquents, and others to get their life stories in their "own" words. Among these early studies was Clifford Shaw's *The Jack-Roller* (1966), first published in 1930. This was the story of a delinquent boy, Stanley, born in 1909, whose petty crimes had landed him in correctional facilities in Chicago—the perfect place at the time to find oneself in a case study. In 1975 Stanley wrote to Jon Snodgrass, then at California State University, and offered to tell a second life story; this story became *The Jack-Roller at Seventy: A Fifty-Year Follow-up* (The Jack-Roller and Snodgrass 1982).

While the life history was used to illuminate individual experiences in local context, the Chicago School social scientists also used interviews as a way of trying to understand different social groups, from hobos to gang members. Although some early Chicago School interviews were in the form of questionnaires or used closed ended questions, others were open ended and more like contemporary qualitative interviews. In a 1939 methods textbook, Pauline Young, who was trained at the University of Chicago, described the essence of qualitative interviewing as the elicitation of stories:

> When people are least interrupted, when they can tell their stories in their own way...they can react naturally and freely and express themselves fully....[Interruptions and leading questions are likely to have the effect that]...the adventure into the unknown, into uncharted and hitherto undisclosed spheres, has been destroyed. (quoted in Platt 2002, 37)

Why Do Qualitative Research?

The reasons for pursuing qualitative sociological research vary historically and locally with the individual, the sponsoring organization, and the contextual political economy. Early Chicago School ethnography was reformist: seeking to bring about social change by altering the environment and—it was believed—the behavior of people raised in poor, criminal, or underclass circumstances. Contemporary qualitative research may be undertaken for similar reasons, or for a much wider range of purposes, including—as you will see later in the text—business research for companies such as Microsoft or Intel.

For many scholars, qualitative research is a kind of personal passion: the satisfaction of a boundless curiosity about the construction of our social worlds. What Reinharz and Chase have to say about feminist interviewers also applies to other qualitative researchers, who "choose research topics that are deeply personal." This type of choice "tends to make the interview [or ethnographic] process emotionally intense for both interviewer and participant" (2002, 227). Even when research topics are chosen because of considerations such as funding, the process of doing qualitative research can engender intensity and a kind of cognitive passion. Warren began to study the mental health/legal system because of grant funding and wrote an ethnography of decision making in a mental health court (Warren 1982). This initial research led to several other research projects, including an interview-based study of 1950s housewives diagnosed with schizophrenia (Warren 1987), and a history of electroshock in America (Kneeland and Warren 2008) using documents and visual images.

A student may be drawn to ethnography, or have a question about human behavior that can only be answered by interviewing—or may simply be expected to do a qualitative study as part of a class requirement. An individual sociologist may wish to pursue promotion and tenure in her department, or (once tenured) make money directly (royalties) and indirectly (increases in salary) by writing a well-received ethnography. The sponsoring institution, a university or college, may or may not reward writing based on qualitative research over that based on quantitative, and may value some research topics over others. The research may be funded or not, the funding level may be large or small, and the funding may come from a variety of local, national, international, private, or governmental sources. Certain topics may be "hot," others cold and dead, often in the context of current media attention to them. But whatever the reasons, and whatever the sponsoring institution or social context, it is important to remember that the motives for pursuing research are connected inextricably with the consequences of that research—that is, all social science research has political implications (Denzin and Giardina 2007; and see Chapter 2).

Contemporary critiques of interviewing processes (Briggs 2002; Gubrium and Holstein 2002; Richardson 1990) illuminate the political consequences of social science methods, a theme we return to in the last chapter. From choosing a topic to selecting respondents to interviewing and analysis, researchers' activities are part of the social order at the micro level, through the interview encounter, and at the macro level, as part of the nexus of knowledge and power. Qualitative methods allow the researcher to both acknowledge power differentials and resist them.

QUALITATIVE RESEARCH AND SOCIAL CHANGE

Qualitative research is connected to social change in two ways: it can be reflective of social change, and it may be focused on bringing about social change. In the early Chicago School, for example, ethnographic and other research used an arrival-assimilation model to study the waves of immigrants that arrived in the city. In the 2000s, the model is globalization. Elijah Anderson gives just one example:

> To understand the new urban immigration…ethnographers must now come to appreciate and learn more about the lives of British Sikhs in California who travel back and forth between New York and extended families in India. (2004, 36)

Some qualitative researchers seek to bring about social change by changing individual behavior; organizational practices; or the laws, structures, and politics of nations—or perhaps all three! Applied sociologists seek to change individual behaviors (such as criminality or drug addiction, or nursing home staff treatment of the elderly), but they may also hope to reform the organizations that deal with these individuals (such as prisons, schools, or nursing homes) and change the laws that govern white collar crime or nursing home administration.

Eric Margolis employed visual documentary methods to explore the "hidden curriculum" in education from a historical point of view.

> While the education literature refers to socialization curricula as "hidden" they are actually quite visible and have readily been photographed. From a critical perspective, class pictures can be viewed as an historical record of certain elements of the hidden curriculum. The photographs show bodies with certain race, gender, age, and ability characteristics spatially arranged in an environmental setting. As social scientists, historians, and educators we interpret these visible relationships as representations of social relations learned about elsewhere: segregation, integration and hierarchy, gender socialization, social class structures. Moreover, we infer that the images were not randomly produced but were carefully

What does this photograph say about the hidden curriculum in this school? *The flag salute to War Relocation Authority, National Archives and Record Service. Dorothea Lange, photographer.*

> fashioned using agreed upon conventions of representation to be symbolic representations of such social qualities and others including: order, discipline, purity, equality, patriotism, and community pride and stability. In these photographs we can see attempts to denote social processes such as socialization, assimilation, and acculturation which cannot be directly photographed. (Margolis 2000, http://epaa.asu.edu/epaa/v8n31)

Margolis later used a similar approach to explore socialization processes in the contemporary "hidden curriculum" of higher education.

Some applied research seeks to implement and/or evaluate social programs or social policies. Although much applied research—often funded by governmental agencies—is quantitative, some qualitative researchers work in applied fields. Social problems and policy research funding tends to follow demographic shifts and changes in political-media focus. In the 1980s, for example, there was an applied research focus on mental illness (as well as on delinquency); one large-scale study of electroshock therapy used interview and ethnographic methods (Lidz 1984). During the 1990s, education was the focus of a good deal of applied evaluation research (Carson 2001; Wright 2001; Peter 2003). The 2000s have seen an expansion in applied geronto-logical research, including Alzheimer's disease (Paterniti 2003; Karner and Hall 2002; Karner 2001). Warren's current research is in applied gerontology (Williams and Warren 2008, 2009).

Other qualitative researchers are more interested in examining the pol-itics of social settings than in implementing or testing social policy. During the 1960s—a time of political change of all kinds—qualitative researchers began to explore a different vision of the relationship between social science and social change. They developed a variety of approaches more politically critical of the status quo than applied research. Some qualitative research-ers continue, in the 2000s, to use qualitative methods not only to under-stand political or social systems (local, national, or global) but also to try to change them. Among these politicized approaches to social change research are action research and institutional ethnography.

Qualitative action research (Whyte 1984) seeks not only to develop understandings of social settings but also to intervene in those settings in ways likely to be helpful to the people being studied. As Denzin (2007, 20) puts it, "acting together, researchers and subjects work to produce changes in the world." Action research has a number of names, including collaborative action research and participatory action research (Kemmis and McTaggart 2000). Action research is premised on the notion that the researchers and the respondents are collaborative equals—the researchers bring sociological expertise to the team, whereas the respondents bring their local knowledge. Both parties are seen as contributors cooperating to accomplish mutually ben-eficial goals. Since doing the research will benefit the researchers (in terms of publication or career opportunities), it should also benefit the respondents both individually and as a class. The researchers participate in the activities of the group being studied, and the respondents participate in research deci-sions at all stages of the process.

Action research by anthropologists, sociologists, or educators is often associated with solving local, national, or global social problems. A good deal of action research has been done in school classrooms, with an emphasis on students' and teachers' perspectives and on the practical help research-ers can offer these participants (Kemmis and McTaggart 2000; Peter 2003). Other researchers, such as Whyte (1984) and Agustin (2007), have done research on behalf of disadvantaged groups such as factory workers, miners, migrant farm workers, and sex workers in the United States and elsewhere. Anthropologists have conducted action research studies both in this country and in third world settings. Kemmis and McTaggart (2000, 595) describe the reflexive "spiral" or process of action research as stages of planning a change, implementing the change, observing the process and consequences of the implementation and change, reflecting on these processes, and rethinking and replanning further implementations (see Box 1.3). The respondents and researchers continue to collaborate and reflect on the processes of change. Action research is not a linear process, but a multiphase progression of reflection, discussion, research, and action (implementation of change).

Institutional ethnography starts not with an idea of change but with a model of relations of domination and subordination in contemporary global capitalist society. Institutional ethnographers such as Dorothy Smith (1987) study organizations and bureaucracies (institutions) such as nursing homes and mental hospitals, because it is there that these relations are played out among clients, lower-level staff, and upper-level staff, in the context of globalization. DeVault and McCoy summarize the purpose of institutional ethnography as a mode of inquiry:

> In contemporary global capitalist society the "everyday world" (the material context of each embodied subject) is organized in powerful ways by translocal social relations that pass through local settings and shape them according to a dynamic of transformation that begins and gathers speed somewhere else (e.g., if the local hospital closes the explanation will not be wholly local).... These translocal relations that

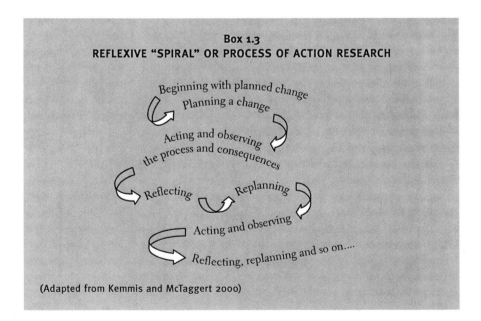

Box 1.3
REFLEXIVE "SPIRAL" OR PROCESS OF ACTION RESEARCH

Beginning with planned change
Planning a change
Acting and observing the process and consequences
Reflecting
Replanning
Acting and observing
Reflecting, replanning and so on....

(Adapted from Kemmis and McTaggert 2000)

carry and accomplish organization and control...[are] "relations of ruling." (2002, 752)

Both action research and institutional ethnography seek social change, but in different ways. Action research has as its purpose the meeting of immediate and local needs, while institutional ethnography attempts to dislocate relationships of domination and subordination. Applied qualitative research follows the Chicago tradition of attempting to change the environments of poverty and crime, thus individual deviance. Both ethnography and the qualitative interview were used by early anthropologists and Chicago School researchers, and both are used in contemporary qualitative research.

Contemporary Directions in Qualitative Research

Although contemporary qualitative researchers are indebted to the Chicago School, much has changed in the three-quarters of a century since. Young's description of the interview as a site for narrative is similar to our understanding of it in the 2000s. In other ways, however, early discussions of the interview differ from today's recommendations and technologies. Tape recorders began to be used for interviewing in the early 1960s, while Young stated that it was best for the interviewer not to even take notes. The issue of the interviewer summarizing the interview material versus trying to record it verbatim was debated among Chicago School researchers (Platt 2002, 37); today it is generally assumed that the respondent's words should be captured as completely and accurately as possible.

The styles and agendas of qualitative research have also diversified since the 1930s from the early commitment of the Chicago School to reform, although reform lives on in qualitative research through the applied, action, and institutional research discussed in the previous section. Erving Goffman, in *The Presentation of Self in Everyday Life* (1959), separated himself from the reformist purposes of qualitative methods, seeking to study everyday life as socially constructed. Both traditions have continued in qualitative research: the study of social life as social construction, and its analysis for reformist purposes. Qualitative research based on the social constructionist work of Erving Goffman (1959, 1961) and the symbolic interactionism of the Chicago, the second Chicago, and California schools is our main focus in this text. However, there are many explorations and experimentations in qualitative research; more than we can cover in this text, so we will introduce you to only two of them: autoethnography, visual ethnography (see also Chapter 8), and the telling of individual and collective stories through interviews.

Autoethnography

Autoethnography puts the self at the center of sociological observation and analysis. Unlike the traditional ethnographer who studies others, the autoethnographer uses his or her engagement in the interaction, or reflections about the interaction, as the data. Autoethnography is about "how looking at the world from a specific, perspectival, and limited vantage point can tell, teach, and put people into motion" and is sometimes seen as a radical approach to bring about social change (Holman Jones 2005, 763). There are two general approaches to autoethnography—emotional (Ellis 1995b, 2007) and analytic (Vail 2002; Kivett and Warren 2002). Emotional autoethnography focuses on the researcher's own involvement in, and feelings about, the setting; analytic autoethnography focuses on involvement, but more on cognition within a particular context than on emotion.

The work of Carolyn Ellis (1995a, 2007) epitomizes emotional autoethnography, although her dissertation research was ethnographic rather than autoethnographic. For her dissertation, Ellis did a study of "Fishneck", a fishing village in the Blue Ridge Mountains; during the research, she was taken in as a guest by one of the large extended families in the village and became quite close to some residents. After her book on the village was published, the people she wrote about recognized the setting, and some of them did not like what she had said about them. Others even felt betrayed. During a return visit many years later, one Fishnecker, Minnie, told Ellis:

> M: "That was a lot of nonsense you wrote. I know you was a writin' 'bout me."...
> E: "How do you know this is about you?...I didn't use your names....How will they know it's you I'm writing about?"
> M: "They'll know," she said confidently...."I thought we was friends, you and me, just talkin'. I didn't know you would put it in no book." (Ellis 1995a, 78–79)

After her return to "Fishneck", Ellis turned to autoethnography as a way of avoiding or resolving the ethical and political dilemmas and consequences of research among strangers. In this quote, Ellis is describing the process of autoethnography to a potential graduate student:

> I start with my personal life. I pay attention to my physical feelings, thoughts, and emotions. I use what I call systematic sociological introspection and emotional recall to try to understand and experience what I've lived through. Then I write my experience as a story. By exploring a particular life, I hope to understand a way of life. (Ellis and Bochner 2000, 737)

Following Ellis's approach, Karner's most recent work "Changing Lens" (2008) is an autoethnographic account of her eye surgery that also includes her photography as data. In 2006, the lenses in her eyes were surgically replaced with manufactured multifocal intraocular lenses, altering, within a span of just fifteen minutes, her sight, her sense of self, and her perspective on the outside world. Having relied for decades on her camera as a means of seeing horizons and distance that her natural eyes could not be corrected to see, Karner found she had an "archive" of her past vision in her photographs. The surgery and resulting changes to her vision, coupled with her use of the camera, provided her with a unique opportunity to explore the impact of shifting ways of seeing at the most personal and experiential level. Changing lenses also underscored her understanding of the primacy of eyesight in the management of the self—physically, cognitively, and performatively—that would not otherwise be readily available for sociological study. Using both autoethnography and photography, Karner turned the sociological lens back on her own experience of sight, disruption, and self to more fully theorize the social aspects of seeing and knowing.

The work of D. Angus Vail (2002) exemplifies analytic autoethnography. Vail studies "tattoo collectors," persons who collect tattoos all over their bodies, in a sort of body suit pattern from neck to wrists and ankles, and then display them to interested audiences. Vail himself is a tattoo collector, with tattoo portraits of Jimi Hendrix, Carlos Santana, and John Coltrane on his legs. His work is, like Ellis's or Karner's, autoethnographic in that it involves himself—and in this case his own embodied experience of acquiring and

In her autoethnographic study of vision change, Karner used her camera to approximate her vision—the left eye before surgery and the right eye after. *Copyright © 2006 by Tracy Xavia Karner. All rights reserved. Used with permission.*

showing off tattoos—in the research enterprise. But it is unlike Ellis's focus in that his interest is in sociological analysis rather than in what he refers to as emotional "navel-gazing." Vail's purpose in studying tattoo collectors is to analyze and convey the perspective of members of this West Coast subculture, not only as he experiences it, but also in a way that represents the social world of other tattoo collectors and artists.

Analytic autoethnographic approaches may also be used when there are no other means of gaining access to social interaction or experience. Douglas Kivett (Kivett and Warren 2002) did an autoethnographic study of social control in "Sweetwater," a group home for delinquent boys where he worked as an assistant. Kivett and Warren were interested in understanding the circumstances under which social control was not exerted in situations that in some sense called for it. Since in this setting there was generally only one staff assistant present, and the decision to exert or not exert social control

Filip Leu tattooing D. Angus Vail. Custom tattoos are measured by the degree to which artist and collector collaborate on a design. *Copyright © 2004 by D. Angus Vail. All rights reserved. Used with permission.*

Tattoo by Filip Leu, Lausanne, Switzerland. Portrait of Carlos Santana. Collection of D. Angus Vail. *Copyright © 2004 by D. Angus Vail. All rights reserved. Used with permission.*

was based on that individual's interpretation, the only source of data on such decision making was the assistant's own thoughts and actions.

Kivett and Warren (2002) follow the steps toward the escalation or de-escalation of trouble and social control within the institution:

> A youth's questionable behavior causes an uneasy feeling in the staff person witnessing the behavior, followed by rumination about what has taken place.... The vague sense of something wrong is defined in local

staff culture as a "gut response," coming "naturally" as the staff member "learns the ropes." (11)

Kivett found that what was crucial to interpreting a boy's behavior as trouble, and thus escalating social control, was staff members' assessment of the intentions and motives behind the boy's behavior. For example, in an instance in which a boy threw a book bag on the floor, they questioned:

> Was the throwing... just that, or was it a meaningful, intentionally negative response to being given an instruction? Was it obedience of the body only, or the totalizing obedience of the truly docile body? Was it, perhaps, in the local culture, "playing games," or perhaps "limit testing"? (Kivett and Warren 2002, 12)

From such moments, social control (and emergent meaning making) in our society is shored up or defused.

VISUAL ETHNOGRAPHY

Qualitative research has a strong and growing tradition of visual social science: using or making still or moving photographs, or analyzing existing visual images (see Chapter 8). Douglas Harper (2002) is a prominent visual sociologist who uses still photography in his work. He notes that "there are at least two alternatives for visual sociologists" (2002, 729). One is to use the camera for observing just as fieldworkers use fieldnotes; these visual observations then become the basis for developing concepts. In his visual sociology of agriculture, Harper displays a photograph of a barn, a silo, and apple trees—one of which is being climbed by a man—and notes that

> Howard Becker suggested several years ago that sociologists learn to analyze photographs by first concentrating on the act of looking itself. Rather than glancing and moving on, give yourself five minutes. Look beyond the quirky, almost humorous construction of the image. See that behind him are a small barn and a silo big enough for the corn of a ten-acre field. Who filled the silo and what animals will it feed? Behind the farmer are two more apple trees. These suggest the family's self-sufficiency.... The farmer works alone on a winter day.... This reading is only the surface, a scratch at the meaning of the image, but even at this level the photo suggests the contours of a biography. (Harper 2002, 9)

Another approach of visual researchers is to use photographic elicitation to "confirm and develop existing theory" (Harper 2002, 729). This method involves taking photographs and showing them to cultural informants to see what the images elicit. For example, Harper showed Italian informants his photographs of bicycles and other traffic taken while he was riding a bicycle

Douglas Harper's photograph of a farmer in front of a barn documents both a vanishing kind of farmer and farm. *Copyright © 2004 by Douglas Harper. All rights reserved. Used with permission.*

in Italy. He asked them to comment on what the photos showed them about the role of the bicycle in Italian society. One informant commented:

> The bicycle stands for: rapidity, convenience, physical exercise, danger, risk, challenge, reduction of stress, increase of stress, cancer in the lungs, cold in the winter, hot in the summer…flexibility of the [traffic] rules, aggressiveness, attention, negotiation, social conscience, no pollution, autonomy. (2002, 725)

In ethnographic video the visual imagery is the vehicle by which the analysis is communicated. Several of Warren's students have, over the years, combined ethnographic writing with film or video. Laura Scheerer and Jim Whitney, two students of Warren's in Los Angeles, collaborated during the 1980s to do fieldwork on what they at first called "homelessness." As their setting the students chose a public parking lot next to the beach in Venice where many "homeless" people lived in vehicles ranging from wrecked, immobile Volkswagens to large, movable RVs. They found that the people who lived in this setting did not regard themselves as homeless because, after all, they made their homes in their vehicles. Scheerer and Whitney's

"Bicycling in Bologna" by Douglas Harper. *Copyright © 2004 by Douglas Harper. All rights reserved. Used with permission.*

ethnography focused on the hierarchy of vehicle dwellers that arose from the conjunction of vehicles ranging from the wrecked to the middle-class, and on the "privatization of public space" that occurs whenever the homeless, or vehicle dwellers, settle in any number in public spaces. Scheerer and Whitney called their film *Addressless* (http://www.sagemtnfilms.com/filmmaking.html).

Eric Margolis (http://courses.ed.asu.edu/margolis), a sociologist and documentary filmmaker, sees film, audiotape, and videotape as ways to more fully represent the spoken traditions of local communities. In his documentary work with coal miners in Colorado, Margolis found:

> The use of non-print media offers opportunities for the investigator to record social processes directly, to explicitly enter into the process, and to record the effect of that interaction. At the same time that I "studied" coal miners, I intended to explore the developing relations between what I was doing and the miners. Not only do cameras and tape recorders open up new possibilities to record social interaction and for sociologists to present their findings, they also have the potential to reduce the dualism experimenter/experimental subject. Reflexive research designs

utilizing non-print media have the potential to provide checks on the work by encouraging "subjects" to participate actively in the research and take a critical role in the presentation of research findings. (Margolis 1994, 130)

The use of either still or moving images in qualitative research poses special problems in the protection of human subjects. As you will see in Chapter 2, researchers are required, in most cases, to promise confidentiality to their respondents; where photographs or videos are used, this promise can be neither made nor kept. Researchers who use visual images—such as Harper (2002), Duneier (1999), Greenblat (2004), and Nugent (2007)—all display the identity of respondents.

THE INDIVIDUAL AND THE COLLECTIVE STORY

As Gubrium and Holstein (2002) note, we live in an interview society. All kinds of interviews are featured on TV; we could probably be watching an interview at any time of the day or night. We may be interviewed for admission to colleges or for jobs. Although face-to-face qualitative interviews are likely to be less common in our everyday lives than survey questionnaires, we are familiar with the basic question-and-answer format of the interview. From a social constructionist and symbolic interactionist perspective, interviews are the primary method by which researchers facilitate *narrative*, or the telling of stories.

In interview narratives, selves and individual histories are "continually reinvented in the service of contemporary psychological and political aims" (Rosenwald and Ochberg 1992, 4). Thus, interview narratives are more than a simple mirror of life events; they are embedded in temporal, geographical, political, cultural, and social fields—all of which lend shape and form to the story. In addition, these stories reflect and define both the interviewee and the social context. "Narratives allow us to create who we are and to construct definitions of our situations in everyday interactions" (Riessman 1992, 232). All interviews, then, tell both a collective and an individual story, but the analysis of interviews may focus more on one or the other. When social scientists, historians, or folklorists use narrative to explore the collective story, they refer to interviews as oral histories, folklore collections, or ethnographic interviews. When they want to examine the individual story within the collective narrative, they refer to life history narratives or biographies.

Oral history interviews provide "firsthand testimony that may assist [scholars] in describing historical events or the experience of social process" (Smith 2002, 711). Scholars who use oral histories are well aware that "in common with other types of evidence, interviews contain a mix of true and false, reliable and unreliable, verifiable and unverifiable information"

(Smith 2002, 712). Thompson suggests that oral history interviews should be used in historical research with the same cautions that apply to all historical research: (a) assess each interview for internal consistency; (b) cross-check information found in interviews with as many other published, oral, and archival sources as possible; and (c) read the interview with as wide a historical and theoretical understanding of relevant subjects as possible (1988, 240–241).

Similarly, folklorists are interested in the collective story. In many cultures, stories are like gifts, "lovingly imparted" and "associated with prior tellers, keeping their wisdom and influence alive" (Narayan and George 2002, 824). In American culture, collective stories include not only our own American history, but also fairy tales such as Cinderella and Jack and the Beanstalk. Folklorists' interviews can illuminate both the cultural and individual meaning of tales. In an interview study of women's and men's memories and meanings of fairy tales, the researcher found that women remembered these tales more than men did. In addition:

> Girls and women sometimes chafed at the messages in fairy tales, and some also reworded the stories to carry alternate endings. So, for example, a 9-year-old girl who preferred the character of Jack in "Jack in the Beanstalk" to Cinderella suggested that perhaps Cinderella could recover her slipper from the prince, and then "maybe she doesn't marry him but she gets a lot of money anyway and she gets a job." (quoted in Narayan and George 2002, 824)

Ethnographers use informant accounts to gain understanding of a particular culture and way of being. Anthropologists conduct ethnographic interviews as part of their fieldwork; the "ethnographic interview is a bid on the part of a researcher to get an interviewee to converse openly about a set of issues of concern to the researcher" (Narayan and George 2002, 820). Spradley notes that the "ethnographer's main tool for discovering another person's cultural knowledge is the ethnographic interview" (1979, 60). He identifies thirty or more types of ethnographic questions that can be asked in an interview, the most important of which are *descriptive, structural,* and *contrast* questions.

Descriptive questions are designed to elicit examples of the informant's language, which is the basis of cultural meaning. These are, according to Spradley, the easiest to ask (1979, 60); his example is the question "Could you tell me what you do at the office?" *Structural questions* reveal what Spradley refers to as "*domains,* the basic units in an informant's cultural knowledge"; an example is, "What are all the stages in getting transferred in your company?" (1979, 60). *Contrast questions* elicit cultural meaning directly, by asking for the "dimensions of meaning which informants employ to distinguish the objects and events in their world." A typical contrast question would be, "What's the difference between a *bass* and a *Northern pike*?" (Spradley 1979, 60).

Since all individual stories are embedded in culture and in history, in some sense—as we have already noted—there is no distinction between the collective and the individual story. However, some interviews seek to highlight individual biographies, either for therapeutic or for research purposes, or some combination. Karner (1994) explored the individual narratives of inpatient Vietnam veterans to understand their personal stories: their understanding of United States culture and the impact the Vietnam War had on their lives. However, because individuals are dependent on the cultural resources at their disposal to tell their story, qualitative interviews allowed Karner to focus analytically on both the individual story and its reflection of the collective story. For example, without cultural resources (such as language, common understandings, shared experiences), certain experiences can remain outside the bounds of telling. For example, some of the veterans' traumatic combat situations were considered "unimaginable" and "unspeakable"—that is, they defied narration. A qualitative interview can facilitate both telling the personally unspeakable events and reintegrating the individual experience into the social context:

> The word *context* literally means to weave together, to twine, to connect. This interrelatedness creates the web of meaning within which humans act. The individual is joined to the world through social groups, structural relations, and identities. However, these are not inflexible categories to which individuals can be reduced.…The general constructs of race, class, and gender are essential, [but] they are not rigidly determinant. Context is not a script. Rather, it is a dynamic process through which the individual simultaneously shapes and is shaped by her environment. (Personal Narratives Group 1989, 19; emphasis in original)

By telling stories to and about each other and ourselves in interviews, we "fashion ourselves and our worlds" (Shoemaker 1991, 356). Indeed, interview narratives constitute the "ideological terrain" of self-representation and formation (Ganguly 1992, 29). As representations, stories are not just the recounting of past experiences or memories; they are a cultural device for the expression of self and experience. The narrator reconfigures him- or herself with each story and with each telling.

Life history interviewing is another term for the interpretation and representation of individual (within the collective) experience. As Atkinson notes, an "individual life and the role it plays in the larger community are best understood through story."

> A life story is the story a person chooses to tell about the life he or she has lived, told as completely and honestly as possible, what the

person remembers of it and what he or she wants others to know of it....The...life story is the narrative essence of what has happened to the person. It can cover the time from birth to the present or before and beyond. It includes the important events, experiences, and feelings of a lifetime. (2002, 125)

In studies of self-help groups (see Irving 1999; Denzin 1989a) and of people-changing institutions over the past ten years, qualitative sociologists have noted the linkages between individual stories told in these settings and the ideologies promulgated by them (e.g., Miller and Holstein 1996; Loseke 1992). In a study of a battered women's shelter, Loseke (1992) explores the process by which a woman is defined in the setting as "a battered woman" and eligible for "intervention." Using an ethnographic approach, Loseke traces how the broader collective stories about battering and abuse are used by the staff members to interpret and typify help-seeking women's narratives—that is, how a woman comes to be defined as an eligible victim in need of assistance as opposed to a woman who is just having a spousal disagreement.

In his work on interpretive biography, Denzin (1989a) links the personal story to the collective story—and ethnography to storytelling—with examples from research on and membership in Alcoholics Anonymous. He points out that the stories told by AA members are individual, with their own events and turning points, but they are also collective. Denzin transcribes a story told at an open AA meeting by Bill, a self-defined alcoholic, and explores its dynamics:

As Bill speaks, he throws his story out to the audience who hears it. This audience becomes part of the story that is told. A third structure emerges. Not only is Bill talking about his alcoholic self, he is telling his stories to other alcoholic selves. A group self is formed; a self lodged and located in the performative occasion of that "open meeting." (1989a, 72)

And, one might add, a fourth structure emerges as Denzin writes his book, that of the academic meanings of individual and group stories and selves. The four structures that emerge in Denzin's analysis provide a striking example of the complexity of qualitative inquiry.

As a student, you are just beginning your qualitative methods journey. Your use of this textbook may be limited to finding out about qualitative research, or perhaps doing one or two exercises such as observing and writing field-notes, doing an interview, or analyzing a set of magazine advertisements. If, however, you are assigned to do something a bit more ambitious—even, perhaps, a paper based on fieldwork, interviewing, or text and image analysis—you may find that you too are drawn to the method. We certainly hope so. But whatever the level of your involvement in qualitative research, it is important to understand that it is framed within the set of ethical, legal, and political issues we discuss in Chapter 2.

Suggestions for Further Reading

Becker, Howard. 1998. *Tricks of the Trade: How to Think About Your Research While You're Doing It.* Chicago: University of Chicago Press.

Bulmer, Martin. 1984. *The Chicago School of Sociology: Institutionalization, Diversity, and the Rise of Sociological Research.* Chicago: University of Chicago Press.

Denzin, Norman K., and Michael D. Giardina, eds. 2007. *Ethical Futures in Qualitative Research: Decolonizing the Politics of Knowledge.* Walnut Creek, CA: Left Coast Press.

Nugent, Stephen. 2007. *Scoping the Amazon: Image, Icon, Ethnography.* Walnut Creek, CA: Left Coast Press.

Chapter 2

The Law, Politics, and Ethics
of Qualitative Research

Social research does not occur in a vacuum; it takes place under specific sociohistorical conditions. And in the twenty-first century, those conditions include a set of important legal, ethical, and political issues surrounding both the subjects of social research and the researchers themselves. These issues, in addition to various laws pertaining to social research, affect all funded and unfunded student and professional social science research.

What constitutes a "human subject" of qualitative research is not entirely clear. It is obvious that if you interview a person face-to-face, you are dealing with a human subject. But what about historical records of persons recently dead whose offspring are still alive? And internet participants such as those posting to blogs, Facebook, or Myspace? Over the past few years, there have been various attempts to include historical and internet data under the "human subjects" umbrella. Organizations such as the American Association for the Advancement of Science have been grappling with the issue of human subjects regulations and internet research (Frankel and Siang 1999). The Center for Information Policy Research now has an online "Internet Research Ethics Clearinghouse" that has relevant debates and publications for internet researchers (http://www.uwm.edu/Dept/SOIS/cipr/irec.html).

The politics and laws of doing research with human subjects also vary by the researcher's discipline. If you are a journalism instructor or student interacting with or talking to "human subjects" for the media, you may ask any questions you wish and use the names of the subjects in your published research; your work is protected by the First Amendment and your notes are protected by law from subpoena. Your only obligation to your subjects is to identify yourself as a journalist. If you are an anthropology or sociology student or instructor, however, you may not interact with or talk to respondents unless you have received permission from your college or university's Institutional Review Board (IRB). You are not protected by the First Amendment, and your notes are not protected by law from subpoena.

Both social scientists and journalists have professional associations with ethical guidelines for the treatment of human subjects; sociology's is the American Sociological Association (ASA). The entire text of the ASA code of ethics can be found on the internet at www.asanet.org/members/ecoderev.html. The basic principles elaborated by this code of ethics are given in Box 2.1.

Despite the existence of professional codes of ethics and of IRBs, debates continue over several issues in field research, including overt versus covert participant observation and the general issue of deception in social research. Various discussions of whistle-blowing have also occurred in ethnographic research under circumstances where the fieldworker becomes privy to illegal or unethical behavior by people in the setting. These and other issues in qualitative research are not easily resolvable by guidelines and codes, because everyday life is not governed by guidelines and codes, but rather by the unfolding of situations. However—and also like the rest of everyday life—anything a qualitative researcher says, does, or writes during the course of research can render him or her liable to legal action by respondents.

Box 2.1
BASIC PRINCIPLES OF THE AMERICAN SOCIOLOGICAL
ASSOCIATION CODE OF ETHICS

- Research should not harm respondents
- Participation in research must be voluntary, and therefore respondents must give their informed consent to participate.
- Researchers must disclose their identity and affiliations
- Anonymity or confidentiality must be maintained for respondents unless explicitly and voluntarily waived.
- The benefits of a research project should outweigh any foreseeable risks.

(http://www.asanet.org/members/ecoderev.html)

The Law and Qualitative Sociological Research

The law is relevant to the conduct of ethnographic research in two contexts: complaints or legal action against ethnographers by people related to the setting, and the subpoenaing of fieldnotes by legal representatives. One well-known ethnographer, William Foote Whyte, was the subject of a complaint to the American Sociological Association by the adult offspring of one of his key informants for the book *Street Corner Society* (1943). As with many such complaints, the central issue was one of seeming betrayal by the ethnographer, in this case Whyte's key informant, "Doc." After Doc's death, his two sons were interviewed about his reaction to the book:

> The oldest son answered, "Mr. Whyte would not be pleased to hear what my father had to say. My father considered the book untrue from the very beginning to the end, a total fantasy." I was extremely puzzled and remarked that on various occasions Whyte had mentioned that his father had gone line by line through the drafts and had approved of them.... They answered that their father did not even know that Whyte had written a book on their [sic] research. (Boelen 1992, 29)

Naming "Doc" as Ernest Pecci, Whyte claims that they did go over the manuscript of the book together (Whyte 1992, 59–60). He says however, "As I expected, when the book came out, he undertook to distance himself from it," mainly because of the possibility of other street corner society members identifying him and themselves in the text and not being pleased with the portrayals (Whyte 1992, 60). Whyte adds: "Doc's sons state that I had exploited their father. While I grant that I got more from the relationship than he did, that was not my intention" (Whyte 1992, 61). Although this and several other cases did not eventuate in full-fledged litigation, they serve as a reminder that not only disgruntled respondents, but even the offspring of disgruntled respondents may use the law to express their sense of betrayal.

FIELDNOTE SUBPOENA CASES

A number of attempts to subpoena the fieldnotes of qualitative researchers in the United States have resulted in court trials, and others were settled out of court. If your instructor wants you to undertake actual field research or interviewing, you should be aware of three published sociology graduate student cases in order to make a realistic assessment of possible difficulties. These are the Brajuha (Brajuha and Hallowell 1986), Scarce (1994), and Leo (2001) cases. The Zink (2003) case involved an anthropology professor, Dr. Sheldon Zink (www.ahrp.org 2003).

In the first graduate student case, Mario Brajuha, a graduate student at the State University of New York, was conducting field research in the 1980s while working as a waiter in various New York restaurants. One of these restaurants was destroyed by fire while he worked there, and arson was suspected by investigators. Brajuha's fieldnotes were subpoenaed by federal and county district attorneys. He refused to turn them over, but did agree to provide copies edited for confidentiality; eventually the subpoena demands were dropped (Brajuha and Hallowell 1986).

In the second case, in 1992, Rik Scarce was doing dissertation research in the sociology department at Washington State University on the radical environmental movement. Upon receipt of a fieldnotes subpoena for a grand jury investigation, he invoked (a legally nonexistent) "academic privilege" under the First Amendment. The judge rejected his argument and held him in contempt of court; his appeal against this conviction was unsuccessful, and Scarce spent 159 days in jail (Scarce 1994).

Richard Leo, the third student case, had done dissertation field research in police interrogation rooms in 1992–1993 in a "large urban police department" in California (Leo 2001, 262). Six months after he had finished his research, a public defender learned of his observation of the interrogation of his client and subpoenaed Leo to appear at a preliminary hearing. Leo did appear at the hearing, and did "betray...my promise of confidentiality" to the detective involved in the case by turning over his fieldnotes and testifying (2001, 276).

The Zink case involved an anthropology professor, Sheldon Zink, who was studying and taking fieldnotes in the operating room when a patient died while receiving an artificial heart transplant (http://www.ahrp.org/infomail/0303/09.php 2003). The widow subsequently sued the hospital and the manufacturer of the artificial heart; the lawyers for these organizations subpoenaed Zink's notes, which she refused to turn over, saying

> I think it is a trust issue with researchers in the field and [sharing field notes] would not be the way we do our research.... It would put the subject in jeopardy and we should protect them as much as we can.

Dr. Zink is "prepared, though hardly anxious, to go to jail."

In the Zink case, it was not possible to conceal the identity of the heart transplant patient, while the three graduate student cases, with their different contexts and outcomes (although all involved fieldnotes dealing with some kind of illegal behavior), underline the significance of writing fieldnotes that conceal the identities of the persons being observed. It has long been seen as important to protect confidentiality in published qualitative research, but it is now necessary to begin the confidentiality process earlier, at the point of fieldnotes. Actual names and clearly identifying details should be removed or changed in all written materials pertaining to qualitative research.

In addition, these cases point to the necessity for sociologists to have the umbrella of First Amendment protections given to journalists. Although journalists are not completely protected by the First Amendment, they are on much firmer legal ground than sociologists when it comes to the inviolability of their notes and sources. The protection of human subjects is important—as we will see below—but so is the protection of researchers by some kind of "academic privilege" equivalent to "journalistic privilege."

The Protection of Human Subjects

The federal government sets standards for the protection of human subjects in social as well as biomedical research; colleges and universities must institute procedures implementing these standards. College and university IRBs are charged with overseeing research with human subjects to ensure their protection. In order to conduct funded or unfunded research on campus, even observation of public places, the sociologist—professor or student—must write up a proposal for the IRB detailing the research design and procedures. Qualitative researchers, whose research always involves observing, interacting with, or talking to respondents, are particularly affected by human subjects regulations. Some qualitative researchers are adamantly opposed to human subjects regulations (Denzin and Giardina 2007). Nevertheless, any research that is either publicly funded or takes place in an academic or organizational setting is subject to them.

Although some IRBs are not particularly concerned with field research in public places, others restrict even this seemingly harmless form of research. Field research in quasi-public places (such as restaurants or bars), workplaces of other kinds, and private places (such as clubs or families) often requires the permission of those in the setting being studied as well as the sponsoring institution. Some settings, such as health service organizations, mental hospitals, and prisons, have their own IRBs to which potential researchers must submit their proposals. Thus, for a single research project, the researcher may have to gain the approval of a number of IRBs. In a study of managed care organizations that Karner (Montgomery, Kosloski, and Karner 1996) participated in, nine separate IRBs had to give their approval before data collection could begin (four managed care IRBs—even though three were part of the same larger organization—four state agency IRBs, and one university IRB). IRB committees require specific documentation of various components of the research process, a requirement more closely suited to quantitative than to qualitative field research. See Box 2.2 for a list of the components required in most IRB proposals.

If researchers wish to interview as well as (or instead of) interact with respondents, the proposal to the IRB must include a list of the questions that will be asked, and anticipated behaviors to be observed. Many times field researchers are unaware of the questions that they will want to ask or all the

Box 2.2
COMPONENTS OF AN INSTITUTIONAL REVIEW BOARD PROPOSAL

- Research design and aims
- Methods and data collection procedures
  - Data collection instruments and questionnaires
  - Interview questions
- Informed consent procedures
  - Proposed consent forms
  - Proposed consent "scripts" used in informing potential subjects
  - Written information to be given to subjects agreeing to participate
    - Subjects' rights
    - Clear idea of procedures and aim of research
    - Any benefits the subject will receive
    - Any potential harm to subjects
- Any potential harms to subjects
  - Argument for necessity of data collection plan
  - Plan to minimize any anticipated harm
- Debriefing procedures or services offered to subjects that might be needed due to participation

types of behaviors they will encounter in a setting prior to entering the field, which makes this sort of prior documentation speculative at best.

Federal guidelines also specify certain populations as "special" ones to whom special protections are extended. To do research with individuals at either end of the age spectrum—children and adolescents under 18, and some elderly populations—the researcher will generally need to obtain the approval of guardians, who may be parents or adult children caregivers. These populations are seen as not fully capable of consenting to participation. Research with prisoners is often not permitted, since their social situation implies that they are not free to voluntarily consent. However, Anita Wilson (2007) was able to conduct prison ethnography in England, so it is sometimes possible. Furthermore, research into "sensitive" topics such as sexual behavior, drug use, or combat activities will generally receive closer scrutiny by IRBs than research that seems less sensitive, such as preferences for ketchup brands.

As Frankel and Siang (1999, 1–2) note, people communicate via the internet "on a range of subjects, some trivial, some controversial, and some intensely private"; they also have the "expectation... [or] illusion of privacy." One key question for qualitative internet research is whether internet data requires the informed consent of participants, or, rather, is in the public domain where there is no expectation of confidentiality. And are there harms from internet research from which the subjects should be protected?

Protection from Harm

What are the human subjects of social research being protected from? One protection is from stigma—the possibility of being "found out" by published or unpublished research as a criminal, drug user, child molester, or other guilty party. Elaborate procedures have been devised to avoid the identification of subjects in published, and even unpublished, research. In order to send out a survey (and resend it if there is no response by a given date), a quantitative researcher has to know the name of the recipient, but once the survey document is received, the respondent may be further identified only by a number. Thus, by the time survey research is published, there is little reference to anything other than numbers. Survey researchers can promise their respondents both confidentiality and anonymity with little difficulty.

But the issue is different for qualitative researchers. Research in "a reasonably comfortable office environment does not present the same challenges and ethical issues that fieldwork does" (Rogers-Dillon 2005, 440). Qualitative researchers observe, interact with, and talk to people, and in many cases know their identities and sometimes even their families and where they live. The data of qualitative researchers are people's words and appearance. So, qualitative researchers cannot promise respondents anonymity, but they can provide confidentiality. Confidentiality involves not only obvious things like not using respondents' names and addresses, but also less obvious things like not describing respondents in enough detail so that they could be identified by others—while not changing details so much that the meanings associated with persons are lost. When it comes to visual research, neither anonymity nor confidentiality can be promised, creating interesting challenges for researchers with cameras.

In internet research, the human subjects involved may protect their own confidentiality and anonymity through the use of pseudonyms, and perhaps (for various reasons) the masking or altering of characteristics such as gender, age, and race. However, if these self-protections are not used—and even, perhaps, if they are—the dissemination and archiving of internet and email data can provide a permanent threat of exposure or stigma (Frankel and Siang 1999, 5–7).

Federal guidelines also seek to protect human subjects from the possibility of distress: being asked questions that provoke emotional reactions such as shame, guilt, or sorrow. In biomedical research, of course, human subjects protections also refer to bodily harm—indeed, it was with issues of bodily harm and biomedical research that our society first concerned itself with the protection of human subjects from researchers.

Human subjects protections as we know them today began, as so many things begin, with media publicity concerning abuse. The Nuremberg trials brought photographs and accounts of the treatment of concentration camp prisoners that made Hitler's genocidal schemes public, and horrifying, to the world. In his camps, physicians had experimented biomedically on adults and children, destroying their bodies and minds in the process. The horrors of Hitler's agenda in Europe, together with ethically problematic research in this country, made twentieth-century politicians and laypeople aware of the need to have strict controls in place for any biomedical experimentation on human beings.

In the United States, the Tuskegee Syphilis Study serves as one of the most egregious examples of ethically problematic research. In the early part of the century, biomedical researchers in Tuskegee, Alabama, received funding from the U.S. Public Health Service to study the impact of untreated syphilis on the human body. For forty years (1932–1972), over four hundred African-American men ill with syphilis participated in this federally funded study. Since the objective of the research was to study untreated syphilis, even after an effective treatment was developed these men were overtly denied the medications. The researchers went so far as to contact the physicians of their participants to persuade them not to treat the research subjects. The study also offered free health care to the participants so that they would not seek care elsewhere. Furthermore, to ensure that autopsies could be done after death, the researchers offered free burial services, thereby gaining access to the bodies without having to gain family consent.

Unfortunately, the Tuskegee study is not an isolated example. In 1963, two physicians at a Brooklyn, New York, hospital conducted a cancer study where twenty-two elderly patients were injected with live cancer cells without their knowledge (Katz 1972). In the Willowbrook Hepatitis Experiment, 1956 to 1972, healthy mentally ill children were given viral hepatitis in order to study the course of the disease (Barber 1976). The journalists who discovered these studies provoked enough public outrage that laws were passed to protect human subjects from such misuses of biomedical experimentation. Controversies also arose in the social sciences during the twentieth century, in response to several social-psychological experiments—including the Milgram (1963) experiments discussed below—that involved persuading research subjects to engage in apparently harmful actions against others.

In 1966, the first federal Public Health Service policy for the protection of human research subjects was issued. It was, however, limited to medical and clinical experimentation (see Warren and Karner 1990). From the 1970s onward, the federal government extended protections for human research subjects to include the social sciences as well. The 1966 policy for biomedical and clinical research served as the model for the federal government's approach to social science research (Reiss 1979). This was a step that many social scientists found—and still find—distressing. Social science research can indeed cause social and emotional difficulties for people: for example, if respondents are engaged in unlawful or stigmatized behavior (such as illegal drug use, excessive violence in combat, or extramarital sexual liaisons) and are identifiable, they could presumably be held accountable by the law, or stigmatized within their own social circles. If they are asked in interviews about distressing subjects—their troubled relationship with their parents, perhaps, or how it is to be biracial—they may become emotionally upset.

However, these kinds of problems are arguably not comparable to Tuskegee or Nazi experiments and are part of everyday life as well as research into everyday life. Social science researchers recognize the importance of protecting their respondents from harm (see the code of ethics in Box 2.1). Qualitative researchers are required to be—and want to be—careful about ensuring that their respondents' identities remain confidential. They are also generally trained to ask questions in ways that are helpful rather than distressing, and to provide information about counseling resources should interviewing (for example) become distressing. However, we agree with many of our fellow social science researchers in the twenty-first century who also feel that the restrictions on social science research have gone too far in this country. On many campuses, even ethnographic research in public places such as bus stops, a few years ago deemed "harmless" by federal and IRB guidelines, is being scrutinized. We also are rather unhappy at being lumped together in the same ethical realm with the Tuskegee research team and Adolf Hitler.

It is also difficult to use dichotomies such as "harm" and "benefit" in the interactional, situated world of ethnographic research. In *Street Corner Society* (Whyte 1943), it might have seemed beneficial rather than harmful for Whyte's key informant, Doc, to become interested in getting out of his lower-class, street-corner circumstances. Doc did not succeed in his ambitions and became frustrated, according to his sons, harmed rather than helped by his association with Whyte. But, surely, the harm (if that) was of a type that affects us all in our interactions with others, every day. Doc was not injected with hepatitis or cancer cells, nor was he left with untreated syphilis or forced to undergo physical experiments without anesthesia; rather, he did not get a job for which he was not deemed qualified:

> When...Frank Harvey...was starting the store-front recreation program, [I] persuaded him to hire Pecci as director of one of the centers. He did an outstanding job, but unfortunately, funding for the program ran out after 6 months....[Later] I learned that Harvey had an opening on his regular staff for a boys' worker. I phoned to urge him to appoint Pecci....Apparently the board was not prepared to appoint a high school dropout, no matter what abilities he had already demonstrated working with boys. (Whyte 1992, 61)

INFORMED CONSENT

IRBs and federal regulations are concerned not only with protection from harm but with *informed consent*—voluntary participation in the research combined with an awareness of its purposes and procedures. IRBs generally require researchers to write an informed consent statement that respondents then sign; situations may occur in which informed consent can be delivered orally and for which the IRB will require a "script." In qualitative research, informed consent forms can be used easily with interview research, but the issue is much different in field research. If you are sitting at a bus stop observing the behaviors and interactions of those around you, it is not possible to request and obtain consent from bystanders and passersby.

The issue of informed consent in field research is one that IRBs and researchers still grapple with today, and it is resolved in different ways at different institutions. Some qualitative researchers are adamantly opposed to human subjects regulation (Denzin and Giardina 2007) and yet must abide by them in order to do research sponsored or funded by organizations.

Some instructors define field research as "student training" rather than as IRB-covered research. Or the instructor may obtain an IRB approval for your class as a whole rather than for each individual project. If you are doing interviews, however, individual proposals will, according to federal regulations, probably have to pass your institution's IRB before the research can proceed. Informed consent may be oral, but it is generally written; examples of letters of informed consent are given in Boxes 2.3–2.5).

Informed consent has itself been a topic for qualitative research. At a university psychiatric hospital, Charles Lidz and his colleagues (1984) observed the interactions surrounding informed consent to electroshock therapy (ECT)

Box 2.3
SAMPLE LETTER FOR INFORMED CONSENT

Dear Ms. X,
The Department of Sociology at the University of X supports the practice of protection for human subjects participating in research. The following information is provided for you to decide whether you wish to participate in the present study. You may refuse to sign this form and not participate in this study. You should be aware that even if you agree to participate, you are free to withdraw at any time. If you do withdraw from this study, it will not affect your relationship with this unit, the services it may provide to you, or the University.

continued

Box 2.3 *continued*

The purpose of this study is to learn more about how individuals with diabetes understand their illness and treatment protocols. **Procedures** for this study include two one-hour interviews with a sociologist where you will be asked questions about your experience of living with diabetes. The interviews will be tape recorded for accuracy and later transcription. We do not anticipate any potential **risks** to participants in this study, nor do we anticipate any direct **benefits** to those who participate.

If you agree to participate, your information will be kept **confidential.** Your name will not be associated in any way with the information collected about you or with the research findings from this study. The researcher(s) will use a study number, initials, or a pseudonym instead of your name. Furthermore, you may withdraw your consent to participate in this study at any time. You also have the right to cancel your permission to use and disclose information collected about you, in writing, at any time, by sending your written request to: Dr. X at the Sociology Department of the University of X. If you cancel permission to use your information, the researchers will stop collecting additional information about you. However, the research team may use and disclose information that was gathered before they received your cancellation, as described above.

PARTICIPANT CERTIFICATION:

I have read this Consent and Authorization form. I have had the opportunity to ask, and I have received answers to, any questions I had regarding the study and the use and disclosure of information about me for the study. I understand that if I have any additional questions about my rights as a research participant, I may call (XXX) XXX-XXXX or write the University Institutional Review Board, University Road, University Town, [State, Zip code].

I agree to take part in this study as a research participant. I further agree to the uses and disclosures of my information as described above. By my signature I affirm that I am at least 18 years old and that I have received a copy of this Consent and Authorization form.

_____   _____

Type/Print Participant's Name   Date

_____

Participant's Signature

Sally Smith, Principal Investigator,
Department of Sociology, University of XXX, University Road,
University Town, XX
phone: XXX-XXXX

Box 2.4
CONSENT FORM FOR AN ONLINE ETHNOGRAPHY CONSENT FORM

Please read the following before continuing to the questionnaire:
The following research study has been reviewed and approved by the Institutional Review Board—Human Subjects in Research, Texas A&M University. For research-related problems or questions regarding subjects' rights, the Institutional Review Board may be contacted through Dr. Richard E. Miller, IRB Coordinator, Office of the Vice President for Research and Associate Provost for Graduate Studies at (409) 845-1811.

We, Sarah N. Gatson and Amanda Zweerink, propose to examine several key issues surrounding the phenomena of community development through the medium of the Internet. The areas we will cover include the nature of the Buffy the Vampire Slayer posting board at www.buffy.com and the community it has spawned; how Internet-based communities may be different from traditional, face-to-face communities; how relationships form between members of this community; and how the community regulates itself and defends its boundaries from outsiders. Ours is a systematic study in the sociological tradition of ethnography. It has grown organically out of both our own experiences as part of the Posting Board membership and our professional interests. In sum, the project links the first two points in the sense that it connects our findings to a larger world of social theory and observation about human behavior, focusing especially on the Internet as a new source of community development and a new research tool and site.

The outlines of the research itself involve Amanda and me as participant observers within the community. As long-standing members, we participate in the activities of the community, and observe the actions of other members, and we record these observations. One important component of this research, and one in which you may choose to participate, is the following survey. The survey is a generally open-ended one in which we also ask some basic demographic questions. The purpose of the survey is to get more directly at your own interpretations of the Posting Board, and your own participation in it. The dates of the survey are currently open-ended, so you may respond at your leisure. You may also choose to contact us to schedule a more in-depth interview, to be conducted over AIM or other Internet-based communications.

The information contained in this survey is strictly confidential, and your participation in this phase of the study is purely voluntary. None of the information we gather will be released in any way that may be connected directly to your real name or position in your life outside the Posting Board. However, because of the public nature of the Posting Board itself, you may wish to select an alternate nickname that the authors may use when referring to, or quoting, your interview or questionnaire. If you do not wish us to use your Posting Board nickname in any form, please say so, and we will then only use your information in the aggregate, or refer to any statements made by

continued

Box 2.4 *continued*

you in as anonymous fashion as is possible. For example, instead of saying "Willa said such and such," we would instead say "One 23-year-old married woman from the Midwest said...." While we need the identifying information to develop an accurate picture of The Bronze and of those members of it who choose to participate in this project in this way (i.e., we need to know who had participated), it is not our intention to share questionnaire information in anything but aggregate form with anyone other than the authors. This is as much a guarantee of privacy as we can make, given that people regularly post personal opinions and information on the PB. If we quote from something posted in the "public" arena of the board, the PB nickname will be used, since that is an area where anyone could see a poster's words, and quote them back at a later time.

I have read and understood the explanation provided to me. I have had all my questions answered to my satisfaction, and I voluntarily agree to participate in this study. I have been given a copy of this consent form. [As this is an Internet-based survey, the filling out of the survey and sending to us constitutes a signature. Please copy and paste this section of the webpage and save it as your copy of the consent form.]

Continue to Survey:

Professor Sarah N. Gatson; Sociology, Mail Stop #4351; Texas A&M University; College Station, TX 77843; gatson@unix.tamu.edu; SarahNic46@hotmail.com
    Amanda Zweerink; Valentine Radford Advertising; 911 Main, Suite 1000; Kansas City, MO 64105; amanda.zweerink@valrad.com

(http://sociweb.tamu.edu/faculty/gatson/consent.html)

between staff and patients. They learned that the degree and kind of explanations offered by staff varied by many factors, including the patient's psychiatric symptomatology and the presence of relatives in the room. They also learned that patients had a variety of interpretations of what they had been told:

> Patients' understanding was...typically incomplete and occasionally misdirected....It seemed often to be idiosyncratic and experientially based....Disclosure by the staff, even when fairly substantial, seemed to play a relatively small part in the patients' understanding....Patients tended to cite their own and other patients' experiences much more frequently than they cited information they had received from the staff in justifying their decisions [to have or not to have ECT]. (Lidz et al. 1984, 317)

This is only one of many examples you will encounter when doing qualitative research (or for that matter living everyday life) on the issue of

Box 2.5

SAMPLE CONSENT FORM FOR VIDEOTAPED INTERVIEWS

PLEASE READ CAREFULLY

Statement of Informed Consent

I understand that this interview is part of research concerning the people's memories of the post–World War II period and the civil rights era in the lower Mississippi Delta. I agree to participate in the interview, and to allow the information I provide to be used to develop a history of the period. I understand that the interview will take at least an hour. I understand that the aim of this research is to develop a fuller understanding of the period, and that it will result in various kinds of publications. I may be quoted by name in publications and other public presentations, and grant permission for the videotape, audiotape, and transcript of the interview to be made available to other scholars and researchers and the public. I realize that I may withdraw without prejudice at any time.

Interviewee: _____   Date: _____

Interviewer: _____   Date: _____

Parental consent: _____

Address: _____

_____

Special conditions:

The project, "Memory and Judgment: Ethnicity and Race in the Lower Mississippi Delta," is undertaken by Jane Adams, Professor of Anthropology and of History, Southern Illinois University at Carbondale. She may be contacted at: Department of Anthropology, (618) 453–5019, Mail Code 4502, SIU, Carbondale, IL 62901–4502, jadams@siu.edu.

This project has been reviewed and approved by the SIUC Human Subjects Committee. Questions concerning your rights as a participant in this research may be addressed to the Committee Chairperson, Office of Research Development and Administration, Southern Illinois University, Carbondale, IL 62901–4709. Phone: (618) 453–4533.

(from Adams and Gordon 2006; see also http://www.siu.edu/%7ejadams/mississippi_delta/mj_frame.html)

interpretation by participants of what was said or done in an earlier situation. In comparing some of our previous research (Karner and Warren 1995), we found that the clinical setting of a Veterans Administration hospital and the psychiatric context of the *Madwives* study (Warren 1987) often led interview subjects to conflate research with clinical treatment despite the fact that they had been informed that they were participating in a research study and different (non-clinically trained) individuals were conducting the interviews. As this illustrates, you cannot assume that the participants' understandings match your own.

Some ethnographic settings are such that it might be possible to obtain informed consent from everyone present; we have seen this done, for example, in small, closed self-help group settings such as Gamblers Anonymous that met once a week. There have also been attempts to make informed consent a continuous part of ethnographic research. For example, in Mitch Duneier's *Sidewalk* (1999), the use of turned-on tape recorders functioned as a continual reminder that the street booksellers' lives and words were being observed and recorded.

Some qualitative researchers, such as Mitch Duneier and Douglas Harper, use still photographs in their research, while others, such as Eric Margolis and Richard Chalfen, use videotape or film. Using the identifiable images of other people in sociological work requires informed consent, although some visual sociologists object to this on First Amendment grounds. It seems odd, they say, that journalists can talk to anyone, and publish anyone's name or image, without requiring informed consent (in most cases), simply because they identify themselves as journalists.

If internet data are part of the public domain, like newspaper articles, there is no need to consider informed consent. But if the expectation of privacy held by many who post on the internet is not just an "illusion" (Frankel and Siang 1999), then how would informed consent be ensured? As Frankel and Siang (1999) propose, the self-protective tactics of many on the internet, such as anonymity or using pseudonyms or disguises, render individual informed consent problematic. See Box 2.4 for an example of a consent form used for an online ethnography.

There are other situations in which individual informed consent is problematic. Anthropologist William B. Trousdale, in his study of military high schools in America (2007), administered a questionnaire and interviewed cadets in several military high schools. He says of his study that "It was unthinkable that I could simply ask a cadet on campus his permission to be interviewed and I never did.... Cadet interviews were normally arranged through the academic dean's office" (2007, 28). In situations where funding is not sought for qualitative research, and respondents' consent is seen to lie in the hands of others (in this case the military high schools' administrators), informed consent may not define the relationship between researcher and respondent.

There may also be situations in which respondents' welfare is not best served by insisting upon informed consent. Researching children in the United States is difficult, if not impossible, without first obtaining the consent of parents or guardians. But matters are different in the streets of Dhaka, India. Conticini (2007) spent a year of ethnographic research with

Box 2.6
SAMPLE OF TWO-STEP CONSENT FORMS FOR
VISUAL ETHNOGRAPHY

LANCASTER
U N I V E R S I T Y
Department of Linguistics
and English Language

Consent Form

We are interested in talking to you about everyday prison life, including what is important to you in your daily surroundings and how you organise the space you live in. We appreciate your help and hope that what you tell us will be able to help other young people get through their time in prison.

Name .... Number ....

I understand what this project is about and I agree to take part   YES/NO

I know that I can stop being part of this project whenever I choose   YES/NO

I know that I do not have to tell the researcher anything I would rather keep to myself   YES/NO

I understand that all information the researchers have about me will be treated as confidential unless there is a concern for my personal safety or the safety of someone elso   YES/NO

I understand that my own name will not be used in any way   YES/NO

If anything is written about what we have talked about I would like to be known as

....

Please sign here .... Date ....

To be countersigned by a [prison] Representative:
I confirm that the project has been explained to the young person and that he understands what is involved.

Signed: .... Name ....

Interviewer's Name ....

Date of Interview: ....

continued

Box 2.6 *continued*

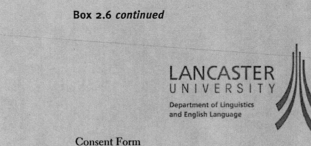

LANCASTER
UNIVERSITY
Department of Linguistics
and English Language

Consent Form

We are interested in talking to you about everyday prison life, including what is important to you in your daily surroundings and how you organise the space you live in. As part of this project we are going to take some pictures. We may have talked to you about this already. We appreciate your help and hope that what you tell us will be able to help other young people get through their time in prison.

Name.. Number.................................

I understand what this project is about and I agree to take part
In the photography   YES/NO

I know that I can stop being part whenever I choose   YES/NO

I am happy for images to be taken of my face/my body/my cell   YES/NO

I understand that all images the researchers have about me
will be used only for this project   YES/NO

I understand that my own name will not be used in any way   YES/NO

If anything is written about what we have talked ablut I would like to be known as
....

I would like to have copies of the photographs that are taken   YES/NO
(subject to approval by the prison)

I would like future information about the project to be sent to me   YES/NO

My contact address is
....
....
....

Please sign here .... Date ....

To be countersigned by a Northallerton Representative:
I confirm that the project has been explained to the young person and that he understands what is involved.

Signed: .... Name..............................
Interviewe's Name...
Date of Interview:

street children there, attempting to establish trust and to help the children, as well as study them. There were no parents involved to provide informed consent, and, arguably, to refrain from this work because of informed consent procedures would have been politically unethical.

CONFIDENTIALITY, PUBLICITY, AND ANONYMITY

When journalists write, they inevitably make public the lives and statements of their respondents without confidentiality. Sociologists, however, are expected to keep their respondents' identities a secret while publishing general information about their lives and statements. These IRB guidelines, as we have seen, are premised on the idea that publicity might harm social science respondents by stigmatizing them in some way, if their identities are put into print. This issue of confidentiality and stigma has been a concern of IRBs, professional associations, and individual researchers for several decades.

In the latter part of the twentieth century, ethnographers who publicized subjects' lives occasionally faced charges of becoming "spokespersons for deviant subcultures" (e.g., see Warren 1972), and a similar ethical debate arose during the early 2000s. Some ethnographers who identified their subjects were criticized for sanitizing or glamorizing the lives of their subjects (Wacquant 2002). If respondents are identifiable by names and even photographs (as in Duneier 1999) in published work, then the sociologist writing about them might be tempted to skew his findings or analysis in ways protective of those respondents. Sociologists who do identify their respondents deny that they are thereby "romanticizing their lives and depicting them as saints" (Duneier 2002, 1552).

As a novice researcher, you can expect your instructor to inform you about any IRB reviews your work might entail: whether your instructor is able to define what you will be doing as training rather than research at your institution, or if a blanket IRB approval will be obtained for the entire class. But whatever the formal procedures, it is incumbent on you to protect the confidentiality of your informants and to try to refrain from distressing them in any way outside the bounds of everyday social interaction. The first issue—confidentiality—is easier in large urban areas than in small towns, where even naming a particular kind of self-help group such as Gamblers Anonymous can narrow the possibilities down to one.

Ethics and Qualitative Research

Over the years, fieldworkers in particular have written extensively about ethics in qualitative research as they encounter issues and dilemmas they see as "ethical" ones. Some of these are mentioned in codes such as the ASA or American Anthropological Association (AAA) guidelines (for example, the issue of sex with respondents, discussed in Chapter 4), while others may not be discussed in any written form but may arise nonetheless. All social science fields face two key ethical dilemmas: the issue of deceptive research, and the Cartesian imperative to treat others (in this case, research subjects) not as means to an end but as ends in themselves. These two key dilemmas take particular forms in qualitative sociological research: the issue of covert versus overt roles in fieldwork, and the clash of citizen versus research roles if abuse is observed in your setting. Both these issues are debated in the context of changing views of what constitutes justifiability in the search for knowledge about society.

Deception in Qualitative Research

There has been an extensive and ongoing debate for several decades over the issue of deception in social science research. Recently, the possibilities of internet research have highlighted the issue of researcher deception in cyberspace. Internet researchers may join chat rooms or blogs as apparent members, without identifying themselves or their particular interests; research ethicists continue to debate this issue (Frankel and Siang 1999).

Psychologists have long relied on experimental procedures in which subjects are not aware of what is really going on—for example, the famous Milgram (1963) experiments in the post–World War II United States. In these experiments, recruits were informed that they were giving electric shocks to research subjects concealed from them, whereas in fact no humans were being shocked in the experiment. Some of these subjects were captured on camera in extreme emotional distress over obeying the experimenter and giving increasingly severe shocks to the concealed (and screaming!) "victim"— but nevertheless continuing to obey.

Although Milgram's work and other such experiments over the next sixty years have been subject to considerable ethical dispute, deceptive research continues to flourish on college campuses in Psych 101 courses, where undergraduates undergo all kinds of experiments, including many involving deception. Like the Milgram subjects, these psychology students are "debriefed" *after* their participation, but the possibility of emotional harm from being deceived has not convinced most campus IRBs to discontinue Psych 101 experiments. The same IRBs, however, would be unlikely to permit covert field research, which has been condemned by the American Sociological Association as well.

The Cartesian insistence that humans should treat one another as ends in themselves and never as means to other ends would, in its most literal interpretation, prohibit all social science research, or perhaps all research not directly beneficial to the respondents involved in it. In doing qualitative research with other human beings, researchers may treat subjects as ends in themselves—be polite, careful, sincere, and interested—but they are inevitably also treating them as a means to the end of understanding and interpreting settings (and, for some researchers, publishing books or articles, teaching, and perhaps amassing some share of fame and fortune). Obviously, since we are sociologists who have done research and we are writing this book, we do not accept a literal interpretation of the Cartesian strictures.

COVERT AND OVERT FIELD RESEARCH

Covert research is passively deceptive in the sense that qualitative researchers either do not reveal their research intentions or are actively deceptive, where they are pretending to be something they are not. For example, Leslie Irving (1999), in studying a Codependents Anonymous group, was not a codependent herself, but attended the meetings anyway and said nothing about her research intentions. On the other hand, Irving could have (though she did not) pretended to be a codependent and participated in telling codependent narratives. Passive deception is more acceptable to many sociologists than active, as this mirrors an approach often found in everyday interactions.

Active deception—someone pretending to be something he or she is not—is doubly problematic. First, it is often impractical, since pretending to be something you are not may entail a good deal of knowledge (which you may not have) and some acting ability (which you also may not have). Second, most qualitative sociologists today would also deem such research unethical, although the matter has been contested for at least the past thirty years. A highly debated study with regard to active deception is that of Laud Humphreys (1970), who dressed in leather and served as a watch queen (lookout) for men engaging in homosexual encounters in park restrooms. He observed the license plates of the participants, had a friend obtain their home addresses from the Department of Motor Vehicles, and then, after disguising himself with a haircut, suit, and tie, approached the men in their homes for a "neighborhood survey." Thus he was able to collect broader background data on the participants than he would have been able to obtain otherwise.

The issue of not revealing one's research intentions is regarded by some qualitative sociologists as ethically problematic, and by others as not. Researchers might join a support group or field setting that they feel they are legitimate members of, but conceal the fact that they have joined specifically for the purpose of research. Some researchers who define themselves as having problems for which there are self-help groups join such groups with mixed agendas, seeking both personal involvement and research opportunities;

several of Warren's students, for example, studied Overeaters Anonymous for both research and self-defined weight problems. Additionally, some researchers find the opportunity for a study arising from their own lived experience, and retrospectively their participation in their own lives could be viewed as unintentionally deceptive as they begin to revisit their former interactions as a source of data.

Public-place field research is almost by definition covert, since one cannot stand at a bus stop or walk down a street informing everyone present or passing by of one's research intentions and status. It is justified, however, both by the public, available-to-all nature of the setting and by the fact that people observe others all the time in public settings. Sociologist Erving Goffman (1959, 1961) has documented in numerous studies of everyday life how people self-consciously present themselves to others, interact with acquaintances and strangers, use public space, and obey or deviate from everyday norms. This body of work is outstanding, and it is unimaginable that human subjects regulations or overly controlling "ethical" regulations might have prevented Goffman from doing this work, or discourage future Goffmans.

Doing overt field research, which is not generally perceived as ethically problematic, means that at least one or some of the members of the group under study know that you are a researcher and have given you permission to "hang around" in the setting. However, this does not mean that everyone at all times knows that you are a researcher. Everyone in a closed, small self-help group might be aware that one in their midst was an overt field researcher, but this would not be the case in a setting where people come and go. Richard Johnson (2002), for example, studied a rural Kansas "sale barn" where local folks auction cattle and various other animal and material goods. Although he was given permission by the owners of the sale barn to hang around on Saturdays when the auctions were in session, not all the sellers, buyers, or members of the sale barn community knew, every Saturday, that Johnson was doing research. Over time, however, many regulars did come to address him as "professor" and ask him how his studies were going.

At a private psychiatric hospital where Warren researched overtly, she soon came to be pulled into the duties of the hard-pressed psychiatric technicians; forgetting her non-tech, research status, the head nurse of the unit tried on several occasions to get her to accept work shifts. Warren did not do so, partly because the hospital was more than a hundred-mile round trip from her house, and partly because she was afraid that as an unlicensed, untrained person she might bring some unintended harm to the adolescents on the ward.

Karner's (1995) field experience on a post–traumatic stress disorder unit at a Veterans Administration hospital presented yet another dilemma of identity. Because the unit routinely had clinical students rotating through for training, some of the unit staff assumed that she was just another clinical student. The veterans Karner interviewed and observed were for the most part unaware of what a sociologist is and had almost no familiarity with social research. Even though the guidelines and procedures for informed consent as sanctioned by both her university and the VA were followed closely, the subjects' lack of knowledge of sociology limited the possibility for fully informed consent.

Punch (1994) proposes that all fieldwork has an element of mutual deceit; both subjects and researchers are practicing impression management. Some subjects may wish to present their most positive aspects, while others may overstate their interest in the researcher's topic. Meanwhile, researchers set out to ingratiate themselves within a community or setting and must develop a sense of rapport and trust with potential subjects that involves both diplomacy and concealment.

RESEARCHER AND CITIZEN

Although federal human subjects regulations may be overly concerned about possible harm done to respondents by qualitative sociologists, it is certainly possible to fear doing harm (as Warren did when she had to deal with disturbed adolescents for the first time) or to observe harmful activities on the part of others. Doing or observing harm is possible in both internet and face-to-face research.

The internet reflects and amplifies innumerable social worlds, as we discuss at length in Chapter 8. Among those worlds are ones considered extremely deviant—people who wish to, or do, cut off their own arms or legs; "thinspo" anorexics celebrating the loss of all body mass; and sexual hunters of small children. If qualitative sociologists, or journalists, study such groups, do they then contribute to the very amplifications of deviance that they are writing about? Are we contributing to these amplifications by writing this paragraph?

Deviant or harmful behavior can also be encountered in real social worlds. The possibility of observing harm is particularly likely in institutions populated by relatively helpless clients, including prisons, mental hospitals, nursing homes and other facilities for the aged, institutions and homes for the developmentally disabled, and general hospitals. Some researchers who have done work in such settings have documented occasions in which their wish to continue researching in the setting has clashed with their wish to "blow the whistle"—to see something done about particular conditions or activities to which they have been privy.

"Blowing the whistle" as a concerned citizen is not something that facilitates continued research access, and several field researchers who have encountered problematic situations in the field have declined to do so, including Stephen Taylor (1987) in his study of a ward for the mentally retarded, and several ethnographers who studied the police. Taylor says that "the ward was a terrible place" (290) in which abuse by the attendants ranged from yelling, threats, and teasing to physical assaults: "It was not uncommon for attendants to hit or slap residents," and

> when attendants were bored or in a jovial mood they compelled one resident to swallow lit cigarettes or instructed another to perform fellatio on one of his peers. (291)

Taylor notes that there were four choices of action facing him when he observed abuse: intervention, leaving, whistle-blowing, and continuing to do the study without any kind of citizen response. He decided on the latter and continued the study. His argument for prioritizing researcher over citizen is that more was to be gained in the long run by accumulating knowledge about issues, problems, and stresses in the field setting than by whistle-blowing in the short run. He notes:

> Drawing on what I had learned about institutions, I have written descriptive reports for use in several court cases and for media exposes. Based on related research, I presented U.S. Senate testimony on conditions in the institutions and the federal government's role in perpetrating abuse.... Had I not continued my research...I would never have had the commitment or knowledge for these activities. (1987, 300)

Studies of illegal police violence by John Van Maanen (1988) and others also highlight the tension between research access and the presumed obligations of citizenship—and, for that matter, between the law and the actual practice of police work. Emerson (2001b, 34–35) describes two ethnographic studies of the police use of illegal force: Van Maanen's fieldnotes on the violent arrest of a drunken bar patron, and Jennifer Hunt's interview with a patrol officer who repeatedly hit a driver who had embarrassed her by driving away while she was trying to ticket him. Emerson comments:

> These descriptions convey a sense of police work as patrol officers might themselves understand and talk about it.... The use of force in circumstances not prescribed by law is not only viewed matter-of-factly, as part of the job, but is assumed to be justified or "normal" in particular contexts and under certain circumstances...but not in any and all. (2001, 35)

Researchers are for the most part uneasy about prioritizing the researcher role over the citizen role, especially in cases where the violations documented are extremely serious. Ken Levi did a series of intensive interviews with a hit man without revealing his identity or crimes to the authorities, and commented on the ethical issues:

> A question might arise about the ethics of researching self-confessed "hit men" and granting them anonymity. Legally, since Pete never mentioned

specific names or specific dates for possible future crimes, there does not seem to be a problem. Morally, if confidentiality is a necessary condition to obtaining information about serious offenders, then we have to ask: Is it worth it? Pete insisted that the hit man had retired from the profession. Therefore, there seems to be no "clear and imminent danger" that would justify the violation of confidentiality, in the terms set forth by the American Psychological Association. (1981, 48)

A number of Levi's colleagues did not agree, and his article precipitated much controversy.

These cases illustrate the kinds of ethical dilemmas intrinsic to ethnography and other forms of qualitative research. If ethnography's purpose is to understand social worlds as the members themselves understand them, then observing abuse of patients or police violence, or interviewing hit men, is likely to be a part of the process of developing such understandings. Furthermore, if sociology's purpose is to develop knowledge about society, then, as Taylor implies, the value of the knowledge gained by continuing to do research is greater than the value of the outcome of blowing the whistle— the termination of research involvement.

There are also matters of gratitude and trust in field research that complicate the role of researcher and citizen. Ethnographers who are permitted, as outsiders, to be part of a setting's activities are often grateful to the people who opened their lives to the researcher, and thus are not inclined to turn them in for any crime. The ethnographer may not wish to violate trust, as Van Maanen (1983) noted in his discussions of the reasons for not blowing the whistle in his police research.

It is no accident that the ethical dilemmas we focus on here are from research done primarily in the 1970s and 1980s. It is much more difficult in the 2000s than it was twenty years ago to obtain access to settings where policy violations or illegal activities might be observed, including police ridealongs, prisons (where Levi located and interviewed his hit man), and institutions for the mentally ill. Although Taylor (1987) was given permission by the institution's administration to research his setting, it is also possible to engage in covert (or only partially overt) research while working for pay or as a volunteer. This is what Timothy Diamond did in his 1990s study of institutions for the elderly, *Making Grey Gold* (1992). Diamond trained and worked as an aide, one of the few men and one of the few nonminority aides in the various settings in which he worked and did research.

So, is it ethical to gain entrée to institutional settings not via IRB approvals but via paid or volunteer work? This brings us back to the issue of covert research. The easy answer is no, since such tactics violate the principles of informed consent and involve deception as to one's intentions. It is reasonable for you to engage in field research in settings in which you already work or that you frequent, such as a bar or restaurant, and you would probably be given IRB approval to do so. But, while you are a student researcher-in-training, do not try to get into a prison, mental hospital, or other such institution as a paid or unpaid worker (or client!). In our view such research should not be undertaken by students. Your instructor is responsible for the conduct of your research, so you should not do anything to get her or him, as well as yourself, in trouble; the same goes for team research and its hierarchy of members.

However, in our view, entering an institution by "the back door" is sometimes justifiable by researchers. One of the major premises of sociology is that we need to understand relationships of power and domination in our society. Sociologists have found over the decades that studying elites is rather difficult, because there is far less access to elites than to nonelites—but some ethnographers have won acceptance among aristocratic, professional, or business circles. Studying the vulnerable and oppressed in society was once much easier, but is now made more difficult by IRB regulations preventing access to settings such as mental hospitals and prisons. It is arguable that research in such institutions is impossible or difficult not because the inmates or clients need to be protected from researchers, but because the owners and managers of such institutions prefer not to be under scrutiny.

One argument for doing the research anyway, covertly by becoming a worker, is that public institutions should be accountable to the public, and anyone should have access to them. And although many of our contemporary care-and-control institutions are private and corporate, including the nursing homes studied by Timothy Diamond (1992), they take public money in many forms. Thus it is also justifiable, in our view, to study private institutions that have been licensed by the state and take state funds such as Medicaid. In short, if you become a professional sociologist and ethnographic researcher, you might want to do as Timothy Diamond did, but not now as a student and researcher-in-training.

Although ethical guidelines and federal regulations are often quite specific about what is or is not permissible in social research, various ambiguities also derive from the ambiguities inherent in everyday life itself. Ethical debates may exist over overt versus covert social research and the general issue of deception, but the field researcher's identity and stated purpose are not simply absorbed and reflected by the people in the setting. And the ethical issues surrounding dilemmas of research and citizenship in qualitative research are not resolvable by general principles, but must be negotiated in the field by individual researcher/citizens. Informed consent, confidentiality, and the absence of risk or danger to respondents are all extremely important issues, but in their actual implementation by IRBs, they may be at the point of hampering or short-circuiting qualitative research. The extension of these human subjects guidelines from face-to-face research to cyberspace is still in flux.

The law, politics, and ethics of qualitative research are as complex as the settings, interactions, and individuals toward which such research is directed. Although the First Amendment protects journalists—indeed, permits them to interview, identify, and name people—it does not protect social scientists, leaving us open to the possibility of lawsuits connected with our qualitative studies. The extension of human subjects protections from biomedical to social research has meant the presence of the long arm of politics (national, local, university, and perhaps international) as well as the long arm of the law in the conduct of qualitative research.

As we said at the beginning of this chapter, research takes place at a particular sociohistorical moment, and within a particular politics. In the 1970s–1980s qualitative research was criticized as inherently conservative, because ethnographers study what is before us rather than invoking visions of alternative worlds. Today, qualitative research is framed as a challenge to conservative definitions of science and scientific evidence (Morse 2006). As Morse (2006, 79) notes, politics involves the acquisition or exercise of authority, whether on the local (your university and community), national, or global level. Angrosino (2007) points out that

> although largely unacknowledged by researchers of past generations, field-work has always been conducted in a politicized atmosphere, whether it was "exotic" anthropology carried out under the auspices of colonial authorities, or urban sociology that was dependent upon the goodwill of the local powers-that-be. This situation has become more visible—and in some cases more readily contested—in the post-colonial world. (108)

Whatever research you undertake or read about—whether conducted on the internet, in East Los Angeles or East Timor—its context is not only legal and ethical, but also political.

As you prepare to enter your chosen setting—having received permission to do your research by your instructor, IRB, or both—think about four issues: (1) be aware that the law is *not* on your side; (2) even if you cannot obtain informed consent from everyone all the time, keep the spirit of informed consent alive by occasional reminders or symbols (such as jotting notes) of what you are up to; (3) protect the confidentiality of your informants by not using their real names, and by not giving descriptions of them that are accurate enough to identify them; and (4) use all the courtesies and kindnesses of everyday life in your interactions in the field—although these courtesies and kindnesses may not always keep others from harm, they are the best we can do in fieldwork, as in everyday life. And if you are doing internet research, keep in mind that the person at the other end of the email, blog, or chat room may or may not be who or what they seem.

Suggestions for Further Reading

Duneier, Mitchell. 1999. *Sidewalk.* New York: Farrar, Straus, and Giroux.

Humphreys, Laud. 1970. *Tearoom Trade: Impersonal Sex in Public Places.* Chicago: Aldine.

Lee-Treweek, Geraldine, and Stephanie Linkogle. 2000. *Danger in the Field: Ethics and Risk in Social Research.* Routledge.

Lincoln, Yvonna S. 2005. "Institutional Review Boards (IRBs), Methodological Conservatism, and Academic Freedom" In *The SAGE Handbook of Qualitative Research,* ed. Norman K. Denzin and Yvonna S. Lincoln, 763–791. Thousand Oaks, CA: SAGE Publications.

PART II

Chapter 3

Field Research

Setting and Entrée

Field research, also known as ethnographic research, is based on interacting and talking with people in a setting. In this chapter, we discuss the first stages of field research: selecting a setting, access to it (sometimes referred to as *entrée*), and ways of gaining access. Geography, time, and financial costs are considered as aspects of choosing a setting, as well as "starting where you are" rather than somewhere unknown. The presentation of self of the researcher—age, gender, appearance—is considered as a factor both in selecting a setting and in gaining access to it. We also consider supplemental or alternative field methods such as the go-along, tour narrative, and shadowing.

"Interacting and talking with people in a setting" sounds simple, but it is not. What is a setting and how should I find one? How should I interact? What should I say and what should I refrain from saying? Will I be the only researcher doing the study or will I be part of a group? Will they let me study them? How will I leave? What should I write down in my fieldnotes? How do I balance field research and fieldnote writing against my other social and academic obligations? All these questions and others are characteristic of the ethnographic enterprise.

To make matters even more complex, as we noted in Chapter 1, there are also a number of different approaches to field research. The approach that forms the basis for this book, and the one that we have practiced in our own ethnographic studies, is what John Van Maanen (1988) calls "realist ethnography." Realist ethnography takes a middle position in the debate over reality versus representation (see Chapters 1 and 10). Realist ethnographers know that a published study is an interpretive representation of a setting, not an exact replica or mirror. But we also think—because we have tried our best to observe the setting and write fieldnotes diligently and for an adequate length of time—that our account represents a reality in which even members of the setting might recognize themselves and their world (see also Emerson, Fretz, and Shaw 1995).

Before considering the first step in ethnographic research—selecting a setting—we want to say a few words about circumstances in which researchers do not choose their settings but rather settings are chosen for them. Sometimes graduate students and possibly undergraduates are hired as part of a team research project of which field research is a part or the whole (Rogers-Dillon 2005). Concerns in earlier decades that "hired hands" might skip details or even falsify data (Staggenborg 1988; Noblit and Burcart 1975; Roth 1966) have prompted team researchers to put safeguards in place. In the mid-1990s, Karner managed a multisite interview project in which she trained several local interviewers in a number of different geographic regions of the United States (Kosloski, Montgomery, and Karner 1999). Local interviewers were selected for their language skills and familiarity with various immigrant groups. Quality control measures such as comparison with other service and family data, regular contact with the interviewers in the field, and a local supervisor were crucial in alleviating "hired hand" concerns.

Students may be assigned their research topics by the instructor, either individually or as part of a group research assignment. Research-methods instructors often assign students to take fieldnotes in open campus settings such as libraries or cafeterias just to have the experience of writing notes and trying to analyze them. But whether for hired hands or supervised field research, the team research supervisor or instructor selects settings that the student can gain access to.

Selecting a Setting

Some students come to classes in qualitative methods prepared with topics or settings that they want to study. In cases where topics such as motherhood or danger have no settings, methods other than field research may be more suitable. What, then, is a setting? This question has been complicated by the addition of online communities to face-to-face possibilities, but the question is not simple even when discussing actual rather than virtual communities and spaces.

Consider, for example, the mental health court Warren studied in Los Angeles, which for the sake of confidentiality she called Metropolitan Court

(Warren 1982). The court is a building on a street; in that sense, the setting is architectural, with floors and walls and roofs. But that is not the "interacting and talking with people" setting. What provides access? This building has one courtroom that provides easy and immediate access to the casual visitor. In the hallways, patient/petitioners wander around and talk with their court-appointed attorneys. Offices abound: the district attorney's office, the public defender's office, the judge's chambers, and offices for bailiffs, court reporters, and mental health personnel Warren had never before heard of when she first visited Metropolitan Court. There are also the bathrooms, cafeteria, and other assorted spaces. So, what is *the* setting?

For the student ethnographer, the most useful answer is this: the courtroom, or *a* courtroom, if the courthouse has more than one. A study of the public rituals of the courtroom would be your best bet for doing a semester or quarter ethnography of Metropolitan Court, or any other court for that matter. Even traffic court can be a fascinating study ethnographically. Warren's fieldnotes from a Kansas courtroom in the early 2000s (see Box 3.1) can give you some idea of what you might find in this kind of public setting. Wider definitions of the setting will take more time; Warren's (1982) study eventually encompassed the judge's chambers, the attorneys' offices, and the hallways. It took her seven years to write about this setting.

What is interesting about the Metropolitan Court example is that it may also be seen as several settings rather than one. Each of the subsettings in the court building—the courtroom, the hallways, the judge's chambers, the district attorney's office—sustained its own patterns of social interaction and talk. In a way, each interactional subsetting was its own social world, a point Jaber Gubrium also made in his study of *Living and Dying at Murray Manor* (1975). In this ethnography, Gubrium described the different social worlds of Murray Manor, a nursing home: the worlds of upper-level staff, of lower-level staff, and of patients.

> Each world provides its participants with a way of looking at and understanding daily life at the Manor. And each has its own logic: its own ideals, sense of justice and fair treatment, method of expedience, prescribed duties, rhetorical style, and proper mode of making decisions. (1975, 37)

If you have the opportunity to choose a setting, one not assigned by an instructor or team leader, be flexible (see Box 3.2 for aspects of choosing a setting). Realize that unless the setting is extremely small and clearly bounded in time and space (such as an eight- to ten-member Smokers Anonymous group that meets once a week on Tuesdays at 6:00 p.m.), you will probably not be able to study it in its entirety. It is acceptable to study one classroom in a school, or one courtroom in a courthouse, especially in a study that will last only a few weeks or months. Although a few ethnographic

BOX 3.1
TRAFFIC COURT AS A FIELDWORK SETTING

I enter the courtroom from the hallway, and find myself in the usual type of courtroom setting: the judge's chair and desk elevated on a platform, with (in this case) her name engraved in large gold letters on a wooden sign, facing the audience. Instead of a witness box there is a podium in front and just to the right of the judge's desk. A middle-aged, white male sheriff, in uniform and with a gun in his holster, hovers around the judge's desk eyeing the crowd and the people coming in.

[symbols of authority and power; the elevated platform, the sheriff, his uniform and his gun to keep order, the judge's name in front of the anonymous crowd. I feel guilty of something although I haven't done anything, my presence in the courtroom is simply to observe.]

And it is quite a crowd. As I walk in I am facing the judge's platform with the podium facing me, and rows of folding chairs lined up on either side of the room. It looks like every chair is full—there are perhaps fifty people in the room of all ages, although only one who might be under 18. I spot one vacant seat in the middle of a row of chairs to the right, and take it. People are still streaming in, looking around for vacant seats. A man in the back by the entry door tells them to sit or lean against the walls, which they do, starting at the back but soon spilling against the sides. The sheriff warns a young woman off a part of the wall that is beyond the rows of chairs and toward the judge's platform.

Most of the people seem to be here by themselves, or at least they are not interacting with anyone, they either stare at the judge's platform in a waiting stance or occupy themselves with shuffling and looking at papers they have brought with them. A few people are talking with one another in a muffled, whispery tone.

A woman sweeps into the room from a door behind the platform, wearing black robes, her eyeglasses on top of her head. She is white, perhaps in her early 40s, with long dark hair and a severe expression on her face. As she begins to sit, the sheriff shouts, "All rise and order in the court!" Everyone shuffles to their feet, and there is pretty instant silence.

[these rituals of authority work; we the audience have to stand before our judge, and we have to be silent unless and until we are invited to speak]

The judge bangs a gavel on the desk in front of her. A man, not in uniform but in khaki pants and a white long-sleeved shirt, comes down the aisle between the rows of chairs and says, "All here in the matter of....[I couldn't hear what he says] please rise, we are going to another courtroom." He opens a door to the right of the room and gestures toward it. About 15 of the people in the room stand up and make their way with various degrees of difficulty through the door. No one else in the room seems to be moving or talking, although a few brave souls who have been standing move quietly to take a couple of vacated chairs....

continued

Box 3.1 *continued*

[Later] the judge said, "Now what I am going to do is I am going to enter a plea of not guilty for you and then when I call your name you will come forward—" she gestures to the podium....[I am intensely surprised by this, as I thought that people in court, even traffic court, would make their own plea, and, indeed, somewhat later still]....the judge calls out a name and a middle-aged white woman comes to the podium. The judge says, "I have entered a plea of not guilty for you." Almost interrupting, the woman says, "Can't I just plead guilty and just get it over with?" [although I could not follow the next brief interchange, I gathered that pleading guilty and getting it over with was not possible]

(Excepted from Warren's fieldnotes)

Box 3.2
EVALUATING SETTING APPROPRIATENESS

- Access
  - Public or private space
  - Internal IRB required
- Geographic issues
  - Proximity
  - Transportation availability
  - Weather
- Interest
  - Of the potential subjects
  - Of the researcher
- Cost
  - Time
  - Money
  - Emotional (dis)comfort
  - Other involvements (schoolwork, employment)
  - Other social relationships (friends, dates, parents)

works are comparative (Sudnow 1967; Lyman 1993), these are generally book-length; shorter studies are usually confined to one setting. So the first principle of choosing a setting for a semester-long project is to be modest in your aims. As indicated in Box 3.2, other considerations are relevant if the setting is public (easy access) or private (may be more difficult) and if the research requires IRB approval.

Sometimes, researchers start with one, bounded setting, but move into other parts of the social world. Loïc Wacquant began his ethnographic research as the only white boxer in a Chicago gym, Woodlawn. But after a while

> the friendship and trust accorded to me by the regulars of Woodlawn were such that I was able not only to blend in among them in the gym but also to accompany them in their everyday peregrinations outside of it, in search of a job or an apartment...[or] cruising with their "homies" from the fearsome housing projects nearby. (2004, 5)

Other researchers study online communities qualitatively. In their online ethnography of fans of the television show *Buffy the Vampire Slayer*, Gatson and Zweerink (2004) used the posting board "The Bronze" as their research setting. Similar to Wacquant's experience, the online setting led to other offline gatherings and interactions, such as Chicagopalooza and Viva Las Buffy parties held in Chicago and Las Vegas, as well as smaller, impromptu gatherings in various cities around the United States.

ACCESSIBILITY, INTEREST, AND COST

A setting may be feasible (public space with no IRB required), but as Box 3.2 also indicates, you still need to think about its accessibility, interest to you, and cost. Public settings are often feasible and accessible, private ones generally less so. You should be able to do an ethnography of a bus stop or a public court-room, but you are not likely to be able to do an ethnography of the West Wing of the White House. This is of course an extreme example—the White House is not only a private space, but a highly secured one as well—but it does illustrate the first principle of accessibility: the public-private continuum of settings.

This example also illustrates the second aspect of accessibility: geographic proximity. Unless you happen to live in Washington, D.C., the White House is an inaccessible setting for reasons of geography as well as privacy and security. A bus stop on campus would probably be a better choice for your field research than a bus stop far from either campus or your residence.

You also might not be interested in either the bus stop or the White House. People's interests come from many places: reading, the media, political participation, leisure, work, and religious affiliation—all different aspects of your personal biography. Sometimes, students are interested in researching something they find fascinating but know little about directly, such as prisons or mental hospitals. Other students are interested in features of their own biographies; for example, a student whose parent is a member of Alcoholics Anonymous may want to study self-help groups.

However, the mental hospitals, prisons, workplaces, and other bureaucracies often of interest to student and faculty researchers are essentially (especially in a one-quarter or one-semester course) off-limits to student field research. Not only does the researcher's proposal have to pass the university's IRB (see Chapter 2), but institutions also often have their own IRBs that further scrutinize researcher proposals. Even if this process is successful—which it well might not be—it might take upwards of a year to get permission for research. By this time your class would be long over!

A student who wanted to study an Alcoholics Anonymous group would face an ethical dilemma. Some meetings of Alcoholics Anonymous and other self-help groups are open to the public, and thus are quasi-public rather than private settings. However, the essential qualification for entry into the meetings is possession of the identity which the self-help group is all about: alcoholic, gambler, narcotics user, smoker, or codependent, among others. A researcher who identified as one of these might have legitimate entrée into the setting; a researcher prepared to pretend such identity would be in violation of ethical standards in place for at least the past two decades (see Humphreys 1970 and Chapter 2). Even the researcher whose entrée was legitimate might be considered ethically compromised if he or she did not identify to the group as a researcher as well. (See Irving 1999 for a discussion of this issue.)

Some settings are accessible in principle, but are difficult to enter if the researcher does not share beliefs or values with the members. Nancy Tatom Ammerman (1987) wanted to observe a Protestant fundamentalist congregation she called Southside. She foresaw problems because fundamentalists were likely to count her, as a sociologist, among the "'secular humanists' who have corrupted traditional ways of thinking" (Ammerman 1987, 10). However, because she was a "committed Christian" able to say "'yes'" to the question "'Are you born again?'" Southside's pastor gave her permission to do the research (Ammerman 1987, 10–11). Patricia and Peter Adler's youthfulness, somewhat hippie appearance, and tolerant outlook on the use of soft drugs made the drug culture they studied accessible to them (Adler 1985, 13).

Public settings such as bus stops or parks are clearly the most accessible, since anyone (at least in theory) can be there, but students often resist studying everyday life settings because "nothing interesting ever happens there." We would like to encourage you to think about studying everyday life in public settings, not just because it is easier with respect to IRBs but also because it is infinitely captivating, as the work of Goffman (1959, 1963a) has shown us. Everyday life pulses with interaction rituals, spatial norms, presentations of self, deviance, sanctioning, and social control all around us in settings such as the bus stop and the grocery store.

Quasi-public settings such as bars and restaurants also present interesting locations for research. They are public in that anyone can enter (although restrictions such as age or dress codes may limit access), but they are owned by and operated in the private sector (or, in the case of an armed forces commissary, by the state). If you are going to do field research as a quasi-customer (rather than as a worker) in such a setting, you will need to be aware of the responses or potential responses of management or owners, often referred to by ethnographers as "gatekeepers," to your presence—as Gary Alan Fine (1996) did when he observed restaurant kitchens (see below).

Another aspect of choosing a setting is cost not only in terms of money and time, but also in less tangible factors such as self-esteem. Some research settings will obviously involve fixed dollar costs (e.g., observing audience behavior in your local movie theater, unless you have free access). Other settings may not have fixed and obvious costs but can come to involve financial elements, as Mitch Duneier (1999) found when he studied impoverished street vendors in New York City who asked him for small loans. You should also calculate the financial cost involved in transportation to or from the setting, and the temporal cost to you of selecting that setting.

Some settings are clearly more costly in terms of time than others. Sociologists and anthropologists who study whole villages have to invest a great deal of time in learning the culture; entire community studies are thus not suitable settings for individual student researchers engaged in one-quarter or one-semester courses. In terms of time, settings where you are already a member may be ideal, although what you learn from them may not be as challenging as would be the case if you became a "stranger in a strange land." Settings that are available all or most of the time and where the interaction is fairly routinized or ritualized are ideal for beginning field research: bars, bus stops, coffee shops, restaurants, book stores, grocery stores, and other such places.

Other costs to consider in some field research settings are physical and emotional. A bus stop, inviting in the late summer at the beginning of the semester, might be less so in the incipient winter at its end. A setting that takes you away from family members used to having you around may take its toll on your personal relationships. And a setting you feel uncomfortable in or ambivalent about might also be one you should consider avoiding. One student Warren had was very uncomfortable with gambling, and was disconcerted by what she regarded as her boyfriend's compulsive gambling. She chose to study a local casino in order to try to understand more about gambling, but was never able to even take good fieldnotes because of her disgust at the activity she was trying to observe.

Angrosino (2007) reminds us that when choosing a setting we also have to consider any costs or burdens our research might impose on the people in that setting. He points out that qualitative researchers

> can overstay their welcome and become nuisances in many ways...being too obtrusive in their observational techniques. If they are living in the community, they must be conscious of the possibility that they are imposing on the hospitality of their hosts, as well as draining their resources. (2007, 9)

Angrosino points out that some settings, such as a contemporary monastery, are designed to extend hospitality to visitors while others, such as "a typical village in Trinidad," do not have accommodations for visitors (2007, 9).

The consideration of costs and burdens on the setting as well as on the researcher is one aspect of the research ethics discussed in Chapter 2.

"Starting Where You Are"

Thus far, we have discussed settings of which you, the researcher, are not already a member. There is a long tradition of field research, however, that relies on varying kinds and degrees of membership or potential membership in the setting to provide entrée, something that Lofland and Lofland (1995, 11) have called "starting where you are." As we pointed out in Chapter 1, a researcher who also wishes to lose weight might join Overeaters Anonymous for both research and personal purposes if she thinks she fits OA's definition of overeater. A student working his way through school by waiting tables at a local restaurant, as Mitch Duneier did in his research for *Slim's Table* (1994), might decide to do field research in that restaurant because he already has access to the setting and is in a good position to understand its patterns of interaction (although he might want to think about this carefully in the light of possible legal issues, as discussed in Chapter 2).

"Where you are" in a setting has a profound impact on the access you will have to the various worlds of interaction and talk within a setting. A worker in a bar or restaurant may do field research on workplace culture, as Spradley and Mann did in the classic study *The Cocktail Waitress* (1975), while a customer is likely to be limited to studying customer-customer and customer-worker interaction (for example, see Cavan 1966). A stranger walking into a bar for the first time will probably have to become a customer—sit at the bar, buy drinks, interact and talk—to understand the patterns of interaction in that setting. In some settings it is really not possible to be or remain an outsider and do field research.

Several of Warren's students over twenty-one have done ethnographies of bars and restaurants where they have been either workers or customers. One bartender-student was in a good position to do a somewhat autoethnographic analysis that focused on the significance of the bartender in bar interaction—as the person dispensing the drinks (or not!), as typifier of customers as *regulars, strangers, funny drunks*, or *on the wagon*, as a focus of talk and interaction at the bar, and in collaboration with the cocktail waitresses. An ethnography of a bar from the vantage point of the bartender will be different than one from the vantage point of the customer.

Many qualitative studies have been done by researchers who are already members of a setting, from Howard Becker's analysis of the world of jazz musicians in the 1960s to Rick Fantasia's (1988) study of a wildcat strike that occurred in an iron foundry to Christine Robinson's (2008) study of social control in a lesbian community. Recently Becker and Faulkner (2008) reflected on the complexities of starting where you are.

> Studying something you are a part of, and interviewing people who you have worked with and will work with again raises difficult questions that fieldworkers in more traditional research situations don't have to address

but, at the same time, offers wonderful possibilities for data gathering not open in the same way to outsiders. (2008, 19)

Other studies are accomplished by the researcher becoming a member of the setting, such as Timothy Diamond's *Making Grey Gold* (1992), a study of nursing homes. Diamond trained as a nursing assistant and worked in several of these homes, usually as the only white male among a staff of African-American women workers. His analysis of how nursing home corporations "make grey gold" out of the pensions and social security of residents, and the minimum wage labor of nursing home aides, is an example of institutional ethnography (see Chapter 1).

Sometimes "starting where you are" is a matter of geographical proximity or even serendipity. When they moved to Southern California to attend graduate school, Peter and Patti Adler (Adler 1985) rented a condominium next to a young man they called "Dave." After hanging out with Dave for a few weeks and noting his drug use and apparent lack of employment, they came to the conclusion that he might be a middle-class drug dealer. They report: "We watched Dave and continued to develop our friendship with him" until interactions with some of Dave's friends made it clear that he was a "member of a smuggling crew that was importing marijuana weekly and 40 kilos of cocaine every few months" (Adler 1985, 14). Thus began Patti Adler's study of drug dealing (1985). The collaborative research team of Gatson and Zweerink (2004) began when they met in an online community devoted to *Buffy the Vampire Slayer*. Both were insiders in the community, and they decided to work together to produce an ethnographic account of The Bronze, the online posting board. So, starting where you are can lead to a collaborative partnership as well as a site for your research.

Your commitment to the setting marks the time to enter or reenter it. If you are a member of a group—a bartender, an Al-Anon member, a lesbian activist, a tattoo collector—your commitment to researching, as well as being part of, that group is in itself a kind of entrée (see Thorne 1980). But if you are not a member, you will have to present yourself to the group as a field researcher: a person in everyday life who looks to be of a particular gender, age, social status, race, or ethnicity.

The Presentation of Self in Fieldwork Entrée

As a method involving everyday interaction and talk, field research is not unlike everyday life. One of the things we have all heard is that first impressions are very important—and this is no different for field research than for any other kind of interaction. The kind of person you look like, the way you dress, your demeanor, voice, accent—everything about you affects first impressions in field research (or interviewing) as in other arenas of everyday life. In large-scale interview research, interviewers are trained in how to dress and how to approach different types of respondents, but presentation of self is often not part of the direct training of sociological fieldworkers (although anthropological fieldworkers studying non-Western societies are generally more aware of the issue; see Warren and Hackney 2000). Crowley (2007) says that

> if researchers present themselves in ways that resonate with their poten-
> tial participants, then their studies are likely to proceed. If, however, the
> researchers' self-presentations do not align with the participants' image of
> their own worth and valuation, then their proposed studies are likely to
> be rejected. (2007, 606)

As we will see in subsequent chapters, entrée is not a one-time event but rather a concept with a number of different meanings. In this chapter we will consider two of these meanings: agreement by the people in the setting that the researcher will be permitted to do field research (an unnecessary step if you are doing fieldwork in a public setting such as a bus stop or in a setting of which you are already a member), and the moment at which the researcher enters the flow of everyday life in the setting to join in the inter-action and talk. Both aspects of entrée depend on the researcher's presenta-tion of self.

Your presentation of self, or front, in Goffman's (1959) terms, is made up of things you cannot change and things you can; things you do change and things you do not. Some of the things you cannot change (at least not eas-ily) include your gender, height, age, and skin color. Anthropologists studying non–first world societies have found that gender, age, skin color, and nation-ality are particularly significant embodiments when seeking entrée to societies structured by these ascribed characteristics (see Warren and Hackney 2000). Race, ethnicity, and gender are also significant ascriptions in contemporary American culture, and can function to shape or defeat entrée.

EMBODIMENTS IN FIELDWORK

In our American culture, the embodiments of gender, age, ethnicity, race or nationality, and apparent social class are significant aspects of interaction in everyday life; it is not surprising, then, that they are equally significant to the conduct of field research, from first impressions onward. Federal law forbids discrimination in employment, housing, and other areas on the basis of gen-der, race, and in some cases sexual orientation, but this does not mean that the settings you might be interested in researching operate without any such discrimination. Ethnographers have written about various aspects of embodi-ment in the conduct of field research in places other than the Western world; anthropologists have stressed ethnicity and nationality, age, and gender, while sociologists have stressed gender. This does not mean that age, race, and other ascribed statuses—and first impressions—are not important in sociology. But especially since the 1970s, with an increasing cognizance of gender in sociology, women and men doing fieldwork (often young women and men doing undergraduate or graduate-level research) have been a focus of ethnographic discussion.

Whatever your embodiments of age, race, gender, and appearance, they will shape your fieldwork access and entrée, facilitating or preventing your doing research in particular settings. If you are a woman, for example, you are unlikely to gain entrée into male homosexual bathhouses, although you could probably hang around some male gay bars. In other settings, either a man or a woman could gain access, but they might be treated very differently according to gender; this has been the experience, for example, of field researchers who study police.

In his study of military high schools in America, anthropologist William B. Trousdale had to ask the ten schools he studied if he could talk to African-American cadets—they sent him only Caucasians as interviewees. It is almost certain that a woman could not have conducted this study of educational institutions for males, and possible that an African-American male would not have been successful either. While visiting a church across from one of the schools, Trousdale was approached in a welcoming manner by a woman congregant. He mentioned that he did not see any blacks in the congregation, and she replied, "'There *are* no Blacks in the congregation...and there never will be.'" (Trousdale 2007, 245).

One qualitative research area that has flourished during the past ten years is research into lesbian and gay settings (Esterberg 1997; Robinson 2008). Here the gender of the researcher is obviously of paramount significance in gaining entrée. Some settings in this area may be completely or almost completely closed to one gender: women's music festivals, for example, are open to lesbians and to other women, but may be closed to men and to transgendered males-to-females or females-to-males. One of Warren's students, in a study of a women's music festival in Minnesota, found that the only men permitted in the grounds were those associated with cleaning crews; when they came into the grounds to clean, the women were warned away from them. This setting, clearly, would not be one for a male to attempt to enter.

In recent decades, the body itself has been a site for qualitative social research, both historical and contemporary. In his ethnography of boxing, Loïc Wacquant (2004) argues for taking seriously "the fact that the social agent is before anything else a being of flesh, nerves, and senses" (vii). Wacquant reminds us—as existential sociology did twenty years earlier—that we are not simply a collection of embodied statuses; not just race, gender, and age shape us, but also bodily sensations. Wacquant discusses anger, hunger, and "food, sleep, sex: the Holy Trinity of the pugilistic culture" (2004, 241). Similarly,

Tyson Smith's (2008) ethnography of wrestlers "explore[s]the bodily skills that wrestlers cultivate to handle a context of ever present pain" (131).

Race is an important aspect of embodiment. In thinking about doing ethnographic research on homeless African-American book vendors in New York's Greenwich Village, Mitchell Duneier felt that he would have to "bridge many gaps between myself and the people I hoped to understand" (2001, 168). These gaps included race, social class, religion (he is Jewish), and occupation. He concluded that "none of these differences seemed to be as significant as that of race. Actually the interaction between race and class made me uneasy, although I was unaware of that at the time" (168). One of the book vendors, Hakim Hasan, wrote a note to Duneier that said he was suspicious of him:

> My suspicion is couched in the collective memory of a people who have been academically slandered for generations....African Americans are at a point where we have to be suspicious of people who want to tell stories about us. (Duneier 2001, 169)

After a couple of months of informal meetings in which Hakim and Duneier discussed issues of race and research, Hakim said that Mitch could start his ethnographic observations at his book vending table.

Though Duneier was able, despite his different race and class, to produce a successful ethnography, other researchers have not been. As a "hired hand" research assistant during graduate school, Rogers-Dillon found that her race got in the way of the research.

> After observing a meeting at an all black church in Philadelphia for *Unequal Childhoods*, I found that my presence (I have light blonde hair and pale skin) drew too much attention. For the next observation...the research team decided it would be more appropriate for an African American RA to conduct the observation. (Rogers-Dillon 2005, 444)

DEMEANOR

Embodiment as a race-d, class-ed, gender-ed and age-d person is the first entrée consideration for fieldwork seeking acceptance among strangers; the second is demeanor. Before you seek entrée to a setting in which you are a stranger, be sure that you have some idea of expected dress and behavior. In his study of a Hollywood talent agency, Stephen Zafirau made some "strategic decisions...about how to present myself," including

> leaving my 1987 Nissan Sentra parked at home when I went to do fieldwork, and borrowing my spouse's much newer car, as well as taking several trips to the mall to update my wardrobe. (2008, 106)

Our general advice is to conform, politely, to the standards of dress and behavior expected within the setting. If you are to study a law firm, you might consider dressing as "professionally" as the people who work in the firm. If, on the other hand, your setting is a construction site, a hardhat and tools might help you to fit in, but also might look odd if you are not working at but only researching the site. In that case, jeans and a T-shirt would probably be adequate. Whatever the setting, it is advisable to dress and conduct yourself in a manner fitting local expectations (as well as upholding the good name of your educational institution). To do otherwise invites a rejection of your interest in entrée.

Sometimes field researchers have to decide how much they are willing to give up, or compromise, to achieve an appropriate presentation of self for a given setting. Warren had a female student with a shaved head whose chosen setting was a beauty parlor. Although she preferred her shaved head to a head of hair, she was willing to grow her hair back in order to be able to fit in with the workers and customers at the beauty parlor. It was the view of the class members, including Warren, that her entrée without hair would have been much more problematic than with hair.

In Richard Leo's research into police interrogations, he knew he was getting into a setting that is "tightly knit and intrinsically conservative....Any outside observer or researcher of interrogation practices may thus be viewed as a potential whistle-blower" (2001, 262). Leo tried in several ways to gain the trust of the officers he wanted to observe, including what he called a "chameleon strategy" (Leo 2001, 266) of attempting to fit in. He not only cut his hair short and shaved closely, he also pretended to share their "personal, administrative, and political biases" (267). Leo's chameleon strategy involved adapting not only his clothing, but also his talk to the setting:

> I feigned conservative politics; I openly shared their bias against abortion and in favor of the death penalty; I affirmed their antipathy toward homosexuality; and I described my intimate relations with women in the same crude manner and sexist language that is common in police culture. In short, I fabricated a nonthreatening research persona in order to establish rapport with the detectives, acquire their trust, and gain observational access. (2001, 267)

Not every setting requires chameleon-like adaptation, but most profit from courtesy. Politeness is part of the smooth functioning of everyday life, and this is no less the case for ethnographic settings (exceptions might include, for example, biker bars). As an individual or a representative of your college or university, you want to approach others with courtesy, not like the student who introduced himself at an AA meeting by saying, "I'm here to study boozers."

Over decades of ethnographic work, field researchers have found that they can as often as not achieve entrée into their chosen settings as long as they are polite and try to fit in. Sometimes, however, entrée does not go as planned. Warren had one student who wanted to study a health care facility that served low-income Hispanics. She spoke Spanish fluently and dressed and presented herself appropriately; however, she never achieved entrée to the setting as she had conceptualized it. What she wanted to study was interactions between health care providers and patients—interactions that took place in private rooms in the clinic. Although she never did gain access to these rooms, she became a fixture in the waiting room of the facility and was able to write an ethnographic paper on waiting room interactions. Once again, this student's experience illustrated the principle that "a setting" may consist of several different social worlds.

Approaching the Setting

Chapter 2 detailed the formal steps necessary before beginning some, if not all, ethnographic research. These preparatory stages of field research involve attempting to gain entrance into the setting during the same time period in which you are negotiating with your institution's IRB: there is no point in gaining IRB permission to do a study of a setting that will not let you in. After you have dealt with questions about embodiment and demeanor, it is time to approach the setting.

Gaining admission to a setting in which you do not already have a role and where people do not know you begins with the first contact. This first contact may best be made by your instructor or supervisor or by you, depending on the setting and what your instructor thinks. Among the possibilities for seeking admission are telephone calls, letters, email, or a personal visit. Which one is used depends in part on the comfort level of the researcher with a given approach, and in part on the nature of the setting, including its formality or informality, IRB requirements, local customs, and the historical time period during which the research takes place. More than twenty years ago, Warren initiated research contact with a psychiatric hospital serving adolescent patients (a formal organization) by visiting the hospital in person and asking to see the hospital administrator. It is possible that such a direct and informal approach would not work today.

Karner has developed a formal, businesslike approach to contacting individuals in larger organizations. She often calls or emails (and this works best if you have been identified through a third-party introduction) to request an informational meeting with key persons in potential settings. As students, you can often contact potential subjects and tell them you are interested in learning more about their work or organization. Most people are quite receptive to interested students. A student of Karner's sought a meeting with the CEO of a large energy corporation; she called repeatedly, leaving messages with his secretary. Her tenacity eventually won out, and the CEO returned her call and facilitated her entrée. Though it took the student over a month to achieve her goal, it is unlikely that she could have invested that kind of time showing up at his office (if she could get past the security guard each day).

For bureaucratic settings such as large businesses, formal approaches may be customary and, perhaps, better received. Yet much field research takes place in settings not as formally organized as a psychiatric hospital or energy corporation. People in settings such as coffee shops or gyms may be more receptive to students who show up and ask to talk with them rather than to emails, phone calls, or letters. It is much easier to put someone off with these more "distanced" approaches. Whichever approach you use, it is important to discuss beforehand with your instructor what you will do, say, or write since you, as fieldworker, are also a representative of your college or university.

In approaching a setting, you should take into account anything about the setting that might be relevant to either allowing or denying you access—if you have this information. Some settings, such as police departments or mental hospitals, are liable to fairly frequent controversies, political battles, and other difficulties, which can make them inhospitable to ethnographic research. In September 1969, W. Boyd Littrell (1979) proposed a study of the administration of criminal law in Fairfield County, New Jersey. His project was approved by Fairfield assistant prosecutors, but

> in November 1969 William T. Cahill, a Republican, defeated the Democrat Robert Meyner in the gubernatorial election. A new prosecutor from a different political party would soon be appointed and the entire project would have to be cleared again. I realized then that my project and I were part of the patronage granted by New Jersey Democrats. (1979, 237)

This change in gatekeepers required that Littrell renegotiate, and even redesign, his research.

GATEKEEPERS

Gatekeepers are those individuals or groups who can grant or deny initial access to a setting—usually a formal organization—and if you are lucky they won't change while entrée is being negotiated. In Warren's (1982) research with a mental health court in Los Angeles, the contact person was the judge—as is the case with any study of courtrooms. In Karner's (1995) research in a Veterans Administration hospital, the contact person and gatekeeper was a professional staff member on the unit she wished to study. Zafirau (2008) enrolled in a local university's film school to facilitate Hollywood contacts; once there, he met a partner in a Hollywood talent agency who gave him ethnographic entrée as an intern. In other kinds of organizations you might have to find out whom to contact—the manager-owner of a restaurant, say, or the top administrator of a nursing home. If these gatekeepers accept your presence as a researcher, other people in the setting will have little choice other than to extend at least a courtesy acceptance to you (more on this in Chapter 4).

Gary Alan Fine (1996) describes the steps to his research entrée into four restaurant kitchens in a large urban area using the restaurants' gatekeepers. He contacted people he knew at each restaurant from a prior stint at a culinary institute (three head chefs and a manager) and sought introductions to head managers or owners. To this second level of gatekeeper, Fine clarified that he had the chef's approval and that he would not evaluate the restaurant (i.e., he was not a food critic in professorial disguise). He told these gatekeepers that he just wanted to stand and watch, and that if they felt his presence interfered with the business he would terminate the research. All agreed, although one requested a formal letter. Fine spent a month observing in each restaurant for six days a week, and reported no problems with the gatekeepers.

In his study of police interrogations, Richard Leo (2001) did not have such an easy time with gatekeepers. Like Littrell (1979) some twenty years earlier, he was initially blocked from doing research because the chief and the captain "feared my study could generate negative publicity for the orga-nization" (Leo 2001, 264). However, when his PhD adviser was asked to do an evaluation study of the police department, this "created a strong incentive for the police chief to be in the good graces" of this adviser. Leo was then permitted to undertake his research, but still had difficulty persuading indi-vidual detectives to allow him to observe their interrogations (2001, 264).

Once having been accepted as a researcher by the "powers that be," you may have a date and time of entrée set for you, or you may have some choice in the matter. Once his gatekeepers—owners, managers, and chefs—had agreed to Fine's kitchen observations, he chose a day to begin his research, one based on prior knowledge of the contingencies of the setting. He began his research at a time that he knew the kitchen staff would not be busy, so he could explain to all of them individually what he was doing. No one refused to allow him access to their work lives, and everyone he asked for an interview said yes: "Like the head chefs, they were flattered that someone of 'importance' was interested in their lives" (Fine 1996, 244).

If you are given a time and place to enter the setting, be punctual. You can also expect that your gatekeeper will give you a tour of the setting, then perhaps leave you in the hands of an assistant or someone else who will feel a sense of responsibility for "entertaining" you. Over time, in general, that sense of responsibility and entertainment on the part of setting-members will fade, and they will go about their business, getting used to your presence in the meantime.

Warren's research subsequent to her 1982 ethnography illustrated several of these issues in acceptance and entrée. A few years after the ethnography of this court was published, she became interested in studying court hearings in which potential electroshock patients sought to avoid being given that particular treatment. Instead of approaching the new judge (whom she did not know), Warren approached (in person) the head district attorney in the court, whom she had known from earlier research. He said he would check with the judge, and then called her to say her research had been approved and she should show up the following Monday at 8:30 a.m., when an ECT hearing was scheduled.

The following Monday at 8:30 a.m., Warren showed up promptly to learn that this hearing had been canceled, and that few electroshock hearings were even scheduled. Thus, while hoping that an ECT case might occur within her lifetime, she decided that it might be useful to spend time looking at the court records of past cases. Her interest in entrée was not only into the courtroom to observe interaction, but also into the files to gain some understanding of the background to these cases. IRB permission to do this was not an issue at this time (the mid-1980s). The district attorney gradually allowed Warren access to these records. At first, he pulled them by case number and read them to her. Then, he pulled them by case number and let her look at them. Some months later, he gave her free access to the files, allowing Warren to pull and return them as she saw fit.

This anecdote illustrates the provisional and dynamic quality of entrée: it may not be a one-time event, accomplished once and for all for the remainder of the research. The researcher is first accepted as an observer, then appears somewhere in the setting. But once in the setting, access to different parts of the setting may require further entrée activities; in the court, Warren had access to the district attorney's office and the courtroom but not, this time around, to the judge's chambers. In addition, the point of entrée is to enter into not only physical settings but also the social meanings, which requires more than simply the copresence of researcher and setting members. If Warren had access to the district attorney's office, but whenever she was there the attorney felt compelled to go elsewhere to discuss their cases (which is what happened at one point in the first phase of her Metropolitan Court research), then her entrée would mean little. These continued entrée processes are part of the long-term conduct of field research, which is discussed in Chapter 4.

It is clear from the discussion of field research so far that issues such as entrée and access are common to all settings, but also that a variety of issues occur in different settings. While it is not possible for us to cover all the possibilities that might arise in your field research, some aspects of the research process are common to various types of settings. In many settings, but especially in bureaucracies and other organizations, key informants play a role in introducing and sponsoring the fieldworker. And in other settings, but especially in community studies, the go-along with key informants provides insight into the meanings a setting has for individuals within it. In still other settings, including but not limited to ones in other countries, the researcher may initially be seen as a spy.

KEY INFORMANTS

In some settings, including organizations, key informants may smooth your way into different situations and connections. Some of these key informants are the gatekeepers who initially permitted entrée into the setting, and indeed, gatekeepers may remain key informants as the research progresses. Other key informants may emerge during the process of research, providing access to new settings or other parts of a setting. Wacquant (2004) was introduced to the gym where he studied boxing by a friend; once at the gym and involved in serious training as a boxer, he was befriended by the trainer (ix–x).

During Warren's Metropolitan Court research she became interested in visiting the mental hospitals from which the court drew its petitioners. She got to know one of the visiting mental health counselors responsible for connecting patients who asked for *habeas corpus* writ hearings with court personnel who could schedule those hearings. After some socializing and discussion of Warren's research interests, this mental health counselor invited Warren to ride along as she went back to the hospital and continued her work with the patients. Warren was very grateful, and took her up on her offer. The opportunity to see the interactions between counselors and patients before they came to court was a valuable step in further understanding the organizational network within which the court was one part.

Though it is not unusual to identify helpful individuals in settings, sometimes their desire to assist the researcher can outweigh their allegiance to their own organizational protocols. While still a young and somewhat naive graduate student, Karner approached a staff member at a local AIDS foundation about the possibility of meeting and interviewing individuals with HIV. The staff member enthusiastically offered to have Karner accompany her on home visits to clients of the foundation. When the director of the organization discovered the staff member's activities, she nearly lost her job, which put an end to Karner's access. Thus, it is wise to be wary of eager offers to help, for many reasons.

Generations of field researchers have, in fact, warned novice fieldworkers that key informants may be problematic in some ways. It is a truism of anthropology and everyday life that members of a setting who are immediately warm and welcoming may be outsiders in their own circles looking for acceptance among newcomers. The twelfth grader who immediately looks for friends among incoming tenth and eleventh graders is one example among many. It is no use cultivating a key informant who is somewhat of a pariah among her or his own people. The rule of thumb in settings where key informants present themselves is to wait and see, at least for a while.

Key informants are not always pariahs in their own worlds; they may be friendly people who are welcoming to any stranger who comes along, including ethnographers. And in some settings, such as bars, friendliness to strangers is encouraged and facilitated by the loosening effect of alcohol. Friendliness and sociability do not always mean truth telling, however, as Box 3.3 indicates. Key informants are perfectly capable of inventing stories and giving the researcher various kinds of runarounds.

Ethnographers have sometimes found key informants in a setting who understand or are connected in some way with the research enterprise. This kind of understanding can greatly facilitate entrée. Esther Newton, an anthropologist interested in studying male drag performers in Chicago in the mid-1960s, sat in on drag shows—then quite "taboo" (Newton 1972, 133)— and also wanted to interview performers. She approached one impersonator who "replied that he had majored in anthropology in college and…would willingly talk to me" (Newton 1972, 134). This man became, over time, "at least as dedicated to the study as I was" (Newton 1972, 133). A student of

---

BOX 3.3
KEY INFORMANTS AT PLAY

Another…problem sometimes occurs when community members know that a sociologist is doing research—they put you on. This is not a problem confined to prostitute respondents who are paid for giving data and feel they have to give the poor john a really good story. Especially in a community where sociability is the main activity and putting people on is one of the happenings, this can happen very often and certainly happened to Warren from time to time. Here is one example from Warren's *Identity and Community in the Gay World* (1972, 170–171):

> Gene said to me in conversation at the bar this evening, "There was this guy from Local College doing research as he called it, and he was really gorgeous, really groovy, and straight. Well, we all really gave him a bad time, told him all of these things, like we used bananas up our ass, and he wrote it all down—for weeks. It was fun." I asked Gene why it was fun, and he indicated that it provided a change from the same old routine at the bar.
>
> Alex told me with a straight face this evening that he and Jake get their kicks sitting on their roof with raincoats and boots on. I saw a certain gleam in his eye when he said it, and he added, "Tell that when you write your book."

Warren's who was studying—and also a member of—the Society for Creative Anachronism, found a key informant in a fellow SCA member who was also an anthropologist.

THE RESEARCHER AS SPY

A researcher who has gained entrée to a setting through one or a group of key informants may find that he is initially assumed to be a spy by other people in the setting. This presumption is particularly common in non-Western societies with a colonial history. In field research in this country, the spying presumption is most likely in hierarchical organizations, where conflict and antagonisms may occur within and between groups. When Gary Alan Fine did his study of restaurants in *Kitchens* (1996), management had allowed his entrée. He comments:

> One day early in the research one of the kitchen workers whom I had not previously met, seeing me constantly jotting in my notepad, inquired if I was conducting a time study.... Paul, the head chef, jokes about me being a spy, adding that "he's watching to make sure we work." (1996, 234)

Management's interest was in ensuring that the kitchen workers worked up to speed, and did not eat—"steal"—the food. However, Fine's fieldnotes often documented these forms of "minor deviance":

> Felicia...eats a piece of the roast beef that had been trimmed off and giggles when she sees me watching. She says to me laughing: "Are you going to put this in your book?"...Lee, a dishwasher, takes some of the beef and jokes to me: "Which part will we steal today?" I am expected to legitimate their deviance, or, better, to participate in it. (1996, 234)

Over the course of the research, according to Fine, the question of who he represented remained unclear to the workers, although it was clear that he did not report to management (1996, 234). Fine did, however, refer to himself and his fellow ethnographers as "spies...like myself" (1996, 233).

Barrie Thorne's (1971) experience studying the draft resistance movement in Boston in the late 1960s provides a political example of the researcher as spy. "The issue of betrayal of trust was thrust upon me in a direct and painful way," Thorne writes, "when I eventually realized that some of the movement members had come to regard me with great suspicion, wondering if I was a 'Fed'" (1983, 227). Within the movement, infiltrators from the FBI were referred to as "Feds." Given her role as a researcher, Thorne reflected on the similarities between her activities as a field researcher and what a "Fed" would do:

> I also was myself doing a kind of spywork not unlike what I imagined a Fed would do, I was systematically observing; I kept my ear out for

a range of information and detail....I asked the kinds of questions a
Fed would also want to know: "When did you turn in your draft card?"
"What led up to that decision?" "What organizations had you been in?"
And I listened attentively, committing the responses to mind for later
recording. (1983, 229)

Good fieldwork does have many of the elements of spywork.

Though Thorne's study was of a radical political group, similar dynamics
may also occur in mainstream organizations. Bureaucracies are hierarchies,
and as such may be rife with cliques, gossip, backstabbing, and other activities of great interest to "spies." In her ethnography of police work, Jennifer
Hunt found that her informants initially viewed her with suspicion. Hunt
notes that any stranger doing research on urban police is liable to be seen as
a spy, but a woman even more so. Not only was the police department she
studied embroiled in a lawsuit charging gender discrimination against female
officers, but she also found that

> the role of spy was consistent with my gender identity. As a civilian
> and a moral woman I respected the formal order of the law and the
> inside world of the academy. As both FBI and police internal security
> also represented the formal order, it was logical to assume I was allied
> with them. In addition, no policeman believed a woman was politically
> capable of fighting the department to promote honest research. Instead,
> the dominant elite would use me for their own purposes. (1984, 289)

Unlike Thorne, who began as a member then became a researcher in
the radical political group, both Fine and Hunt were given entrée to their
settings by gatekeepers, and consequently were initially seen as spies by those
lower in the hierarchy who did not, however, have any choice in the matter.
This was also true of Warren's Metropolitan Court research; although anyone
could attend hearings in one of the two courtrooms, it was only by the permission of the judge that she was able to wander around the "backstage" area
of offices. At times, as in Warren's research and Hunt's, some of this initial
suspicion remained, and some interactions were hidden from the researcher.
At other times, as in Fine's study, suspicions of spying were replaced by a
greater trust and acceptance.

Go-Alongs, Tour Narratives, and Shadowing

In addition to—or instead of—gaining entrée to a particular space, researchers
may move around in a space with respondents, combining ethnography with
interviewing, conversation, or videotaping. In the go-along, the researcher
walks or drives around with respondents, informally interviewing them and

discovering what various aspects of their environment mean to them; in the tour narrative this is combined with videotaping. Shadowing is used where the respondent is engaged in work activities such as caregiving, where he or she must focus on aspects of the setting other than the fieldworker.

Go-alongs have been used in communities in the Los Angeles area by UCLA ethnographers. In her Hollywood research, Margaret Kusenbach found that going along with people who lived in the community illuminated the biographical meanings of community membership to residents, something not ordinarily highlighted either by ethnography or by off-site interviewing. For example, Kusenbach walked through the neighborhood with a realtor, who spoke of the property values and resale histories of the houses they passed; to him, the meaning of the neighborhood was intertwined with his occupation as realtor. As she walked with a retiree, Ross, who had worked in the city's department of street lighting, he noticed the lighting:

> Ross points out something to me that I have never noticed before: the fact that the street lights in Gilmore Junction are installed on only one side of the street and that there are only three of them in the entire block. He tells me what this particular type of lamp is called, "Cobra," and he also says that these lamps are much too high....Ross also says: "I always take notice of the lights!" He tells me that when he traveled in Venice (Italy), the hometown of his wife, he realized that the streetlights were very yellow, unlike in the U.S. (Kusenbach 2003, 473)

Ross also "likened the property on the corner of his block to a 'jungle'" because of its wild, dense foliage. He did not approve of this jungle look, preferring "civilized" and tidy gardens. Another go-along, Jill, a musician in her late forties, used the same term, "jungle," to refer to the garden, but in her case the term was used approvingly; she "just loved" how it looked (Kusenbach 2003, 475).

Studies of urban space can be done from the standpoint of the stranger-observer, as Lyn Lofland has done in her ethnographic work (1998). But the go-along enables the fieldworker to gain access to the individual, as well as the collective, meanings of participating in public interaction. As Kusenbach summarizes:

> The position of the lonely, outside observer well suits studies of public space because anonymity reigns here and the dominant principles of interaction are based on categoric, not personal knowing. But it takes a more familiar, intimate vantage point to understand the dynamics of interaction in communal (and private) realms—and this is where walk-alongs have a considerable edge over ethnographic methods. (2003, 472)

Sara Pink (2007) used what she calls "walking with video" in her study of a community garden. Pink accompanied her respondent to his garden, asking questions, joining in the enjoyment of landscape and seasons, and document-ing with videotape. She notes that the "integration of video" into the go-along "can serve as a catalyst for creating ethnographic understandings of other people's experiences, and represent...those experiences to a wider audience" (Pink 2007, 240).

Shadowing staff can help the researcher understand individual experi-ences within organizations. In a recent study with Lynn Snow (Snow et al. 2007), Karner shadowed care staff in a dementia unit of a long-term care facility. Beginning with the LPN who was the unit supervisor, Karner fol-lowed nursing assistants as they went about their patient care tasks. These staff members functioned as key informants by explaining the various aspects of their role—the insider knowledge needed to do their tasks—and the social worlds of the unit. As part of a larger study that included qualitative inter-views, surveys, and patient records, the shadowing data in this project was used to contextualize the organizational factors that influenced how care was accomplished and interpretations communicated (see also Williams and Warren 2008).

Once having selected and been accepted into a setting—or at least to go-along for a while—you are in a position to begin your field research in ear-nest. If you are studying an organization, permissions have been granted both formally and informally, gatekeepers have been helpful, and perhaps they remain available to you as key informants. Alternatively, you have been in as a member already, for weeks to years, but now you are in as a researcher, changing the ways in which you observe and interact with people in the setting. You may have decided to do visual ethnography using a still or video camera, or an autoethnography, or a "realist tale." With any of these approaches—as stranger or member, as ethnographer or autoethnographer—you are going to have to pay a different kind of attention to the setting as a qualitative researcher than you do in everyday life. You will find yourself attending to things with intensity and in ways that are unfamiliar—and typi-cally quite tiring. You will find yourself making and unmaking various kinds of relationships with informants, and taking on or being cast into various social roles (Chapter 4). And you will be writing fieldnotes (Chapter 5).

Suggestions for Further Reading

Hine, Christine M. 2000. *Virtual Ethnography*. London: Sage.
Mitchell, Richard G., Jr. 2002. *Dancing at Armageddon: Survivalism and Chaos in Modern Times*. Chicago: University of Chicago Press.
Robinson, Christine M. 2008. *The Web: Social Control in a Lesbian Community*. Lanham, MD: University Press of America.

Wacquant, Loic. 2004. *Body and Soul: Notebooks of an Apprentice Boxer.* New York: Oxford University Press.
Additionally, there are journals within the social sciences that publish contemporary ethnographic research as well as methodological discussions, including the following: *Journal of Contemporary Ethnography; Qualitative Sociology; Journal of the Society of Symbolic Interaction; Ethnography; Qualitative Inquiry; Field Methods; American Ethnologist; Cultural Anthropology;* and *Ethos.*

Chapter 4

Roles and Relationships in Field Research

This chapter is about doing field research once you have achieved initial entrée, or—in the case of preexisting membership—once you have begun to explore the field as researcher as well as member. The key issue for the field researcher as stranger is the development of new roles and relationships; for the member or "indigenous" researcher, it is how existing relationships develop and change. For the stranger-ethnographer, what is problematic in interaction is figuring out who is who and how to fit in; for the member-researcher, it is how to maintain existing roles and relationships while adapting them to research. In this chapter, first we will explore the incorporation of the stranger and second the reincorporation of the member.

In the case of undergraduate students, field research may be limited to a semester or less, while graduate students or professors may conduct field research for a year or more. Warren studied Metropolitan Court for a total of seven years, although she visited the court only a few times a week for a few hours at a time. But however short or long your stay in the field, interacting and talking with its members is likely to have a profound influence on you, and perhaps you will have some influence on them, as well. As in all other arenas of social life, the personal, culturally meaningful characteristics we discussed in the last chapter, such as gender and nationality, shape the roles and relationships occurring in the field.

The term *role* refers to the individual's place within a social setting or network of social relationships. The fieldworker who enters a setting takes on (from his or her perspective) the role of fieldworker. Other setting members, however, may assign to the researcher the role of mascot, apprentice, or other roles, associated with embodiment. The fieldworker may also develop particular kinds of relationships with setting members, which in published ethnographic research have included everything from enmity (not a good idea in field research) to sexual liaisons (ditto). The ethical standards and guidelines discussed in Chapter 2 should be reviewed as you continue your fieldwork, because the intersections of roles and the development of relationships inevitably bring with them ethical dilemmas in the conduct of fieldwork.

Incorporation refers to the ways in which people in a setting define the researcher and accord her or him a particular role or social place in that setting. This process has to do not only with the personal and social characteristics of the researcher but also with the setting and its members as things go along, and change, over time. Since most of you will probably be doing your research in the surrounding community rather than abroad, we will confine our examples mainly to research conducted in the United States rather than (as typically occurs among anthropologists) in the third world or other countries where both language and nationality are issues.

Since the 1960s, the literature on incorporation into roles and relationships in field research has identified a number of key themes. One theme is the significance of personal characteristics, or *embodiment*, in the process of fieldwork. Gender and race have received the most attention in the methodological literature in sociological field methods, particularly the issues confronted by women studying a variety of settings, and men—black and white—studying race. Certain common themes appear in these discussions, including the setting members treating young women researchers as mascots and young men as apprentices. Sex in the field has been discussed for thirty years in sociology, longer in anthropology, in themes ranging from consensual sex to sexual harassment and rape. The issue of danger sometimes appears in these sexual narratives, and at other times in narratives of males researching violent subcultures.

Incorporation and Research Roles

The ways in which a field researcher is incorporated into the field—as well as the ways he or she is granted or denied entrée, discussed in Chapter 3—are dependent on many factors, including the researcher's race, age, appearance and demeanor, and gender. Anthropologists who study highly gender-stratified and even gender-separated societies have long noted the importance of gender in ethnographic research. In 1885, anthropologist Edward B. Tylor stated that

> to get at the confidence of the tribes, the man of the house, though he can do a great deal, cannot do it all. If his wife sympathizes with his work, and

is able to do it, really half the work of investigation seems to fall to her, so much is to be learned through the women of the tribe which the men will not readily disclose. The experience seemed to me a lesson to anthropologists not to…ward the ladies off from their proceedings, but rather to avail themselves thankfully for their help. (quoted in Wax 1979, 517)

At that time, the researching "ladies" were often the wives of ethnographers rather than trained ethnographers themselves.

In some settings, opposite-gender researchers may have an advantage. In Elliott Liebow's fieldwork with homeless women, he described how being a male was useful to the conduct of his research, while his age (late middle age) and Jewishness did not seem to be problematic (1993, x). He noted, "Most of the women probably liked having me around. Male companionship was generally in short supply and the women often made a fuss about the few male volunteers" (1993, xi).

Other characteristics of the gendered body have also been the subject of discussion among ethnographers. Liebow said of himself: "I am 6'1" and weigh about 175 pounds. I had a lot of white hair but was otherwise nondescript" (1993, x). Who knows what might have happened had he been young and handsome, or black and weighing 400 pounds? Anthropologist Rosalie Wax, in her analysis of gender and age in fieldwork during the 1940s through the 1970s, noted that in her study of a World War II Japanese internment camp, "perhaps the fact that I was a strapping five feet ten and weighed (then) about 180 pounds helped a bit" in enabling her to evade danger and threat (1979, 521).

The ethnographic tradition of male ethnographers writing about men and masculinity (Winlow et al. 2001) is fairly recent, as are gender studies. However, a longer tradition exists of Anglo, white male ethnographers (and some African-American male ethnographers) writing about race. Many of these works are set in Chicago, since the university campus is on the edge of a black ghetto area. Early Chicago classics in this genre include William F. Whyte's *Street Corner Society* (1943) and Elliott Liebow's *Tally's Corner* (1967); more recent examples are Loïc Wacquant's *Body and Soul* (2004) and Sudhir Venkatesh's *Off the Books: The Underground Economy of the Urban Poor* (2006). Research using the urban Chicago style, but set elsewhere, include Mitchell Duneier's *Slim's Table* (1994) and Elijah Anderson's *Streetwise* (1990) and *Code of the Street* (1999). These works analyze racial differences and similarities of race, class, and ethnicity as they affect the conduct of field research done by and about men.

Mitchell Duneier (who is white) recounts an occasion on which he went with an African-American photographer, Ovie, to a bookstore to have a picture taken of some major ethnographic books. Ovie thought that they should ask permission of the bookstore's manager to clear a shelf of its for-sale books and replace them with the ethnographies, but Mitch did not want to bother. This event taught Mitch something about being black, or white, in public space:

> In a very sensitive way [Ovie] pointed out something I knew in theory but had not acted on in the situation: As a white man I go through life believing I can take liberties that black men would never think of taking. One can only imagine what would have happened if a black man had been seen putting books in a bag....I felt stupid. If anyone should have been aware of the situation, it was a sociologist who was writing about black men. (1999, 166)

As we saw in Chapter 3, there were other occasions of ethnic and racial differences between Duneier and his male respondents in his New York study of homeless African-American street book vendors (1999). He used tape recorders, continually running, to capture the interaction that took place at the vendors' tables. At one point during his absence from the scene, a conversation was recorded that questioned his research motives in the context of race, ethnicity, and class. The vendors were wondering why he did not study rich people who have yard sales, instead of them:

> He's not questioning them....He's questioning us! He want to know how did the homeless people get to do it....Not really trying to help us. He's trying to figure out how did the homeless people get a lock on something that he consider *lucrative*....You gotta remember, he's a Jew, you know. They used to taking over. (1999, 337)

It is not surprising that Duneier concluded, as he was publishing his study as a book, that at times he thought that "the truce I thought I had developed [with the book vendors] was nothing more than an illusion" (1999, 14). In ethnography, race and ethnicity, like gender, may be deeply and dichotomously divisive in our culture, as in our social institutions.

As an apprentice boxer and a Frenchman, Wacquant (2004) was more sanguine about his genuine acceptance among male Chicago African-Americans. He says that "being the only white member in the [boxing] club...could have constituted a serious obstacle to my integration"—but it did not, partly because of his ability and willingness to learn boxing, and partly because he is French. Among the nicknames bestowed on him by the other boxers were "The French Hammer" and "The French Bomber" (2004, 11).

Being of the same gender and ethnicity as one's respondents does not, however, guarantee an ethnographic experience free of difficulty. Dorrine Kondo, a Japanese American woman, studied family and workplace in Japan during the 1980s.

> My ambiguous insider/outsider position in the field may have made the issue of identity and selfhood especially acute, but other studies by white

female ethnographers and by Japanese American men suggest that my experience was not a unique one. (Kondo 2001, 199)

Although she was Japanese by heritage, Kondo did not speak perfect Japanese, she had not been socialized into Japanese gender norms, and she was an American citizen. Thus it was culture and nationality, not ethnicity or race, which formed the basis of ethnographic difference for her.

Over the past thirty years, qualitative social scientists have analyzed patterns in ethnographic relationships that involve differences in gender and age between setting and researcher. Young women have experienced being treated by powerful males in various organizational settings as mascots—that is, when, as "dancing daughters," they could avoid the sexualization of interaction that sometimes also occurred. Young men have reported being treated by powerful males in similar settings as apprentices: people eager to learn about the setting in possible preparation for becoming a member. That is not to say that women are never defined and treated as apprentices, or men as mascots or sex objects, during the process of field research, just that these have been the most commonly inscribed experiences.

RESEARCHERS AS MASCOTS, APPRENTICES, AND DANCING DAUGHTERS

Liebow referred to his gender in the homeless women study as a "resource" (1993, xi). Many women fieldworkers have documented gender-as-resource in a variety of settings, including the fieldworker as mascot, sexual object, or dancing daughter. More than thirty years ago, Arlene Kaplan Daniels, engaged in fieldwork and interviewing with military psychiatrists, noticed that her male respondents treated her like a mascot: someone nice to have around, but not taken very seriously. Daniels recounts how one officer explained her presence: "She's a great girl. She's our mascot. She studies us" (Daniels 1967, 286). Ten years later, Lois Easterday and her colleagues noted that the research "mascot is accepted simply for 'being'" rather than for research competence (1977, 343). More than twenty years later, Laura Adams noted the same patterns in her research on bureaucrats in Uzbekistan. She became a mascot to these middle-aged men, being a "good girl" in dress and demeanor, and "approving of [her hosts'] nation-building projects" (Adams 1999, 340–342).

For men, the functional equivalent of mascoting female researchers seems to be apprenticeship. William Foote Whyte (1992) noted this research role in his retrospective discussion of his own fieldwork among "corner boys" several decades earlier; he was an apprentice to the art and task of "hanging out" on the corner. In his ethnographic, videotaped study of pawnshops, Geoff Harkness (2003) noticed that the pawnshop owners and managers identified him, and identified with him, as a fellow heterosexual white male interested in making a buck. They presumed that his interest in the pawnshop extended not only to videotaping but also to possible work as, or investment in, pawnbroking. Burke Forrest, in discussing his apprenticeship research in "hidden worlds" such as spiritualist groups, comments:

> Apprenticeship is largely a matter of attitude and…can be carried out in almost any setting.…The apprentice attitude is one of sincere questioning with a willingness to be taught about the meanings behind the actions in a given milieu. (1986, 437)

Wacquant (2004) went so far as to subtitle his book *Body and Soul: Notebooks of an Apprentice Boxer* (emphasis added).

How a researcher is perceived can also vary by whom one is interacting with even within the same setting. When Karner was researching a unit of a Veterans Administration hospital where clinical interns were common, she was treated as an apprentice. Her key informant, who did not have internship supervisory responsibilities, took great care to place Karner in this role, introducing her to the Veterans Administration procedures as well as explaining and elaborating about treatment philosophies. Other clinical staff members on the unit who routinely supervised *real* interns—and knew Karner was not one—viewed her as a mascot of her key informant. In contrast, however, the veterans seemed to see her role quite differently. One veteran dubbed her the "translator." If they could have Karner understand their combat experience and its aftermath, she could then translate it to the rest of society. Thus, the veterans treated her more like an apprentice—but one seeking knowledge or awareness rather than skill. As Karner's experience illustrates, it is not that women could not be treated as apprentices, nor men as mascots in some field settings, it is just that, thus far, women have written mainly about mascoting and men about apprenticeship.

The "dancing daughter" is, like the mascot, associated with women rather than men, but while mascoting represents the response of men in the field to women, the dancing daughter represents a strategy of women researchers in a field of men. The "dancing daughter" attendance upon the powerful male(s) in the setting is busy, cheerful, and just out of reach. Warren used this strategy in the early 1980s with the judge of Metropolitan Court (Warren 1982). More than a decade later, Laura Adams (1999), who was also treated at times as a mascot during her research in Uzbekistan, reported that the former administrator of a television company told people that she was his "little daughter" (1999, 361). The "dancing daughter dances to attract her 'field father's' eye and keep it paternally (not sexually) on her" (Warren 2001, 217).

SEX AND QUALITATIVE RESEARCH

The literature of fieldwork has considered sex as well as gender as an aspect of field relationships. This literature refers to several aspects of sexuality: consensual sex, sexual objectification or harassment, and sexual danger, as well as sexual orientation. Erich Goode (1999, 2002) notes that although emotions, intimacy, and sexuality are often part of field research as they are of everyday life, social researchers rarely discuss this issue in the articles and books they publish (1999, 302), although there is plenty of gossip among ethnographers about "lurid assignations, couplings, trysts, and other linkages between ethnographers and those they 'observe'" (Fine 1993, 283).

One of the few sociologists who has written about his own sexual behavior in the field is Erich Goode (1999, 2002). Goode describes his sexual experience in three research endeavors, including an ethnographic and interview study of the National Association to Aid Fat Americans (NAAFA; by 2002 renamed the National Association to Advance Fat Acceptance). He says that "sex represented my unconditional entry into NAAFA....Only by dating was I seen as a full-fledged member of the organization"; however, dating "recklessly and promiscuously" was also his "undoing" as a NAAFA member (Goode 1999, 314). The point of revealing these sexual activities, according to Goode, is that "sex was a central fact of my investigation of that setting, and any honest account had to take note of it" (1999, 314). A critic of Goode, Clifton Bryant, finds Goode's and others' justifications of their sexual activities in the field "far from persuasive," and states

> there is little real evidence that sex with informants...actually enhances the researcher's integration into the community, facilitates the research process, or sharpens or enriches research insight. Instead, the accounts...would seem to be essentially self-serving, methodologically spurious, and an effort to normalize hedonistic tendencies. (1999, 327)

Most of the literature on sex and gender in fieldwork during the past half century was written by women fieldworkers and is focused on issues of sexualization, sexual objectification, sexual harassment, and even sexual danger in the field. For many women fieldworkers, being treated like a mascot or dancing daughter is preferable to—and may head off—being treated as a sexual object. Although the term "sexual harassment" was not in general use thirty years ago, Joy Browne documented the sexualization of interaction that occurred while she did research in a used car lot during the 1970s:

> As I progressed with my project, it became important to note that I was a young woman. Irrelevant as it might have seemed at the outset, the fact that used car lots have little shacks that can cozily accommodate a salesman (nearly all are men, and all those I encountered were men) created a methodological problem. I had to develop a method of convincing a sometimes over-eager informant that I did not want to be that kind of participant. (1976, 78)

By the 1990s, fieldwork accounts of being treated as sexual "fair game" had become less oblique, and were framed as sexual harassment. Terry

Williams and his colleagues noted that in their urban street ethnography project and in other settings,

> several female ethnographers have had their fieldwork severely constrained or have had to terminate it completely...due to the sexual expectations and demands of other males in the research setting. The threat of sexual assault or rape is a real concern for most female ethnographers and staff members. (1992, 363)

One of these female ethnographers wrote that when treated as "fair game," she usually would "just move away or shift to a conversation with someone else" (Williams et al. 1992, 355).

As Angrosino (2007, 105) notes, "it is impossible to legislate—let alone enforce—a single standard of appropriate behavior" among qualitative researchers concerning sex in the field. But the consequences of sex with respondents can range from lawsuits directed at the researcher and the sponsoring institution to sexual danger. And such liaisons can affect, as many aspects of fieldwork do, relationships with other people both inside and outside the setting. Despite his own experiences and revelations, Goode (1999), too, warns that sex in the field can be dangerous to the researcher in a number of ways, especially for women. One survey he cites reported that 7 percent of female anthropologists reported rape or attempted rape against them in the field. Goode notes,

> For all researchers [sexual liaisons] may make a research enterprise less viable, close off avenues of information, and upset and anger participants.... Sex on the job traverses much of the same landmined territory. (1999, 314)

With regard to potential sexual aggression, a researcher needs to use common sense and social awareness in the field as in everyday life. This is also the case when studying settings where other forms of violence may occur.

VIOLENCE IN QUALITATIVE RESEARCH

It is not only women who can be endangered by sexual—and nonsexual—violence in ethnographic research. Men who research settings in which male violence is commonplace may also face the consequences of such immersion. While studying motorcycle gangs, Hopper and Moore (1990) were threatened with physical violence when events did not unfold as the bikers liked. The bikers did not like questions, uninvited comments, or humor directed against events that they took seriously, such as wrestling on TV. For example,

> At times when we were not expecting any problems conditions became hazardous....One morning in 1985 we walked into an area where bikers

had camped out all night. Half asleep and hung over, several of them jumped up and pulled guns on us because they thought we might be members of a rival gang that had killed five of their "brothers" several years earlier. If Grubby, a biker who recognized us from previous encounters, had not interceded on our behalf, we could have been killed or seriously injured. (1990, 368–369)

Although these two male ethnographers escaped actual violence, others have not been so fortunate. Sanchez-Jankowski (1990), who studied gangs in New York, Boston, and Los Angeles, was subjected to physical violence by gang members.

The ethnographer may not only be endangered but may also endanger others. In a British study of bouncers (men, and sometimes women, who are hired to keep order in bars and nightclubs), Simon Winlow and his colleagues focused their analysis on the male working-class parameters of social worlds such as those of bouncers. They comment, "In this field doing research was dealing with violence, and sometimes doing violence" (2001, 537). Bouncers are not paid very much, and

the real benefits of the occupation are grounded deep within masculine working-class culture and self-identity...with its powerful appreciation of bodily power, personal and group respect and violent engagement....Being a bouncer allows a demonstrative cultivation of a hyper-masculine persona: from body language to the cut of their clothes to the way they smoke their cigarettes. (Winlow et al. 2001, 541)

The one member of the research team who got a job as a bouncer was liable to violence by bar customers, and also had to engage in violence when the job conditions made this necessary: "It was impossible to avoid problematic interactions with bar customers, who might well be drunk or under the influence of drugs, and it was impossible just to stand and observe" (Winlow et al. 2001, 543). Incorporation into the social world of the bouncer involved, inevitably, participation in violent encounters.

Danger in field research may involve sex, violence, or violent sex, for women or for men fieldworkers. However, there are also dangers in fieldwork that do not involve violations of the body, most notably the danger of arrest when studying illegal behavior. Although he did not think about this issue at the time, Laud Humphreys (1970) could have been arrested, under sodomy laws of the time, for being an accessory to felonious sex acts. The Adlers were afraid of being arrested during their research into the "wheeling and dealing" of drugs in the context of their own drug use. They comment, "We broke the law ourselves....It would have been impossible for a nonuser to have gained access to this group" (Adler 1985, 24). The Adlers did not get arrested, and they completed their research successfully.

Incorporation: Finding a Place

By now it should be clear that incorporation into the setting is a matter of negotiation between the embodied researcher and the members. The literature on incorporation from the 1970s onward (although the process was not referred to as incorporation in the 1970s in sociology) discussed entrée (see Chapter 3), choosing a research role, and other themes such as the research bargain (more recently referred to as the useful researcher), going native, being proselytized to convert (generally to a religion or cult), emotions in the field, and leaving the field.

In early (1970s and prior) sociological field research, the presumption was that the researcher chose the role he or she would play in the field—a presumption that was behind the discussion of covert versus overt roles. By the 1980s, sociological ethnographers had come to the realization (as their anthropological colleagues had done earlier) that incorporation into the setting involved more than the researcher choosing and acting out a role. The respondents had their own definitions of the situation, ones that might vary greatly with the researcher's self-definitions. Gary Alan Fine, in his ethnography of restaurant kitchens, introduced himself as a sociologist who was writing a book. His respondents kept the book part in focus, but also imagined movies; further, they interpreted him as a psychologist rather than a researcher. One cook said, "The book will be *Portrait of a Cook*. I'll have my name up in lights. The movie will be filmed in an insane asylum." Others saw Fine as a "psychologist" or "psychoanalyst," judging "are they crazy or sane?" (1996, 236). Informed consent (see Chapter 2) may require respondents to hear about the researcher's intentions and identities, but it does not force them to define the researcher according to his or her revelations. People outside university settings often do not make distinctions between social science disciplines such as psychology and sociology.

Fine describes incorporation as partly situational and partly a series of stages. He notes that in the four kitchens he studied for one month apiece, it was "a continuing stream of joking" that transformed him "from researcher to worker, from observer to full participant" in the eyes of the cooks (1996, 236). At times he was not permitted to observe, including nights when less expensive specials were served, and times when workers were being trained by observing the kitchen (when it was too busy and too crowded for the ethnographer). Further into the research process, though, Fine writes, "I was present on equally busy nights....Later in the research, when another server was being trained, I was allowed to observe" (1996, 235).

Incorporation into the social world of one part of a setting may mean estrangement from other parts, as Warren found in her research in Metropolitan Court. Acceptance by the judge and the district attorney's office meant, almost automatically, nonacceptance by the public defender's office.

Even in leisure rather than work settings the researcher can be torn between different cliques, as Warren found in her research thirty years ago in the gay male community of a Southern California city (see Box 4.1).

Other issues of incorporation into settings have been written about by ethnographers in various contexts. There may be research bargains in which the researcher is expected to be useful in the setting in return for continued access. *Going native*, a possibility in research where the setting somehow "fits" the researcher, has been seen as a problematic feature of field research since the Chicago School. Acceptance into the field may itself tempt some researchers to glamorize their respondents, an issue that has dogged authors' ethnographic research with poor or minority respondents (Wacquant 2004; Venkatesh 2008). In some religious cults or sects, the fieldworker (no matter what he says) is perceived and treated as a potential convert who is expected to go native. Thus, leaving the field can be a relief (as in a setting where there is escalating and unwanted pressure to convert), or it may be continually delayed in the face of what can become almost an addiction to one's setting.

BOX 4.1
COMPETING RELATIONSHIPS IN FIELD RESEARCH

The gay community is made up of multiple cliques, whose members shift and change, and which do not necessarily get along with one another....I got to know several cliques quite well, but kept some distance from them in order to move into other situations....Sometimes these tactics were successful, and at other times they did not do as well.

> Dick called me up and invited me to go to Beach Town for Sunday brunch with that new set of 'wealthy queens' he's always talking about, so of course I accepted. Justin called almost immediately afterward and suggested that "our group" get together for Sunday brunch....I knew that Justin resented Dick's defection from "the crowd" so I indicated unspecifically that I had another engagement, which bugged him. Joe, I hear, has been commenting to some of his friends, "Carol's too good for us now, she's always up at Beach City with those rich bitches up there." When I called and invited him over, he was quite cold, and claimed he had something planned "every weekend for the next three months."

....As I got to know more people I was invited to more and more homes, often at the same time, and had to weigh increasingly carefully the question of where to go, making sure that I didn't always go where it would be most fun, where everybody liked me, or where I felt most at home.

Warren, Carol. 1972. *Identity and Community in the Gay World*, 173–174. New York: Wiley-Interscience.

RESEARCH BARGAINS

Ethnographers have written extensively over the last thirty years about the research bargain that is part of fieldwork. Incorporation into a setting—being permitted to hang around, interact, and talk with people—is a gift of time and attention. Both fieldworkers and respondents may see this gift as something that needs repayment. People in some settings may seek information or even intervention from researchers perceived as experts. Other settings are so busy and active that anyone around, even the overt fieldworker, is pressed into service of some kind. This aspect of incorporation into a setting—essentially making use of the researcher—is sometimes referred to as the *research bargain*, and the researcher as a "useful" one.

Gary Alan Fine refers to the circumstances of the bargain as "The Plimpton Effect," recalling a "journalist-essayist who briefly participated as a member of professional sports teams" (1996, 236). In his ethnography of restaurant kitchens Fine peeled potatoes, retrieved food from storage, strung beans, and stirred soup when asked. As the research continued, he was jokingly asked to "work the window," mop, cut meat, and "take over" (1996, 237). Agreeing to do these tasks was his "gift" to the workers who were willing to let them into their lives and give him information; their "gifts" to him came in the form of "pleasant little bribes" of food (1996, 237). Fine comments on the place of the research bargain in organizational ethnography:

> The cooks liked me, and I became, in some measure, a member of the group; yet, simultaneously I was and would remain an outsider, potentially affecting their lives and reputations. By bribing me and telling me about their lives they hoped to gain my support. Because they work in scenes that they do not entirely control, and because I have access to those who control them, they were at my mercy. I, in turn, was at their mercy to the degree that I was allowed to operate, briefly and marginally, as one of them. (1996, 238)

Leo (1995) sought access to interrogations of suspects by research bargains with detectives ranging from taking them pastries to listening sympathetically to their "war stories." He also helped out in the office by answering phones or doing other minor bureaucratic tasks, since unoccupied observers just hanging out seem suspicious in police settings. In his research on a Hollywood talent agency, Zafirau found that his "status as a researcher often seemed less important to those at Limelight than my proficiency in making copies, answering phones, and running packages" (2008, 107).

Dorrine Kondo describes the processes by which she, as a Japanese American who did research in Japan, was incorporated into the work and home lives of her hosts. In return for initial and continued research access, Kondo was "bombarded with requests to teach English, a story familiar to any American who had been in Japan" (2001, 198). However, she was also required, over time, to be more and more incorporated into

> the demands and obligations of Japanese social life....People asked me to take part in many social gatherings....Though at the beginning stages of my field research I welcomed all such invitations, the requests and solicitous care shown to me occasionally elicited feelings of invasion. I felt bound by chains of obligation, to my sponsors, my relatives, my friends, and my co-workers. (2001, 198)

In settings where social life is stratified by gender, gender may shape the demands of the research bargain. Kondo was also asked by her host family to help out with the cooking and serving of food. Although she did not mind doing these domestic chores, she was disturbed by the expected behaviors of the men she served, who would "ask for a second helping of rice by merely holding out their rice bowls to the woman nearest the rice cooker and maybe, just maybe, uttering a grunt of thanks in return for her pains" (2001, 193). Similarly, when Warren was doing field research in a residential drug rehabilitation center in Los Angeles in the early 1970s, she was put to work in the kitchen, washing dishes. Such activity was part of her incorporation, as the norms of the setting required that everyone be doing something (even the fieldworker); Warren was put to work in the kitchen because that is where the women in the setting worked.

Other research bargains involve the seeking of goods or money. In his ethnography of *Tally's Corner*, Elliott Liebow (1967) found that the poor street-corner men he was studying asked him for small amounts of money, a request that he found difficult to refuse. Thirty years later (and at the same age of 37), Mitch Duneier (1999) confronted the same issue during his ethnographic research with African-American street magazine and book vendors. As time went on, he was asked for money more often and for larger amounts. Two of his key informants told him that "these men asked me for money on a regular basis because they thought that as a college professor and a Jew, I was 'rich' enough to afford the donations" (Duneier 2001, 184). Although Duneier at first handed out small change willingly, he was not "rich" ("I could hardly afford the tapes I was using to record the street life") and eventually had to limit the scope of his "donations."

Duneier's respondents also sought to use what they perceived as his expertise and high position in the social structure to navigate their lives. He was asked what he regarded as "simple" things such as what the law might be in a given area, and more complex ones such as providing a reference, or finding (and paying for) a lawyer. He even intervened in the setting: together with an Australian architect he designed a "new and improved" vendor cart for the book salesmen. A food cart manufacturer they approached refused to make the book carts for the vendors on the grounds that the local business and legal controllers of Greenwich Village "want to get all the [vendors] off the street...[but] you want to put them on, Mitch! Why you making so much trouble, Mitch?" (Duneier 2001, 186).

As a novice researcher, you may find yourself in situations where your basic human sympathies are brought into play or where, as Fine notes, you are asked to perform services to "cope with the [members'] frustration of seeing the researcher standing around, watching, 'doing nothing'" (1996, 237). It is fine to do small favors for respondents—giving them a few cents for a phone call, perhaps—but it is probably best to refrain from offering major assistance. Giving rides in cars could result in accidents, or bringing someone into your home could have negative consequences. Again, this probably sounds old-fashioned—and it is. But as our old-fashioned relatives used to say, "better to be *safe* than *sorry*."

GOING NATIVE

"Going native" refers to being immersed in the field to such an extent that the fieldworker becomes a member—or at least sees her- or himself as a member. Going native has been regarded as problematic because it may result in the field researcher setting aside the research and becoming a member of the group instead. This may or may not be a good thing, depending on what the group represents and the values of the person doing the judging. Warren had a student who was doing field research at an air traffic control facility; he subsequently dropped his sociology graduate studies and passed the air traffic control exam, becoming an air traffic controller. He did not regard this instance of "going native" as a problem, and neither did Warren, since he seemed happier as an air traffic controller than he was as a sociology student.

Field researchers often do regard it as problematic, however, when their students "go native" into religious cults or other deviant or stigmatized groups. Another student of Warren's, for example, was tempted by the religious cult among whom she was doing overt research (but who, naturally, regarded her as a potential convert). She had just moved away from her family to Los Angeles and was lonely and without close ties. As it became clear that going native was a real danger, she switched to another setting.

In addition to being personally problematic, going native—also referred to as overinvolvement or overrapport—may be dangerous to analytic integrity. As Adler and Adler summarize,

> Becoming too closely aligned with one group in the setting may prevent the researcher from gaining access to the perspectives of other groups in the scene...[and] bias researchers' own perspectives, leading them to accept uncritically the views of the members...as their own. (1987, 17)

Over the decades since the Chicago School, ethnographers have urged their students not to get overinvolved, even lost, in the setting, noting that a balance of immersion and distance is possibly the best place from which to represent others' worlds (Emerson 2001b).

The concept of going native implies that the field researcher has willingly become a member of the group, as did the student who became an air traffic controller. But some settings, from cults to gangs, actively seek to convert the researcher, trying to persuade her to become a member. Sometimes conversion efforts are successful, from Bennetta Jules-Rosette's (1975) conversion to an African cargo cult that she was studying to Venkatesh's (2008) acting as a gang member and leader. More often, field researchers expend an enormous amount of energy and strategizing avoiding the conversion attempts of the religious or political groups they study. In a 1980s study of the Jesus People, David Gordon (1987) comments:

> Field research with proselytizing groups presents difficult problems for field researchers. Such groups usually expect commitments from those who are knowledgeable about their point of view. Should the field researcher fail to make this commitment there is the possibility that further access to the group will be ended... [or] continuous proselytizing directed at the researcher can create emotional responses that adversely affect field relationships. (1987, 267)

Several other researchers have commented on the discomfort (Rochford 1985), tension (Robbins, Anthony, and Curtis 1973), or annoyance (Peshkin 1984) they felt in the face of continued conversion attempts. One way to deal with these attempts is to go native; another way is to pretend to go native by acting like a member, a strategy attempted by Peshkin (1984). From the point of view of the leadership of a cult or sect, the refusal of the researcher to convert, especially over time, may also become annoying. In John Lofland's (1966) research with the Moonies, or Divine Precept cult, once the leader of the group he was studying decided that Lofland was not going to convert, she wanted control over his research. He eventually left the group.

Gordon (1987) notes four possible responses to continued pressure to convert: (1) feigning conversion and switching to covert research; (2) going native or studying a group whose beliefs one already holds; (3) remaining a nonbeliever and refusing to discuss one's own beliefs with the group; or (4) remaining a nonbeliever and discussing one's beliefs with the group. In discussing his use of the fourth strategy, Gordon notes the problems associated with it:

> Six months into my study, the leader of the group asked me if I "knew the Lord yet." When I replied, "no," he said, "Well, why not? You've had plenty of time. You know it says in the Bible that Jesus is like a stone and either you will trip over it someday or it will crush you... you've been coming here and hearing all about Him, and one of these days you're going to have to face up to Him."... These are the kinds of pressures

that lead field researchers to experience fear of expulsion, anxiety, and guilt. (1987, 272)

As Gordon (1987) notes, gaining entrée into and developing initial relationships with members of proselytizing groups is easy precisely because they want converts. Maintaining relationships over time, however, depends on the members' notions of a proper time frame for conversion, which the informant quoted above saw Gordon as beginning to violate. Gordon responded to pressure by joining more group activities such as prayer meetings or singing, but the members also stepped up the pressure by involving him in more and more detailed discussions about his beliefs in contrast to theirs (1987, 275–276). Finally one member said to him: "Why don't you just throw all this stuff [his tape recorder and notes] away and get saved? I think we're going to bring you downstairs and just hold you down until you get saved" (1987, 276).

The older methodological literature framed the research role as a matter of the ethnographer's choice, for example between covert and overt research (Humphreys 1970). But during the past decade or so, ethnographers have become more attuned to the ways in which respondents incorporate them into the setting, according them a role or social place. Although you can control your appearance, demeanor, and presentation of self, you cannot control the ways in which others interpret your presence, or how they see you. Although Warren always introduced herself in the mental health court as a sociology professor from the University of Southern California doing field research, she was almost inevitably interpreted and introduced to others as either a law student or a nursing student. Most young females who came around the court were law students or nursing students, so in the worldviews of respondents, she was as well.

Emotions in Qualitative Research

In this chapter we have touched on some of the emotional aspects of doing fieldwork: the intensity of the experience, the closeness of the relationships that can develop, the play on human sympathies that can occur, and the tension of resisting conversion while maintaining a role in the setting. In Chapter 2, we also discussed some of the emotional stress brought about by covert research and the emotional energy needed to maintain social "fronts," as well as the ethical dilemmas that researchers have wrestled with when observing cruel and hurtful behaviors in the field. Yet, students are often surprised to find they have emotional responses to their experiences in the field. Sanders advises that we should not shy away from emotional responses:

> If our ultimate goal is to truly comprehend the rich variety of perspectives and experiences that shape interaction processes, however, we must not avoid involving ourselves in, and empathetically sharing, the sorrow and joy, pain and conflict, that are integral features of social life. (1998, 192)

In doing fieldwork, the goal is to understand the setting from the inside—to gain an understanding that is as close as possible to that of those being studied. It is a process of achieving closeness, both in physical proximity and emotional insight. The balance of experience-near fieldwork—"how ethnographers 'do closeness' on the one hand and 'do distance' on the other" (Emerson and Pollner 2001, 240)—alternating periods of immersion in the setting with periods of reflective withdrawal (perhaps to write fieldnotes), is the dance of the fieldworker, and it can be an emotionally challenging one. Because you, as the researcher, take on a social role in the setting and initiate and negotiate interactions, it is never a passive process; it is one fraught with all the social and emotional aspects of everyday life—only intensified. In Box 4.2, Karner's fieldnotes document her emotional response to a particularly disturbing interaction that she witnessed. As a researcher, you are

---

Box 4.2
EMOTIONS IN FIELDWORK

Later as I was leaving, I saw the veteran who had just been discharged in an unpleasant and intense staff meeting, he had gone to his room and was now dragging his guitar behind him. As soon as he saw me, he started "those goddamned mother fucking fools," etc. I pretended not to notice and went down the back stairs.

(at lunch yesterday, a unit nurse said that this veteran reminded her of a little boy with his dad's shoes and hat on...trying to be a man...a little cowboy trying to be a big cowboy...the way he tucks his pants into his boots and he drags this guitar around)

At the bottom of the stairs I found the tall, thin vet with long, curly, dark hair....."Is it always this intense?" I asked shaking my head, overwhelmed (the discharge meeting had been very emotional for me—I heard this little boy pleading for what he saw as his last or only chance at having himself back).

The tall vet patted me on the back, "This is the easy stuff, wait 'til you get into trauma [therapy] group—there are just so many triggers, everything seems to pull someone's trigger."...

I said, "I'm just so overwhelmed...I just...."

Another vet answered, "Yeah, just wait until you get to trauma [therapy group], you think this is intense—that gets into some real heavy stuff that you've thought about for years and you've wanted to talk about but couldn't."...

Asking another veteran who was nearby how to make sense of all of this—he said, "You just keep listening hoping something will fall through the cracks and will click for you....Just keep listening." [He must be a qualitative researcher at heart!]

(Excerpted from Karner's fieldnotes)

looking to gain entrée, wanting to be accepted as an insider and confidant, exploring new worldviews and belief systems. Your ethnographic agenda, however, does not protect you from responding as a person. You are still you, with all your own sensitivities, insecurities, needs, and desires. And any personal interactions have the potential to be problematic.

Some researchers will be drawn to the unknown, to settings that seem exotic to their own lives. This sense of exoticism, Rosalie Wax warns, can leave the researcher "so fascinated by the new, exciting, and significant things he is learning, that he may spend months passionately and persistently thinking of nothing else" (1983, 192). This is the emotional and compelling nature of fieldwork. Other ethnographers will be drawn to settings that allow them to somewhat safely learn about their own lives. One of Karner's students sought out a support group for adult survivors of childhood sexual abuse for her fieldwork site as a means of understanding her own experience by studying others with similar backgrounds. Karner believes that her initial interest in studying violent veterans was an attempt to understand the male violence she had witnessed in her own life.

Still other scholars write about their fieldwork experience as personally transformative. In *Missing Pieces: A Chronicle of Living With Disability* (1982), Irving Zola documents his fieldwork in a town in the Netherlands where everyone was physically disabled and no one was stigmatized due to physical limitations. Zola credits this experience with his subsequent acceptance of his own disability. However, other researchers report less positive emotional responses. John Johnson makes two major points about the conduct of fieldwork:

> First, in any complex social setting the personal relations between an observer and the individuals he studies will emerge gradually and will be problematic.... Second, the complicated personal relations involved in field-research project[s] will necessarily create patterns in the field observations. (1983, 205)

As people with feelings and responses, fieldworkers are never passive observers no matter how unobtrusive they attempt to be.

Emotional responses to respondents and to oneself are reflexive in complex ways. In looking back over her experience doing fieldwork at a holistic health center, Kleinman acknowledged feeling both angry and frustrated with the participants, as they did not live up to her political expectations. The consequence of her emotional response, Kleinman believed, caused her to delay the start of planned individual interviews.

> In close relations with participants, we only expect [to feel] good will. When we break the feeling rule by failing to have those good feelings, we may accuse ourselves of empathetic incompetence. (Kleinman and Copp 1993, 28)

Having negative responses in the field led Kleinman to doubt her abilities as a fieldworker, but through reflection she later came to consider her feelings as a tool that added depth and complexity to her analysis.

Fieldwork occurs in a social setting—within the "mini-dialectic of personal relations" (Johnson 1983, 205)—and has all the opportunities for emotional response that are present in everyday life. Wearing your researcher hat does not protect you from reacting to your experience in an emotional—that is, a very human—way. We can only remind you, as a beginning researcher, that fieldwork can be an emotionally compelling experience. Ideally, you will not be surprised to find yourself entranced by the wonder of learning about your setting, though for many of us, this is exactly the draw of the experience-near work that we do. This draw is one reason why ethnographers may at times be unwilling to leave the setting they are studying.

Leaving the Field

Eventually all things, good or bad, come to an end. The rule of thumb for leaving the field is this: your observations are no longer yielding new and interesting data. Warren left Metropolitan Court the first time, for example, when she realized that during her observations of *habeas corpus* writ hearings—having observed more than a hundred by this point—her attention was wandering. Because of Warren's mascot status with respect to the judge, she was not going to gain entrée to the meaning-world of the public defenders' office. Thus, figuring that she had spent enough time in the district attorney's and judge's offices, Warren left the field.

Leaving the field sometimes has emotional as well as practical elements. Field researchers often become very attached to "their" settings and the people in them, partly because of the intensity of the observational experience in comparison with everyday forms of social attention (which are often mixed with large doses of inattention). One of Warren's graduate students, Richard Johnson, studied sale barn auctions in the rural Midwest and found it difficult to stop going to the Saturday auctions he had attended for a year, even though it was time to focus on writing the ethnography. He had become a quasi-member of the setting, socializing with the members and even being pressed into service as an auctioneer (a "useful researcher" kind of research bargain we discussed earlier in this chapter).

At other times the emotions generated by leaving are related to people rather than the setting itself. As Emerson notes,

> Many ethnographers have noted the difficulties of extrication and disengagement from the field due to the...intense interpersonal ties between fieldworker and informants:...Leaving the field will typically transform

these relationships, in some instances ending them entirely, in others diminishing contact to the point that informants feel abandoned. (2001, 140–141)

Negative as well as positive emotions may surround the process of leaving the field. Taylor (1991), who was disgusted by the way in which staff treated the mentally retarded at the state institution he was studying (see Chapter 2), says that he

> began to feel terribly inauthentic. I found it difficult to keep up the facade, yet could not confront the attendants without blowing my cover and letting them know I had misled them about my true feelings. So, without even calling an end to the study in my own mind, I simply stopped visiting. (1991, 244–245)

Although in fieldwork the "stages" of research, fieldnote writing, and writing of the ethnography overlap, they don't overlap so much as to permit you to remain in the field beyond the period of useful observation. This point in time varies depending on the complexity of the field project, but it does come. As indicated above, some field researchers do go native—perhaps usefully in the case of getting a job, perhaps dangerously in the case of joining an extremist group. But in most cases, and certainly for undergraduates studying in the social sciences, it is necessary to leave the field either when you have become very familiar with it, or when your instructor suggests you should leave.

Even after leaving the field, the ethnographer may not sever ties with all its members, but may continue to maintain contact with one or more of them for some time afterward. The Adlers point out that fieldworkers sometimes

> continue to form friendships, especially with key informants, that are lasting. Through these people they can manage contact with the group for several purposes, including follow-up research and future re-entry. (1987, 79)

But leaving the field, like doing the research, is not just about the researcher. Riemer notes that leaving the field thoughtlessly can have consequences for future research and researchers. To "get out quickly" and "with little thought for the persons they used for the study" can cast discredit not only on the researcher but also on the profession or discipline as well (Riemer 1979, 177).

When Karner began preparing to leave the Veterans Administration hospital, she timed her departure to coincide with the final staff meeting to evaluate the last veteran she had been interviewing. This meeting typically occurred on the day before the veteran would leave the unit as well. This scheduling provided a natural closure for both the unit staff and the remaining veterans, and also gave Karner the opportunity to publicly express her gratitude before leaving the field.

Reincorporating the Nonstranger

The fieldworker who is doing fieldwork in a setting he or she is already a part of faces somewhat different challenges of incorporation than the stranger-researcher. The Adlers' (1987) discussion of membership roles in field research highlights the possibilities available to the nonstranger. But whatever the researcher's role in the field (bartender or customer in a bar, say), the ethnographer must decide to either keep the research agenda private (a kind of covert research role) or reveal it to all or some of the setting's members (an overt research role).

In her ethnographic study of a lesbian community in a midwestern college town, Christine Robinson (2008) initially decided that she would not share her research agenda with her respondents, a position acceded to by the university's IRB. She had moved to the college town to work on her PhD in sociology and had affiliated with the lesbian community in town before deciding to do her ethnographic dissertation on the community. Later in the study, however, she decided to end the covertness of her participant observation and let people know that she was doing the study.

Field researchers who also want to interview members of their group must, of course, reveal their research agenda. The decision to do interviews as well as field research was one of the factors that convinced Robinson to let her respondents know what she was doing. Similarly, Kristin Esterberg, who refers to herself as an "open lesbian" (1997, 5), did interviews and a survey as well as field research among lesbians in the "small eastern community" she studied. She reports no consequences or difficulties either for the research process, the data, or her own social circles in her switch from member-only to member-researcher.

The way in which the field is understood and interpreted may also be affected by being a member in it. At first glance it would seem useful for the researcher to be a member of the setting, since the purpose of field research is understanding members' meanings. And, indeed, various problems of entrée and accessibility are solved by membership. But the member may take so much for granted in the setting that fieldnotes end up as thin descriptions. A graduate student of Warren's who was a nun was also doing field research on her own order for a PhD dissertation. In her first set of fieldnotes she wrote, "we prayed." This meant something very specific to her, and something so familiar that she did not write it down as a nonmember would. So Warren had to ask her: What do you mean by "we prayed"? Did you kneel down? Bow your head? Recite aloud? Contemplate silently? Eventually a thickly descriptive account of praying was derived from the question-and-answer session.

"Membership Roles" in Field Research

A number of qualitative researchers have written about the range of membership roles in field research, from the complete participant to the detached observer, with various possibilities along the continuum between these extremes. The Adlers (1987) note that complete membership roles in field research are of several types: (1) the "master status" of the fieldworker is the same as those in the setting; (2) subcultural, recreational, political, or occupational statuses are shared; and (3) the researcher has gone native or converted (1987, 69). In contemporary fieldwork, it is often option 1 or 2 that constitutes the context of student research.

Twenty years later, Angrosino (2007, 107) refers to "membership roles reconsidered" suggesting that "field researchers and the people they study do not inhabit the same perceptual space." He notes that researchers' involvement is both voluntary and temporary, which makes them different no matter how much empathy or rapport is developed, and adds that "even indigenous researchers studying their own people have probably gone away for training and thus entering a situation in which they have not been continuously participating" (2007, 107).

Some qualitative research is applied or social justice–oriented, and the role of the researcher is, at least in part, to bring about social change. Laura Maria Agustin (2007) studied sex workers who migrated to Spain and other European countries, contrasting the economic and moral implications of sex work with the other jobs available to migrants: domestic and "caring" labor. She says of her place in the lives of those she and her colleagues observed and interviewed:

> In Europe, I deliberately located myself on the border of bothgroups, the migrants and…all those claiming to research them and work on their behalf—spending time in brothels, bars, houses, offices, outreach vehicles, conferences, and "the street" in its many incarnations. (2007, 151)

Students interested in gender, social class, ethnicity, race, body type, sex work, or sexual preference, and who share "master statuses" with respondents, may choose to study settings in which they are "indigenous" members (Denzin 2007). There is a tradition, for example, of lesbian or gay researchers studying lesbian or gay settings (Krieger 1983; Esterberg 1997; Robinson 2008). Helen Rose Ebaugh (1977), a former nun, did research on religious orders. Jennifer Hackney (1996) and others who have struggled with issues of body and weight have done research in settings such as Weight Watchers or Overeaters Anonymous.

While "master status" settings are one aspect of "starting where you are," settings such as workplaces are another. Ethnographic research on bars has illuminated social relations both from the point of view of workers (work members) and customers (leisure members). In their study of *The Cocktail Waitress*

(1975), James Spradley and Brenda Mann studied a bar in which Mann was already a member, employed as a cocktail waitress. They found that cocktail waitressing was a good example of "woman's work in a man's world," in which the waitresses were subordinate to both the bartender and the clientele.

In the member role of customer, Sherri Cavan (1966) visited a number of taverns in San Francisco, investigating both types of bars and social interaction within bars. Her typology of bars included "marketplace" or pickup bars (both homosexual and heterosexual) and "home territory" bars of the sort immortalized in the 1980s television series *Cheers*. Within different kinds of taverns, various types of customers ranged from "the stranger" to "the regular," and different social interactions flowed from those statuses. Both Spradley and Mann (1975) and Cavan (1966) highlighted the significance of gender in bars as workplaces or leisure places, and the role of alcohol in loosening up social behavior.

What do you think you might find in a similar study of bars in the 2000s?

Fieldwork roles are negotiated between the ethnographer and the members of the setting, and may change over time. No matter how the ethnographer wants to present him- or herself—overtly or covertly, as savior or as spy—incorporation occurs at the pace and in the ways of the setting. Fieldwork relationships begin with first impressions and continue in a variety of directions, some wanted and some unwanted. Or they begin where one lives, studies, or works. The substance of fieldwork interaction—and thus the data of fieldnotes—emerges from this nexus of roles and relationships in the field, and ends only when—and if—the researcher leaves the field and has not remained as native or convert. During the process of fieldwork, the researcher may decide to interview some of the respondents as well, as Krieger (1983) and Robinson (2008) did in their studies of lesbian communities. As we shall see in Chapters 6 and 7, interviewing, the second major qualitative method, has its own roles and relationships as well. But first, we turn to a discussion of the documentation of fieldwork, the writing of fieldnotes.

Suggestions for Further Reading

Emerson, Robert M., ed. 2001. *Contemporary Field Research: Perspectives and Formulations*. Prospect Heights, IL: Waveland Press.

Katz, Jack. 1999. *How Emotions Work*. Chicago: University of Chicago Press.

Warren, Carol A. B., and Jennifer Hackney. 2000. *Gender Issues in Ethnography*. Thousand Oaks, CA: Sage Publications.

Whyte, William F. 1943. *Street Corner Society*. Chicago: University of Chicago Press.

Chapter 5

Writing Fieldnotes

This chapter is about writing fieldnotes, the data of ethnographic research. Writing fieldnotes is necessary to the successful conduct of field research and is a part of research that anthropologist Clifford Geertz ([1973] 2000) and others refer to as *inscription*. The inscription of fieldnotes is a time-consuming activity that requires commitment on the part of the researcher, as well as memory and organizational work. In this chapter we discuss how to write and keep track of fieldnotes, the use of computers in qualitative research, and the reading and rereading of fieldnotes that is essential to ethnographic analysis. We also explore some of the historical and epistemological aspects of fieldnote writing, from the Chicago School to postmodernism.

In some ways it can be both easy and exciting to do the observational work of ethnography. To gain entrée into and be accepted by members of a setting, to engage in the type of focused observation characteristic of ethnography, to feel the first stirrings of belonging and acceptance—these are the exhilarations of field research. But writing fieldnotes is its necessary drudgery. In this chapter, we discuss what fieldnotes are, the process of writing them up from observations and from earlier inscriptions such as jotted notes, and what constitutes good and useful as opposed to inadequate and not very useful fieldnotes. Since we live in a computer age, the various uses of the computer in generating and using field research are also discussed at various points. But first, we place fieldnotes in the historical context of early anthropological research and the case studies of the Chicago School.

Fieldnotes have been used in qualitative social research for decades, perhaps generations if one counts traveler and missionary precursors to anthropology and sociology. Anthropological ethnographers such as Bronislaw Malinowski wrote about their encounters with "natives" in the field as they went about collecting kinship and economic data, also inscribing some of their (not always positive) opinions about these natives and their cultures (Emerson 2001d, 7). Malinowski wrote in 1922 that in fieldnotes

> belong such things as the routine of a man's working day, the details of his care of the body, of the manner of taking food and preparing it; the tone of conversational and social life around the village fires, the existence of strong friendships or hostilities, and of passing sympathies and dislikes between people; the subtle yet unmistakable manner in which personal vanities and ambitions are reflected in the behavior of the individual and in the emotional reactions of those who surround him. (quoted in Emerson 2001d, 7)

University of Chicago researchers collected fieldnotes as part of their set of case study methods, using them along with survey, documentary, and interview data. As Emerson notes, field research was an "optional component of the case study approach" rather than the sole method. He adds that even in case studies that relied extensively on observation, such as Nels Anderson's *The Hobo* (1923),

> the primary value of direct contact and observation lay in allowing the researcher to see for him or her self rather than in providing access to subjective meanings or perspectives. (Emerson 2001d, 12)

In contemporary research, fieldwork may also be used as an adjunct or background to other methods such as the interview. In Williams and Warren's (2008, 2009) applied research on the mostly women residents of four assisted living facilities, for example, interviews were focused on the residents' satisfaction with the facility, depression, memory, and other aspects of their everyday life. Field observations were made in the four facilities concerning staff-resident ratios, facility décor and cleanliness, food quality, and other background factors that might contribute to residents' lives.

The use of fieldnotes in the late nineteenth and early twentieth century was not particularly self-conscious or reflexive; the relationship between what the observer saw and what she or he wrote down was seemingly obvious. It was not until the movement toward postmodernism in academia began in the late 1960s and early 1970s that the issue of representation (see Chapter 1) and the subjectivity of the ethnographer emerged as an issue, and thus the issue of fieldnotes—since fieldnotes, as contemporary scholars point out, are one form of representation. It is not just the finished ethnography that is a representation of the field, the fieldnotes are a prior representation of it. As Geertz says,

> The ethnographer "inscribes" social discourse; *he writes it down*. In so doing, he turns it from a passing event, which exists only in its own moment of occurrence, into an account, which exists in its inscriptions and can be reconsulted. (Geertz 2001, 67; emphasis in original)

In his discussion of fieldnotes as the inscription of thick description, Geertz set the epistemological framework—and, indeed, the practical standard—for fieldnote writing in the coming decades of qualitative research.

Writing Fieldnotes

To reiterate, fieldnotes are inscriptions (written representations of what has been observed), and they are, ideally, thickly descriptive. Contrast, in Box 5.1, a thin with a relatively thick (much more could be written) description of the ROTC building on a university campus. The researcher is entering the building in order to conduct an ethnography of the student lounge, which is

---

Box 5.1

THIN AND THICK DESCRIPTION OF A CAMPUS ROTC BUILDING

Thinly Descriptive Fieldnotes

I walked into the ROTC building and asked someone for directions to the student lounge, and went upstairs.

(MORE) Thickly Descriptive Fieldnotes

The ROTC building, as I approached it, looked as if it were built in the 1920s out of native stone. Above the door that I was approaching a Roman eagle was carved, wings outspread. The door had a pane of glass in the center, and on the glass was taped a typed list of (many) rules of conduct to be observed in the building, a list I did not read but decided I would read carefully when I came out later.

As I entered, I observed that there was much upon the walls. There were glass cases to my left that stretched from about waist height to head height (of a six footer) and contained many sports trophies and photographs. To the right, photographs in frames adorned the walls: displays of the faces of white men (mostly) in uniform, grouped, seemingly, according to rank, with the leader or commander at the top of the frame. That list of typed rules appeared in several more places on the walls....

upstairs in the building. Thick descriptions take account of context, including season of the year, time of day, weather, buildings, and anything else of relevance for "setting the stage" of the setting.

Thick descriptions are based on attending to as much detail as possible in the setting—"Write down everything that you see or hear going on" is what we tell students, although we acknowledge that writing down everything that you see or hear is as impossible as seeing and hearing everything that is going on. The observer sees and hears within horizons of meaning, which encompass geographical and social location, and observational choices as well. To illustrate these horizons of meaning we use Warren's research on the steps of the campus building where she works, steps that serve as both entry and exit points, and as smoking areas for the students and workers who come in and out of the building (see Box 5.2).

Social location also shapes what kinds of things are noticed within the setting and thus what gets into fieldnotes. In group studies of interaction in public and semipublic places, students attend to different dimensions of that interaction. One student might be fascinated by the apparent spatial rules of waiting at a bus stop or riding on a bus, noting which standing and seating places were occupied and which left open. Another might take note of conversations, writing down what she heard people talk about in a crowded deli. What is observed in ethnographic settings is likely to be a variation of what is observed in everyday life that, in turn, is the outcome of biographical experiences.

Emerson, Fretz, and Shaw (1995), in *Writing Ethnographic Fieldnotes*, give a vivid depiction of differences in fieldnote descriptions of checkout lines in grocery stores. While all three examples they provide of such notes are thickly descriptive, each attends to different features of checkout lines. They note that one set of fieldnotes

> describes the line *spatially* in terms of individual people (particularly physical appearance and apparel) and their groceries as laid out before being rung up. (1995, 6)

In another,

> The observer describes moving through the line as she experienced the process on a moment by moment basis, framing her accounts of others' behavior as she received, understood, and reacted to them. (1995, 7)

And a third,

> In these notes the observer initially writes himself into a prominent role in the line but then he moves himself offstage by spotlighting another character who says and does a number of flamboyant things as he waits

and then gets checked out. This express line becomes a mini-community. (1995, 8)

The first set of fieldnotes reflects the noticing of spatial relations, physical appearance, and apparel; the second focuses on temporal sequences; and the third presents interactions and personalities. That said, the reader may wonder whether there is any right way to write fieldnotes, or, if fieldnotes vary with horizons of meaning, is there any way to differentiate between well-done and badly done fieldnotes? Yes: well-done fieldnotes are those written as soon as possible after the events in the setting have transpired, and for which as much time as is needed has been taken. The fieldworker, to write

---

Box 5.2
SMOKERS' STEPS: THE PROCESS OF WRITING FIELDNOTES

On these steps, where smokers gather to smoke and chat with one another, fifteen minutes of observation can result in ten or more double-spaced pages of fieldnotes. I have also found that writing jotted notes while I observe to prompt my memory later prevents me from observing for the full fifteen minutes, because in the act of looking down to jot notes I lose moments of observation. And I have found that in the few minutes it takes to go up in the elevator from the ground floor of my building to the seventh I have already forgotten some of the details of what I just observed.

What I see and hear as I observe the steps depends upon where I am: standing close to the building looking out, sitting on one of the steps—a lower or higher one, a right or left one—or beyond the steps, at the side of the pathway that leads to the road. Thus, what is seen and heard depends partly on geographical location—where the observer is at any given moment. Furthermore, once one is settled into a location, there are many things going on, so that choices are made of what to observe within the ongoing flow of interaction. As I sit on the top step and observe and watch and listen to the smokers do I also attend to the passersby, and if so, until what point—the end of the steps, the end of the path, the street beyond? Do I watch an interaction all the way through, or shift my attention to different parts of the setting as I alternately look up and around, and look down to write my jotted notes?

What I see and hear also depends partly on social location—where I come from in the cultural scheme of things. As a late-middle-aged professor, I notice students in a fairly undifferentiated manner—they are identified by me by their backpacks, their casual clothes, their youth. But I have found over the years of having my students observe campus settings that *they* make fine distinctions between students that I cannot, literally, "see." While I can differentiate roughly between graduate students (leather book bag, somewhat less casual clothes), they can differentiate between freshmen, sophomores, juniors, and seniors from cultural clues built into clothing and demeanor that are invisible to me.

thickly descriptive fieldnotes, has to make a commitment to thick rather than thin description, to sooner rather than later fieldnote writing, and to taking a good deal of time to write the fieldnotes. Technical assistance, from jotting notes to using computers, can help (or sometimes hinder!) the process of writing fieldnotes.

TIME AND MEMORY

No matter what one has observed within horizons of meaning, the inscription of these observations in fieldnotes requires holding them in memory. A few settings—mainly those in which writing itself is normative behavior— lend themselves to writing notes while observing. A college classroom is a setting in which the presence of someone writing on a lined tablet will not be attended to as out-of-place. However, typical behavior in a college classroom also includes focusing one's eyes on the instructor rather than gazing around at others, so that the observational behavior of an ethnographer in the classroom might seem odd.

Even where taking full fieldnotes in the setting is possible, it is not necessarily desirable, since it is virtually impossible to continue to observe closely while looking downward taking notes. But neither is it necessarily desirable to take *no* notes in the setting, since relying solely on memory can result in large gaps in thick description. The general advice to the field researcher is to take brief jotted notes in the setting. These jotted notes may be taken overtly—in front of the members—in settings where such behavior does not seem odd, for example in a courtroom or a classroom. Where any writing might seem disruptive or odd (for example in a bar), the researcher can leave the setting for a while and write on a notepad or enter notes into a laptop.

Noting and remembering becomes more problematic as the setting becomes more complex and time spent in it greater. In the smokers' steps example, the setting is a public one, with interaction in public places the focus. Fifteen minutes or five hours on the steps would yield observations of similar kinds of interactions, the kinds observed by Goffman in *The Presentation of Self in Everyday Life* (1959) and other works. In the mental health court, in contrast, the complexities were much greater, starting with different subsettings that ranged from the courtrooms (two) to the judge's chambers (one) to the district attorney's and public defenders' offices (one of each)—and these are just a few examples. The analytic focusing that takes place during fieldwork may make the task of remembering and inscribing easier, however. As she focused on the issue of social control in the everyday interactions of a lesbian community, Robinson (2008) took fuller and richer notes on these types of interaction and less on other activities such as political work.

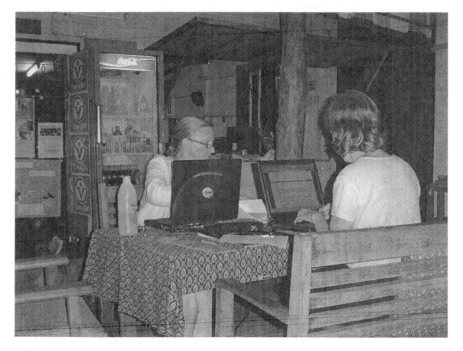

After a day in the field, Karner and her colleague Rita Litwiller return to their guest house to type up their fieldnotes in Mae Sot, Thailand. *Author's collection. All rights reserved. Used with permission.*

Observation sessions in different settings could take a few hours or an entire working day, at the court or at a lesbian community event. In the smokers' steps research, Warren found that a half hour of observation followed by an immediate retreat to her computer upstairs was optimum for memory. After Robinson learned that social control was commonplace in social occasions such as parties, she focused on those parties in her observational and fieldnote-writing activities. And Warren, if she were to do courtroom observations again, would observe for no more than a couple of hours at a time and use an audio recorder as soon as possible after observing. Recordings, computers, and other technical aids can help with problems of time and memory.

The use of recording devices in interviews is quite common (see Chapters 6 and 7). Depending upon your setting, a recording device may also be helpful as an additional memory aid to your jottings in writing up fieldnotes. In a recent study Karner (Snow et al. 2007) used a recorder as she observed in a long-term care facility. Using a wireless mic with a digital recorder, Karner placed the main microphone on the staff member she was shadowing (see Chapter 6), and the secondary microphone on herself. Thus the recorder picked up their conversations as the staff member went about her care tasks. The recorder picked up much of the background sound as well. Karner found that playing back the recording was invaluable to the research. The recording provided cues for sequencing of events, voice for direct quotes of conversations, and other background activities.

A recorder worked well with the shadowing design that Karner used, but in a setting where you are attempting to observe discreetly, a recorder could draw unwanted attention. In deciding whether to use a recorder, you should consider whether the sounds in the setting will be helpful in some way and if the recorder would have an impact the comfort of individuals in the setting. Technology can be an asset in some settings, and inappropriate for others: in a complex and chaotic environment, a recording might not be helpful. Whenever recorders are used, their use should be certified by involved IRBs (see Chapter 2), and they should never be deliberately concealed.

COMPUTERS

Before the computer era, fieldworkers wrote their fieldnotes by hand on lined pads or, later, typed them with manual and then electric typewriters. Both these forms of inscription make it difficult to alter the content or sequence of fieldnotes, although strategies were developed, such as leaving the left-hand page of a bound notebook blank for later entries and remembered insertions (Warren 2000). Computers, however, facilitate the addition and rearrangement of inscription when something once forgotten is later remembered. In addition, audiotaping fieldnotes for later transcription can be useful in situations where it is impossible to write full notes immediately after observing.

The dissemination of computer technology during the past three decades has helped enormously in writing fieldnotes (for other uses, see Chapter 9). It is a rare student—and an even rarer professor—who does not have access to a personal computer or, at a minimum, one provided by a computer lab at the academic institution or workplace. Once out of the field, the qualitative researcher makes a beeline for the computer, to get fieldnotes down as quickly as possible using whatever word processing program is preferred. The ability, when using computers, to move text and add materials is useful for field researchers as one memory is retrieved and unlocks another. Visual representations of the field, such as the spatial relations between people waiting at a bus stop, can be prepared using computer software as well. And multiple copies can easily be made, preparing the way for coding and analysis (see Chapter 9).

Laptop computers can also be used to inscribe fieldnotes, either away from the people we are interacting with, or in front of them. Although it seems that using a laptop while observing would facilitate thickly descriptive fieldnotes, Angrosino warns that this practice might not facilitate interaction or acceptance:

> Laptops certainly have the advantage of allowing researchers to type their notes directly, without going through the intermediate step of having to decipher written scrawl. But if hiding behind a pad creates barriers to optimal social interaction, how much more off-putting might be a researcher parked behind a keyboard? (2007, 73)

PREPARING AND LABELING FIELDNOTES

Researchers use many strategies to prepare and label their fieldnotes. Some researchers prepare several sets of documents, one set a thick description of the setting, another an account of researcher responses—emotional and otherwise—to what went on, and the third an analytic memo, noting conceptual ideas and connections as they occur. Other researchers prepare one narrative, in which reactions and analytic points are bracketed off from the descriptive text. As an example, we return to Warren's smokers' steps:

SMOKERS' STEPS FIELDNOTES, OCTOBER 22, 2002

There is a lone smoker on the steps as I walk out into the crisp, almost cold fall afternoon air. She [YWF] is sitting on the second step from the bottom, to the right as I exit.... She is about 5'3" and 190 lbs, long blond hair, no jewelry or makeup, no glasses, wearing jeans and a tucked-in white cotton shirt, thin and somewhat dirty white sneakers on her feet, white socks showing. She is drinking a Coke from a can, and reading a hardback book placed on the step between her legs and feet [I wonder if she is a student or a janitor? No backpack, but a hardback book; looks like the "uniform" of the women janitors in this building].

Useful shorthand for writing fieldnotes are abbreviations such as "YWF," which means "Young White Female," abbreviations that make it unnecessary to write this kind of phrase out fully each time a stranger appears in the fieldnotes. Some researchers object to these gendered and racial characterizations, finding them stereotypical; however, what we first notice about strangers in everyday life tends to be their embodiment—as women or men, race, age, height, weight, and clothing—and this is what we then also first notice about strangers inscribed in our fieldnotes. Note that social class and university membership are also implicit in this excerpt; there were various markers of social class and student or janitor status in this observation, but these were not as apparent as gender and age. Similarly, if you observe a man and a woman with a small child in your setting, rather than assuming that they are a family, describe them as a man and a woman with a small child [presumably a family]. Although abbreviations are not as "technological" as computers and audio recorders, they are among the techniques that make fieldnote writing go somewhat more smoothly than otherwise.

Computers are also useful in keeping track of fieldnotes. One of the urban legends of ethnography is the one about a young ethnographer who went to the field for three years. On his return, he loaded his box of handwritten fieldnotes into his Volkswagen, stopping at a store to pick up a few groceries. As he was in the store the Volkswagen was hit by another car, exploded, and burned up, destroying the box of carefully taken notes with the car. Although this story may be apocryphal, the message behind it is not: you don't want to put an enormous amount of time and effort into fieldnotes only to have them disappear.

We both write our fieldnotes on our computers, saving to the hard drive or external drive (see Box 5.3). Once finished with the batch of notes, we

---

Box 5.3
ORGANIZING YOUR FIELDNOTES

Warren says: On my computer disc and hard drive I use terms for the setting (Smokers' Steps, SS), fieldnotes (FN), the number of the notes (1 for first, and so on). So I have: SSFN1.txt. I put the hard copies in file folders labeled the same way as I label the outside of my discs: FNSS1–5 for example. This works for me. If you take more than one set of notes, for example, you might reverse the order: SS (Smoker Study), FN (Fieldnotes), R (Reaction Notes), A (Analytic Notes) for three sets of files; SSFN1, SSR1, SSA1.

Karner says: My primary organizing tool for research materials is the use of the directory structure on my hard drive, which I supplement with backup copies to my external hard drive while the project is in progress and then make a final back up to a disc at the completion of phases of fieldwork. I begin with a directory for each project, then a subdirectory for fieldnotes, subdirectories for observation locations, and then separate files for each observation. I use a word processor that allows for longer file names so I can be as descriptive as I desire. So, my computerized system of organization looks something like this:

C:/Research/VA project/observations/family therapy/ 3Oct.doc
C:/Research/VA project/interviews/staff/psychologist-1.doc
C:/Research/VA project/interviews/patient/John Smith Interview1.doc
C:/Research/VA project/notes/identity issues.doc

I also create notebooks for my hard copies that are organized in the same directory structure, using dividers and color-coded notebooks (blue for fieldnotes, red for staff interviews, green for patient interviews, etc).

make a hard copy and also a backup copy from the hard drive to the external drive. Periodically, every few months and definitely at the end of a fieldwork phase, Karner also backs up her entire set of fieldnotes and project materials to a DVD as well. Thus we end up with multiple copies of our data: hard copy, external drive, hard drive, and DVD. Since keeping track of documents involves being able to find them as well as not losing them, it is important to make your labels for these materials clear, so you can remember what they were called and how to find them again. There are almost as many ways of organizing fieldnotes as there are researchers doing fieldwork. What is most important for you is to find an organizing strategy that is meaningful to you and fits with the software and hardware you are using.

Computers are also useful for assembling materials other than fieldnotes for your study. If you have a scanner, for example, you can scan in relevant documents, such as a magazine article on the different policies universities have regarding smoking in, outside of, and around buildings. Visual records of your settings can also be scanned (or taken with a digital camera) and stored on your computer or a CD. Of course, it is important to remember that your organizing system and computer are tools for completing your research—if your organization process gets too complex you will have to make and keep lists of where all your files are and how you may have used abbreviations!

What Fieldnotes Look Like

What do fieldnotes look like? We have given you some examples in this chapter. And there are other sources of fieldnotes for public reading, including the quotes selected for illustration in ethnographies—any of the published ethnographies we refer to—fieldnote archives, and internet fieldnotes.

Anthropologists in past decades have donated their fieldnotes and other papers to archives. Leopold (2008) lists 850 collections of notes in archives, including those of Ruth Benedict (1887–1948), Margaret Mead (1901–1978), and Gregory Bateson (1904–1980). He also notes that the Smithsonian archives hold an additional 640 sets of papers. Fieldnotes of other qualitative researchers may be searched in archives and libraries through the internet, although in disciplines other than anthropology it has been uncommon to share fieldnotes.

Fieldnotes are also published on the internet in various blogs and other sites, making examples of them available to anyone. An anthropology graduate student researching music education in Belize writes of his first encounter with a key informant in the village of Santa Familia:

> George is the head of a large family of musicians....When I first met George, it was a humid and slightly rainy morning...around ten...[which]

was George's usual resting time for the day...after he worked all morning on his farm, where he grows coconuts and plantains, though he still seemed very happy to talk to me. (www.anthro-liz.livejournal.com, May 21, 2007)

So there are lots of examples of what fieldnotes look like—but what *should* they look like?

First, fieldnotes should be thickly descriptive and fully narrative (see Box 5.1) rather than terse and listlike. Second, they should be contextualized as to time and place. If you are not able (as the noted anthropologist Margaret Mead was and many are not) to take note of the minute-by-minute timing of things, at least take note of what time you entered and what time you left the field. If you are working as a lone researcher, you might include this information at the beginning of each set of notes. However, if you are working as part of a research team, where colleagues will be reading each other's accounts, it can be helpful to put together a "face sheet" form that should be filled out for each set of notes (see Box 5.4). This allows each person to get a quick overview of the notes just by looking at the face sheet. Whether you choose to embed this information in your notes or in an attached face sheet, it is crucial to have it documented so that you will have as full (or thick) a context as possible within which to analyze your field data. For example, Warren's fieldnotes on the smokers' steps begin and end: "I walked out of the building on to the steps at 10:05 a.m....I went back inside at 10:35 a.m." They have a heading and a context:

SMOKERS' STEPS FIELDNOTES, OCTOBER 14, 2002

I walked out of the building onto the steps at 9:03, just after the time, as I have learned, that the janitors get their second break. The weather was windy, cold and overcast, discouraging the enjoyment of smoking or doing anything outdoors on the steps. Two smokers (YBM and YBF) were standing with their backs to the building, shoulders hunched, nobody on the steps in the wind [the dedication to smoking must be considerable to come out here in this weather in order to smoke].

As this extract shows, fieldnotes are a cumulative enterprise; the ethnographer learns more and more about what goes on in the setting as time passes. By the time of this observation, two months into the research, Warren had learned that student smokers appeared on the steps during the minutes between classes, janitors during scheduled work breaks, and professors and administrators more or less whenever they wanted to (highlighting both social class and bureaucratic frameworks for interaction on the smokers' steps). By then, she had also learned some of the social types: which smokers were janitors, which students, which professors. As part of the

Box 5.4
SAMPLE "FACE SHEET" FOR FIELDNOTES

Public Utilization of Green Space Project

Fieldnotes completed by:

___ John Smith   ___ Peter Tu
___ Betsy Hernandez   ___ Margaret Chou

Observations site:

___ Memorial Park   ___ University Park
___ Veterans Park   ___ City Zoo Park

Location of researcher within site:

Time entered the field: _____   Time exited the field: _____

Subjects observed:

Activities observed:

Team Notes:

university and the building, Warren was already a member and before starting the research had a stock of knowledge on which to draw, which was also displayed in her notes:

SMOKERS' STEPS FIELDNOTES, NOVEMBER 4, 2002

As I leave the doorway, I see a familiar trio sitting on the steps: Chrissy, the MAWF [middle-aged white female] secretary in my department, together with the two secretaries from the Other Department (YWF1 and YWF2) she often smokes and talks with. They are all smoking, C on the top left step, YWF1 to the right of her on the next step down, YWF2 to the left of her (from where I stand). I say, "hi," they all turn their heads in unison and say, "hi," then go back to their animated conversation. I hear the words "thermostat turned down to 68 degrees" in a tone of indignation from one of the three [I feel the same way about this interoffice memo]. I pass the trio and head down the path....

One thing **not** to put in fieldnotes is the real names of people you encounter during your research, although this has been done in some published studies, especially those that use photographs. In public or quasi-public settings from beaches to university campuses you will encounter both strangers and people whose names you know. "Chrissy" is not the real name of the smoker on the steps. Although some fieldworkers use real names in fieldnotes and change them when writing for publication, because of the legal issues discussed in Chapter 2, we believe it is wiser for names to be changed at the point of fieldnote writing. Although fieldworkers often use *pseudonyms* with the same first letter as the real name—pseudonym Chrissy for the real name Cathy, for example—not doing so is even more protective of confidentiality than same-letter pseudonyms. When using pseudonyms, many researchers keep a separate log of the actual names and the pseudonyms locked up in a safe place, as memory may or may not hold for a long, complex project. However, should you chose to do this, we remind you once again of the cautions discussed in Chapter 2.

A finished fieldnote set, thickly descriptive, resembles an essay or narrative with a heading, a beginning, a middle, and an end. Although there are different ways to write fieldnotes, the most effective way, we believe, uses many of the narrative conventions, including the use of correct grammatical forms, full sentences, paragraphing, and the use of quotation marks for statements that are rendered close to verbatim. All these requisites for fieldnotes are debated among qualitative researchers, but the use of quotation marks for verbatim speech is probably the most contested.

The argument against the use of quotation marks in notes and publications for verbatim speech is that it is not really verbatim: the speech is heard, interpreted, remembered, and inscribed, but there is a lot of "slippage" away from verbatim during this process. The observer may mishear, misinterpret, or misremember, yet still use quotation marks to represent verbatim speech. Although slippage is clearly inevitable, the use of quotation marks is in our view preferable to eliding speech; thus, "The YWM leaned over to the YWF and said, 'Are you going to class today? I'm not going, I don't want to walk over there in the rain'" rather than "The YWM asked the YWF if she was going to class today and said he was not going because of the rain." Trying to recapture talk verbatim encourages the researcher to include more thickly descriptive details. Fieldnotes, and sometimes published writing, often include maps and other visual aids for understanding and visualizing the setting (see Gubrium 1975, for example). A researcher who is writing about interaction in a library may draw a map of the library—its stacks, reference desks, student study desks, and so on—and may also include the placement of various students and employees at various times in the stacks or at the desks. Warren often mapped the engagements and encounters between smokers and others (see Box 5.2) on the steps. A map can serve as an organizing structure for locating your remembered observations as well as a way to easily reference the spatial locations of observations in your notes. Photographs of the setting can be helpful in this regard as well—if they are devoid of human subjects (that is, no identifiable individuals are in the resulting images), then IRB issues would not apply. However, you may need permission of the facility manager.

As we noted above, a set of fieldnotes resembles a story, with a beginning, middle, end, and many pages in between. With a computer, the researcher can add remembered details to the narrative at any point, while initially writing up the notes or at a later time. CD and hard drive copies of your notes can be single spaced, while we recommend that hard copies be printed double spaced, with wide enough margins for you to make comments as you read and reread your fieldnotes. As important as writing fieldnotes is, the reading and rereading of them is of equal importance.

Reading Fieldnotes

Fieldnotes are the qualitative research equivalent to quantitative researchers' "raw data." Quantitative researchers take numbers and turn them into statistical tables, while qualitative researchers take fieldnotes, interview transcripts, images, or other documents and turn them into further inscriptions. But between inscription and reinscription is the reading and rereading of fieldnotes, always by the ethnographer, and sometimes also by others, whether team field research supervisors or course work instructors. Reading fieldnotes is a stage in ethnographic research; it is also an epistemological issue in relation to the audiences for our writing.

It is a truism of qualitative research that it is less linear in process than quantitative research. In quantitative research, the researcher has a research design with theory, hypotheses, quantitative methods, quantitative analysis, and write-up of findings (see Chapter 1). In ethnography, the researcher enters the field and takes notes, reenters and takes more notes, reflects and analyzes, continues in the field, writes up some thoughts—and so on, in an overlapping circle of activities. But there are still some rough stages between entrée and leaving the field. At the end, you will have a (we hope large) body of fieldnotes, some already partially analyzed, to read and reread.

Why all this reading and rereading? At the time you inscribed the first, tenth, or seventeenth set of notes, you were becoming more and more familiar with the setting—but not yet with the connections between the setting and concepts from your discipline. On reading or rereading, these connections may emerge. Christine Robinson, for example, recorded innumerable instances in her notes of conversations among lesbians in the Brownville community that went something like this: "Great to see you here today! We really missed you at the last potluck," or "Where's Ann? I haven't seen her for a long time," or "We were sorry you couldn't make it for the party last week, we had a lot of fun." As her PhD research supervisor, Warren read these field-notes and marked them, in the margins, "social control," because these kinds of comments seemed to indicate members' interpretations of past and present behavior, as well as attempts to influence future behavior. At the time, Warren was doing research on Cub Scout activities and had noticed many of the same kinds of comments by members of the scout community. (While lesbian and Boy Scout groups may be substantively different, in formal terms, such as the activities of social control—see Simmel 1950—they appeared pretty much identical.) In the end, everyday life social control (an important issue in 2000s sociology) became the focus of Robinson's (2008) ethnography.

Without thickly descriptive fieldnotes, conceptual connections cannot be made in this manner. Although Robinson's research interests were not focused on greeting rituals, she did write down what she heard (and she heard socially controlling rituals over and over again in many places), not just what was already of interest to her. She did not remember the greeting rituals, either, since they were not important to her until she conceptualized them as an aspect of social control. But she had made a commitment to writing and reading fieldnotes, did so diligently, and reaped the conceptual rewards of her diligence. Thus, the fieldworker should always read and reread her own notes even if there is no supervisor to also read them. Rereading notes throughout and after the process of fieldwork can lead to a chain of new insights that further shapes the inscription of ethnographies.

Writing the Other, Inscribing the Self

As inscription, fieldnotes are intended to describe what anthropologists call the Other—other cultures, other meanings. But since they are inscribed by selves, they also reflect those selves. This is clearly true where fieldnotes are routinely read by other people (Warren 2000). But it is also true where the notes are likely to be read only by the fieldworker. Emerson, Fretz, and Shaw argue that the stance from which fieldnotes are written is shaped in part by the "intended or likely audience," which is generally "herself as a future reader" (1995, 44). The possibility of legal action in relation to ethnographic fieldwork (see Chapter 2) may also make the inscription of fieldnotes attentive to the possibility of unwanted audiences (Warren 2000).

As Sanjek (1990, 34) comments, fieldnotes reveal about the writer "the kind of person you are"; they reflect back to the reader the writer's personal and pedagogical self, as well as the others of the field. In a personal context, "fieldnotes can reveal your childish temper" (Jackson 1990, 22) or become a forum for complaints about your field setting, respondents, or life. While studying and working in a tourist pub in rural Ireland, anthropology student Kaul (2004, 1) wrote in his fieldnotes:

> I've been lamenting ad nauseam the fact that I've worked so much this summer....I would imagine most fieldworkers would consider my summer half-ruined because I've spent half of the summer doing brainless work serving plates of food to complaining tourists instead of "getting out there," interviewing people, doing surveys, blah blah blah...

In the pedagogical context, novice and student fieldworkers may worry about fieldnotes "not being done well": that they are skimpy or verbose, unfocused, or not looking at the "right" things (Jackson 1990, 27)—especially if they are to be read by other people such as supervisors or team members. One consequence of the fear of audience reaction is the censoring of notes. Emerson, Fretz, and Shaw suggest that if a student is afraid of the responses of supervisors, he or she should produce one set that includes all the material of interest, and another in which it is censored; the censored set of fieldnotes goes to the supervisor (1995, 222). Several of our students in field methods classes have admitted that they have turned in censored fieldnotes and kept uncensored ones (Warren 2002, 88). Censored materials include those involving the other, and those involving the self. Generations of qualitative researchers have written down the "NEXT worst thing" that they did, or that happened to them, in fieldwork.

Generations of sociologists and anthropologists have also admitted censorship of fieldnote materials that might cast discredit on "their people," perhaps an incident of sexual harassment, perhaps the "embarrassing or illegal activities of poor urbanites" (Obbo 1990, 291). Fieldnotes taken in contexts where the fieldworker, supervisors, and members of the field setting are all known to one another may be censored for gossip or other linkages of personal behavior with identifying characteristics, which would then have made the notes themselves into a form of gossip (Warren 2000, 189).

But fieldnotes inscribe the self as they inscribe the other, so that censorship of the self may occur as it relates to the field. Beyond "childish tempers," fieldworkers may want to conceal aspects of self that might be discrediting or stigmatizing. In earlier decades, this was often the case with qualitative sociologists who studied lesbian or gay subcultures. But even today, some lesbian or gay graduate students who intend to continue into academia may conceal their sexual identities as they write supervised fieldnotes about lesbian or gay others, fearing problems with hiring and tenure (Warren 2003).

At times, rather than censoring, the ethnographer writes about himself for the fieldnote audience. As supervisors of fieldnotes, we have found that students use them to communicate directly with us, as in the following example from a student's research on a group home for delinquent boys:

> Jack [one of the boys] got defensive, but that only makes sense. It makes sense that he would want to retain the attitude so as to appear consistent. In other words, retain the *fake* attitude as a way of showing off for Colin [another inmate]. Consistency would mean his attitude was real, not just performance. (Sorry I am low on detail here. Am I lacking?). (Warren 2000, 194)

This note was more like an analytic memo than thick description. In response to it, Warren asked the student to avoid glossing over the specifics of interaction by using words such as "defensive," and tell the reader what was said and done by Jack to lead the writer to that conclusion.

Sometimes—indeed quite frequently—students write about various aspects of themselves in their fieldnotes as they observe and react to interactions in their setting. One student, as she wrote about the ethnicity, clothing, and appearance of members of the Hispanic health care setting she was observing, also marked her own:

> Maria wore a red blouse and "skort"...splashed with bright yellow, pink and orange tropical flowers. I felt that she looked typically colorful and Hispanic, while I in my cobalt blue and white striped sweater and denim jeans looked typically pale and conservatively Anglo. (Warren 2000, 195)

In their fieldnotes, students or team members have—either purposely or as part of the way they write—given us all kinds of information about themselves: sexuality, ethnicity, clothing, appearance, self-confidence or a lack of it, and life events. Although there are very few examples of communication of the self via notes in the published literature, there are a few. Here is an extract from anthropologist Don Stull's notes during his team field research in Garden City, Kansas:

> No one but me tries to set and keep common agendas. But then I think everyone looks to me to play that role. Then again, maybe I am just too anal....I am getting surly in my dealings with other team members. (quoted in Erickson and Stull 1998, 33)

Fieldnotes—through inscription and reinscription, reading and rereading—are the key to successful ethnographic research. If the researcher is either a team member or doing research supervised by an instructor, an external authority is insisting on those notes. If, however, the fieldworker is not supervised by anyone, there is no external prompt to write fieldnotes. But the writing of them is necessary. As we said in the beginning of this chapter, writing thickly descriptive fieldnotes is time consuming and requires a commitment on the part of the researcher. Do not rely on your memory of events instead of writing fieldnotes—and do not rely on your memory of your fieldnotes instead of reading them. They are as important to your qualitative research as are the transcriptions of qualitative interviews, discussed in the next chapter.

Suggestions for Further Reading

www.anthro-liz.livejournal.com

Emerson, Robert M., Rachel I. Fretz, and Linda L. Shaw. 1995. *Writing Ethnographic Fieldnotes*. Chicago: University of Chicago Press.

Sanjek, Roger. 1990. *Fieldnotes: The Makings of Anthropology*, 34–44. Ithaca, NY: Cornell University Press.

Van Maanen, John. 1988. *Tales of the Field: On Writing Ethnography*. Chicago: University of Chicago Press.

Chapter 6

The Interview

From Research Questions
to Interview Questions

The second major qualitative method, used together with fieldwork or by itself, is research interviewing. Today we are all familiar with different types of interviews: the job interview, the medical interview, the psychiatric interview, the journalistic interview seen on television. Interviews may be face-to-face, by telephone, or conducted electronically as "virtual interviewing" (Fontana and Prokos 2007).

Non-research interviewing shares with research interviewing the intent to get to know the interviewee better, but the purposes of *getting to know* are different. In the job interview, the employer wants to fill a position. In the medical or psychiatric interview, the person taking the case history wants to arrive at a diagnosis. In journalistic interviewing, the interviewer does—like the research interviewer—want to use the interview to contribute to a body of knowledge. But the body of knowledge developed by the journalist is generally of the storytelling or whistle-blowing kind, while that of the social scientist has conceptual or theoretical import.

Research interviewing is a special kind of conversation in which the interviewer questions the respondent on a topic of interest to the interviewer, and of some relevance to the interviewee. You may be familiar with the survey interview, which will not be covered in this chapter since it is part of the quantitative rather than qualitative research tradition.

There are several types of qualitative interview. One is the oral history approach, in which respondents are questioned in the context not so much of their individual biographies, but as witnesses to the historical events that occurred during their lifetimes. Used by historians and other social scientists, oral histories focus on interviewing eyewitness participants for the purposes of historical reconstruction (Perks and Thompson 2004). The use of oral history techniques allows a researcher to amass substantial data on aspects of social and personal experience that are not usually covered in formal histories of groups or organizations (Cockcroft 2005). Oral histories capture the experiences of average people, rather than the well-documented lives of government officials and elites, as part of the historical record.

In this chapter we will focus on the qualitative interview, sometimes called the *in-depth* or *intensive* interview, which centers on the meanings that life experiences hold for the individuals being interviewed. Such interviews typically involve one interviewer and one respondent, but other forms include the focus group, in which one interviewer questions more than one respondent. Interviews may be conducted face-to-face, over the telephone (Shuy 2002), or on the internet (Mann and Stewart 2002). We will confine our discussion, in this chapter and Chapter 7, mostly to the qualitative face-to-face research interview with one or more respondents. As Kvale describes it, this type of interview is

> a conversation that has a structure and a purpose. It goes beyond the spontaneous exchange of views as in everyday conversation, and becomes a careful questioning and listening approach....It is not a conversation between equal partners, because the researcher defines and controls the situation. The topic of the interview is introduced by the researcher, who also...follows up on the subject's answers to his or her questions. (Kvale 1996, 6)

Research interviews today are often single events, with the social scientist interviewing a respondent only once. Interviews can also be part of longitudinal research designs, in which they are used to trace the development of social meanings over time. In Warren's work on schizophrenic women in the late 1950s and early 1960s (Warren 1987), the eight interviewers interviewed seventeen women and sixteen of their husbands for up to three years (with a follow-up interview for some twelve years later), at intervals ranging from weekly to monthly. These interviews showed the changes in the women's understandings of their psychiatric diagnosis and mental hospitalization from admission through discharge, and life after institutionalization.

Interviews in one form or another have been used in many ways and in many places and times. The origin of the interview, like that of field research, is sometimes traced to the journeys of Herodotus (Bailey 1995, 7) or the dialogues of Socrates (Kvale 1996, 21). Its modern origins, however, are more commonly located in the social reform studies of the nineteenth century. In the 1830s, for example, Harriet Martineau interviewed women and men throughout the United States, concluding that there was some similarity between the lives of women and of slaves at that time (Reinharz and Chase 2002, 222). Martineau was also an early participant observer in the lives of American women (Bailey 1995, 7). These and other nineteenth-century qualitative and reformist studies in the United States and Europe formed the background to the development of the Chicago School.

The Qualitative Interview

The Chicago School continued the traditions of urban social surveys and reform politics in their case studies of the early twentieth century. Interviews were used, together with quantitative social surveys, documents, and field-work, to illustrate the local conditions of the times and to suggest what might be done to ameliorate those conditions. Early Chicago methods texts distinguish between what we now call qualitative interviewing and interviewing done with a questionnaire or schedule (Platt 2002, 36). Pauline Young, in a discussion of interviews published in 1939, recommended that the interview be based on "a considerable degree of rapport...[and] the mutual discovery of common experiences" (quoted in Platt 2002, 36). Young also discussed the value of the interview:

> The personal interview is penetrating; it goes to the "living source." Through it the student...is able to go behind mere outward behavior and phenomena. He can secure accounts of events and processes as they are reflected in personal experiences, in social attitudes. (quoted in Platt 2002, 36)

The focus of sociological research shifted after World War II to the quantitative survey interview and away from fieldwork and qualitative interviewing, with several major studies of the armed forces. While the primary concern was still finding out about and ameliorating social conditions—at first, the condition of the armed forces—the methods were increasingly quantitative rather than qualitative, applied rather than historically based. Although qualitative interviewing remained as a major method in anthropology, it was over-shadowed in sociology by survey interviewing until at least the 1980s. Several textbooks on qualitative interviewing in the social sciences were published in the 1990s (Arksey and Knight 1999; Kvale 1996; Weiss 1994), while a major *Handbook of Research Interviewing* (Gubrium and Holstein 2002) was published in the early 2000s. From the Chicago School until today, researchers have explored important issues in qualitative interviewing, beginning with the question of when to use qualitative interviews instead of, or in addition to, other methods.

WHEN TO USE QUALITATIVE INTERVIEWS

Qualitative interviews may be conducted as part of ethnographic research, as part of a larger research design, or as the sole method of a study. The decision to do an interview study, or to have an interview component in a larger study, is based on the kind of research questions you wish to answer. As a rough rule of thumb, if you are interested in behavior and interaction, use the ethnographic method; if you are interested in biography and accounts, use the interview method; if you are interested in both, use both methods.

The use of multiple methods is illustrated by Karner's (1994) study of inpatient Vietnam veterans diagnosed with post-traumatic stress disorder (PTSD). In this longitudinal research project, Karner employed ethnographic observation and qualitative interviews. On a Veterans Administration hospital unit for the treatment of combat-related PTSD, she observed the various therapeutic activities that took place including small therapy groups, educational classes, recreational activities, formal and informal discussions between staff members and veterans, and the veterans interacting among themselves in unstructured activities. Karner was able to raise issues and ask questions in the small therapy groups she observed, giving her access to the opinions and insights of the veterans as they talked. This component of her study, similar to an informal focus group (see below), allowed Karner to focus on behavior and interaction, whereas in the later stages of her project she began a sequence of intensive interviews collecting the veterans' biographical accounts. By using multiple methods, Karner was able to contrast what was *said* (accounts) with what was *done* (behaviors) by the veterans and staff. She was also able to see the differences between the veterans' accounts and presentation of self privately (in interviews) with their public interactions (small therapy groups). These contrasts provided a much broader understanding and thicker description than had she employed only one method.

What sets the interview apart from the other kinds of conversation found in field research is its formal structuring: the development of a set of specific questions to be asked of respondents, the selection of respondents, and the audiotaping (or sometimes videotaping) of the interview. It is these elements of the interview-as-conversation that require the separate consideration of an interview study component, or interview study, as part of human subjects IRB review. We will deal with these issues in the rough time order in which they generally occur: conceptualizing the topic, framing the research question, developing the specific questions, the IRB review, deciding on the interview format, sampling respondents, and planning the interview. In Chapter 7, we will discuss the process of interviewing as social interaction and speech event, what happens after the interview, and transcription. The subject of analyzing interview transcripts will be discussed in Chapter 9, together with the analysis of fieldnotes, images, and other documents.

From Research Topic to Interview Questions

Many interview researchers, like ethnographers, select topics because of some biographical connection; they want to find out how other people have thought or felt about, or handled, some particular issue or problem. For example, Ryan Moore (2007) became interested in the commercially independent (or Do-It-Yourself) cultural production of a punk music subculture he frequented in San Diego. Other researchers—especially those in research teams, and sometimes students in classes—are assigned interview topics by supervisors, instructors, or granting agencies. Karner and Hall (2002), for example, were asked by their funding agency, the Administration on Aging, to design and conduct a study that would systematically document the service insights of staff members of community service organizations.

Whatever the topic of the interview, a general research question, or set of research questions, should be framed from it: How do nursing home staff members decide if patients who cannot communicate are in pain (Snow et al. 2007)? How do individuals newly diagnosed with diabetes handle the lifestyle changes associated with their illness (Karas and Karner 2005)? What is it like for an older woman to be married to a younger man (Warren 1996)? From these general research questions the interviewer develops a set of ten to fifteen open-ended research questions. Examples of specific research questions can be seen in Boxes 6.1 and 6.2. The questions in Box 6.1 may seem vague, and those in Box 6.2 mundane, but both sets of questions elicited a wealth of respondent narratives. In Box 6.1, question 3, for example, was designed to elicit information about whether the couple rented or owned a home, if the home was owned by the woman (which it generally was), and who moved in with whom (generally the man moved in with the woman). Questions such as number 10 in Box 6.1 are typically asked at the end of an interview in case there is something on the respondent's mind that the interview has not yet elicited.

Interview questions have to be developed prior to submitting a research proposal to IRBs, since these committees will want to know what you are going to ask the respondents. The level of specificity necessary to satisfy the committee may vary by institution. The interview guide that Karner was

---

Box 6.1
INTERVIEW GUIDE FOR A STUDY OF OLDER WOMEN
AND YOUNGER MEN

1. When did you first meet...? [name of spouse or cohabitee]
2. How did it go between you at first?
3. When and where did you first live together?
4. When did you get married?
5. How is being married to...?
6. Do you have or are you planning to have children?
7. How do you get along with her/his family?
8. How about her/his friends?
9. When you think about the future, how does it look?
10. Is there anything else you would like to add?

(Warren 1996)

Box 6.2
INTERVIEW GUIDE FOR A STUDY OF NEWLY DIAGNOSED
INDIVIDUALS WITH DIABETES

1. Please tell me a little about yourself—where you grew up, your family, hobbies, occupation, or anything else you want to share.
2. Please tell me about when and how you were diagnosed with diabetes.
3. What did you know about diabetes at that time?
4. What was it like to find out you had diabetes?
5. Did your physician have any recommendations for you to address the diabetes?
6. What it is like to live with diabetes on a day-to-day basis?
7. Has having diabetes caused you to make any changes in your life?
8. Has the way you think about diabetes changed since you were diagnosed?
9. When and why did you decide to join this diabetes support group?
10. Is there anything else you'd like to add?

(Karas and Karner 2005)

---

required to develop for the IRB process at a Veterans Administration hospital that was unfamiliar with and somewhat reticent about the use of qualitative methods can be seen in Box 6.3. However, Box 6.3 represents only the first of a four-page listing of interview topics for the proposed six hours of interview time, and thus one quarter of the material insisted on by the Veterans Administration hospital IRB.

Box 6.3
IRB INTERVIEW GUIDE FOR STUDY OF VIETNAM VETERANS WITH PTSD

I will be following the format of intensive interviewing, which is more like a guided conversation than a formal questionnaire. I will be interested in three main areas of the veteran's life experiences: childhood, Vietnam, and post-Vietnam. I will ask the veterans, in broad general terms, to describe their experiences and how they felt at the time. The veterans will be able to answer these open-ended questions with as much specificity as they wish. I will follow up with elaboration probes when appropriate, such as "What do you mean by...?" or "How did that make you feel?"

My main purpose will be to elicit the veteran's memories and understandings of his experiences. I will be using the topics listed below as a broad guideline for the material to be covered. These topics are not inclusive; rather, they will be used to facilitate an open dialogue between the veteran interviewee and myself.

Interview Series Topics: During the first session, I will be attempting to get acquainted with the veteran. I will answer any questions about the study that he might have and give him a general outline of how the series of interviews will proceed.

Basic Demographics and Current Situation

Date of Birth

Sex

Race or ethnic background

Current marital status

Number of previous marriages

Number of children, sexes and ages.
   Do any *live* with him?

Age at time of Vietnam tour

Was he drafted or did he enlist?
   If enlisted, rationale

Length of tour

Main military duties,
   in and out of country

Branch of service

Date of tour

Was he wounded in combat?

Length of total military service

First memory of arriving in Vietnam

How does he remember his tour
   (briefly)?

In general, how did his service in
   Vietnam impact his life?

How often does he think about Vietnam?

Does he think that most people
   understand what Vietnam was
   like?

What is the greatest misunderstanding
   about Vietnam?

Has he visited the memorial in
   Washington, DC?
   Under what circumstances?

Does he read books or see films
   about Vietnam?
      Why or why not?
   Are any of the portrayals accurate?
   Did he find any of them emotional
   or moving?
      In what ways?

Does he feel comfortable talking
   about Vietnam?

continued

Box 6.3 *continued*

Does he speak of Vietnam often?
  If so, to whom?
How did he come to be in the PTSD unit?
  Is this his first time?

Is he service-connected for PTSD?
  If yes, at what percentage?
  If no, does he have a claim
  pending?

In equal detail, the IRB proposal goes on to list topics for each of three main areas of the veteran's life experiences: childhood, Vietnam, and post-Vietnam. (Karner 1994, Appendix A)

FACE SHEETS

Rather than asking about demographic information such as gender, age, and occupation in the interview, you might, instead, develop a face sheet for that purpose (see Box 6.4) for the respondent to fill out as you set up your recording device. This face sheet should have a code keyed to the same code on the audiotape you will use for the interview (much more infrequently, you may be using a videotape), and on the transcript of the interview (more on this later).

There are several things to notice about this face sheet. In a study of people who might include the transgendered, the researcher would include something like "other" as a third category along with M and F; doing so in *this* study would just seem odd. Warren's ordering of M before F is also commonplace in the social sciences (look at any survey you receive); thus, she kept this ordering because to do otherwise might introduce unnecessary error by causing women to check the M box and vice versa. Since this was the face sheet for a study of older women married to younger men (Warren 1996), the exact age was important. Where the specific age is not so crucial, but some idea of age is necessary, the interviewer may use age groupings for the respondent to check (i.e., 18–25), with the parameters of the age grouping set by the likely ages of the respondent. With older populations, it is more useful to ask for birth dates rather than age, as one's date of birth does not change over the years and is more likely to be remembered and reported consistently.

Although (to get at socioeconomic status) Warren asked about education and occupation, she did not ask about income; people are often reluctant to disclose or truthfully report their income. Warren surmised that she would get enough information from the qualitative interviews on income differentials to avoid asking for income on the face sheet. Marital status, previous marriages, occupation, race, and ethnicity were left open (without response categories) on the face sheet so that the respondents could define these as

> **Box 6.4**
> **DEMOGRAPHIC FACE SHEET FOR A STUDY OF OLDER WOMEN/YOUNGER MEN**
>
> Your gender   M_____   F_____
>
> Your age _____
>
> Current marital status _____
>
> Dates of any previous marriage(s) _____
>
> Number and ages of children _____
>
> Education: highest level attained _____
>
> Occupation _____
>
> Ethnicity/race _____

they saw fit. Also, you will see in many older studies that religion was routinely included in demographic data collection, but it is often omitted today; Warren did not see religion as something she wanted to explore with respondents and so omitted it.

DESIGNING RESEARCH QUESTIONS, PROMPTS, AND PROBES

If some questions might disturb the respondent, they should be left until the end of the interview; the easiest and least disturbing questions should come first. This is because of the expectation, seen throughout the literature on qualitative interviewing, that some degree of rapport will develop between interviewer and respondent (more on rapport in Chapter 7); a respondent who might be reluctant to answer a particular question upon first meeting the researcher might be more willing to do so after an hour or more of conversation. McCracken suggests that interviews begin with "grand tour" questions that sketch out the terrain to be covered (1988, 35). This overview function can also be served by the face sheet that has been filled out and handed in to the interviewer, who can then refer to it and ask questions from it: "Oh, I see you have been married four times; can you tell me about the ages of your previous husbands?"

In addition to the relatively small number of planned questions for the qualitative interview, the researcher must be prepared to probe for clarification or prompt for additional details. Because the use of prompts and probes depends on the respondent's narrative, they are difficult to specify in advance.

This is also true of the additional questions that arise as the respondent tells his or her story. McCracken gives an example of the use of probes and additional questions in interviewing:

> [One] device is to repeat the key term of the respondent's last remark with an interrogative tone.

> (Respondent: "So me and my girlfriend decided to go out and get wrecked."
> Interviewer: "Wrecked?"
> Respondent: "Yeh, you know, really, really blasted.")

> If these techniques are not effective, the interviewer can be more forthcoming ("What do you mean 'blasted' exactly?"), but not more obtrusive ("Do you mean 'intoxicated'?"). (1988, 35)

We will return to the issue of using prompts and probes in the next chapter, when we discuss the interview process in greater detail.

Questions that are obtrusive or "lead the witness" should be considered carefully by interviewers, although they are sometimes used to give immediate focus to the interview process. In an ongoing study of memory problems among elderly residents in assisted living, for example, the first interview question was "When did you first notice difficulties with your memory?" Through other studies, the researchers had determined that all the residents they interviewed were concerned with forgetfulness (Williams and Warren 2008, 2009).

Some interview studies that are based on leading—or even bullying—respondents have, however, been criticized as promoting untruthful answers. In the influential mid-twentieth-century Kinsey reports on sexual behavior, for example, pressure was used to get respondents to "admit" to sexual practices:

> It became necessary to say, with firmness, even vehemence, and yet always with kindness, "Look, I don't give a damn what you've done, but if you don't tell me the straight of it, it's better that we stop this history right here. Now, how old were you the first time that this or that happened?" Surprisingly, in not a single case did a person refuse to continue. (quoted in O'Connell Davidson and Layder 1994, 132)

Fifty years later, the use of such tactics casts doubt on Kinsey's findings:

> Considered in the light of research into social conformity and the way in which people tend to comply with researchers who are perceived as authority figures, this makes Kinsey's figures on levels of sexual activity look...suspect. (O'Connell Davidson and Layder 1994, 132)

One alternative to leading the witness is the phrasing of questions that have as little content as possible. Rather than "Didn't that make you feel awkward?" use "How did that make you feel?" The first form of the question assumes that the respondent felt a certain way (awkward), while the second form assumes that she had a feeling. If the narrative that elicited "How did that make you feel?" would lead any competent observer to believe feelings were involved—for example, the respondent has just described how her husband rejected her—then the second form of the question would be appropriate. Where feelings might not be at issue—for example the respondent has just described a dinner with her husband—you might use something like "How was that?"

The purpose of qualitative interviewing is the elicitation of narrative stories from the respondents that indicate the meanings they give to those aspects of their life-world relevant to the interviewer's topic. Such a purpose requires the pre-interview development of questions as a general guide, but it also requires flexibility in using, adding to, deleting, expanding, or in other ways changing the substance or order of these questions. This emergent aspect of the qualitative interview, like the emergent features of ethnography, makes the letter-of-the-law fulfillment of IRB review procedures somewhat problematic. Although the interviewer plans to use probes and additional questions when necessary, it is difficult to plan in advance what these probes and additional questions will be (as seen in Box 6.3).

THE IRB REVIEW

Your instructor may have obtained an agreement from your institution's IRB that your interviewing is part of your training rather than an independent research project. Or you may have to prepare and submit your interview plan to your IRB with the help of your instructor. Either way, it is important to remember the three principles of human subjects protections discussed in Chapter 2: informed consent, confidentiality, and avoiding harm. Informed consent generally requires that you present your interviewees with a letter describing the purposes of your research and its institutional sponsorship (as we noted in Box 2.3 of Chapter 2). Assuring confidentiality requires that although you may—and probably will—know the identity of your respondents (thus you cannot promise anonymity), you will not publicize the names of your respondents, or so many identifying details that they could in fact be identified. Thus you will use codes, rather than names, to identify respondents on data files, transcripts, audiotapes, and face sheets, keeping a master list of names and codes in a locked file, to be destroyed at the end of the research project.

There are some types of respondents, and some topics or questions, which IRBs may not permit you to get involved with. "Protected classes" of people who cannot be interviewed without great difficulty include children and minors, and institutionalized populations such as prisoners. These people are presumed to be unable to provide free and informed consent, children because consent resides with their parents (and will have to be obtained from their parents), and prisoners because they are confined involuntarily and thus cannot truly consent to or refuse anything. Your instructor will let you know, if you are doing interviews, what kinds of people you are going to be permitted, by your institutional IRB, to question—and what topics and lines of questioning you may pursue.

Combinations of topics and populations are particularly problematic for researching with qualitative interviews (e.g., adolescents' sexuality). That is not to say that no social scientist, ever, will be able to interview adolescents about their sexuality, just that the IRB review process is likely to be long and cumbersome, permissions from parents difficult to obtain, and the outcome uncertain. In studies of nonspecial populations that aren't particularly controversial, there may still be specific questions that an IRB will not approve for the researcher to ask, or will want reworded.

Additionally, IRB proposals generally expect the researcher to provide information about any potential harm that might come to the respondent as a result of participating in the interview. This can include even minimal "harm" such as talking about psychologically stressful events like combat or rape. In attempting to get approval for such a project, a researcher should have some sort of support available for distressed interviewees or at least a procedure to follow should the need arise. For example, in Karner's interviews with the Vietnam veterans (1994), where she proposed to discuss stressful events in their lives, she identified staff volunteers on the PTSD unit who agreed to provide counseling support for any veteran who might feel the need during or after the interview. This procedure assured the IRB committee and she received approval, though no veteran ever used this option.

Alternative Interview Formats

Although our discussion so far has focused on one interviewer face-to-face with one respondent, there are other formats. Interviews can take place with one or more interviewers and one or more respondents, and they can be arranged electronically. We are unaware of any studies in qualitative interviewing that use more than one interviewer at the same time, but there are many examples of interviewing more than one respondent, including focus groups and interviews with couples (commonplace in clinical interviewing). Internet interviewing is also becoming an important tool of qualitative research, as well as a source of data (see Chapter 8).

INTERVIEWS WITH COUPLES

Either purposely or circumstantially, research interviews may take place with husbands and wives, or other dyads—making up a triad of interviewer and two respondents. Holstein and Gubrium have explored the dynamics of interviewing two people together, in one instance an elderly married couple that lived in a nursing home (1995, 67–78). Although the focus of the life-history interview was Don, the husband, "as the interview unfolded, it soon was apparent that Sue did not much like Don's version of things because it did not include her" (Holstein and Gubrium 1995, 67). Sue, then, began to direct the interview toward parts of Don's life that included her. Following Don's description of his early life and move to Florida, Sue says, "[sarcastically] 'Why don't you tell her that we got married in the meantime? I'm part of it, too, you know'" (1995, 68). Later in the interview, after Don has described various aspects of their life in the Depression, Sue again intervenes:

> [Chuckling] "Just listen to him. In the meantime we had three more children." [Sarcastically] "Remember that?" (Holstein and Gubrium 1995, 68)

It is clear from this interview, and from clinical interviewing with couples, that the story told in an interview with one person in a marriage will differ not only from the story told by the other person, but also from the story told by both together. In her classic study of working-class families, sociologist and clinician Lillian Rubin decided to interview wives and husbands separately

> because I was interested in understanding the way each experiences the marriage relationship and his or her role in it....The perceptions of husband and wife are not necessarily congruent, and...both perspectives are necessary for understanding the reality of a marriage....Women tend to discuss their feelings about their lives, their roles, and their marriages more freely when men are not present. (1976, 10–11)

Interestingly, triadic issues with interviewing may arise even if the married-couple interviewees are not copresent. In the Bay Area research, with one interviewer interviewing both spouses individually over a period of time, spouses sometimes sought access to confidential information about the other. Mr. Sand was disturbed when he found out that the male interviewer had not shared information with him about Mrs. Sand:

> He asked me if I had talked to his wife that day and when I did not answer at once he repeated the question and I finally told him that I did....He told me that...I knew things about what was going on at the hospital with his wife, and I didn't tell him a thing about it. He brought this up a few times. (Warren 1987, 266)

Focus Groups

Interviews with one or two interviewers and a group of people are referred to as focus groups, and are common in communications, program evaluation, and market research. Although only a few social science research studies used focus groups during the 1980s, by the late 1990s there were over two hundred (Morgan 2002, 142). Focus group market interviewing is generally structured, focused on the product to be sold, program to be assessed, or media event to be analyzed. Social science focus group interviewing is often less structured, focusing, like qualitative interviewing in general, on the participants' rather than the researcher's meanings and interpretations (Morgan 2002, 146–147). Focus groups have some advantages over individual interviews for social scientists, including lesser costs in terms of time and money (Fontana and Prokos 2007, 34). Focus group interviewer David Morgan describes his "ideal focus group":

> The ideal group would start with an opening question that was designed to capture the participants' interest, so that they themselves would explore nearly all the issues that a moderator might have probed. Then, just as the allocated time for that question was running out, one of the participants in the ideal group would spontaneously direct the others' attention to the topic for the second question by saying something like, "You know what really strikes me is how many of the things we're saying are connected to...." (Morgan 2002, 148)

Focus groups offer a data collection strategy that allows for the involvement of a larger sample in a shorter amount of time. They are generally thought of as a highly efficient means of collecting informational data that is not of a sensitive nature. For example, what services would parents like to see in their neighborhood parks? How satisfied are students with their educational experience at a particular college? What are some ideas for increasing efficiency in an organization or business? After conducting numerous focus groups, Hollander (2004) began to analyze focus group process from a sociological view—that is, she studied these events as the site of a specific kind of small-group interaction. She argues that focus groups also provide an excellent site for analyzing the processes of social interaction because

> the social contexts of focus groups—that is, the relationships among the participants and between the participants and the facilitator, as well as the larger social structures within which the discussion takes place— affect the data that are generated in ways that have not yet been widely acknowledged by focus group researchers. (2004, 603)

Focus groups are artificially formed for the researcher's project, making them contrived social events; that is, unlike many sites of interaction, focus groups do not occur naturally. Focus groups include approximately four to twelve (though six or seven is thought to be ideal) participants with specific characteristics germane to the research, and one or two leaders or moderators who ask questions of the group. In focus groups with two interviewers, one researcher usually takes the lead and asks most of the questions, while the other researcher may play a more supportive role—noting "talking points" on a blackboard, introducing prompts or probes, and interjecting questions or feedback infrequently.

What is said in focus group interviews may differ from what is said in dyadic ones, just as dyadic interviews differ from triadic ones. In a study about community violence, Hollander (2004) found the conversational context of a focus group of both men and women encouraged specific kinds of stories while silencing others. Women in the groups voiced concerns about violence, whereas the men expressed lack of concern. In her veterans study, Karner (1995) found great variation in the men's presentation of self as strong and tough in public forums to emotionally distraught in the dyadic interviews. If you want to study how context might influence behavior or narrative, then focus groups can provide an ideal setting and format.

INTERNET-BASED INTERVIEWING

Though marketing, communications, and media researchers were the early adopters of online data collection methods, internet-based research is becoming more common in social science investigations as well. Internet-based interviews may be synchronic (the researcher and respondent use the connection simultaneously) or asynchronic (the connection is used at a different time). Online interviewing is becoming so common that some researchers are interested in studying its implications for response rate, response quality, and in comparison with face-to-face interview formats (Fontana and Prokos 2007, 107–109).

The world wide web offers time- and cost-effective strategies that allow for including hard-to-reach populations all over the globe. Some researchers have developed online environments as cultural contexts within which to study virtual interaction (Hine 2000), while others have adapted traditional field methods focus groups (Murray 1997) and interviews (Shields 2003) for online use. As with all new methodologies and technologies, new ethical considerations have come to the fore as well (Robson and Robson 1999).

Many aspects of the online environment can be seen as conducive to good research—invisibility of physical characteristics (race, class, gender, age) of the interviewer (no need for "matching"), anonymity of respondents (ensured confidentiality), and the resulting disinhibition that can lead to more honest comments. These elements make the internet ideal for interviewing stigmatized and deviant social groups (Stewart and Williams 2005) or disenfranchised individuals with computer skills (Shields 2003). However, these same features create questions about the validity of the data collected (which we will talk more about in Chapter 9). Unless the researcher has some way of knowing who is participating in the focus groups or is responding to the interview question, he will have a hard time understanding the data in any meaningful way.

Using a listserv format where members must sign up with identifying information or creating password-protected access to the interview website are two ways that researchers can address some of these concerns. However, most of these solutions are beyond the beginning student researcher and fraught with enough IRB and ethical issues that we encourage you to start your interviewing practices with the traditional face-to-face interview, which has several formats and plenty of complexity for a semester course.

Your choice of interviewing people one by one, in pairs, in focus groups, in person, or via the internet will depend on the kind of information you expect to elicit as well as your costs in time and money. As Rubin's (1976) classic study has shown, if you interview married couples about their marriages, you are likely to get different responses from the wife, the husband, and in a joint interview situation. Your choice in this case would depend on your research questions: Do you want to be able to compare husbands' and wives' views of marriage? Do you want to see how the couple interacts as well as hear what they have to say? Or, do you want to compare responses across different interview formats? Whatever you decide about how many people to interview at one sitting, your next task will be to decide what the parameters will be for respondent selection in terms of age, gender, class, and other social statuses.

Sampling Respondents

Qualitative sampling strategies have a different underlying logic than the strategies used by quantitative researchers: what is called theoretic rather than random sampling. Random sampling is used in positivist, quantitative research, to ensure the generalizability of findings to the populations from which the sample was drawn. Theoretic sampling, by contrast, seeks in respondents only the criteria specified by the research questions: individuals newly diagnosed with diabetes in Karas and Karner's (2005) study, first admissions of white women with children to Napa mental hospitals in Warren's study of *Madwives* (1987), or caregivers of family members with Alzheimer's disease (Karner and Bobbitt-Zeher 2006). Within the context of theoretic sampling, the researcher has to decide the number of respondents she will interview (which may change as the research progresses), what types of respondent to interview (using criteria such as gender, age, and class), and how to locate specific respondents using these criteria.

NUMBER AND TYPE OF RESPONDENT

If you are a student or employee, the number of respondents you will interview may be preset by the instructor or research design; we both require students in one-semester classes to do ten interviews for a qualitative interviewing paper. Published research on one type of respondent (e.g., "older women" or homecare workers or veterans with PTSD) may be based on as few as 15 or as many as 100 or more respondents. The original *Madwives* (1987) research was based on thousands of interviews, but with fewer than 50 people, including 17 wives, 16 husbands, and a variety of psychiatric hospital personnel. By contrast, Diane Vaughan (1990) interviewed 103 people for her book on *Uncoupling*, and Carole Brooks Gardner (1995) interviewed more than 500 respondents for hers on public harassment, including minority and nonminority women and men.

The social characteristics of the people interviewed will depend on the research questions that you have derived from your topic. When Karas and Karner (2005) decided to study how individuals think about their lifestyle choices after a diabetes diagnosis, they chose to sample individuals with diabetes from local diabetes support groups. As they were primarily interested in changes a person may or may not make after diagnosis, they sampled only those diagnosed within the previous year (who were also the most likely to attend disease-specific support groups). This was the only restriction they put on their sample. Diane Vaughan, who wanted to study the experience of divorce and other kinds of uncoupling, interviewed "young and old, male and female, gay and straight, married and living together" (1990, 197).

Since the topic you have chosen for your interview research may have some biographical importance to you, it is likely—and may be a good thing—that there will be similarities between you and your respondents. There is a considerable literature, for example, on the gender of interviewers and respondents; although with some topics this may not matter, with other topics it may matter a lot. In interviewing men who had been recently divorced, Terry Arendell found that

> from the initial point of contact, the interview became a proving ground for masculinity and a site for the exercise of male dominance displays against ex-wives (and sometimes against all women). (1997, 342)

These men immediately "took charge" of the interview topic and attempted to "place" Arendell as married or unmarried, available or not, male basher or nice girl (Warren 2002, 96). Interviews between matched interviewers and interviewees will elicit one kind of interaction and narrative, whereas a very different interaction and narrative may emerge between an unmatched dyad. It might seem that interviews with divorced men, from the Arendell experience, would go better if it were a man doing the interviewing—but then again, they might not.

Finding Respondents

A common means of finding people to interview involves locating a social setting in which they can be found, either in the community or over the internet.

Karas and Karner (2005) found their respondents with diabetes at two local diabetes support groups, where Karas introduced herself and the study to prospective interviewees. She handed out a form for the support group members to provide their contact information if they would like to be contacted about the research project. This gave the researchers the opportunity to talk to support group members individually, discuss the project more fully, and, if they consented, arrange for an interview. Karner has repeatedly found that working with local organizations is a very successful way to access respondents. By locating her veterans study on an inpatient unit of a Veterans Administration hospital, she obtained many willing participants who looked forward to the interviews as something to break the boredom of institutional life. When studying homecare workers, Karner (1998a) was able to solicit interviewees through the homecare agency, which also provided a location for the interviews. In their studies of community service providers (Karner and Hall 2002) and nursing home staff (Snow et al. 2007), Karner and her colleagues employed the same strategy of gaining access through cooperating institutions.

However, finding actual respondents to interview within the parameters the researcher has set up, without the assistance of a cooperating organization, can be a daunting task. Vaughan (1990) describes her first strategy for trying to obtain respondents to interview concerning uncoupling. She sent one hundred letters to individuals and couples selected from newspaper divorce listings one to five years before the research started: "Four responses trickled back...but no one agreed to be interviewed" (1990, 198). Warren had a similar lack of response when she attempted to find elderly people to interview who had had electroshock therapy. Warren posted flyers in nursing homes and other places where elderly people were present, and in psychiatrists' offices and hospital waiting rooms, but to no avail.

The only way Warren eventually found her interviewees—and the main method used by Diane Vaughan—was through snowball sampling. This term refers to the process of accumulating interviewees from within interlocking social networks, beginning with an initial contact. Moore used a similar strategy for his research on punk rock.

> Initially, I had few contacts, so I used the snowball technique for arranging interviews: at the end of each interview, I would ask, "Who would be a good person to talk to about this scene?" and the interviewee would frequently offer to arrange an introduction with someone they knew. (Moore 2007, 444)

The internet is useful not only for interviewing respondents, but also for locating them. Researchers often turn to the internet to locate respondents through internet organizations. Joos and Broad (2007), for example, sought their email interview sample from an internet organization for the offspring of lesbian, gay, bisexual, transsexual, and queer (LGBTQ) parents.

Most discussions of sampling for interviews presume that the respondents obtained will be strangers; this is even reflected in the title of a textbook on qualitative interviewing, *Learning From Strangers* (Weiss 1994). However, the topic of interviews is often of mutual interest to respondent and interviewer. Especially when snowball sampling is used, the interviewer may find herself interviewing within her own interlocking social circles, as Moore (2007) did with some of his respondents from the punk music scene. Sometimes, as in Robinson's (2008) ethnographic and interview study of a lesbian community, the researcher finds herself studying friends and acquaintances, co-members of the same groups or communities. At other times, as in Warren's research on electroshock, although electroshock had no biographical relevance to her (she had obtained a grant, with others, to do the study), the snowball sampling technique with which she found respondents meant that she was interviewing the relatives of friends and colleagues.

When it comes to obtaining interview data, interviewing nonstrangers sometimes may mean that respondents do not answer our questions in detail, because as we have heard many of them say, "Why are you asking me that? You know all about that!" But sometimes more than the interview is at stake. Shifting from a purely sociable or personal to a research agenda may have consequences for the researcher's social relationships as well as for the data gathered. Interviewing people with whom one is familiar may take unexpected turns and have unexpected consequences. For one thing, respondents may be annoyed at being asked questions that they know the interviewer knows the answer to but is trying to get "for the record" (Harkess and Warren 1993). In addition, the topic of the interview may bring tensions into the relationship between interviewee and interviewer.

When Warren was doing interview research on electroshock therapy with elderly psychiatric patients, she interviewed a friend concerning the psychiatric hospitalization and planned electroshock treatment for her mother. During the interview, this respondent became very upset with both herself and Warren, accusing Warren of accusing her of abusing her elderly mother with electroshock. The interview questions did not give her that impression— they were quite bland—but her prior knowledge of Warren as a sociologist and critic of institutional psychiatry did. This episode had a negative impact on the friendship for some months after the interview, even after the friend's mother had been discharged from the hospital without receiving ECT. Richardson reported similar issues with a friend whose comments she had used in a book about another friend's dying:

> One friend who took exception said that she was surprised that I had taken what she had thought of as a private conversation and put it in my book. I was surprised at her surprise....Have I alienated a dear friend of twenty-five years? (2007, 172)

Planning the First Face-to-Face Interview

Once respondents have been identified and have agreed to be interviewed face-to-face, it is time to set up an appointment with them. As a courtesy, respondents should be consulted as to what date, time, and day of the week is convenient for them, and what kind of place they would like to be interviewed in. It is difficult enough to get respondents to make and keep interview appointments; if you also ask them to come to campus (with the search for parking and similar problems), you are making their job and thus yours all the more difficult. You may also not want to interview respondents in their homes, especially in the case of male-female dyadic interviews. Often a public place is the best choice, such as a table at the library, a quiet cafe or bookstore whose owners do not mind you interviewing at one of their tables, or, in nice weather, a park bench. Sometimes the respondents may ask you to come to their workplace or office for the interview, and that is often a very good choice, especially if the interview is about their work.

Herzog (2005) reminds us that the choice of the interview location (who chooses and what place is chosen) is not just a logistical issue. In her study of Palestinian women, she states that "the choice of interview location reflects the attitudes, tactics, and negotiations of the interviewees within the parallel power structures of research....gender....and nationality" (2005, 28–29). Indeed every "participant who consents to being interviewed is raced, gendered, and classed" (Warren 2002, 90). The choice of location can reinforce or attempt to equalize power relationships. For example, in a study of students' rights, Nairn and her colleagues (2005) decided (after one failed interview) to hold all further interviews off school grounds to lessen the inherent authority structures in the high school setting. Thus it is important for student researchers to be sensitive to the complexity that can occur in choosing a location.

Yet a place (see Box 6.5) for the interview must be selected, and you will want to choose a location that will maximize the respondent's physical comfort as well as your own. Also keep in mind that you would prefer that

---

Box 6.5
KEYS TO SELECTING GOOD INTERVIEW LOCATIONS

- Convenient for the respondent
- Comfortable and safe
- Quiet and free from distractions
- Private

the location be quiet and generally free of distractions. You will want to be able to sit comfortably for an hour without being interrupted. A table is also helpful for placing the recording device between the two of you as well as for taking notes. Privacy is also key to conducting a good interview. When selecting a time for the interview, make sure that your respondent will have enough time to talk without feeling hurried. We have also found that it's best to avoid mealtimes, as you do not want your interview curtailed by hunger. Avoiding mealtimes also saves you from having to negotiate invitations to join respondents for meals. In addition, you should select a time when you are *sure* that you can arrive on time. It is important for you to be there when you said you would.

You should also consider any special needs or challenges your interviewees may present. For example, in her study of older women who had survived breast cancer, Hall (2008) identified a number of challenges in interviewing this particular population. Older women in her sample preferred to be interviewed in their own homes, which required extra time and travel for the interviewer. Additionally, they often required memory or communication assistance from family members and were often dependent upon others for transportation. Perhaps the greatest challenge Hall found was the difficulty in recording frail, elderly voices clearly, which at times necessitated the assistance of an active note-taker during the interview. If your chosen sample has transportation or communication or other special needs, it will be up to you to both anticipate and address as many as you can.

Your preparations for the interview include self-presentation. When you first meet the respondent, how you present yourself and what you say are significant in helping the respondent crystallize his or her perception of both you, as an interviewer, and the experience of the interview as well. Therefore it is important to pay more attention than you usually might to specific details, common amenities, and cultural sensitivities. You will want to present yourself as an interested listener: empathetic, trustworthy, polite, nonjudgmental, and professional. However, you generally do not want to be perceived as an authority figure (do not wear your power suit) or as someone completely alien (from a different class, culture, or with dissimilar values). Try to dress somewhat like your respondents, but more conservatively. It is important for your respondents to feel that you can understand them and their attitudes, beliefs, and values, or they will not feel comfortable sharing them with you.

Your dress should be appropriate to the situation. If you are interviewing members of a biker gang, for example, it makes no sense to go to the interview in a suit and tie; the reverse may be true if you are interviewing attorneys. A rough rule of thumb is that your dress should not echo the respondents'—do not dress as a biker if you are not one—but should respect their choices. Thus, a sports coat might be appropriate for a man interviewing an attorney, and jeans and a T-shirt for a man interviewing a biker. Your demeanor should be unfailingly polite; although a calm, nonjudgmental stance will probably work with both bikers and attorneys (at least, work better than confrontation and hostility), a more easygoing approach would probably be appropriate with the bikers and a more formal one with the attorneys.

Before you travel to your first interview, use a preparation checklist (see Box 6.6). You may need maps to get to the interview location, and information on parking once you get there, especially if you are going to offices or educational institutions. Anything you need to actually conduct the interview should be listed, including paper, pens, and any audio or video equipment you intend to use.

Box 6.6
INTERVIEW PREPARATION CHECKLIST

Directions

- Clear directions to the interview location
- A plan for where you will finding parking, if needed
- Coins to feed the meter or credit card for parking lot
- Name tag or sign, if interviewee is unknown to you

Forms

- Consent form with extra copies
- Face sheet with extra copies
- Copies of interview guide (questions)

Recording

- Recording device
  - Check working order
- Microphone, if needed
- Extra batteries
- Extra tapes or memory sticks
  - Labeling pen

Supplies

- Notepad
- Pens, pencils
- Business cards, optional

Interview Technologies

Although some interviewers (and ethnographers) use videotape, most pub-lished interview research is based on audiotape or digital recordings. Be sure that you have good quality, pretested audio equipment: a recorder with two sets of fresh batteries and an electrical cord, and an adequate supply of tapes or memory sticks (twice as many as you think you need). If you are using tape, take along a selection of thirty- and sixty-minute tapes, starting with a one-hour tape and moving to a half-hour tape if the one-hour one runs out. With a digital recorder you need to have extra memory sticks and a way to back them up or transfer data if you are doing a number of interviews in the field. Some digital recorders only come with internal memory so you are lim-ited to a certain amount of recording time before you must transfer the data to your computer. Depending upon the memory space on such a recorder, the interviewer may need to have a computer at the ready to download data between interviews. You always want to have twice as much, if not more, memory or tapes than you believe you will need ready at the beginning of an interview. Many researchers are now using their iPods, smartphones or PDAs to record their interviews. Some of these devices can even be used for low-resolution video recording.

Whatever recording device you choose, be sure to test your equipment thoroughly before the interview, at least once at the site where you are going to be doing the interview, to see if you are going to plug in the recorder or use the batteries, and to situate it and test for sound pickup. You can check for little things like placing the recorder on top of a notepad for cushioning to cut down on vibration noise, or how to position the recorder to avoid excess noise from a circulating fan. Using a microphone might be necessary in situa-tions where there is likely to be a lot of background noise. Karner has a wire-less mic set up that she finds works very well in these situations, whether she is doing video or audio recording. The microphone set comes with a remote mic for the interviewee and a background mic that can be used for the inter-viewer. The recorder can be of any style or size, but must always be visible to the respondent as well as to you to ensure that it is still functioning. The most common interviewing situation is for a respondent and an interviewer to be across from each other at a medium-sized table, with the recorder and microphone placed between them to record both questions and answers.

Setting up the Interview

Arrive at your first interview (and each subsequent one) at least fifteen min-utes before the prearranged time to set up your recording equipment—and to ensure (generally) that you are waiting for the respondent rather than vice versa. You will want time to construct your interview environment. You want to sit close enough together so that your respondent can easily see any notes you have so you do not seem deceptive. You want to be comfortable; you want privacy; and you want to be free from as many distractions as possible. Keep these things in mind when first sitting down and arranging the interview environment. It is very disruptive to the flow of talk if you need to readjust things midway.

For an interview with someone you don't know, you might wear a name tag so that the respondent can identify you; you might even want to hold up or have on the table a larger sign with your name or the project title on it (not the respondent's as is done when a stranger is being met at the airport). When the respondent spots you, get up (if you have been sitting), smile, and introduce yourself. How you introduce yourself is important—use Mr., Ms., or Mrs. when addressing the respondent unless the respondent asks you to call him or her by another name or title. Showing respect is important, especially if you are younger than the respondent. When saying your name, avoid titles. For example:

> "Hello, Mrs. Doe. I'm Jane Smith and I'm one of the interviewers for the diabetes experience project. It's very nice to meet you."

Make sure the respondent is seated comfortably across from you, giving him or her time to settle in (stowing purses, coats, etc.) as you make pleasant small talk about the weather or the traffic. When the respondent is comfortable and gives you eye contact, it is time for the formal interview to begin.

You should begin by explaining the purpose of the interview. Respondents who believe in the importance of the research and especially its relevance to their own situation are more attentive and provide more productive interviews than those who are uninterested. So remember that in telling them about the interview project, you are, to some extent, informing them about its importance. You should keep the explanation as straightforward as possible. For example:

> This interview is part of a study to see how well the Sunshine Day Care is working for the people that use it. We are trying to find out if people are satisfied with the services so we will know what to change in the future. We are also looking at different types of experiences with caring for older persons, so we have some questions that ask about your experience of caring for your mother.

Be sure to allow respondents to ask any questions they may have or voice any concerns. Take any concerns expressed seriously and answer them fully. You want the respondent to feel listened to, even before starting the formal interview.

At this point you are ready to ask the respondent's permission to turn on your recording device. You might also tell the respondent that he or she should feel free to turn the recorder off at any time if there is something that he or she would rather not have recorded. We have never had this happen, but it offers the respondent some sense of control. Another thing you might try is enlisting the respondent's assistance in making sure the recording light stays on so you can explain why you will be checking periodically (especially if you have a recorder, like Karner once had, that silently runs out of tape). After you have the go-ahead to begin recording, you can give the respondent the consent form to sign, with a copy for each of you to keep, so that you will have an audio record of any comments that are made about the form. Then present the respondent with the demographic face sheet, if that is how you have decided to get basic information about gender, age, and so on (see Box 6.4). You should have your list of questions (show the respondent on request) in your hand, and a lined pad and pen or pencil to take notes.

Your interview has begun.

Suggestions for Further Reading

Fontana, Andrea, and Anastasia H. Prokos. 2007. *The Interview: From Formal to Postmodern.* Walnut Creek, CA: Left Coast Press.

Gubrium, Jaber, and James Holstein. 2001. *Handbook of Interview Research: Context and Method.* Thousand Oaks, CA: Sage Publications.

Kvale, Steinar. 1996. *InterViews: An Introduction to Qualitative Research Interviewing.* Thousand Oaks, CA: Sage Publications.

Mishler, Elliott G. 1986. *Research Interviewing: Context and Narrative.* Cambridge, MA: Harvard University Press.

Chapter 7

The Interview

Interaction, Talk, and Text

A survey interview and a qualitative interview may look alike to the casual observer, with prepared, trained interviewers asking questions and recording answers. But for the qualitative interviewer the interview is not only a method, it is a social interaction of the very type that qualitative methods were designed to study. Thus, the qualitative interview as social interaction has been the subject of numerous methodological analyses over the past few decades.

The qualitative interview has also been studied from a sociolinguistic perspective as a "speech event," since it consists of talk between two native speakers, or various combinations of native speakers, non-native speakers, and translators (Briggs 2002). The presumption in this chapter is that of an English-speaking interviewer and an English-speaking respondent. The complications that arise when the interviewer and respondent speak different languages (the interviewer is not fluent in the respondent's language, or a translator has to be used) are beyond our scope—and of most student research.

In this chapter, we explore the interview as social interaction, and as a process with a beginning, middle, and end. We then consider the challenges of transcription, or taking talk and turning it into text. Finally, we take a look at the epistemology of the interview: how qualitative researchers have interpreted the interview as a source of data and of sociological knowledge. Since interview transcripts will join fieldnotes and other texts as the subject of analysis (see Chapter 9), it is important to understand what kind of data they represent.

The Interview as Social Interaction

Interviews are a special form of social interaction in which "the interviewers' desire to know something impels the interaction" (Dick 2006, 91). Discussions of the interview as social interaction—and indeed speech event—have taken place at least since the Chicago School. As Vivien Palmer said in 1928,

> Any interview constitutes a social situation between two individuals; it is a process of continuous, spiral interaction in which one person's response to the stimulation of another in turn becomes the stimulation for another response. (Palmer 1928, 171)

Although this more than seventy-year-old perspective on the interview as a social situation is still at the heart of contemporary definitions, many of the other ideas about interviewing proposed by Palmer and other Chicago School researchers are quite different. Unlike many of today's qualitative interviewers, for example—especially feminist ones—Palmer advised the research interviewer to maintain an objective "detachment as a scientific investigator" throughout the interaction (1928, 175). Today some qualitative sociologists, particularly feminists, recommend a more participatory role for the interviewer, and for the interviewee as well.

The interview as social interaction, like other social interactions in everyday life, can range from disastrous to mutually rewarding, depending on the talkativeness of the respondent, the topic of the interview, the functioning of the recording device, and the interview process itself. In addition, the interviewer's disposition and ability to improvise in the back-and-forth of question asking and answering can greatly influence the outcome of an interview (Nairn, Munro, and Smith 2005; Russell 2005). Some respondents may not want to talk much and give brief "yes" or "no" responses; others may be intimidated (perhaps because of class disparities), or would prefer to avoid the topic. This is where the interviewer's preparation (in terms of planned prompts and probes) and rapport-building skills come into play.

While most interview topics are of mutual interest to respondent and interviewer, some topics may be interesting but uncomfortable to the respondent. For example, Watson (2006) found eager respondents for her study of teacher identity and discipline in the classroom. Though the teachers were initially enthusiastic, the discrepancies between their sense of themselves as "good" teachers and their accounts of using "the belt" came to light, their interest in continuing with the research project waned considerably. As Watson discovered, not all topics contribute to interview rapport.

There is a range of interview interactions, from the ideal interview described by Rubin and Rubin (2004) to the other extreme, the interview in which only monosyllabic responses are obtained. The monosyllabic-response interview is probably worse from the interviewer's point of view than a refusal, since the investment of considerable time (and perhaps money) in the process has not resulted in a usable narrative. Failure to obtain a "good" (narratively rich) interview may reflect defects in the training, preparation, or approach of the interviewer. Indeed, some researchers have found that as their confidence as interviewers increased, the quality of the interview data also improved (Nairn et al. 2005; Russell 2005). Or it may reflect the social situation or attitude of the respondent at the time of the interview.

Although the interviewer may have decided on the format of the interview, actual interviews may involve interaction with a range of people other than those originally planned for. This is especially true of interviews that take place in a household or at a place of work. Children needing their mother's attention frequently interrupted the Bay Area expatient interviews. Interviewers may or may not regard such interruptions negatively; although they break the flow of narrative, they also provide opportunities to observe the life-world of the interviewee. In her informal interviews with high-school students with "academic or emotional difficulties," Russell (2005, 186) found that a number of students who had not been selected for her study would "purposely act unruly in my presence with the hope that I would notice them and ask them to participate [in the research]." Heying Zhan's (2000) interviews with individual family members in rural China were regularly interrupted by other members of the family as well as neighbors who would come to join in the conversations. Since Zhan's interest was in intimate family caregiving duties and expectations, the public nature of the interview situation, she found, compromised her responses considerably. Given the cultural norms of the villages, she was unable to hold any private interviews.

THE INTERVIEW PROCESS

The interview process has a beginning, an unfolding or natural history, and an ending, all of which are dependent upon the interaction of interviewer and respondent. If you are doing an interview study by yourself, the choice is you. If, however, you are an investigator recruiting interviewers, you have to decide what qualities of the interviewer—including age, gender, and appearance—will best facilitate interaction, the development of rapport, and the elicitation of good data. As we will see, qualitative researchers' ideas about the ideal interviewer have changed over the past eighty years.

As we saw in the last chapter, the interview process is facilitated by the interviewer's and respondent's ease with the setting and the technology. Throughout the interview, the researcher engages in active listening, as well as questioning, while—hopefully—developing rapport with the respondent.

The point of the whole process is the development of rapport, from which will flow truth, truths, or at least stories. Interviewers and respondents may also, unexpectedly perhaps, experience emotional reactions to the topics or processes of the interview. Once rapport has been established—or not—and questions answered, the end of the interview is near; the social interaction, however, may continue after the interview.

THE INTERVIEWER

The interview, like field research, involves an embodied researcher of a particular appearance, gender, sexuality, race, class, and age; one or more respondents with their own social characteristics; and a topic that may be of interest to both participants but a threat to one. No matter what the previous understandings or initial rapport, and no matter who is doing the interviewing, certain topics, or even certain questions or subtopics within a general topic, may stymie the interview process.

While speculating about lack of interviewee responses in a study of New Zealand teenagers, Nairn and her colleagues (2005) noted that sexuality was "out of bounds" for this age group within the Pacific Island cultural perspectives of their respondents. Similarly, Adler and Adler discuss an interview with a drug dealer's "old lady" that had to be terminated because of her discomfort:

> We thought that she liked and trusted us and that, as a graduate student in cultural anthropology, she understood and respected academic research. However, as soon as the interview began, we realized that she felt uncomfortable discussing the drug trafficking of her friends: She ducked our questions, feigned sleepiness, and avoided direct answers. We politely left and lost all future access to her. (2002, 525)

Perhaps because the Adlers were focusing on illegal activities, their withdrawal from the situation was the appropriate response. If, however, the topic was one without legal ramifications, a skillful interviewer might use the respondent's reticence to redirect the questions to uncovering the source of discomfort. For example, "I know this is an uncommon experience, but if you could help me understand why some people have a difficult time talking about it—that would really help my research." The interviewer can "talk around" the topic and focus on the interviewee's approach and emotional response to the issue. Another approach might be to ask about the differences between those who are willing to talk about the topic and those who are not. If the interviewer broadens the reference group (using "some people" or "other people" rather than "you"), the interviewee is given some emotional and personal distance from the topic and may be much more comfortable talking around his or her own experience in this more general way.

As we saw in Chapter 6, both survey and qualitative interview researchers may seek to "match" respondents on such characteristics as gender and race in order to (they hope) maximize rapport. In their study of New Zealand youth, which included indigenous and immigrant groups, Nairn and her colleagues (2005) speculated that not matching the interviewer to respondents could account for a "failed" interview.

It could be concluded that a "40-something" Pakeha interviewer was inappropriate for the interview...[with students from diverse Pacific Island backgrounds but no Pakeha students] and this explains why the interview "failed." (2005, 226)

Nairn's research team, however, decided that such thinking would only reinforce essentialist assumptions which could mean that "only women can interview women, only Maori can interview Maori and...only young people can interview young people" (2005, 226). After more careful and thoughtful reflections, they decided that having teachers (authority figures) "recruit" their student subjects may have had more to do with the interview challenges. Through their body language and their relative silence, the student interviewees demonstrated a lack of desire to participate in the interview. Interviewing respondents who don't really want to be interviewees is not in keeping with informed consent (that we discussed in Chapter 2) and definitely counter to facilitating a productive interview. Though interviewer characteristics such as age, gender, height, nationality, accent, and level of experience interviewing can all influence the research (Russell 2005), other factors such as the consent and recruitment process may also play a role.

Most scholars acknowledge that matching respondents and interviewers on key characteristics may not be the most crucial element in planning a successful research project. Indeed, the matching theory of rapport has not always been the dominant one. In many of the early Chicago School texts, the gender of the interviewer was often left unspecified; given the focus on interviewer "objectivity," it presumably did not matter who did the interviewing. But when gender was mentioned it was the male interviewer who was preferred, because of his greater presumed empathy, friendliness, and authority (Warren and Hackney 2000). This preference lasted at least until Kinsey's studies in the 1940s and 1950s; as O'Connell Davidson and Layder note, "Kinsey's assumption that women would tell the truth about their sexual lives to male interviewers now appears as dated" (1994, 130). By the 1970s and 1980s, women interviewers were presumed to be the empathic "sociability specialists" who could extract the truth from women and men informants (Warren and Hackney 2000) due in part to their nonthreatening presence (Russell 2005).

Social class, as well as gender, may affect the interview process as it is read through the bodies of the participants (demeanor, accent, dress, and so on). The social class of the interviewer as well as of the respondent has been at issue during the decades of twentieth-century interviewing. Kinsey, for example, refused to

> employ women, Black people, or people with Jewish names...because he believed that "only WASPs [White Anglo Saxon Protestants]...could interview everybody." (O'Connell Davidson and Layder 1994, 130)

Although the Kinsey research team considered matching interviewers with respondents on such features as class, occupation, and race, they concluded that "the qualities of the interviewer, not his sex, race, or personal history, were the important variables" (O'Connell Davidson and Layder 1994, 130). Today researchers would probably attend both to the matching of social statuses and to the personal attributes of potential interviewers before hiring them.

Respondents of lower social status and education may be reluctant to talk with someone they perceive as an authority figure—or they may feel obliged to talk with the authority figure but give monosyllabic answers. Respondents of higher social status and occupation may be reluctant to talk with an interviewer not because they have nothing to say but because they do not have enough time to say it in, such as the physicians interviewed by Grace DeSantis (1980). People who are just busy may not be able to find the time to be interviewed, or, if they are interviewed, hurry to get the interview over. In the Bay Area study, some of the women did not want to be interviewed in the post-hospital phase of the study because they did not want to be reminded of the stigma of having been mental patients, while others were willing but were busy with housework and childcare (Warren 1987).

The issue of matching interviewers to respondents based on social characteristics raises similar issues to those of incorporation of the fieldworker, discussed in Chapter 4. Much as the stranger fieldworker faces different challenges to incorporation than the member fieldworker, interviewers that are matched confront issues that differ from those an unmatched interviewer will meet. Furthermore, matching may not be static (Naples 1996); it may be dynamic and permeable as individuals become acquainted with each other and find commonalities as well as differences. In interviews about children, parenthood of both parties may be more important than similarity with regard to race or age. De Andrade (2000) found that even though she was a member of the ethnic community she sought to interview, respondents continually questioned her background and connections as her status was evaluated and negotiated during her fieldwork.

Another interpersonal issue is the ability of the interviewer to grasp the meaning of what the respondent is saying. Zinn (1979, 159) was an early proponent of the notion that "minority scholars" could "ask questions and gather information that others could not." However, we believe based upon our own research across difference that unmatched interviewers of different races, classes, ages, or genders, through careful and active listening coupled with respect, can conduct successful interviews.

As Rubin and Rubin (2004) point out, the interview is as much about listening as it is about talking, and the first thing an interviewer has to be is a good listener. A good listener is an active and attentive listener. Interviewers with this skill do not expect the recorder to pick up everything for them while their mind wanders; instead, they listen carefully to everything the respondent says, in both words and body language, and respond accordingly. Active listening lets respondents know that you are interested in what they have to say, and that you are not just there to collect data for your own research needs—it is a demonstration of your respect for what insights they have to offer. A good listener, and thus a good interviewer, will use both nonverbal (nodding and eye contact) and verbal ("I see," "oh yes," "ah, that makes sense") encouragements while listening.

QUESTIONS AND ELICITATIONS

Qualitative interviewers begin with their interview guide, which consists of a number of open-ended questions (see Boxes 6.1 and 6.2). These questions point the respondents to specific topics of discussion but "the objective is to bring the respondent to consider an issue in his own words, leading the interviewer towards the areas of greatest import for the respondent" (Dick 2006, 93). This format allows respondents some control over the degree of exposure they are comfortable with (Sinding and Aronson 2003). Retaining some control may reduce "ego threat," so that the respondent feels comfortable in answering honestly.

You may want to emphasize that there are no "right" or "wrong" answers; even if you do, however, some respondents may need reassurance that they are answering the questions correctly or in a helpful and interesting manner. Comments such as "you are doing fine" or "that is so helpful" or just nodding and saying "good" can help alleviate apprehension. These gestures demonstrate a respect and concern for your respondents that can help build a sense of trust and rapport.

In addition to your questions, you should use prompts to clarify or expand on various topics. Box 7.3 demonstrates how prompts were used with Karas and Karner's (2005) interview guide (Box 6.2). Interviewees may not always respond immediately to your open-ended questions. If a response is not offered, it may be that the question requires thought and the respondent merely needs some time to think. An interviewer may prompt: "I know it is a complex question and you might want to think about it." The interviewee will probably let you know if that is the case or if there is a need for clarification. Furthermore, this prompt gives the respondent permission to pause and think. The second option might be to further clarify the question you've asked, or ask if the question makes sense. You can easily say, "Does that make sense?" For example, "I know that some people see caregiving as just part of being a loyal spouse, but I wonder if there are some things that you find yourself doing now, that you didn't do before…" would be a way of clarifying a question about different kinds of care.

Sometimes an interview respondent seems hesitant to answer. Though we will talk in greater detail below about resistance due to perceived threat to self, here we will cover the less problematic kinds of respondent resistance. There are many forms of resistance to answering the interview questions. One comment you might hear is, "Didn't you already ask that?" or "You already know that, why are you asking?" Always begin by agreeing with the respondent: "Yes, you are right, I do know that, but I need to ask you 'for the record'" or "Yes, this does sound similar, but it is a different question."

At some point, the respondent may say "I don't know" to one of the questions. Dick (2006) reminds us that in qualitative interviewing a response of "I don't know" is not necessarily problematic, as it illuminates what information the respondent considers meaningful (to know or remember) and what she finds unimportant (not noticed or paid attention to). As an interviewer, you will have to decide what information an "I don't know" response is offering your study.

If you are asking something factual—"When were you diagnosed with diabetes?" for example—"not knowing" by a respondent would mean something different than if you were asking "How was that for you, when you found your best friend had been wounded?" An interviewer might respond with: "I realize this question may be difficult to answer without some thought. What can you tell me about your experience?" Again, you are giving the respondent permission to think about the answer and acknowledging that it is a challenging question.

If you are asking something factual, the date of some occurrence, for example, and the respondent is still reticent to respond, you may say, "I don't have to know exactly, but what is your best guess?" This is especially helpful if you are asking about when something long ago occurred. Or if the hesitance comes from being asked to estimate something in the future, you can answer: "Well, of course nobody knows for sure, but given the way things look now, what do you think or what is your best guess?"

"What do you mean by that?" is another possible respondent question. The interviewer should treat this as a simple request for clarification. The problem is to communicate the meaning of the question without suggesting an answer and without changing the meaning of the question. If the respondent does not understand the question, you can ask: "Can you tell me what it is about the question that you're not sure of?" Perhaps it is just the wording or language usage that is confusing, or the respondent may not be sure of the referent.

As qualitative researchers, we are active partners in the elicitation of the narrative (Gubrium and Holstein 2003). How we ask the question, how many times we interview the respondent, and whether we probe for clarification can all have an impact on the resulting narrative. Even if the respondent, like Ramsey (Box 7.1), believes he is telling the truth, his account may vary

Box 7.1
SELF ACCOUNTS AND TRUTHS

This excerpt from Karner's (1995:58–60) "Medicalizing Masculinity: Post Traumatic Stress Disorder in Vietnam Veterans" illustrates how *truths* shift and evolve with each telling of self. Karner writes,

In the *first interview,* Ramsey spoke, with great regret and sorrow, about the individuals he felt he had killed needlessly. He recalled having remorse at the time and he contrasted that to other soldiers' joy in killing. Ramsey unfolded his story in contradictions, first mentioning what happened and then claiming that he could not have done it. "I should've if I was like somebody else that was brought up different than me and didn't have any feelings about human life then I would have come back bragging and said 'oh I killed somebody today.' You know as though I'd marked the little part on the helicopter you know that I got a kill today." Ramsey also mentioned during the initial interview that he had "kind of went off the deep end, the extreme opposite of being a very sheltered Christian—I went to the extreme opposite!" However, he gave closure to each event narrated by withdrawing from the aggression and willfulness of the event. He mentioned what happened and then concluded with "I feel so guilty." At various times during the interview, Ramsey paused to ponder, "I don't know if you call it murder or kill, I don't know for sure, at times I call myself a murderer." He contemplated the appropriate label for his behavior and could not accept either word.

During the *second interview* [two days later], Ramsey told some of his stories from the perspective of Scott, the other door gunner in his helicopter. "I tell you, I had a problem with that. I didn't go back and brag about it with the other guys. The other guys would brag about it....It wasn't any problem for Scott, because Scott had done a lot of killing....He whooped and hollered." Then Ramsey mentioned later in the second interview, "I didn't perceive myself as being someone who could kill somebody and then laugh about it and feel good about it." He paused briefly, then added, "I didn't." Ramsey was still narrating through negations. He had forgotten the candor of his first interview and, when pressed to talk about the time when he had killed a woman and the child in her arms, he could not. Ramsey talked around the event and tried, but ended with "I can't come out and say it."

The telling of traumatic memory was inhibited by its lack of language, but it was also a process much like the construction of a puzzle. The veteran gave clues in multiple ways, all but telling without telling, while he remained unable to speak of it directly. Approximately six weeks later, during the *third interview,* Ramsey had become much more vocal. He had been able to tell his stories in "trauma group" and now had a language to help him integrate them within himself. Ramsey began by disclosing, "Well, I wasn't telling myself exactly the truth because I really enjoyed killing that woman...because I

continued

Box 7.1 *continued*

was so angry about my friend being killed." Later he broadened his statement, adding more pieces to the puzzle, "I've learned just to go ahead and tell the truth that I enjoyed killing." The main focus of this interview became Ramsey's desire to kill...He spoke of his enjoyment and euphoria in Vietnam, being able to kill at will....Ramsey had decided that his feelings were acceptable in light of the rationale that he only wanted to "put to death people who deserve it." When asked directly if he would kill again, Ramsey answered ambiguously, "I wouldn't admit that, there's no way I'd admit that." Ramsey had started to let some of his traumatic experiences unfold. From his narrative, it seemed that he had mentally placed all the times he had felt like killing within his Vietnam experience. Thus when his combat memories began to unravel, his other, similar memories came to the forefront as well.

During the *fourth interview,* about a month later, Ramsey was willing to address one more element of his traumatic experience. In all the earlier interviews, he had identified the death of his friend Mike as the impetus for his entire excessive combat killing. "Mike is someone that I argued with and hoped that he would get killed and he got killed." Ramsey's motivation for revenge was no longer there, but rather a feeling that his wishes had been fulfilled. Thus, at this point, Ramsey had been able to speak about the moral issues that had been dividing his self. Ramsey believed that the person he had been in Vietnam was the "extreme opposite" of whom he had been brought up to be. Having enjoyed killing and continuing to want to kill presented him with ethical dilemmas that made him either a "killer or murderer."

Ramsey spoke directly about knowing himself internally as a killer while simultaneously trying to project the image of a good person to himself and others. "I can put on a front that people think is really me, that I'm a nice person, real tender hearted and all that. And I think I really am....Underneath the face I am someone, I know I am a killer."...

For Ramsey..., as well as for many others, issues of trauma were as much about the portraits they painted of the self as the horror and atrocities that exist in the world. Their difficulties in remembering and telling their stories focused on protection of themselves from negative judgment. The ambiguities centered on the moral vacuum of their combat impromptu selves and their inability to reconcile the actions of those selves with the noncombat ethics of society.

considerably from that of other observers and even from his own retellings. Thus the notion of truth, much like the issue of accuracy of internet web pages that we discuss in Chapter 8, can be seen as situational. Rather than empirically verifiable statements, the actions and the accounts that emerge provide the "texts of expression" that constitute social data that can be analyzed. From this perspective, all interview responses do contain both a "truth and a secret." And even outright, obvious lies may contain social truths and useful data.

Rapport in the Interview

The development of *rapport* between interviewer and respondent was an important theme in discussions of both survey and qualitative interviewing in the decades between the Chicago School (Palmer 1928, 172) and the 1980s. The purpose of establishing rapport was to find out truth; without rapport, it was feared, problems of untruthfulness and evasion would occur. In the 1920s Palmer indicated that the purpose of the interview is to elicit the respondent's "experiences and attitudes as they actually have occurred or exist" (1928, 173–174). Similarly, in the 1980s, Jack Douglas said that his "ideal goal" in interviewing "is the revelation of the complete truth about human life" (1985, 95–96).

We see interviewing as a means to facilitate the telling of individual accounts within the context of interaction and talk. Thus, there is always a situated "truthfulness" in the interaction that is reflective of broader social truths even though the actual information conveyed may have a limited intersection with any empirical reality (Watson 2006). We will discuss this further when we turn our attention to the epistemology of the interview.

Establishing rapport remains an essential component in successful interviewing (Fontana and Prokos 2007). Indeed, how to establish and maintain rapport with respondents was the subject of discussion during the six decades between Palmer and Douglas. Palmer proposed in the 1920s that rapport would be broken if the interviewer talked too much, suggesting the use of body language instead:

> Gestures, the nod of the head, smiles, facial expressions which reflect the emotions narrated are…very important. They also aid the interviewer in escaping pitfalls; if the response is put into language it can more often lead to disagreement and misunderstandings which break the *rapport* between the interviewer and his subject. (1928, 171–172, emphasis in original)

Some sixty years later Douglas argued that the key issue in rapport is warmth, something that he says "is not my trump card…but…can be learned" (1985, 106). We would argue, in contrast to Douglas, that respect (from which warmth may also follow) is the essential component of building rapport—respect for your respondents and respect for the knowledge and perspectives they have to offer.

As we noted in Chapter 6, first impressions are important in interview as well as ethnographic research. If first impressions are "too bad," Douglas cautions, "everything that follows…may not follow at all" (1985, 81–82). Further into the interview, a respondent's voice tones, gestures, or silence might indicate a breakdown of previously established rapport. Under such circumstances the interviewer might, for example, change the order or type of questioning until the respondent seems more comfortable, or reengage in small talk (Douglas 1985).

Interviews are like conversations, but they are not the same as social conversations. How much to interject into the discussion, and how much self-disclosure about one's personal life the interviewer will make, must be carefully thought out. In analyzing the use of disclosure in their own data sets, Abell and colleagues (2006) found that respondents did not always interpret interviewer self-disclosure as rapport building. An interviewer's personal comments may illuminate difference in social status or experience rather than similarity with the respondents, having a negative impact on the subsequent interview dialogue.

In other studies, sharing information about one's life, such as family situation or name of hometown, can help build trust and rapport (Russell 2005). However, the balance of self-disclosure must be negotiated carefully. Karner had a student who felt that she was conducting some wonderful interviews. She believed that her technique was to share a lot of her own opinions and experiences to build rapport. When it came time to analyze her data, she found she had substantially less data to work with than her classmates, and that none of her respondents had provided any information that was contradictory to the views she had espoused, rendering all of her data problematic. Balancing rapport and what sociologists refer to as active listening is as important in interviewing as the research questions themselves.

Some researchers argue that the rapport has to be exactly right, not underrapport but not overrapport either. Underrapport might lead to untruths, refusal to answer, or short yes or no responses. Overrapport, however, might lead to the respondent trying to please the interviewer with a socially desirable answer rather than a true one—that is, telling the interviewer what she wants to hear (like Karner's student discussed above). Palmer suggests that a "detached attitude" can guard against overrapport "distorting the story of the person interviewed, against causing him [the respondent] to express himself in terms of the interviewer" (1928, 175). Another issue with the idea of rapport is that discussions of it are based entirely on the interviewer's determination that it has or has not occurred. In an interview between sexologist Alfred Kinsey and "an older Negro male" the following exchange occurred:

> Kinsey...inquired if he had ever "lived common law."
> The man admitted he had, and that it had first happened when he was fourteen.
> "How old was the woman?" [Kinsey] asked.
> "Thirty-five," he admitted, smiling.
> Kinsey showed no surprise. "She was a hustler, wasn't she?" he said flatly. At this, the subject's eyes opened wide, he smiled in a friendly way for the first time, and said, "Well, sir, since you appear to know something about these things, I'll tell you straight." (quoted in O'Connell Davidson and Layder 1994, 131)

From Kinsey's point of view he had established rapport with this respondent by showing he "knew the score." O'Connell Davidson and Layder question this interpretation:

> Why did [Kinsey] not consider the possibility that the man was exaggerating the age difference, or that the smile and wide-eyed "Well, sir" could have been a straightforward mockery of Kinsey's rather transparent line of thought? (1994, 131)

Did Kinsey achieve overrapport, so that the respondent told Kinsey what he wanted to hear? Or did Kinsey underdevelop the rapport, resulting in mockery? As readers we are generally left with only the interviewer's assessment of whether he or she has established rapport or is being subtly mocked or manipulated. Rapport might be more appropriately conceived of as the basis for telling accounts, rather than truths. Without some sort of rapport, very limited telling will occur. With rapport, a rich textural accounting can unfold. This most often occurs when researchers approach potential interviewees with respect and genuine interest.

We offer an excerpt from an interview sequence Karner conducted (see Box 7.1) that demonstrates the complexity of rapport and truth. In interviewing men diagnosed with PTSD, she found that

> telling about traumatic memories was a process of revelation of the self to the self and to others. Veterans often recounted their experiences in an emotionally stressful, contradictory, and fragmented manner that undermined their credibility and thereby maintained both *a truth and a secret*. Moreover, the aftermath of trauma is always expressed, if not in words, then in actions or symptoms (van der Kolk 1988). The veterans' nonverbal process of retelling was manifested in their hypermasculine pursuits of drinking and drug use, recklessness, and outbursts of anger, whether the veteran consciously willed it or not. Lives became the *texts of expression*. (Greenspan 1992, 146; quoted in Karner 1994, 216; emphasis added)

As reflected in many past and present textbooks on qualitative interviewing, the ideal interview is one in which rapport is established and a rich narrative emerges. The ideal interview is also on a topic of mutual interest to researcher and interviewee (Kvale 1996). Many individuals are quite willing to talk and will agree to be interviewed. As the Rubins state,

> At a basic level, people like to talk about themselves; they enjoy the sociability of a long discussion and are pleased that somebody is interested in them....You come along and say, yes, what you know is valuable, it should not be lost, teach me, and through me teach others. (Rubin and Rubin 2004, 103)

Indeed, we have both had students doing interviews where respondents continue to offer the researcher insights long after the formal interview ceases. If a researcher takes the time to express genuine and respectful interest, respondents will often want to make sure that the interviewer understands fully. At other times, however, talking does not come so easily. Strategies and issues related to maintaining the flow of talk during the interview include impromptu prompts, respondent resistance, and emotional content. (See Box 7.2 for a brief summary of these techniques.)

Box 7.2
COMMENTS FOR ELICITING RICH NARRATIVE ACCOUNTS

Impromptu prompts

(Permission to take time to think)
I know it is a complex question and you might want to think about it...

(Clarifying difference between spouse caregiving and illness caregiving)
I know that some people see caregiving as just part of being a spouse, but I wonder if there are some things that you find yourself doing now, that you didn't do before...

(Clarifying if the respondent understands the question)
Does that make sense?

Respondent Resistance

(But you already know that...)
Yes, you are right, but I need to ask you "for the record."

(Didn't you already ask that?)
Yes, this does sound similar, but it is a different question.

(Oh, I really don't know....)
I realize this question may be difficult to answer without some thought.
   Or
I don't have to know exactly, but what is your best guess?

(I don't know the future, how could I know?)
Well, of course nobody knows for sure, but given the way things look now, what do you think or what is your best guess?

(I'm really not sure....)
Can you tell me what it is about the question that you're not sure of?

Emotional Content

(If respondent seems emotionally overcome...)
I can see that this is difficult for you; would you like to take a moment?

Box 7.3
USING PROBES AND PROMPTS

**Interview Guide with Prompts and Probes for a Study
of Newly Diagnosed Individuals with Diabetes**

1. Please tell me a little about yourself.
   Prompt: Where you grew up, your family, hobbies, occupation, or anything else you want to share.
2. Please tell me about when and how you were diagnosed with diabetes.
   Probe: When was that (probe for date)?
   Probe: How did you come to be diagnosed?
   Probe if necessary: Did you have any symptoms before being diagnosed?
   Probe if necessary: Did you suspect that you were diabetic at that time? If so, why?
3. What did you know about diabetes at that time?
   Probe: Does your family have a history of diabetes?
4. What was it like to find out you had diabetes?
   Prompt: What reaction did you have when you were diagnosed?
   Probe: How and when did you tell your family and friends about it?
   Probe: How did they react?
5. Did your physician have any recommendations for you to address the diabetes?
   Prompt if necessary: Did s/he recommend that you change your diet, physical activity, anything else?
   Prompt if necessary: Did s/he recommend that you monitor your glucose levels? Explain.
   Probe if necessary: How closely did you follow what s/he recommended?
   Prompt if necessary: Do you follow them to the same degree today as you did when you were first diagnosed? Explain.
6. What is it like to live with diabetes on a day-to-day basis?
   Probe: How often do you think about diabetes in an average day?
7. Has having diabetes caused you to make any changes in your life?
   Prompt if necessary: Besides diet and exercise, in what other ways has diabetes changed your life?
   Probe if necessary: How have your family or friends given you support since your diagnosis?
8. Has the way you think about diabetes changed since you were diagnosed?
   Probe: In what ways?
9. When and why did you decide to join this diabetes support group?
   Probe: What advice would you give to a new member of the support group?
10. Is there anything else you'd like to add?
    Probe: Is there anything I may have forgotten to ask about that you see as important to understanding your experience?
    Prompt: What advice would you give to someone just diagnosed with diabetes?

(Karas and Karner 2005)

EMOTIONS IN THE INTERVIEW

Rapport is one emotion that interviewers seek to engender in respondents; yet other emotions may emerge from the interview interaction or topic. During the interview process questions may invoke an emotional response from the respondent, while some answers may precipitate an emotional response from the interviewer. Every interviewer should be prepared for emotional reactions—even if you don't think you are asking emotionally stressful questions. A graduate student of Warren's was interviewing a biracial man about the experience of being biracial when it became clear that the topic itself caused him distress about his ambiguous identity and place in the world. Since almost any topic can be emotionally charged for someone, you will need to be sensitive to this possibility. We can never be fully sure that our questions or responses will not evoke some unintended discomfort for the interviewee (Sinding and Aronson 2003)—or for ourselves.

If the respondent is overcome by emotion or starts to cry, you need to set down your pencil and give him or her some time. You might offer to postpone the rest of the interview for another time: "I can see that this is difficult for you; would you like to take a moment? Or we could finish the rest of the interview another time." Usually, if given a moment, respondents will want to continue—but you need to acknowledge their pain and give them the choice. It is best not to marshal them through the interview if it becomes obvious that they are upset. There may be circumstances under which you should terminate the interview in the face of respondent upset; this occurred with the biracial student interviewed by Warren's student.

The end of the interview occurs at some point after the last question or probe by the interviewer, perhaps question 10 in Box 6.1 (Chapter 6): "Is there anything else you would like to add?" From such questions the interview tends to wind down, with shorter answers and longer pauses leading to comments from either the respondent or the interviewer such as, "Well, that is probably about it for now." Sometimes respondents are eager, and sometimes reluctant, to end the interview; in fact, it is not necessarily easy to determine when an interview is over and ordinary leave-taking rituals begin. In practice, interviewers often see the end of the interview as the turning off of the recording device, a point at which another phase sometimes begins: interaction after the interview.

AFTER THE INTERVIEW

From the interviewer's point of view, once all questions are asked and the recorder is turned off, the event is complete and it is time for leave-taking rituals. Some interviewers, however, do recommend a period of what Kvale calls "debriefing" after the interview:

> At the end of the interview there may be some tension or anxiety, because the subject has been open about often personal and emotional experiences and may be wondering about the interview's purpose and how it will be used. There may perhaps also be feelings of emptiness; the subject has given much information about his or her life and may not have received anything in return. (Kvale 1996, 128)

From the point of view of the respondents, the end of the interview may be a welcome relief, something to prolong if possible, or anything in between. Respondents vary from extremely busy people who have squeezed in a half hour to respond hurriedly to questions, to elderly or isolated people who are lonely, desire company, and do not want the interviewer to leave (of course these responses may also be situational, with the same people busy at some times and not at others). In research Warren did with some colleagues and graduate students on the period after the interview, we found that respondents' behavior varied depending on their life circumstances, once the recorder was turned off (Warren et al. 2003). Some, at that point, seemed willing to say things they had not said while being recorded; for example, when Harkness (2003) videotaped pawnbrokers they expressed sympathy for their customers. Once the videotape was turned off, they expressed stigmatizing views of those same customers. Comments such as these, though not recorded, should be detailed in your fieldnote descriptions.

Other respondents sought to continue the conversation with the interviewer once the recording device was turned off rather than proceeding to leave-taking rituals. If you are receiving pertinent information and want to continue, you should ask if it is okay to turn the recorder back on. In other cases, respondents just want to engage the interviewer in more balanced conversation. This was true in many of Karner and Bobbit-Zeher's (2006) interviews with the caregivers of recently deceased elders, who wanted to talk about their experiences more, get advice and referrals, or ask about the experiences of others in the same situation.

Leave-taking can be even more difficult after longitudinal studies or multiple interviews. At the end of her study of high-school students, in which she spent substantial time with each student and at each school, Russell (2005, 196) held a "farewell and thank you" gathering during her last day at each school. This was partly to ease her own guilt at leaving the research relationships that had become an intense part of her daily life, as well as to mark the end of the time for the students and the teachers. The point of the leave-taking process is for you, as an interviewer, to be sensitive to the cues given by the respondent as you are engaging in concluding the interaction, and perhaps be willing to give a little more of your time if debriefing seems needed. Eventually, however, the interview *does* have to come to an end.

After you and the respondent have parted company, you should spend some time writing up notes about the context and conduct of the interview, either where you are (in a cafe, say), or as soon as possible after you return to your home or to campus. You should write down everything you can remember about the context of the interview: where it took place; how the respondent was dressed, looked, and behaved before, during, and after the interview; any body language that would not be captured in an audio recording; and your interpretation [set off in brackets like these] of the respondent's appearance, demeanor, and body language. If you interviewed the respondent in his or her office, home, or other space (and it may be safe to interview respondents at home under some circumstances, say, if the respondent is a relative or friend), describe these places in some detail. As we saw in the ROTC building example (Chapter 5), physical context can say a lot about the social life that transpires within.

Transcribing the Interview

The issue of transcription—how to get the recorded interview into the form of a written text—has been the subject of discussion since the Chicago School researchers used the method on a large scale. In the days before audiotape recording of interviews, the interviewer was advised to jot down notes during the interview to use as memory prompts later, and to write out the interview from memory as soon as possible, before it has "gone cold" (Palmer 1928, 177). This is essentially the same advice that is delivered today with regard to fieldnotes (see Chapter 5). Interviewers were advised to try to make their written transcriptions reflective, so far as memory permitted, of the respondent's own words:

> If the interview is reported in the first person, in the actual phrases and language used by the informant it will furnish better data....When the research worker makes the report in his own terms, when he translates the expressions of the informant into his own language or summarizes them in trite generalizations or common concepts, he...has so transformed the original narrative that it has lost its exactness. (Palmer 1928, 176)

The use of audiotape equipment in interview research began during the 1950s and 1960s; indeed, the interviewers received machines halfway through the Bay Area project (Warren 1987). Today, recording is seen as a necessity for the transcription of interviews, whether the research is by teams or individuals. In large-scale funded studies, transcription may be done for you; your audio- or videotape is whisked away from you to a transcriber who then returns a textual copy to you and/or to your supervisor, ready for coding. But most students, both undergraduate and graduate, will need to transcribe their interviews themselves. And this is a good thing to do: if you did the interview, you are able to visualize the physical setting, remember what the respondent said if parts of the recording are unclear, and above all, relearn by relistening to what the respondent said. In the process of transcribing you will need to

> listen carefully and think deeply about the recorded voices and the inter-view context, using sensory and other memory. Transcribing provides an opportunity to critique one's own interviewing performance. (Park and Zeanah 2005)

Some academic departments have tape players with foot-pedal devices (misleadingly called transcription machines) that can be used in conjunction with a computer to help you with transcription by not requiring you to move your hands from keyboard to audio device. But even with this help, transcribing traditional taped interviews is an extremely time-consuming and labor-intensive task—which is why it is often done so unsatisfactorily by hired hands (who also do not have access to memories of the interview). It may take four to six hours to transcribe a one-hour interview, or even more. Digital technologies promise to alleviate some of the time-consuming and tedious task of transcription, and we will discuss those options in more detail below.

It is important to transcribe everything that is said during the interviews, including your own questions and probes, because these shape the respondent's answers. It is also important to transcribe everything the respondent says, including things that do not seem important or relevant to the topic, because what seems irrelevant at one stage of interviewing might seem much more relevant at a later time during the analysis phase. And it is also important to preserve the narratives—the voices—of your respondents in as much detail as possible.

Although these are the general principles of transcribing, it is well known that even the most diligent and motivated of transcribers will leave things out. For example, if you are interviewing an adolescent about his standing in his peer group, he may digress to a lengthy description of an episode of *American Idol* that probably has some connection in his mind to the fact that you have just asked him about what his peer group is wearing this semester, but has no relevance in yours. The best thing to do is to transcribe the entire episode—you may, on rereading, see the connections that the adolescent was making—but at least put in parentheses what was going on (["here Respondent M3 talked for 15 minutes about an episode of *American Idol*"]) rather than just simply skipping over the strip of talk ([....]).

Transcription Technology

There is some hope among researchers that the tedious typing process of transcription may someday be a thing of the past. The innovation of digital recorders that, with expanded memory cards, can now record hours of dialogue, coupled with advancing technology in speech-to-text (voice recognition) software, may lead to a decline in hours spent at the keyboard. Karner has had one student who has experimented quite successfully with this approach.

Halbert (2003) used a digital recorder to conduct impromptu interviews with people attending informal music events. He spoke with a number of different individuals, with a variety of speech particularities, was able to input the digital recording (through a USB port) to his computer and ran it through a speech-to-text program. This program then generated a lengthy textual document, which Halbert read through and edited for accuracy while listening to the recording. Halbert estimates that the software is about 85 percent accurate, misinterpreting punctuation, capitalization, slang, speech idiosyncrasies, and homonyms most commonly used. While proofreading, he edited the materials to denote speaker (interviewer or respondent), enter punctuation, and assure accuracy. Halbert claims that it took an average of less than two hours to fully transcribe and format a one-hour interview, including the time it took to download the audio into the computer.

However, when Karner decided to test the same voice recognition software that Halbert recommended, she was not as successful in speeding up the process of translating voice to text. The first thing she discovered was that the software needed to be "trained" to recognize her voice. This meant that Karner had to read numerous software-selected texts into the USB microphone plugged into her computer so the program would learn the peculiarities of her voice.

The second issue for Karner was that the software was useless with non-native English speakers. At the time, Karner was interviewing English-speaking but accented Burmese refugees in Thailand, and the software could not recognize their speech. Subsequently, Karner and her colleague Rita Litwiller relied on a "channeling" procedure suggested by Halbert. They listened to the recorded interview through headsets and repeated (or channeled) the respondents' comments into the microphone for voice recognition. Then each proofread and edited the other's transcript. Neither found this approach particularly enjoyable, but it did cut the transcription time down by approximately 40 percent.

In a study of the use of voice recognition software, Park and Zeanah (2005) came to a similar conclusion that the "listen and repeat" method of transcription was the most productive way to use the software. They also noted the need for a good-quality digital microphone and a quiet room, both of which are essential for streamlining the transcription process and reducing the operator frustration!

Karner's 2003 version of voice recognition software required the speaker to add punctuation and line return commands verbally. In the promotional literature for the current version of this same software it says that the punctuation is now inserted automatically and that the voice training is no longer needed; the voice recognition will now work "straight out of the box." Even though using voice recognition software has not been easy or straightforward, we are hopeful that in the future it will successfully revolutionize the transcription processes.

TRANSCRIPTION ACCURACY

Whether you use digital technology, a foot-pedal transcription machine, or just listening, the accuracy of the final transcript is essential. Although the transcription of interviews has been undertaken by generations of researchers and is a vital step in qualitative studies using interviews, "it does not yet appear to be standard practice for qualitative researchers to consider transcription quality prior to their undertaking the analysis of textual data" (Poland 2002, 630). Although transcription is supposed to generate a verbatim record of what has been said (transcriptions often cannot communicate how it has been said), even the most careful researchers generating their own transcriptions have identified lapses in their capturing of "the original language and flow of the discussion" (Poland 2002, 632). Poland points out that seemingly minor details, such as the placement of a period or comma, can change the meaning of utterances. He comments,

> "I hate it, you know. I do" carries a different meaning from "I hate it. You know I do." Although the original meaning and intent *may* be clear from the intonation and pacing of speech in the audiotape, it may be much less so in the transcript. (2002, 632; italics added)

Other problems in verbatim transcription include turning run-on talk into sentences, identifying occurrences of respondents' quoting other people, and the mistaking of words for other similar words. Poland (2002, 632) gives examples from his own transcriptions in which the word "consultation" was substituted for "confrontation," and "an evaluation model" was translated as "and violation of the model." Transcribers typically check for errors and omissions in their work by going backward and forward on the tape; this process can itself generate omissions by not going backward or forward far enough and thus missing parts. Poland's example reads:

> In one case "I lost a very close friend to cancer" should have read "I lost a very close friend to lung cancer." The omission of the word

"lung" was significant given the focus of the study on smoking cessation. (2002, 632)

Transcription by hired hands can generate even more problems in the text than transcription by researchers concerned with accuracy, either because of carelessness or the opposite. Poland describes a case in which a transcriber "(a legal secretary) took it upon herself to tidy up the discussion so it would *read* better, just as she would have been expected to do with dictated correspondence at work" (2002, 633; italics in the original). As Poland (2002) notes, verbal interactions are quite different than written statements, and can look quite messy when they appear on the printed page.

There is some debate in the literature over the ethics of tidying up respondents' speech in transcription. Some researchers worry that lower-class or minority respondents may be made to sound inarticulate or linguistically incompetent if their words, pauses, grammar, and so on are transcribed verbatim. If protection of human subjects requirements have been adhered to, the respondents would not be stigmatized as individuals for their language, but as members of a particular class or ethnic group. Other researchers worry that if vernacular, grammatical errors, and other features of speech are "tidied up" in the transcription, then some of the original meaning of the talk will be lost. Poland suggests a compromise: not changing talk to protect respondents at the point of the transcription but doing so at the point of publication, taking "care that what is removed does not appreciably alter the meaning of what was said" (2002, 634).

After the first interview and the first transcription, review what has gone on in order to make any necessary changes for your next interview and transcription. Was the cafe you met in too noisy? Change the locale. Did it take six hours to transcribe a half-hour interview? Try to find one of those foot-pedal machines or look into the availability of digital technology at your school. Continue this review process with each subsequent interview. If two respondents raise their eyebrows and pause at question number 3, look at this question again to see what might be puzzling or confusing about it, and perhaps try asking it another way. At the end of this process you will have a body of interviews, transcribed and ready for analysis, that represent an accumulation of knowledge not just about the topic, but about the process, too. You are ready to analyze your data—but what kind of data does the interview generate?

Interview Data: Epistemological Considerations

In the literature on the epistemology of the interview from the 1970s to the 2000s, there has been an ongoing debate over the kind of knowledge generated by interviews: can interview data be used for interpreting social life that occurs outside of it? There is a continuum of perspectives on what kind of knowledge can be legitimately generated from qualitative interviews, beginning with the "snapshot" theory of knowledge espoused by positivists (see Chapter 1). This view is in some ways echoed in our discussion of rapport, since rapport has been framed as necessary to the elicitation not only of answers, but also of truthful answers from respondents.

Whenever methodological discussions turn to the idea of truth (truth about behavior, true opinions, etc.), the snapshot theory of knowledge is in operation. The other end of the continuum is the radical opposite of this snapshot theory of knowledge generating truth. This radical opposite is the belief that since the interview is a form of social interaction, it can generate knowledge only about the interview, not about anything beyond it, and certainly not any objective, empirical truth. A radical interpretation of Arendell's (1997) interviews about divorce with divorced men would, for example, see these interviews as saying nothing about the men's divorces, but everything about the interaction between Arendell and the men. Obviously most qualitative interviewers do not share this extreme view; otherwise they would not be doing interviews in the first place.

In the middle of this continuum—where we and many other qualitative researchers feel most comfortable—is the position that interviews can tell us about the social interactions of the interview, but they can also provide accounts of circumstances outside of it. In Holstein and Gubrium's terms, the interviewee is not merely a "vessel of answers" from which truth can be ladled by the interviewer. They note:

> Meaning is not merely elicited by apt questioning nor simply transported through respondent replies; it is actively and communicatively assembled in the interview encounter. Respondents are not so much repositories of knowledge—treasuries of information awaiting excavation—as they are constructors of knowledge in collaboration with interviewers. (Holstein and Gubrium 1995, 4)

This notion of collaboratively constructed knowledge positions the interview as a social interaction, a speech event, and also (still) about a particular topic of interest to the interviewer (and ideally to the respondent as well).

As we mentioned in Chapter 1, although ethnographies and interviews are both qualitative research methods that seek to understand the meanings of social life to respondents, they have epistemological differences. Ethnographic research is based in observation of interaction in what has been called the ethnographic present. Interview research can be focused on the present, past, or future of the respondent, but it cannot be focused on behavior (see Box 7.4). The data gathered by interview methods are accounts of behavior, biography, TV watching, or whatever the interviewer is interested in;

they are not reflections of behavior. Although some behaviors—notably sexual behaviors (O'Connell Davidson and Layder 1994)—have been the topic of interviews, this is only because observation of such behaviors is private and virtually precluded, not because of a belief that accounts of conduct are preferable to observation of it. For example, see a discussion of the confusion of terms, accounts, and behaviors (Warren 2002) with one of the interviews of one woman in the Bay Area study that we include in Box 7.4.

Proceed with caution when claiming or encountering the claim that accounts of behavior reflect actual behavior, especially behavior involving cultural taboos, stigma, lawbreaking, or moral outrage. Such behavior may be "forgotten" or may be lied about to the interviewer. Although the Kinsey researchers were very concerned to ferret out negative lies—denying sex behaviors—they were unconcerned about the possibility of positive lies—claiming sex behaviors that they had not engaged in (O'Connell Davidson and Layder 1994). Both negative and positive lies about behavior are more than possible in interview research.

The epistemology of the interview is important to the interviewer because one's position on this continuum of interaction determines what one feels justified in doing with the data. A survey researcher who defines respondents as

---

Box 7.4
ACCOUNTS OF BEHAVIOR IN INTERVIEWS

As this example demonstrates, if Messinger and Warren had taken the interviewee's account at face value, they would have misinterpreted both the meaning of the term "homosexual" for her as well as what kinds of behaviors were being referenced. Warren (2002, 98) writes,

> In the Bay Area Study, sociologist and interviewer Sheldon Messinger talked approximately twenty-five times between November 1957 and July 1958 with "Kate White" (Messinger and Warren 1984). Among the "delusions" that precipitated Kate White's diagnosis and hospitalization was the idea that she was "homosexual," and her husband was homosexual too.
>
> In the commonsense meanings of the 1950s (and 2000s for that matter), homosexuality referenced same-gender erotic preferences, attraction, or behavior. But, taking the interviews with Kate White as her story, it became clear that what she was talking about was not desire or eroticism but social role: she wanted to work outside the home, and men did that, so perhaps she was homosexual. During her hospitalization, her husband had enjoyed keeping house and taking care of the children, a woman's place, so perhaps he was also homosexual. For Kate White, homosexuality referenced gender roles not sexual desire (in fact she was having an affair with a man at the time).

vessels of answers need not pay attention to the social circumstances under which these answers were ladled out, as long as they *were* ladled. In practice, of course, survey researchers are not so naive about the process of interviewing (see Dick 2006). A researcher who holds the radically opposite point of view, that the interview as a social interaction cannot reflect any realities outside the interview, will either not do interviews or analyze them only as interviews.

The middle-ground position is that interviews generate a kind of grounded knowledge that can be used as data about social life, but with two caveats. First, the knowledge gained from the interview is the outcome of a situated encounter between embodied interviewer and respondent rather than a ladling of answers out of a respondent by an interviewer. Second, the knowledge gained is in the form of accounts of social life, not of observed behaviors or truths. These accounts, or stories, are the ways in which individuals explain themselves (Hertz 2006), which may be quite different from what they do or how they act. If you want to find out what people do, it is necessary to observe. If you want to find out what people *say* about what they do, what they *say* they believe or value, what they *say* their opinions are, then the interview method is ideal.

Interview data can also provide insights into the broader social and cultural contexts within which individuals develop their stories. Interview accounts can reflect broader values about what it means to be a man (Karner 1995) or female gender aesthetics (Bordo 2003). Individuals construct their narratives, but they do so within a specific time and place, and their stories draw on the resources available to them (Watson 2006). Those of us who take the middle ground are willing to use interview transcripts as accounts of the other, subject to these caveats, and analyze them as such.

Face-to-face and internet interviews are one way in which data can be elicited from individuals, while ethnographies seek an understanding of social settings. Many studies use both interviews and field research to capture the experience of individuals within settings. However, in addition to interviews and settings, there is a whole world of data that may not involve face-to-face or present-time involvement. In the next chapter, we explore that world: historical, visual, and internet data that can be used to illuminate cultural and social worlds that otherwise might be closed to us.

Suggestions for Further Reading

Denzin, Norman K., and Yvonna S. Lincoln, eds. 2005. *The Sage Handbook of Qualitative Research.* Thousand Oaks, CA: Sage.

Gubrium, Jaber, and James Holstein. 2003. *Inside Interviewing: New Lens, New Concerns.* Thousand Oaks, CA: Sage Publications.

Holstein, James A., and Jaber F. Gubrium. 2003. *Postmodern Interviewing.* Thousand Oaks, CA: Sage Publications.

Rubin, Irene, and Herbert Rubin. 2004. *Qualitative Interviewing: The Art of Hearing Data.* Thousand Oaks, CA: Sage Publications.

Chapter 8

The Textual and the Visual as Qualitative Data

Documents, Images, and the Internet

As we have seen in previous chapters, qualitative researchers seek data not only in face-to-face interaction but also from the media: in the printed word and in visual images, in magazines and newspapers, videos and film, historical documents, and on the internet, including websites, blogs, and photo sharing sites. There are several ways in which researchers study media, including quantitative (and sometimes qualitative) studies of media consumption and its impact on audiences (Becker 2002), ethnographies of how media are constructed, and qualitative analyses of the cultural meanings of media representations. Our focus in this chapter will be on using media as data for studying culture, and on the creation of media—as in still images used for photo-elicitation—to explore meaning and experience.

The qualitative study of media representations may be interdisciplinary (including the humanities as well as the social sciences) and is sometimes referred to as cultural studies or cultural analysis. The term *culture* refers to the material and nonmaterial social artifacts and representations that surround us, from TVs and computers to the structure of language and the proscriptions and prescriptions of social roles. Qualitative researchers who focus on such social artifacts are interested in analyzing them in roughly the same way as other qualitative sociologists analyze observations of social groups or interviews.

Cross-cultural and trans-local comparisons can also be made by using documents, something that can be useful in an increasingly global environment. Local newspapers from the midwestern, eastern, and western states can be compared for the political perspectives they espouse. American magazines can be compared with Japanese magazines for what they say about the place of ethnic features in contemporary fashion—that is, providing you know Japanese. Or they can be analyzed visually (designs, gestures, contexts, poses) if you do not know the language. One of the problems in doing cross-cultural research is addressing the issue of language. But at your stage of research, as a student, you will be able to find mountains of material to use for cultural analysis in the language of your choice.

Documents of many kinds can be used for qualitative research, including public documents published by local and national government bodies. Other documents useful for sociological research are magazines and newspapers, which can be analyzed for both their editorial content and their advertising. Magazines and newspapers can generally be found easily on the shelves (and in the microfilms, for earlier years) of public libraries. Some (such as the *New York Times*) can be found in all or in part on the internet. Although many other kinds of documents can be studied by qualitative researchers, everything from minutes of business meetings to legal statutes, we will begin our discussion in this chapter with magazine advertising.

Magazines and Advertisements as Data Sources

The use of advertisements as data sources has a long history in qualitative research. Erving Goffman, whose observational studies of everyday life and of total institutions have been read and used by generations of researchers, also wrote one of the first cultural analyses in qualitative sociology, *Gender Advertisements* (1979). In this work, instead of studying the presentation of self in everyday life, or interactions between mental hospital staff and patients, Goffman studied the ways in which women were represented in magazine advertisements during the 1970s. This tradition has been continued by many qualitative sociologists and other scholars, including Susan Bordo in her books *Unbearable Weight* (2003) and *The Male Body* (1999).

The study of magazines, both articles and advertising, is interesting and useful for cultural analysis because what is depicted in these sources are often the cultural ideals to which the media and the marketplace would like us all to aspire.

> Advertisements, therefore, are narratives whose primary function is to tell entertaining stories that appeal to what preoccupies consumers and offer some use of, or symbolic context for, the product being advertised. (Grady 2007, 214)

Magazines cater to virtually every category of person and interest, from the large-circulation magazines for women or adolescent girls to small-circulation magazines directed at particular interests, leisure pursuits, sports, or sexual orientations. And countercultural "zines" direct their adherents' attention to the culture by publicizing transgressions of it.

Why are these marketing- and media-linked representations of culture important to qualitative researchers? First, they are an easy-to-access source of data in a research era in which regulations on human subjects can hamper face-to-face forms of qualitative research. Second, they are not just easy to access; they are a rich source of data on idealized cultural representations. They offer examples of the types of body and appearances marketed to, and thus often sought by, teenage girls or boys, or adult women or men. Advertisements also provide a window into changing social attitudes, for example in terms of racial integration (Grady 2007) or how women of different races are portrayed in fashion (Millard and Grant 2006). Although it is not possible to prove the impact of these representations *on* culture, we can study them as representations *of* culture.

STUDYING CULTURE

Qualitative sociologists are increasingly interested in the study of various aspects of culture, including embodiments such as gender and race, and how the media portray the body. Magazines—their editorial content and their advertising—are interesting sources for cultural studies, including changing (and less changing) views of gender and age.

Many studies of magazines and advertising have followed Goffman's lead and analyzed the representation of gender in magazines aimed at adolescent or adult women. In *Unbearable Weight* (2003), Bordo looks at the content of magazine and other print advertising, both in the late twentieth century and in earlier decades. She notes, as have many other feminist scholars, that the feminine ideal body, although somewhat variable over time, is a site of intense social control. This control is sometimes direct, for example, as in enforced sterilization, but it is often indirect, operating through media representations. As Joan Brumberg also shows in her book *The Body Project* (1997), since the 1920s the ideal body for women has been slender. The details vary: representations of the 1920s flapper show an elongated neck, overlarge head, and flat chest; the 1950s girl has breasts that are pointed and rigid, her slim waist encircled by a tight belt, her hips hidden under a flaring skirt. But the requirement for slenderness remains the same.

As Bordo (1999, 2003), Brumberg (1997), and other scholars of the culture of gender have shown, the means proposed for attaining the ideal woman's body include dieting (since the discovery and publication of the measured calorie in the early twentieth century), exercise, pharmaceuticals (diet pills and aids), and, increasingly, plastic surgery. One way to attain the modern ideal figure—slim, muscular, and big breasted—is to have breast enlargement surgery. And the youthfulness as well as the slenderness of the magazine-advertisement ideal has to be maintained, again through diet, exercise, pharmaceuticals, and cosmetic surgery.

Other scholars use advertisements for the study of race or ethnicity in culture. John Grady (2007) analyzed advertisements in *LIFE* magazine from 1936 to 2000 to document the depiction of blacks as an indicator of social segregation and later integration.

> Between 1936 and 2000 blacks are represented in two dramatically distinct ways in this sample. The first—the iconography of segregation—appears in a mature form in 1936, when *LIFE* magazine began publication, and disappears by 1960. The second—the iconography of integration—emerges in 1967 and continues to evolve through the present. (Grady 2007, 225)

The iconography of segregation, Grady notes, is characterized by showing African-Americans as dark-skinned males in service functions. "Whether as porters, waiters or personal servants, they are often characterized broadly and commonly speak in an implausible black dialect" (225). In contrast, the advertisements after 1967 celebrate a world of achievement in the iconography of integration. African-Americans are seen as sharing the rewards of the consumer society, exemplifying earned success, and participating in a broader community of family and friends. These advertisements also "depict a more varied black community: more women and mixed groupings, a wider array of skin tones, and a more diverse representation of age groupings" (228).

In addition to advertisements, magazines offer other images and texts for analysis. Millard and Grant (2006) studied fashion photographs from *Cosmopolitan, Glamour,* and *Vogue* to see if racial stereotypes were still evident. In a content analysis of the images, they found that African-American models were more likely to be shown in submissive poses, but less likely to be in overtly sexual poses than white models were. Though that was an interesting finding in itself, Millard and Grant decided to explore how young adults viewed these fashion photographs. They were surprised to find the respondents' impressions to be "counter stereotypic," that is,

> submissive black models and explicitly sexual white models in photographs used to illustrate fashion articles were judged to be more intelligent and achievement oriented than their counterparts in the opposite pose. (Millard and Grant 2006, 671)

While many magazines are directed at adult women or teenage girls, other publications such as *Men's Health* or *GQ* are aimed at men in both their articles and advertising, which has also been of interest to cultural analysts. During the late 1990s, some scholars turned their attention to advertising and other representations of men's bodies. Women in advertisements often appear in relation to men and the private sector—as domestic functionaries, doing cooking or laundry; as goddesses, preparing the face and body for cosmetic perfection; or as companions. Men in advertisements, by contrast, appear in scenes: at the helm of a boat, in the midst of a corporate deal, busy and successful in the public realm. These are generalizations, of course, and exceptions can readily be found: advertisements that show older people wearing trendy Gap clothes, a woman in a business meeting, or (rarely) a man doing the laundry. But pick up any magazine at, say, your doctor's office and flip through it; we think you will find that the generalizations made by Bordo, Brumberg, Grady, and others reflect the majority of contemporary advertisements in mainstream publications.

Magazines can also be used to study change in the culture over time, as in Grady's (2007) study of racial iconography in *LIFE*. Some magazines, like *Seventeen* (Massoni 2005), have had seven decades within which to compare trends and differences, as well as similarities, in the representations of gender and age: appearance, clothing, sexuality, etiquette, occupational and educational concerns, dating, courtship, and cigarette smoking. In her analysis of the myths of the American family in "The Way We Never Were," Stephanie Coontz (2000) traced images and beliefs about marriage, courtship, and dating in magazine articles and advertisements. She also examined college handbooks, textbooks, etiquette books, and advice columns in newspapers and magazines.

> In the older courtship system, a young man was invited to come "calling" at the girl's home; the initiative lay with the girl and her family. Etiquette books were firm: It was as improper for a male of the early 1900s to suggest that he would like an invitation to call as it was for a girl of the 1950s to hint that she would like to be asked out. (Coontz 2000, 196)

Family, gender, age, race—all of these can be studied in the 1920s as well as in the 1990s. But how do we best find them? The answer is related to which magazines we sample from, and then which issues of the magazine we use for data sources.

Sampling from Documents

If you use documents such as magazines or advertisements for qualitative research, you have to decide how to sample the documents themselves—which years of *LIFE* magazine, and which advertisement within each selected year of *LIFE* magazine? Although random sampling is seldom used in qualitative sociology (because the purpose is not statistical generalization to larger populations), it is important to be thoughtful and systematic in your choice of data sources. If you just grab whatever magazines are available on the table of your physician's office, your selection of advertisements or editorials to study will reflect an unknown variety of audiences to which these magazines are aimed, from young women to Christian readers to car enthusiasts. Your analysis—what you can do with such data—will suffer greatly without an understanding of the purpose and context it was created within. Do some research to determine what ranges of magazines are likely to have advertisements that reflect your interest.

Once you have identified the range of magazines, the next question is what specific magazine or magazines should you study? Match your magazine choice to the topic you are interested in: *Seventeen* if you are interested in young women and change over decades; perhaps *Boy's Life* if you are interested in shifting depictions of youthful masculinity over time. Then, which issues of the magazine? If you are interested in comparing the decades from the 1970s through the 1990s, then you might consider looking at all copies of monthly magazines from 1970 to 1999. If your time frame is longer, you might want to sample fewer issues, say every other month, or four per year. For example, in Grady's (2007) study of advertisements in *LIFE* magazine from 1936 to 2000, he sampled nine time periods of two years each and then analyzed every image containing a black figure for a total sample of 590 images. The point is to balance a fair amount of coverage, systematically selected, with a reasonable workload.

Your final choice is about which advertisements to analyze from the magazine issues you have selected. At this point, use theoretic sampling to identify those advertisements that most exemplify the themes you are looking for. In this type of sampling, the opposite of random sampling, you look for texts or images that epitomize the broad themes you have identified. If, for example, you want to make the point that advertisements in men's magazines generally show the men alone, in some leisure, adventure, or business setting, or with a woman, but rarely in male pairs, find advertisements that exemplify each of these images. But also be sure that, if you do find an unusual advertisement, you include it for contrast. If you want to make quantitative points, you are going to have to count all the advertisements in the issue (e.g., if you want to find out what percentage of household labor advertisements feature women versus men, or what percentage of advertisements featuring males are set in adventure contexts). You are also going to have to tell the reader how you decided, methodologically, to distinguish a household labor advertisement from one that is not, or an adventure context advertisement from one that is not.

To illustrate this point further, think about the claim that sex sells. Since the 1950s at least, when cars were advertised with young women in the picture, both laypersons and scholars have made claims concerning the sexuality of the advertisements (e.g., see Kilbourne 2000). If you want to study the sexuality of advertisements, you are going to have to decide what constitutes sexuality: what, in the images you see in the advertisements, can be regarded as sexy or sexual. If you are doing comparisons over time, you will note that the definition and extent of sexiness as displayed in advertisements changes. One body part that was important in Victorian times, for example, was the arm. The outline of women's legs was covered to the ankle with long skirts, but the arm, although covered by long sleeves, was outlined by clothing, and the outline could be seen! As a consequence, you will see a great deal of attention paid to sleeves and cuffs in fashion magazine advertisements of the 1890s, something you would probably not see for the 1980s. And we no longer think that if we do not cover the legs of pianos and other furniture, men will get so sexually aroused that they might attack the women present or perhaps even the furniture itself.

Historical Documents: Voices from the Past

This discussion brings us to primary historical documents. As with magazines, a great deal of historical material can be culturally analyzed and used for comparisons over time and across space between different societies or nations. Historical documents can most generally be found in college or university libraries, sometimes in special floors or buildings set aside for rare documents or collections of books and documents, or archives. A research librarian at one of the branches of your college or university library is the best source of information on easily available historical documents. Primary historical documents can also be found on the internet.

What makes a document historical? If you are going to do historical research as part of your training in qualitative sociology, your instructor will probably tell you where the dividing line is between what is and is not historical. Warren, for classroom purposes, chose 1970 as her dividing line, so that her students must find documents earlier than that date for their papers. Karner, on the other hand, takes a more project-specific approach to designating what is historical. This sounds somewhat arbitrary, and in some ways it is. From a commonsense perspective, everything prior to this moment is past, and thus in a way historical—and yet we regard the last minute or two, or last week, as the present. We would all agree that the 1400s represent the historical—but how about the 1980s? Again, your instructor will provide guidance in time boundaries.

What makes a historical document primary? Although the matter is not always so clear-cut, in general, a primary document is one generated during the time period of interest. For example, if you want to study seventeenth-century Puritan sermons, your primary documents are copies of the original sermons, not books or articles written about the sermons in later years. Later books about sermons (or anything else historical) are referred to as second-ary sources. Qualitative sociologists who do historical research use primary sources as data, and secondary sources for background information.

The farther back in time you propose for your study, the more difficult it generally is to find primary documents. So, in practice, we both encourage our students to do research with documents from the mid-nineteenth to early twentieth centuries. This is a good period for analysis because there is a wealth of materials from this time period, and yet it is far enough in the past that cultural differences, as well as similarities, can be seen. For example, David Armstrong (1986, 1993, 2002) used medical textbooks, journal articles, and hygienic instructions to explore how notions of appropriate behavior for patients and healers shifted over time, how medical categories came into being, how differences between safe (pure) and dangerous (diseased) were defined, and how hygienic regimes were constituted. Using a constructionist approach, Armstrong (2006) traced the evolution of medical ethics through these historical texts. "The principal task of ethics," Armstrong states, "was to 'police' the boundary around the profession, ensuring the integrity of profes-sional identity" (2006, 877).

In his study, Armstrong charted the development of the medical profes-sion by paying close attention to changes in discussions of ethics. The earli-est modern document of medical ethics is thought to be a 1803 pamphlet by Thomas Percival. Ethics, in this early context, concerned how medical practitioners should treat each other. Yet, by the mid-twentieth century the code of medical ethics had shifted its focus to how doctors should treat patients.

> The shift from an ethics based on the relationship between practitioners to one based on the relationship with their patients is viewed as a major advance brought about by a more enlightened society engaging with the consequences of new [medical] technologies. (2006, 866)

Using historical documents as a source of data means that we tend to hear certain kinds of voices rather than other kinds. The further back we go in the past, the smaller the proportion of people who could write; thus we expect to find documents from those kinds of people who could write— generally upper- rather than lower-class people, educated rather than not, in professions that emphasized writing, and men rather than women. Also, only certain kinds of documents have been preserved through time; others have either been thrown away, become lost, been burned accidentally or purposely, or in other ways been rendered unavailable. Upper-middle-class men as well as women in ancient Rome were literate, because soldiers wrote to their wives and the wives wrote back. But only the soldiers' letters were preserved, because in the culture of the times what was important was the public world of men, the military battles that carved out empires—not the domestic world of the wives who wrote replies.

Historical documents, then, provide for the qualitative sociologist particular representations of culture: not the idealized, market and media representations found in magazines and newspapers, but expert, often medical, religious, or legal perspectives. As an example of this difference from the late nineteenth century, take the issue of corsets for women. If you look in the pages of women's magazines from the era, you will note innumerable advertisements for all kinds of corsets, which nipped the waist in (the purchaser hoped) to the 16 inches proposed as the ideal. These advertisements encouraged the reader to purchase and wear corsets. But if you look in the pages of medical journals during the same time period, you will see something different: many physicians were concerned and discouraged women from wearing corsets. They wrote that corsets damaged the women's internal organs by pushing them downward into other parts of the abdomen. Women's lungs were compressed so that they could not breathe; some of them could not even get up off the sofa. A few physicians, however, were willing to cooperate with the corset wearer by surgically removing ribs—something that is reputed to have been done by popular culture "stars" within the last decades of the twentieth century.

What is striking and interesting about qualitative research based on historical documents is the interplay of continuity and change in our culture. If you look at American women's magazines from the eighteenth century, for example, you will see many of the themes still present in contemporary magazines: the focus on fashion, on body image, and on attracting and keeping men, for example. But the content of these themes will have changed significantly: from long sleeves and intricate embroidery to spaghetti straps; from wasp-waisted with spine thrown forward to thin and muscular; from virginal and retiring to sexually experimental and actively seeking dates.

LOCATING HISTORICAL DOCUMENTS

Locating older historical documents is somewhat different than seeking twentieth-century magazines and newspapers because of the differential preservation of texts, and the actual rarity of some of them. Students usually begin with a topic they want to study historically, for example, nineteenth-century prison reform. Since this particular topic is quite a large one, it could be narrowed down to the United States (some historical studies are Anglo-American, but to go much farther than England the student will have to know other languages). It would even be possible to study prison reform in one state if that state had a good deal of interest in the topic, as did, for example, Pennsylvania and New York.

What kind of documents would you find for such a topic? You would find several types, the most fruitful of which would probably be proceedings of commissions of inquiry or other bodies given the task of investigating prison conditions and suggesting reforms. Such texts are generally found in the government documents sections of university and other libraries. You can also find monographs written by prison reformers through the general catalogs of libraries, for example, those of Franklin Benjamin (*Prison Science Versus Prison Discipline: Reminiscences of Six-and-Thirty Years*, 1900) or Elizabeth Fry (*Observations, on the Visiting Superintendence and Government of Female Prisoners*, 1827). Of additional interest might be Oscar Wilde's writings from prison as well as on prison reform (*De Profundis*, 1907). University and museum libraries often have a wealth of both well-known and little-known, underresearched documents such as Wilde's prison reform materials.

Prison reform is one of innumerable fascinating historical topics; aging is yet another. Warren's research on aging in premodern Western society shows her interest both in the general interpretation of aging by experts of the times, and in the specific issues of gender within aging. For this research, Warren drew from various kinds of texts, including advice and self-help treatises and manuals from ancient Greece and Rome into the Enlightenment (Warren 1998).

Warren found throughout the centuries certain themes common to the philosophical and medical discussion of aging. In contrast to the romantic notion that "in the old days" people revered the elderly, she found that this was not the entire story. Aging, and the elderly, were viewed in Western culture ambivalently at best, and with hostility at worst. Listen to a seventeenth-century description by Sir Francis Bacon of the old:

> dry skinn'd and impudent, hard bowelld, and unmercifull; bleare ey'd, and envious; downlooking, and stooping…trembling limbs, wavering, and unconstant, crooked finger'd, greedy and covetous, knee trembling, and fearefull, wrinkled and crafty. (quoted in Warren 1998, 23)

Aging women were even more liable to this kind of commentary than old men, since the cessation of menstruation during menopause was seen by premodern physicians as a kind of toxicity.

SAMPLING HISTORICAL DOCUMENTS

As in the example of ethnographic research, some topics provide easier access than others in doing historical research. Getting into a mental hospital is more difficult than sitting at a bus stop, and studying thirteenth-century Irish monasteries is likely to be more difficult than studying nineteenth-century American prison reform. In terms of historical time, the closer the period you are interested in is to the present, the more materials will be available.

We often suggest studies of the late nineteenth century to students because in this time period there was a great deal of interest in public hearings, documentation, and the gathering of statistics, both in America and in Europe. There are some topics, for example in the sociology of medicine, for which eighteenth-century documents can be found easily enough to make projects feasible for undergraduates. But it is difficult to study periods much earlier than the mid-eighteenth century without special research and language training, especially for the pre-Enlightenment era in Europe, when the language of choice for published work was often Latin.

Historical documents can be found in rare book collections and other libraries here and there, locatable through card catalogs or browsing. But there are also systematically collected (although not always fully catalogued) archives and collections of books, often left as a group to a library. Spencer Rare Books Library at the University of Kansas, for example, contains archives from the Irish Republican Army, and also from the personal library of a man named Brodie, who left his mostly eighteenth-century collection of eclectic books to a relative, who in turn gave them to the Spencer Collection (http://spencer.lib.ku.edu/sc/irish.shtml). Another assemblage of interest might be the Wilcox Collection (also at the University of Kansas, http://spencer.lib.ku.edu/kc/wilcox.shtml), which has one of the largest compilations of left- and right-wing United States political literature from 1960 to the present. Many such rare and varied collections are accessible to undergraduate researchers. If you are interested in doing qualitative research with historical documents, the best place to start is with the research librarian at your local library.

The most important thing to remember about historical document research is to be flexible; sometimes you can start on one topic with historical research, and as you browse, end up with something else entirely. One of the reasons for this might be the paucity of documents in your local area for a given topic (interlibrary loan may be too slow for a semester's project), while another may be that in some old volumes all kinds of articles and essays are bound together. Following all available leads is the best strategy in historical research.

Images in Qualitative Research

What can qualitative researchers do with photographs, films, or videos? The use of images, both still and moving, has a long history within social research. From the pencil sketches and watercolor drawings of premodern travelers to the photography used by early anthropologists, images have played an important role in conveying culture and experience. Anthropologist Robert Flaherty filmed Eskimos in the 1920s, while Margaret Mead and Gregory Bateson filmed everyday life in Bali in the 1930s (Faulkner 2007). Still photography was used in anthropology in the late nineteenth century, and an article on anthropological photography appeared as early as 1893 (Nugent 2007, 43). The author of that article, Everard Thurn, staked out the terrain of ethnographic photography for anthropologists as against tourists or other casual photographers, a position we have encountered today:

> Thurn, who used photography as part of his field research in Guiana, addressed the Anthropological Institute after returning to London, complaining that poses of native people taken by outsiders were "merely pictures of lifeless bodies" and stating that "the ordinary photographs of uncharacteristically miserable natives...seem comparable to the photographs which one occasionally sees of badly stuffed and distorted birds and animals." (Nugent 2007, 43)

Contemporary visual sociologists (see www.visualsociology.org) and anthropologists (http://www.visualanthropology.net) categorize images in three primary ways: researcher created; subject produced; or preexisting. Drawings, paintings, photographs, film, or video may be made by the research subjects, made by the researcher either about the subjects or to document the subjects, or already exist in a visual archive somewhere, perhaps a research library. Each of these categories of images can be interrogated using Marcus Banks's three sets of questions for analysis (Box 8.1) and/or may be used to facilitate open-ended interviewing called photo-elicitation. There are also images to be found on the internet, which we discuss in a separate section, below.

Box 8.1
THREE SETS OF QUESTIONS FOR SOCIAL RESEARCH WITH PHOTOGRAPHS

One

a. What is the image of?
b. What is its content?

Two

a. Who took it?
b. Who made it?
c. When and why?

Three

a. How do other people come to have it?
b. How do they read it?
c. What do they do with it?

(Adapted from Banks 2001, 7)

RESEARCHER-CREATED IMAGES

In an overview of his experience using visual methods, Steven Gold (2004) claims that taking photographs is useful in various ethnographic tasks.

> When starting a field study, photographs are useful for recording information about people, locations, and events of interest. For example, photographs can document what environments look like, how they provide a context in which groups interact, and who is present at events. The resulting images can be reviewed to assist in recording, coding, and analysis of field notes. (1554)

The taking and sharing of photographs can also be helpful in gaining entrée (see Chapter 3) and building trust and rapport (see Chapter 7). Making "photographs gives a field worker a basis for meeting and interacting" with people in the field and presents opportunities for return visits to share the images (Gold 2004, 1555). For his longitudinal fieldwork in Bolivia, Jerome Crowder

Soviet Jews look at photographs Steven J. Gold made of their community. *Copyright © 2004 by Steven J. Gold. All rights reserved. Used with permission.*

Anthropologist Jerome Crowder documented the lives of the villagers he studied in El Alto, Bolivia. *Copyright © 2000 by Jerome Crowder. All rights reserved. Used with permission.*

(2007) began photographing during his first visit to the El Alto in the early 1990s. Crowder used photography to become a part of the community. He photographed "graduations, weddings, baptisms, funerals, and other special events" ensuring that he would be included in all the important moments in the village (2007, 182). As he gained entrée, and became more accepted, Crowder was then able to visually document the everyday life of this migrant community.

Douglas Harper (1982), a visual sociologist, used his camera to study tramps in the late 1970s and early 1980s. Howard Becker says that Harper's photographs "contain, and express, ideas that are sociological in their origin and use, and thus may not be as transparent to an immediate reading as other photographs" (Becker 1995). For instance, a photograph of a man shaving needs to be seen in context as evidence that refutes the common notion that these men are bums who don't take care of themselves and don't share conventional standards of decorum. As he says, when we see these men with a two-day growth of beard we should realize that that means that they shaved two days ago (Becker 1995).

Visual sociologist Cathy Greenblat used photographs she had taken in Mexico (2003) to gain entrée to a dementia care institution in the United States. Staff members were moved by the respect and dignity of her images

In his work *Good Company* (1982), Douglas Harper portrays the circumstances and experiences of tramp life in images and text. *Copyright © 1982 by Douglas Harper. Excerpted from Good Company. All rights reserved. Used with permission.*

and thus granted her access to their facility. This allowed her to complete the groundbreaking visual study of individuals with Alzheimer's disease in an institutionalized setting. In *Alive with Alzheimer's* (2004), her black-and-white images document the life worlds of Alzheimer's sufferers who are still living and thriving, albeit in a new and different manner. Given the disease process, individuals with Alzheimer's disease are less able to tell their experience in narrative or interviews. Thus, Greenblat's choice to employ photography gives visual expression to an experience that could not otherwise be documented or shared.

Heather hums quietly to Helen. *Copyright © 2004 by Cathy Stein Greenblat. Excerpted from* Alive with Alzheimer's. *All rights reserved. Used with permission.*

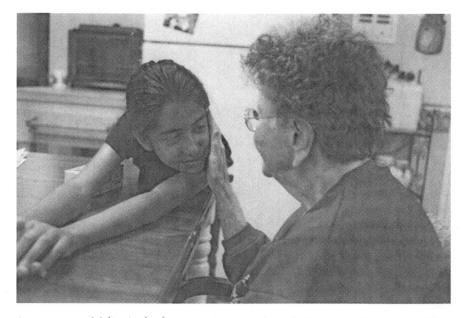

Anna caresses Melissa's cheek. *Copyright © 2004 by Cathy Stein Greenblat. Excerpted from* Alive with Alzheimer's. *All rights reserved. Used with permission.*

In her study of post-colonial "whiteness" in Hong Kong, Caroline Knowles (2006) wanted to examine the relationship between seeing race and photographing race. Knowles sought out Douglas Harper to help her document the "racialization" of everyday life in its "more mundane and unspectacular moments" (517) in the lives of her British key informants, Lyn and John, along with their newly adopted Chinese baby and their Sri Lankan nanny, Nana. Knowles conducted observations and interviews, and worked with Harper to capture

> the (raced/ethnicized) intimacies of lived proximity and a tableau of "doing" which sometimes contradicts the things people say about themselves and their world as migrants in Hong Kong, but are anyway much richer than non-visual accounts. Intimate social relationships are an intangible effectively captured by the lens: a point of access to race/ethnicity as spatially performance forged and animated in bodies and lives. (Knowles, 2006, 519)

Knowles and Harper collaborated to create images that trace the particular and the specific—the situated knowledge within which race as a social

Douglas Harper worked with Caroline Knowles to document the lives of her British key informants, Lyn and John, along with their newly adopted Chinese baby and their Sri Lankan nanny, Nana. *Copyright © 2006 by Douglas Harper. All rights reserved. Used with permission.*

practice is created and acted upon. In Harper's images, we see moments of daily life. Nana feeds the baby in one image, while Lyn holds the baby in another. We see the sharing of the small kitchen as well as care of the baby by these two women, both immigrants making lives in an unfamiliar culture. These photographs, Knowles (2006, 527) argues, document the "qualities of the social relationships composing what we call race" that go beyond mere words or text.

In contrast to Knowles—who looked at race in a culture unfamiliar to her—Jerome Krase (2004) uses his camera to explore "ethnic vernacular landscapes" within his own neighborhood of Brooklyn, New York, and compare them with prior visualizations. He says that

> we can use photographic surveys in comparison with historic photographic archives to see and record how differing constructions of space and spatial practices [impact] the landscape of new immigrants transform the city. We can photograph, film, or video ethnic enclaves to both document and illustrate how particular spaces are changed by their new

Russian Brighton Beach. *Copyright © 2004 by Jerome Krase. All rights reserved. Used with permission.*

Chinese New Year. *Copyright © 2004 by Jerome Krase. All rights reserved. Used with permission.*

occupants.... Visual methods make it easier to examine new construction, as well as alterations of existing spaces. (Krase 2004, 10)

Krase's work provides a compelling record of globalization, migration, and transformation as various ethnic groups move in and out of the urban environments. Some groups are more visible, while others "merely blend into the background" (2004, 21). In some cases, Krase notes, "seeing is the only way of knowing" as he documents the artifacts of transition—shop signs, merchandise, national flags, cultural emblems, and religious effigies.

Using a camera is one way of transcending academic abstractions and categories—such as labeling all people without houses as homeless, or all hairdressers as "service workers." In order to create meaningful and informative images of the occupation of interest, the researcher must think more specifically about the life world of the participants. Visually documenting everyday life relies on an understanding of the situated knowledge associated with the setting and tasks (Harper 1992). Making photographs in the field "can offer a corrective to...academic distancing" (Gold 2004, 1554)— although, as Nugent (2007) points out, photography is complicit in the portrayal of all Amazonians as "forest people."

West Indian stone work. *Copyright © 2004 by Jerome Krase.*
All rights reserved. Used with permission.

SUBJECT-PRODUCED IMAGES

Some visual researchers seek collaboration with the people they study by using subject-produced images. These images enable people to document their life worlds with limited direction by researchers. Prosser (1998, 102) notes that "there has been a move by critical and interpretative visual anthropologists, visual ethnographers, and visual sociologists, to reflexively *engage* with those they study." For example, Worth and Adair (1972) taught filmmaking to their Navajo subjects and asked them to visually depict their culture, traditions, and rituals. Chalfen (1974) used a similar approach with eight groups of children aged five to sixteen from different socioeconomic back-grounds. He asked each group to "make a movie" and then documented the processes by which they created their "socio-documentary." Damico (1985) had schoolchildren take photos as a means of exploring the racial composi-tion of their worlds. Ziller (1990) asked subjects to document "meanings of self" in various contexts (war, peace, country, culture) and life events (release from prison, relationships).

Visual researchers have explored the meanings of workplaces and home spaces. In a series of studies about home, mobile, and office work spaces, Felstead and colleagues (2004) requested that subjects take photographs or

Mother of two sons. Auto-photograph by Viktoria Gotting, 2003. *Copyright ©*
2003 by Viktoria Gotting. All rights reserved. Used with permission.

videos of their working environment for one week to ten days, individually or in teams. These subject-created data were then used in conjunction with researcher-created photographs and video to provide a visual and narrative understanding of contemporary work spaces. Milligan (2003) used photographs of home restoration to understand how homeowners make choices about change and preservation of older structures, while Rae (2003) had urban co-op owners document the changes that they had made to their residences since gaining ownership of the building.

Caroline Wang is a proponent of what she calls "photovoice," which she defines as

> an innovative methodology that puts cameras in the hands of rural women and other constituents who seldom have access to those who make decisions over their lives. As an educational tool, the practice of photovoice has three main goals: (1) to empower rural women to record and reflect their lives, especially health needs, from their own point of view; (2) to increase their collective knowledge about women's health status; and (3) to inform policymakers and the broader society about health and community issues that are of greatest concern to rural women. (Wang, Burris, and Xiang 1996, 1391)

Grounding their approach in a feminist epistemology, Wang and Burris contend that "photovoice allows people to document and discuss their life conditions as they see them" (1994, 171). In *Participatory Video: Images That Transform and Empower,* White (2003) provides an overview of the work of numerous individuals and organizations who use subject-produced visuals in their work as applied social scientists—that is, work that is intended to bring about positive social change.

Richard Chalfen and Michael Rich (2007) undertook two applied visual case studies of medical conditions. In a research method Chalfen and Rich call Video Intervention/Prevention Assessment (VIA) (www.cmch.TV/via), chronically ill children and adolescents are given the opportunity to create video diaries of their illness experience. The children are asked to "teach your clinicians what it means to live with your condition" (55). Developed for use with children suffering from asthma, VIA provides "invaluable ethnographic" information about home conditions and the presence of asthma triggers. An early study found that the routine narrative medical history conducted by clinicians missed approximately 95 percent of patients' exposures to triggers, which led to "major changes in medical history-taking" practice (61).

In using VIA to study obesity, patient-generated videos showed unconscious eating behaviors and poor food choices that contributed to weight problems. Watching the videos facilitated increased awareness in the patients; thus VIA itself served as an intervention. The VIA data provided new information to clinicians, helping them to work with their patients effectively.

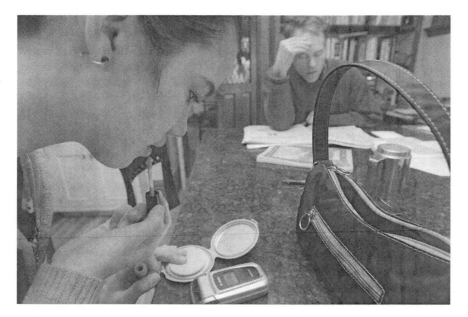

Photographer and researcher Dona Schwartz studied the interaction among teenagers in her series *In the Kitchen* by photographing her children and their friends. *Copyright ©️ 2005 by Dona Schwartz. All rights reserved. Used with permission.*

VIA provides patients with opportunities to construct their own narratives, to describe and comment on "backstage" aspects of their illnesses—what their physicians have not seen and do not know (Rich and Patashnick 2002, 63). Subject-created photographs and videos have the potential both to engage participants and to provide insights that would not otherwise be available to researchers.

ARCHIVED IMAGES

Some research relies on *preexisting images* in archives or personal collections, such as postcards, photoblogs, and family snapshots or movies, to understand various aspects of social life. These images can be "useful for 'backward mapping' but often lack important contextual information such as the relationship between the photographer and the subject, why a photograph survived when others did not, and the photographer's intention in making the image" (Prosser and Schwartz 1998, 122). If you are working with images from an archive or collection, they can be approached much like the historical documents that we have discussed above, and they have the same limitations as other forms of history.

In a study of "interracial intimacies," France Windance Twine (2006) asked white birth mothers of African-descent children to share their family photo albums with her. Twine used the album-viewing experiences collaboratively with the mothers, defining the interviews as "racial tours of an interracial marriage" (491) and the family photographs as "primary data to map the racial networks" of affiliations (490). In considering her conversations with one of the mothers, Twine notes how different "readings" of her life were offered at various times over the ten-year ethnographic study.

> The differences in her analysis of the significance of "race" and "racism" in her life are linked, in part, to the dynamic nature of her relationship with her husband and her in-laws. Photo-elicitation interviews generate data that can complement and challenge field notes, participant observation, and racial consciousness interviews. They provide a rich source of empirical data that can advance theories of how race and racism are negotiated in the context of…class mobility, heterosexual marriage, racial hierarchies and gender inequality in longitudinal studies of interracial intimacy. (508)

Family photographs, as Twine found, provide rich materials for prompting stories and recollections—what Annette Kuhn refers to as memory work. Kuhn's (2007) work with photographs centers on how individuals' memories "intersect or are continuous with shared, collective, public forums of memory" (283). The task of the visual social scientist engaged in memory work, Kuhn states, is not only to analyze the image but to come to understand it—"that is, to try to enter into the memory-world" of the object (284).

Kuhn (2007) advocates a three-step method: the first step is descriptive and interpretive; in the second, the researcher opens the interpretation to a group or workshop for broader interpretive discussion and analysis. In the third step, an "oral-photographic method" is used, whereby individuals unconnected to the image are asked to do a "performative reading"—weave a speculative narrative of what they perceive in the images—of the photograph or album. Through this three-step approach, Kuhn traces the connections between individual stories and memories and broader cultural, national, or social narratives.

Kumin (2007) did a fascinating study of early images of nineteenth-century Brazilian Indians. She found, in an archive in Switzerland, the initial drawings that were made in the field by the first outside explorers of these tribes. Using these field images, she was able to identify how they were reconstructed to match Victorian gender assumptions for public consumption in printed volumes. For example, in one original drawing, a woman was engaged in hunting activities, yet the published image shows the woman in

Bath Houses and Boulevard, Galveston, Texas.

Postcards can reveal what was considered unique about the city and worthy of pro-
motion. This postcard shows off the bath houses and beach resort area of Galveston,
Texas. *Copyright © 2000 by the Special Collections and Archives, University of Houston
Libraries. All rights reserved. Used with permission.*

a more passive pose, carrying supplies behind her male partner, while all the
remaining elements of the image match the initial drawing.

Judith Friedman (2003) studies postcard images to understand what
aspects of local environment and community are deemed important enough
to celebrate in this format. In addition to postcards collected by individuals,
archives such as the collection of historic Texas postcards are available online
through the University of Houston Libraries (http://info.lib.uh.edu/sca/digital/
texpost/histexpc.htm). Other interesting images can be found in museums,
such as the mourning stamp collection at the National Museum of Funeral
History in Houston, Texas. This unique museum also has the group photographs of early funeral directors' conventions (where Karner was surprised
to note the presence of women) as well as the Smithsonian's collection of
mourning photographs. The Library of Congress American Memory Project
is an excellent Web source of historical images of all kinds (http://memory.
loc.gov/ammem/browse). These images provide an interesting insight into the
"backward mapping" of communities and social rituals.

Visual anthropologist Michael Ball (2005) calls attention to another site
of "found" photographs—surveillance cameras in public spaces. Ball looks at

automatically generated photographic and filmic visual documents that are used in the practical work of police in regulating traffic flow. In the police context, such images are treated as evidence of illegal acts; for the qualitative researchers, the police interpretations of these videos are data. In contrast to the older film cameras that could store up to 400 images, "the contemporary state of the art digital speed cameras can store records of some 56,000 speed violations" (513).

Photo-Elicitation

While photographs can be analyzed as reflections of various social scenes, they can also be used as visual prompts during qualitative interviewing or as part of a set of qualitative methods. One term for this strategy is *photo-elicitation*. Initially described by Collier (1967), photo-elicitation is a "very simple varia-tion on the theme of open-ended interviewing" (Harper 1994, 410). The researcher assembles photographs selected on the basis of their potential sig-nificance to interviewees. The photographs are then "shown to individuals or groups with the express aim of exploring participants' values, beliefs, atti-tudes, and meanings, and in order to trigger memories, or to explore group dynamics or systems" (Prosser and Schwartz 1998). Photo-elicitation can be accomplished with subject-produced, researcher-created, or preexisting images. Sometimes photo-elicitation is used in the context of a focus group, where images are presented to elicit memories, narrative accounts, and discussions.

In exploring historic photographs of a 1914 tent city near the mining town of Ludlow that was subsequently attacked by the Colorado militia, Margolis (1988) sought to more fully understand the remaining images by comparing them with other data. Using the photographs as elicitation devices, Margolis wanted to find any living residents who had been in the area at the time of the attack. One particularly poignant image showed a lone tent left standing, with the caption, "Typical miner's family fearlessly facing the guns of the militia" (Margolis 1988, 45). However, when interviewing Emma Zanetell, an eighty-nine-year-old woman who had lived in the tent city, Margolis learned of a different meaning of the image.

> "That's my tent," she exclaimed, "I'm there sick in bed." The story emerged that, a day or two before the picture was made, she had given birth to twins who died. Her husband and relatives had gone to Trinidad to bury the babies, leaving the tent colony undefended. While they were gone, the militia tore down the tents and burned them. Two soldiers came into Emma's tent; one told her to get up so they could set fire to her tent. Too sick to move, she overheard the other soldier threaten to kill his companion if he harmed her. Mercy, not fierce determination, explains why...one tent [was] left standing. (Margolis 1988, 45)

Images can provide a way to remember and retell experiences that interview questions alone might not elicit.

Using visual methods as a complement to other qualitative approaches, Radley and Taylor (2003) employed subject-directed image making as a catalyst for better understanding the patient recovery experience in a hospital ward. They requested that postsurgery patients take twelve pictures of anything on the ward that was (positively or negatively) significant to them, then used the images in two photo-elicitation interviews—one interview as soon as the images were developed and then another a month after the patients had left the hospital. Box 8.2 includes an example of the patients' images and their reasons for selecting that aspect of their recovery for inclusion.

The images themselves are mundane—beds, windows, shower rooms, and bathrooms. Yet the meanings the patients attached to the images, or how they "read" them, to use Banks's term (Box 8.1), yielded "something that was already in the experience of the patients, things about which they might not have spoken beforehand or could not easily speak about in an

---

Box 8.2
IMAGES OF RECOVERY

"Sites, sources, and channels of treatment and care"

Twelve images by a 48-year-old woman patient taken on the eighth day after her surgery:

Image	Reason for Photographing
1. Chair next to bed	I was looking forward to sitting on it
2. Window in ward	I looked out to a lovely view
3. Bathroom & toilet (looking in)	I was left in there struggling after the operation
4. Bathroom & toilet (looking out)	I was left in there struggling after the operation
5. Bed in 4 bedded room	It made me feel good
6. TV room	I had space and was able to cool down
7. View from window in TV room	[no comment]
8. Fish tank in dayroom	It was very calming
9. Shower room	An effort and long awaited
10. Restaurant downstairs	Went with boyfriend
11. Notice board	I could see from my bed & noted slanted writing
12. Name details on bed	My name was spelled wrong at first

(From Radley and Taylor 2003, 92, 84)

interview" (Radley and Taylor 2003, 90). For example, one characterized a picture of a clock as "time stands still" and another referred to a picture of the stairs as "escape route." The patients' photographs offered nonpatients a new perspective on the ordinary objects and spaces on the hospital ward. In the act of photographing and explaining their images, patients "articulated into significance" the unseen experience of the "sites, sources, and channels of treatment and care" (Radley and Taylor 2003, 92). Taking a more general theoretical stance, the hospital researchers proposed that "the anesthetic device of medicine extends beyond the actual drugs used," and in the hospital context "the person dulls his or her senses against the stimuli of the medical setting and the interventions that it supports" (Radley and Taylor 2003, 94). The patients' photographs and narratives bring to light the "onslaught on the whole sensorium" of the hospital experience, which reinforces passivity and compliance (Radley and Taylor 2003, 95).

Sampling Visual Images

How a researcher chooses which images to select or compose for a study is influenced by the research questions and the overall research design of the project. If, for example, you have decided to give your subjects cameras, the images produced constitute your sample. This means that your sampling decisions occur when you select the subjects or settings (which we discuss in Chapters 3 and 6), rather than with the photographs. Likewise, if you are working with preexisting images, for instance in a photographic archive, your sampling frame will follow the topic of interest and what materials are available. You will then develop a systematic approach, balancing the need for coverage with a feasible workload, as we talked about earlier.

For example, Jerome Krase (2002) studies "ethnic theme parks": urban areas that have become recognized as part of the immigrant tourist industry. Over the past three decades, Krase has studied and photographed a wide range of internationally recognized ethnic neighborhoods where one finds ethnic festivals and other spectacles. Often these neighborhoods and events are listed in city guidebooks, reinforcing ethnic stereotypes as well as the "authenticity" of ethnic experiences. Krase has documented Chinatowns as well as other ethnic theme parks around the globe. We include three of his photographs, within which you can see that he has used the symbolic, architectural boundary marker of the entrance gate as one thematic means of image selection.

Researcher-made images require careful thought about what is presented and meant. In choosing to construct the images—whether by taking photographs or making videos—the researcher recognizes

> the added complexity introduced when making images in the course
> of conducting research...[and also feels] compelled to consider issues

Chinatown in Philadelphia. *Copyright © 2002 by Jerome Krase. All rights reserved. Used with permission.*

regarding "empowerment" (of subjects), and "ownership" (of data and findings), especially in regard to photographs. We accept that making pictures can be a threatening act (amply demonstrated by the metaphors photography invokes: we "load", "aim" and "shoot") that yields an artificial product, an artifact of the idiosyncratic relationship among photographers and subjects, the medium, and the cultural expectations it generates. (Prosser and Schwartz 1998, 119)

Visual images communicate powerful messages that can be immediate and direct. How a researcher selects and constructs the images that will

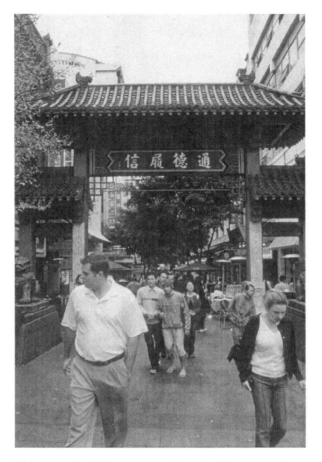

Chinatown in Sydney. *Copyright © 2002 by Jerome Krase.*
All rights reserved. Used with permission.

be included in the study, at each point in the process, allows for possible manipulation or mediation of the social event. Photographs are sites of interpretation and expression, not merely reflections of some external social reality. In employing visual methods, sampling concerns may be relevant throughout the data collection process. Attending to the epistemological foundations of qualitative methods that we have discussed throughout this text is an important aspect of applying visual technologies to social science research.

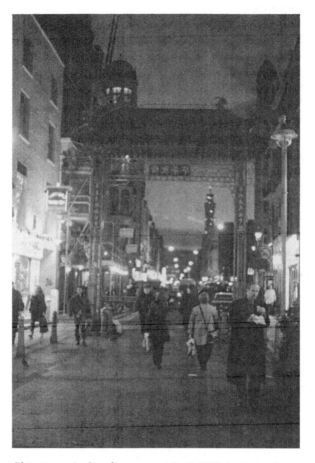

Chinatown in London. *Copyright © 2002 by Jerome Krase.*
All rights reserved. Used with permission.

DISSEMINATING VISUAL RESEARCH

In qualitative work, the written narrative is still how the majority of research is shared with our colleagues and other interested communities. We will talk about writing qualitative research papers in Chapter 10. While there are a growing number of journals that will include photographs (i.e., *Visual Studies* and *Visual Anthropology*), video work or larger photo essays are better suited for other formats. Given today's technological advances, researchers working with visual materials have a number of options for sharing their research.

"Emerging technologies," Douglas Harper notes, "have revolutionized the use of imagery in social science" (Harper 2005, 750).

Lovejoy and Steele (2007), two ethnographers working for Microsoft, created photostories while in the field. At the end of each day of fieldwork, these researchers sorted through their notes, audio recordings, and photographs to develop an overview of the key points of their work using software (Plus! Photostory) to create a narrated slide show with audio quotes from the field. (You might think of these photostories as multimedia "memos" or "analytic notes," which are part of the qualitative analysis process we discuss in Chapter 9.) The researchers then uploaded these photostories to Microsoft's intranet, where other company ethnographers working on similar issues in other parts of the world could view the work and share feedback. Lovejoy and Steele's experience not only points to the engaging format this technology offers, but also to the wonderful possibilities for global collaboration it makes possible.

Visual anthropologist Jay Ruby demonstrates that you do not have to be a corporate ethnographer with access to Microsoft's resources to utilize these advances with his Oak Park, Illinois, project (http://astro.temple.edu/~ruby/opp/). Ruby created his own website as a forum for sharing his thinking about the project, his interviews, photographs, fieldnotes, progress reports, and video segments. He also created a listserv for residents of Oak Park to provide feedback or comment about the study. Though he concluded the study with a final report in 2006, published on the website, Ruby has continued to maintain the website, using it as a tool for the dissemination of his research results.

Other researchers have used technology to create CD-ROM or DVD versions of their work. Perhaps the most well known is *Yanamamo Interactive* (Biella, Chanon, and Seaman 1997), which features an interactive version of the classic ethnographic film by Chagnon and Asch, *The Ax Fight*. *Yanamamo Interactive* contains three versions of the film (unedited, and two edited versions), biographic details on the participants, maps of the villages, timelines, genealogical charts, ethnographic explanations, and numerous still photographs of the fight. All this information is interactively linked, so that the viewer can click on various aspects within the film to view other text or graphic information in pull-down boxes. It is an amazingly rich display of various forms of data (still and moving images, text, maps, charts). Though such a final project is probably beyond the scope of your semester class, *Yanamamo Interactive* provides a compelling model for what technology allows, as well as strong inspiration to think beyond traditional photo essays, videos, or written papers.

The Internet

The internet is a useful source of cultural representations for qualitative analysis. Indeed, with the world wide web, the "researcher's reach is potentially global, data collection is economical, and transcribing is not more difficult than cutting and pasting" (Markham 2005, 799). In spite of the ease and opportunity the internet represents, we are sure you have also been warned many times not to believe everything that is found there, because often it is impossible to find out where something originates. However, if you treat internet material as data for analysis, not as fact or reality, there is a vast network of topics available to you on the world wide web. The ones we consider here are email research, the amplification of the social world on the internet, and the exchange of words and images through blogs and other forums. But first, we consider an ethical problem for social scientists: the amplification of deviance through the internet and internet research.

THE AMPLIFICATION OF DEVIANCE

The internet, above all other data sources, can reveal to qualitative researchers the amplification of the extreme identities and behaviors we often regard as deviant. Online spaces provide unique opportunities for the construction and presentation of identities outside the mainstream, and for the discussion of behaviors abhorred by most, such as child molestation. Here, we focus on "anas" and "thinspo" sites, and on apotemnophilia.

Internet studies of anorexics ("anas") and of a psychiatric diagnosis "apotemnophilia" illustrate the potential of the internet for the amplification of deviance. Anorexia and anorexia nervosa are psychiatric diagnoses of self-starvation and/or excessive laxative use or exercise; most anorexia diagnoses are of young girls and women, although boys, men, and elderly people are also diagnosed as anorexic. Anorexia nervosa refers to the control of desired eating, while anorexia refers to the lack of desire for food. Anorexia is an example of our cultural focus on thin bodies, especially for women, as purveyed by the media and the marketplace—but in this instance of thin bodies seen by family members and physicians as having "gone too far." The internet is used by anorexics and "wannabes" to fight the diagnostic label and imputation of deviance. "Anas," as the young women (mainly) on these websites refer to themselves, counter the medicalized definitions of anorexia, reframing them as "diets" or "choices." Thinspiration or "thinspo" videos— including the extreme "bone thinspos"—are video documentations of being and becoming skeletal (Heffernan 2008).

Elliott (2000), a journalist, explored apotemnophilia on the internet; a psychiatric diagnosis refers to the desire to become an amputee. Elliott writes,

> In 1977 the Johns Hopkins psychologist John Money published the first modern case history…[distinguishing] apotemnophilia from "acrotomophilia"—a sexual attraction to amputees. (2000, 73)

Elliott used the internet (one discussion listserv had 1,400 subscribers) for the accounts of apotemnophiliacs themselves. They described their feelings about their limbs and what they had done with their arms or legs:

> "My left foot was not part of me," says one amputee, who had wished for amputation since the age of eight. "I didn't understand why, but I knew I didn't want my leg." (Elliott 2000, 20)
>
> In October of 1999...a legal investigator...after being refused a hospital amputation, tied off her legs with tourniquets and began to pack them in ice, hoping that gangrene would set in, necessitating an amputation. She passed out and ultimately gave up. Now she says she will probably have to lie under a train, or shoot her legs off with a shotgun. (Elliott 2000, 73)

Elliott also used newspaper accounts as data on a British physician who, most controversially, was willing to amputate the healthy limbs of apotemnophiliacs (2000, 73). Some apotemnophiliacs attempted to cut off their own limbs using crudely constructed instruments or by lying down in front of moving trains.

EMAIL RESEARCH

Email can be used either as sources of data (the qualitative researcher collects material found on the internet) or as forms of communication between researcher and respondents, such as email interviewing, mentioned in Chapter 6. Richard Hessler and his colleagues (2003) used email diaries to study adolescents' views of risky behavior such as sex, drinking, drugs, and fast driving. They collected daily email diary entries from thirty-one adolescents aged fourteen to eighteen for periods ranging from eight to ten weeks. They discuss three issues in the use of email as a research tool—technical difficulties, privacy issues, and the use of email in the collection of qualitative data—and note:

> Security of data or confidentiality was the common theme running through most of the articles....At the heart of the problem is the fact that these communication methods were not designed to have strong security features...transmitting confidential information was not part of the e-mail plan. (113)

Security problems were the main negative aspect of the study, according to these researchers. The use of email data was cheap, rapid, and facilitated communication between different generations. Emailing was "anonymous enough to override the usual adolescent self-consciousness about sharing sensitive thoughts and actions with adults" (Hessler et al. 2003, 122). However, the researchers also warned that many adolescents are lonely and

> e-mail researchers have enormous potential influence over the thinking and behaviors of respondents....The line between data gathering and

the therapeutic interview is always thin and e-mail fieldwork makes it even easier to cross. Methodological work on controlling the power of this technique should proceed. (Hessler et al. 2003, 124)

Joos and Broad (2007) used email interviewing in their study of adult (over eighteen) offspring of lesbian, gay, bisexual, transsexual, and queer (LGBTQ) parents. They located respondents through an organization, Children of Lesbians and Gays Everywhere (COLAGE), that could be found on the internet. Joos gained permission for the research not only from individual—self-selected—participants, but also from the list managers and the COLAGE executive director. By the time of this study, email interviewing had become so commonplace that the article made no mention of any special issues related to email versus face-to-face interviewing.

The adolescents in the Hessler study, and the respondents in Joos and Broad's study, were recruited from organizations, thus they were likely to actually *be* adolescents or offspring of LGBTQ parents. Email and other internet research is most appropriate, in our view, when controls are in place to ensure that someone is as she presents herself. One of the difficulties researchers face in studying online is "that our expectations remain rooted in embodied ways of collecting, analyzing and interpreting information" (Markham 2005, 815). On the internet this expectation is inappropriate. There is no way of validating claimed identities: a "thirteen-year-old girl" in a teenage girls' chat room may indeed be a forty-year-old man. Even photographs on the internet can be misleading, since the forty-year-old man can most certainly obtain photos of a thirteen-year-old girl and claim that he is she.

WEBSITES AND BLOGS

Among the other possible data sites on the internet are websites and blogs— weblogs that encourage communication. You are probably familiar with many websites, and you have encountered quite a few so far in this book. One example of a social scientific analysis of websites is Margaret Godel's (2007) study of internet memorial websites for stillborn children.

Memorial portraiture in the United States, sometimes called *memento mori*, became common after the invention of the daguerreotype in 1839; relatives believed that the daguerreotype captured some of the life essence of the recently deceased (Godel 2007). Families had images created of their loved ones as a way of keeping them present. Unlike later technologies that allowed for multiple prints to be made from a single negative, daguerreotypes were one of a kind, and might be the only likeness of the deceased the family ever had.

Postmortem photographs that were once shared privately within the family are now being made public through memorial websites. This public expression of grief allows the researcher access to previously private practices of mourning. Godel viewed over one hundred memorial websites—most of them created by the mother or at her request—dedicated to stillborns. This site is typical:

> The welcome page of Ruth's site is mid-blue and accompanied by music…The page is bordered with repeated images of a young girl with angel wings…Romantic and idealized, the figures are surrounded by clouds, or, in one case, bathed in light and picking flowers in a beautiful garden. Music expressing loss and longing, and angelic imagery, are recurring features in both the visual and textual material on this site, as well as on other memorial sites to stillborn infants. (Godel 2007, 260)

By making their mourning public, Godel argues, bereaved parents are creating an identity for their stillborn child by presenting images, artifacts, and narratives that construct the baby as a member of the family to the broader community. These memorial websites provide families with a means to "construct or reconstruct their family biography, and continue to include the baby in their lives" (Godel 2007, 266).

In addition to personalized websites, blogs also communicate words and images between a potentially infinite number of people and interest groups on the internet. As Wakeford and Cohen (2003) note:

> People have kept chronological diaries, journals, and logs for eons. Blogs are the next permutation of this. "Blogs" evolved from "Web logs," which were nothing more than personal journals published on the web for all to see. Blogs have grown quite a bit since the early days (the late 1990's) and now may offer several interactive and multimedia features depending on what the author wants to share. (http://photoblogs.org/faq)

Blogs exist for every conceivable interest and way of life, from sex to politics to cooking to intimate diaries of every moment (Gould 2008). There are over 100 million blog sites, including text, audio, video, art, sketch, and photoblogs. Blogs are either personal or corporate, and there are also fake blogs put out by companies to advertise their products. If you want to search the blogosphere for particular types of blog to study there are search engines such as Blogscope and Technorati.

Photoblogs are photographic web logs that are updated regularly and maintain some chronological structure. In photoblogging, individuals use their digital cameras or camera phones to take pictures of the various activities of their day and post them directly to a photoblogging site, such as http://photoblogs.org. Some photobloggers include diary-type text, while some just have captions with their images. On most sites, discussion and feedback from viewers is encouraged, and some have a running dialogue (like an internet discussion board) between author and viewers. This type of visual log offers a representation of individuals' sense of themselves, and provides rich opportunities for social research. Sociologist Danah Boyd has a bibliographic listing of blogging sites on her page (http://www.sims.berkeley.edu/~dmb/blogging.html), which cites a number of resources for blog researchers.

In an interview study of thirty bloggers, Cohen (2005) finds that in their focus on photographing the mundane aspects of daily life they have the "intention to be unintentional":

> Their interest in picturing " the mundane"—the simple everyday moments of their lives, the otherwise unremarkable events—has led every photoblogger I know to carry their camera with them at all times, or to aspire to this. One photoblogger always carries his digital camera in a holster on his belt. Others carry cameras in their rucksacks and handbags. (890)

Julia Davies (2007) used one of the most popular photo-sharing sites, Flickr.com, to explore issues of identity and online display practices. Using her insider status as a "flickrite," Davies offers examples of collaborative acts in the Flickr community that provide rich social data. For example, one of several interest groups on the site, a group called "What's in your bag?" prompted five thousand members to upload photographs depicting the contents of their bags (2007, 553). Flickrites are encouraged to add "tags" or keywords to their images. Tags signal the contents of the photographs and are searchable.

> Using a tag search I found 5000 images of padlocks; 42,500 images of doors; 3,000 of shopping trolleys (in supermarkets; ditches; hedges, etc.) and 300 car parks, to name just a few of the unusually overlooked spaces and mundane artifacts. (Davies 2007, 560)

Websites and blogs offer many unexplored opportunities for qualitative researchers, as do large internet sites such as MySpace and Facebook that combine text with photos, social networking, and links to personal favorites. New text and visual data sources continue to be added to the more traditional ones—magazines, newspapers, advertisements, and historical documents. Some research with text or visuals is quantitative, such as examining patterns of sales and circulation of magazines, but much of it is qualitative, focusing on culture. And increasingly, researchers work with cameras—still and moving—as well as words.

Visual and textual qualitative research is pragmatically easier to set up than is research based on face-to-face context. And yet, with all their richness, these studies lack the interactional texture of interview and ethnographic studies—so we hope that during your stay in qualitative methods, limited or extended as it might be, you try face-to-face as well as textual or visual research. In the next chapter, the analytic approaches common to all three methods of qualitative research are discussed and illustrated.

Suggestions for Further Reading

Armstrong, David. 2002. *A New History of Identity: A Sociology of Medical Knowledge.* Basingstoke, UK: Palgrave.

Banks, Marcus. 2008. *Using Visual Data in Qualitative Research.* London: Sage Publications.

Harper, Douglas. 2001. *Changing Works: Visions of a Lost Agriculture.* Chicago: University of Chicago Press.

White, Shirley. 2003. *Participatory Video: Images That Transform and Empower.* Thousand Oaks, CA: Sage Publications.

PART III

Chapter 9

Analyzing Qualitative Data

Fieldnotes, Transcripts, Documents, and Images

Qualitative analysis requires a large quantity of thickly descriptive data, good organizational skills, and interpretive ability. When you look around you to see notebooks filled with thick descriptions, lengthy interview transcripts, stacks of images, or piles of document copies, you may feel unsure as you face the task of analysis. As Mauthner and Doucet (2003, 414) comment, "Like other students coming to qualitative research for the first time, we were overwhelmed by the amounts of data we generated." Doucet (2008, 75) warns that analysis involves "physical and emotional exhaustion that most qualitative researchers come to know well." So don't be surprised if you feel overwhelmed as you face your pages and pages of data. In addition to being an organizational feat (see Chapter 5), the analysis of qualitative materials is a creative endeavor. In the process of analysis, the researcher attempts "to filter through the myriad of relationships that make up our social worlds and show how they work together in ways that make sense to those who enact them" (Katz 2002, 72).

Unlike quantitative data that condense huge amounts of information into files that can be maintained, analyzed, and summarized numerically, qualitative data generate pages and pages of text, images, or video. If you developed the kind of organizational system we discussed in Chapter 5, you will be ready to begin this next phase of analysis. However, at this point, we want to reiterate that analysis is not something that begins after the data are collected. Rather, analysis begins as you add bracketed analytic notes while typing up your fieldnotes, as you transcribe your interviews, and as you work with your documents and images. This rereading or relooking process should occur throughout the data collection process; preliminary analysis and analytic ideas should be noted at all phases. Some researchers keep ongoing research journals to record their thoughts and ideas as they conduct their study. Others routinely review their data on an ongoing basis between visits to the field or between interview appointments.

Analysis is time consuming, detail oriented, and at times overwhelming. Many novice researchers assume that collecting their data is the most challenging task they will face. However, once the data are collected and organized, it becomes necessary to focus on your interpretive analysis, conceptualizing, and theorizing. In some cases the analysis can take as much time as the data collection, and sometimes much more, depending on the complexity and wealth of data collected. For her historical analysis of electroshock therapy, Warren estimates that she and her coauthor spent over a decade collecting data, analyzing, and writing (Kneeland and Warren 2008). Richard Mitchell (2002) began his study of modern-day survivalists in 1983, analyzed his data, returned to the field, collected more data, reanalyzed, rethought, and rewrote his work for close to two decades before its publication. The fieldwork for Wacquant's 2004 book *Body and Soul: Notebooks of an Apprentice Boxer* was done in the 1980s.

We offer these examples not to scare the beginning researcher but rather to emphasize the need to allow adequate time for analytic "seasoning." The development of a strong and informed analysis requires many elements: an interesting topic or setting (if these are not interesting to the researcher, they are unlikely to be interesting to the reader); thickly descriptive data that have been gathered carefully over a meaningful space of time; a sound organizational strategy so data can be contextualized and retrieved; a deep and abiding familiarity with the data, setting, and topic; and, most important, time to reflectively engage with the data to interpret the story and to construct a faithful, ethical representation. Perhaps due to the exhilarating aspects of fieldwork and interaction with research subjects, some researchers find themselves physically and intellectually exhausted when they reach the point of intensive analysis. John Lofland (1970, 35, 37) considers researchers who fail to follow through with the laborious detail work of analysis as suffering from "analytic interruptus," which produces "conceptually impoverished" work.

The Analysis Process

A useful first step in the process of analysis is to have some idea where you want to end up. You have been conceptualizing and theorizing while collecting data, so you are not arriving at this stage as completely unaware, but rather in the middle of a process that will now become a more focused endeavor. So, what should you hope to accomplish? What should your final analysis look like? By now you have probably read a number of qualitative studies to see how other researchers have approached similar topics or settings, and how they have structured their written summary of their analysis. Or perhaps you have had the opportunity to read qualitative studies in your other classes that have relevance for your research. When you read these articles and books, you can identify some general patterns about how qualitative researchers write up their studies (which we will talk more specifically about in the next chapter). More important, though, you can get a sense of the kinds of research questions that we try to answer through our work. Gubrium and Holstein refer to these as the "leading questions" of qualitative research.

> Typically at the forefront are the *what* questions. The commanding focus of much of qualitative research is on questions such as *what* is happening, *what* are people doing, and *what* does it mean to them? The questions address the content of meaning, as articulated through social interaction and as mediated by culture....
>
> At the same time, a sensitivity to the ways people participate in the construction of their lives and social worlds has led qualitative inquiry toward equally compelling *how* questions. While not ignoring *what* concerns, those pursuing how questions typically emphasize the production of meaning. Research orients to the everyday practices through which the meaningful realities of everyday life are constituted and sustained. The guiding question is *how* are the realities of everyday life accomplished?
>
> ...There are, of course, other questions, most notably those dealing with *why* things are as they are, *why* people act in particular ways, and the like. Such questions, while not uncommon in qualitative research, are typically deferred until the *what* and *how* questions are dealt with. (Gubrium and Holstein 1997, 14–15; emphasis in the original)

Some qualitative researchers seek to go beyond analytic descriptions of what and how in their analysis, using qualitative data to propose causal relationships (why) at either the micro (individual or group behavior) or macro ("social facts") levels. Causal explanations are tricky at best, regardless of the method used to generate them. In some cases qualitative researchers may want to speculate about causation, but generally qualitative analysis is limited to "the empirical purview of the here-and-now or the there-and-then" (Gubrium and Holstein 1997, 195).

These *what* and *how* questions develop into the steps that will take you from wading through your data to writing a thorough representation. The first step is to organize your data for analysis; the second is to choose your technology. We will take up these topics in turn, alternating between general advice and individual preferences. Once you have an idea of the process you will be moving through, you will have a better idea of how to make organizational and technological choices that will best match your talents, skills, and way of approaching qualitative sociology. Given the interpretive nature of qualitative analysis, it is somewhat individualized in terms of the logistics of each phase of the process. Whether you choose to use computers, colored pencils, or some technology in between, to guard against Lofland's (1970) charge of "analytic interruptus," each step in your conceptual development must be carefully and thoroughly addressed.

Analytic Description

We use the phrase *analytic descriptions* to refer to the development of conceptual understandings of *what* (or *how* or *why*) research questions that your data answer. In earlier qualitative research methods texts, analytic descriptions were sometimes called typologies, classifications, or categories.

Analytic descriptions are one endpoint of qualitative analysis involving the identification of recurrent patterns or themes and attempting to construct a cohesive representation of the data. These recurrent themes are then linked to concerns or issues in the research literature—theoretical, conceptual, or applied—as you develop interpretations of what is happening in your setting (or interviews or documents or images) and what their words or images mean to the participants.

The first stage in your analysis is to become intimately familiar with your data; the point of this step is the generation of analytic descriptions from the thickly descriptive texts or images that constitute your data set. Reading, rereading, contemplating, thinking, and rereading is where you begin. As you are reading and rereading your data, you will begin to notice some similarities or themes. You may also notice that you pay attention to different aspects of the data each time you examine them—this may be due to a recent conversation, class lecture, or journal article that has sensitized you to something in a new way, or you may have identified a key issue in one interview or set of field-notes that you now come to see appearing throughout your data. This kind of realization is why rereading is so important. We both have many stories, our own and our students', of how we missed fundamental themes or issues in our initial readings only to see them with seemingly blinding clarity on later readings.

The insights that come to you as you immerse yourself in your data are the initial steps in identifying analytic patterns and themes; the process is often referred to as "open coding." At this point, the researcher is open to whatever is read from the data. It is important to be "open" so that you do not miss something important by precluding it from your attention too early in the process. Many researchers make margin notations with thematic labels and mark the referenced text throughout with underlining or highlighting. Boxes 9.1 and 9.2 demonstrate different strategies for open coding. In Box 9.1, Karner displays her margin "comments" throughout a page of an

---

BOX 9.1

USING OPEN CODING TO DEVELOP ANALYTIC PATTERNS OR THEMES

Mangum, 106, Interview #1b

Interviewer: you don't have anybody to talk to at home?

Mangum, 106.1 (p.23): ah well my wife, she hasn't been to VN, it's just like talking to that wall.

> Comment: Wife as unfamiliar
> Comment: Able to respond denotes good listener

Interviewer: I haven't been to VN.

Mangum, 106.1 (p.23): well I don't know how to explain it but, many men that's been to VN, man, I don't need that stuff.

> Comment: Contradiction between account and behavior of talking
> Comment: Cultural products for those who weren't there

Interviewer: they lived it they don't want to talk about it?

Mangum, 106.1 (p.23): yeah, and that's where you are and at time I got to, you know I was in such and such a unit and I was in such and such a unit, I went to such and such base, I went to such and such .I can deal with that, but when you start to get to close, I'm gone.

> Comment: Surface talk
> Comment: Meaningful talk
> Comment: Resistance to talk

Interviewer: so you...

Mangum, 106.1 (p. 23): I want to talk but really don't want to talk.

> Comment: Desire for meaningful talk
> Comment: Resistance/fear of meaningful talk

Interviewer: when you think back about VN are there certain memories that come to the forefront?

Mangum, 106.1 (p.23): um hum, certain memories and certain days.

> Comment: Crystallizing memory

Interviewer: can you tell me about any of those...

Mangum, 106.1 (p.23): just like I was telling you about that Christmas eve and Christmas day when we beached into an ambush and they was blowing them back in as fast as they was coming off, guys running up side the bank, bloodied, lost their weapon, don't have no weapon, trying to get back on to the boat, but didn't make it, like I said the operation went on and brought 2 back of Charlie company. Lost 36 navy guys.

> Comment: Memory attached to holiday marker
> Comment: Combat as chaos
> Comment: Human cost of chaos

Interviewer: how do feel when you ...

Mangum, 106.1 (p.23): I don't feel responsible. But it just a, the screams and the hollering, and the blood and the flush, and only one I've, I don't know, I guess feel responsible for is, (but my hands were tied) took a B40 rifle through the gun turret, but we was in a fire fight, I'm on a gun, we hemmed down, and see we all wear headsets, radio, I can't get to him, and when we did get a chance to get to him, he'd bled to death, and that just was tough.

> Comment: Human cost of chaos
> Comment: Guilt over what did not happen—couldn't save friend
> Comment: Trapped in chaos
> Comment: Memory in present tense
> Comment: Summary gloss statement

Interviewer: were you close?

Mangum, 106.1 (p.23): yeah, we met up in San Diego, CA and went through training all together, and uh he lacked about two months from going home.

> Comment: Military bond
> Comment: Time measured in closeness of end of tour—return to "world"

interview transcription. For Karner, the first step in her analysis process is noting, in the margins, the ideas and interpretations that she identifies in her rereadings. Box 9.2 shows Warren's initial analysis of an ROTC building on a university campus from the thickly descriptive fieldnotes shown in Chapter 5. Note that these approaches are the same in that they both represent analytic strategies, but they are also different because we are different people. As we noted above, both organizational skills and individual creativity are part of qualitative analysis.

Before narrowing your focus, you need to have some sense of the "big picture" of your data. This is what you accomplish by open coding. When you feel sufficiently familiar with your data and the sociological answers they imply, it is time to begin to make choices about focus. As you begin to make notations or analytic reading notes, you may notice that you are paying attention to some things and not to others (for example, seeing examples of stigma rather than gender relations in your fieldnotes). Certain aspects of your data will seem more important or interesting to you. Or, as often happens with open coding, everything will seem important and you will be at a loss for how to make your data more manageable. Ask yourself: what is the most compelling aspect of this data? Is there something novel about these settings, interviewees, documents, or images? What is most surprising to you? However you make these decisions, it is important to begin to focus. Once you are *very* familiar with your data and have completed a series of open coding sessions, you are ready to make some analytic decisions about the focus of your paper. It is important not to do this too soon; although no hard-and-fast rule mandates when to begin tightening your focus, eventually you do have to do this!

BOX 9.2
ANALYTIC CHARACTERISTICS OF AN ROTC CAMPUS BUILDING

- It is military (the Roman eagle, the uniforms).
- It is historically grounded or contextualized (the Roman eagle, the many years and decades of photographs of soldier-students and others on the wall).
- It is hierarchical (the arrangement of ranks in the photos from the highest to the lowest).
- It is rule-oriented (the many posted lists of rules of conduct, beginning with the outside of the glass entry door).
- It is organized (everything is organized, neat, symmetrically arranged).
- It is masculine (most of the photographs are of men).
- It is associated with sports as well as war; war and sports are connected (the sports trophies in the glass case).

Recall our example of a bus stop for a field site in Chapter 3. If you had chosen such a setting, you could focus on a variety of aspects of the social life of the bus stop (e.g., *what* occurs there—*who* frequents the bus stop, *how* they use the bus stop, *what* kinds of communication strategies people use to engender conversations or avoid them, *how* space is negotiated). These questions cover a myriad of sociologically interesting themes, and thickly descriptive fieldnotes would allow for in-depth analysis of any one of those. Many beginning researchers believe that everything is of equal import and must be included with the same level of emphasis in their papers. Each of these five examples of what may happen at a bus stop would be worthy of a sociological paper. However, *one* paper that tried to do justice (remember the goal of a loyal and comprehensive representation) to all five topics would be inadequate to the task! Even though there may be overlap among the possible themes, it is wise to focus on one main theme as the primary focal point of the analysis and analyze the "overlaps" in the context of the main point. You should be able to outline the subthemes of your main focus in the manner depicted in Box 9.2.

Once you have identified your focus, you are ready to go back through your data, marking and labeling (sometimes called coding) each occurrence of your central theme and its subthemes. Then, you will want to gather each example of a selected theme or subtheme together. Some people do this by cutting copies (not their original!) of their data into strips and sorting them into thematic piles. Others do this electronically, creating separate document files for each theme.

THE LOGISTICS AND TECHNOLOGIES OF ANALYSIS

The analysis process, as we noted above, can be individualized to match your skills and comfort level. Whatever technology you choose, you must begin logistically: by organizing your data in a manner that matches your technology. What you have to analyze at the end of your ethnographic interview or documentary research is texts: fieldnotes, interview transcripts, photographic images, or photocopied or scanned pages from magazines, newspapers, or old medical journals. For your ethnographic and interview research, your fieldnotes or interview transcripts can be found in three places (see Chapter 5): in files of printed, paper copies; on your computer hard drive; and on a backup copy on a DVD or external hard drive. If you are doing documentary research, our advice is that you scan these materials (if possible) into digital files and have them in the same three places.

Whether you want to work with paper or electronic copies, we offer a few pieces of advice. First, *maintain a main master copy,* that you *do not alter,* of everything, either in notebooks or on DVD. This can save lots of heartache when the unexpected happens, so just trust us at this point: you will be glad that you have done this. Second, *organize your data by type, and within type by chronological order.* For example, we separate our interview transcripts from our fieldnotes and then place each set in the order in which it was collected. In other cases, such as transcripts from a series of interviews with the same subject, you might want to separate your transcripts by interview subject and then place them in the order in which they were conducted. Third, complete a thorough *log or codebook* that includes a master list of your subjects, IRB forms, settings, dates of observations or interviews, and any other documents or materials you have collected. File a complete copy of this log with your master copy of your data for safekeeping. (Some scholars even keep full backup DVD copies of their data in their safety deposit box or a fireproof home safe.) Fourth, decide on a means of backing up or *saving your work at each step* of the process. Yes, this may seem compulsive, but if anything problematic happens, such as a hard drive malfunction or the loss of a file, you will be glad you have a backup copy.

Now that you have organized your data, you are ready to contemplate your technology choices. Contemporary analytic technologies range from the use of colored pencils to the use of specialized computer programs, which can "locate all the data the analyst has previously identified" (Weizman 2004, 146)—though, these programs cannot do the analysis for you. Among the software available for qualitative data analysis are Qualrus, Atlas.ti, NVivo, ts/QCA, interClipper, C-I-SAID, Transana, and HyperResearch (Weitzman 2004), Ethnograph (Nee 2004), MAXqda, N6, and QDA Miner (Lewins and Silver 2006, 2007). In Box 9.3, we provide a general overview of qualitative data analysis software. However, our preference—and that of most published qualitative researchers at the present time—is for the use of word processing, combined, in Warren's case, with colored pencils, and in Karner's case, with digital text-editing tools (as illustrated in Box 9.1).

For reasons of both individual and disciplinary preference, then, we limit our discussion of technologies for analysis to those that facilitate the analyst's (re)reading and rearranging of materials rather than those that attempt to automate various steps in the analysis. Moreover, we both believe that students should learn how to do this manually before thinking about adapting technology to their methods. Researchers who begin with the software rather than the hard copies may not have enough experience to remain true to their analysis, and they may find that the program inappropriately drives their efforts. There are a variety of software programs available, yet they are not all suitable for every task. Lewins and Silver caution that

> some software packages may be more suited to certain types of approach, their purpose is not to provide you with a methodological or analytic framework. The tools available may support certain tasks differently and there is some debate as to whether a particular package may "steer" the

Box 9.3

What kinds of software are available to support qualitative analysis?

Qualitative software falls into two main types: code-based theory building software or text retrievers in textbase managers.

Code-based theory building software assists with managing the analysis in the researcher's application of thematic coding to components of data. This software often contains limited search capacities and usually has memoing functions. Data can be retrieved thematically (by codes), which can allow for development of higher order categories. Some programs offer graphic displays of connections among codes through mapping options.

Text retrievers in textbase managers operate much like a database of numbers only they are organized around units of text. They offer functions to index all words contained in the file, thesaurus tools to search for text with similar meanings, provide word frequency tables, and keyword text retrieval strategies. They offer a quantitative approach to textual data that might be more appropriate for content analysis than creating a faithful representation of life worlds.

What does software for qualitative analysis actually do?

- Most software programs act as containers or connectors to the data files included in the study. Some program files (internal databases) contain all the data you import; others (external databases) create linkages to the original data files but do not change them.
- All programs offer a process for code assignment and retrieval capabilities. They differ in the manner in which codes are visible in the data file, the flexibility of what can be shown, and the interactivity of the various components (e.g., data, coding, thematic categories).
- A project management function occurs through the data organization (before and after importing), tracking of the coding and analysis processes, and multi-user functionality that facilitates team cooperation and communication.
- All software programs involve some way of interrogating the data through different ways of searching the content within the data, including higher-level means of seeing co-occurrences or proximity among codes and categories. Search tools allow researchers to see interpretive coding as well as descriptive or organizational aspects of the data.
- Writing tools are a key component and all packages have a way to attach memos, comments, or annotations to the data.
- Output options vary from tabular breakdowns of code frequencies that can be exported to SPSS or Excel, to reports which contain all the occurrences of specific codes or categories.

Proponents of software that can assist with qualitative analysis believe that using these packages can "aid continuity, and increase transparency and methodological rigor (Lewins and Silver 2006, 5).

(Adapted from Lewins, Ann, and Christina Silver. 2007. *Using Software for Qualitative Data Analysis: A Step-by-Step Guide*. London: Sage Publications.)

way you do the analysis. However, as the researcher you should remain in control of the interpretive process and decide which of the available tools within a software can facilitate *your approach* to analysis most effectively. (2006, 3; emphasis in original)

The essential tool for everyone analyzing qualitative materials (fieldnotes, interview transcripts, and other documents) is, like the transcription of those data, a computer with word processing capabilities. Warren's choice is an old program, WordPerfect 6.0; Karner's preference is the latest version of Microsoft Word. Yours can be any of the various programs available. However, it is wise to use what you are used to, since you do not want to spend the time available to you for analysis in trying to learn new software programs. For Warren, the other essential tool is a packet of different-colored pens or pencils, with at least ten colors. The following examples of how to analyze assume that you have typed your fieldnotes or transcripts into your computer, or scanned documents or images into it, in the various kinds of marked files discussed in Chapter 5.

When the time comes in Warren's research to begin analysis, she prints out a hard copy of everything that has been typed or scanned into the computer. Warren then commences the task of reading and rereading these materials, a set of colored pencils by her side. As she identifies a theme, she selects a color to represent it. For example, as Warren read and reread the Bay Area interview transcripts and fieldnotes (all 30,000 pages of them) in her initial (open) coding, she noticed discussions of ECT or electroshock therapy, which she then marked in green in the margins "ECT." Hydrotherapy, much less frequently mentioned, was blue "Hydro," psychopharmaceuticals purple "Pills," and psychoanalysis or other talk therapies red "Talk." Together, these four therapies clustered into a typology of treatments used at Napa, and the women's (and sometimes their husbands') interpretations of them. For ECT, as Warren continued to reread, she made subtheme notations (more focused coding) in other colors:

MAIN THEME: MEANINGS OF ELECTROSHOCK (GREEN)

1. Subthemes:
    1. to the physicians: medical model (Yellow)
    2. to the patients: memory loss (Pink + Green)
    3. to the husbands: marital social control (Orange)

As coding continues, the researcher may identify a third level of subthemes. For example:

2. Meanings of memory loss to the patients (Pink)
    a. desire to forget their problems (Pink + Turquoise)

b. memory loss as identity loss (Pink + Magenta)
c. puzzling over why therapists urge her to remember but give her ECT to forget (Pink + Grey)

Using a word processing program, Warren then extracted and copied all these references to ECT from the main text, leaving the main text intact and pasting the excerpts into a new ECT document file. To do so she decided how much of the text surrounding the ECT excerpt to include in order to preserve the full, contextual meaning of the segment. Thus Warren could assemble the elements of an analytic (*the meanings*) description (*what was done*) of treatments at Napa in the late 1950s and early 1960s as interpreted by these women patients.

Karner uses the margins of her text for beginning to make notations, memos, and initial codes alongside, and within, the data. Instead of colored pencils, however, Karner works in the electronic files using the text editor and highlighting options in her word processing program. The "Reviewing" tool bar in Microsoft Word allows her to add bracketed analytic memo notes in a different color within the text, highlight themes in the data in up to twelve different colors, and add "comments" on the themes she has identified in the margins. Thus, Karner follows a similar conceptual process as Warren, but limits the number of hard copies necessary. This also means that all her "marked" or coded data are stored electronically and can be saved to DVDs for safekeeping.

After identifying the conceptual themes in the data, Karner also cuts and pastes these data excerpts into a new document, again leaving the original data file intact. Microsoft Word XP and higher allows the user to have a seemingly limitless number of documents open at the same time, so Karner is able to scroll through her primary data file and extract and paste into different thematic files at the same time (she has tested having up to thirty open documents at once). Additionally, while copying the data, she makes use of macros to mark from where the data has been extracted. Macros are recorded keystrokes that are grouped together as a single command. The researcher can then use this "command" to execute the repetitive typing tasks. For example, Karner sets up macros to identify each of her main data files. One macro might contain the text "Ramsey, Interview 1, Page_." With this macro at the end of every extracted data excerpt from this file, Karner executes the command and "Ramsey, Interview 1, Page_" appears in the document, and she then inserts the appropriate page number. This way, with each data extraction, Karner can locate the page in the original data file where the text appears in its entirety and in context (without retyping "Ramsey, Interview 1, Page_" over and over to identify each excerpt).

Now that we have discussed the initial analytic development of rich conceptual themes and some of the technologies used to assist in this task, we offer the following examples of what this process of analysis looks like. How does one move from "data collection [which] often produces a wealth of descriptions that have been created at great pain" to a "coherent narrative" (Katz 2002, 64). "A systematic ethnography needs to take into account the intrinsic orderings through which social worlds are produced and reproduced" (Atkinson and Delamont 2005, 831). To illustrate this process, we offer three examples of analyzing data: fieldnotes, interview transcripts, and documents or images. For the fieldnotes and interviews we use Warren's late 1950s and early 1960s *Madwives* (1987) research. Both the fieldnote and interview texts illustrate how, during this time period in America, psychiatric interpretations of mental illness were based not only on medical criteria, but also (as they are today; see, for example, Wirth-Cauchon 2000) on contemporary cultural ideas about the proper place of women and men in society, in the household, and in the workplace. The documentary analysis we discuss below is also related to gender roles, this time in the late nineteenth century, and is based on materials from Kneeland and Warren's (2008) study of the history of electroshock.

Analyzing Field Notes

These fieldnote examples are from a Bay Area researcher's observation of Napa State Hospital discharge conferences, where a panel of physicians and social workers decides whether the patient should remain in the hospital, be discharged, or be given home leave. The comments that indicate marital, as well as medical, elements in the decision-making process have been italicized for illustration.

Mrs. Peggy Sand's First Discharge Conference, 7/30/58

Dr. C: "Why are you here?"
P: "*My husband signed a petition to have me committed.*"
Dr. C: "*Does he think you are crazy?*"
P: "*The hospital asked him before if he thought I was crazy and he said no. Then he said that the people at the hospital told him I was sick enough to be committed.*"
Dr. C: "*Do you get along with him now or do you still fight?*"
P: "*I can get along with him after a fashion...for the time being I'll go home to him. I've been placed in a position where I'm dependent on him for everything I do.*"
Dr. R: "What do you mean, 'go back home'?"
P: "*Oh, be a housewife, cook the meals, take care of the children.*"
Dr. D: "How do you picture your future?"

P: "Very bleak" (She said this in a matter of fact way, but then her voice cracked and she appeared and sounded a little more depressed and almost on the verge of tears). "But I am tired of beating my head on a stone wall."

Dr. D: *"You say everything depends on him—how?"*

P: (she said something to the effect that, in the first place *she was married to him, and now she is in here and he has so much say over things that happen to her....* Later, after Peggy had left the room, after a brief pause Dr. B asked Dr. D what she thought. She answered, "You mean, is she psychotic?—oh, I don't think so." Dr. C immediately chimed in "I don't think she is psychotic either." However Dr. McG said, "I think she is schizophrenic." He added that she probably has a lot of provocation for what has happened to her. He then concluded in a manner as though looking for some kind of out, "I don't think she's normal." [She was refused discharge or leave of absence. Later the researcher talked to her]

P: "If I was an accomplished liar it would help in cases like that." I asked her how that would have helped. She shrugged and then said, "Oh if I'd been able to say that I'm feeling fine, going out with my sister, get a job right away, file for divorce—then they would say she knows what she wants to do."

From this extract we learn that Mr. Sand, like other husbands in the late 1950s, had the power to sign a petition to have her committed. We also learn that the psychiatrist and the husband confer about her mental status, and make joint decisions about hospitalization that may not include her. The psychiatrist's questioning of Mrs. Sand includes not only psychiatric but also marital issues, about how she gets along with her husband. She is well aware of her legal dependence on her husband, and that the only possible escapes are either getting a job or filing for divorce.

Mrs. Peggy Sand's Second Discharge Conference, 9/17/58

I asked her if she were expecting any particular things to be brought up at the conference. "Oh, I imagine there'll be *questions of how I'll be getting along with my husband,* something like that." (How will you answer that?) "That's a good question—*I get along with him all right, as long as I let him have his own way. I expect to go to work in two or three weeks, I think that will help—me anyway.*" (How will that help?) "Well, when you are doing *clerk-typist work* you can't keep your mind on your job and something else at the same time. *Housework gives you too much time to think.*" (What are you afraid that you might think about?) "Oh, *if I start on housework*—I usually think of something someone has done to me a

long time back—and if I keep at it I work myself up into a boiling rage."
At which she laughed. . . .

Dr. H: [first question of the conference] *"Isn't it true that you had an argument with your husband* one day last week when you weren't there to meet him?"
P: "Yes."
Dr. H: "What do you think you have accomplished in the time you've been here?"
P: "I've learned to face things more realistically."
Dr. H: "What do you mean?"
P: *"Well, before, I was bound and determined to get a divorce—there was nothing else. Now, I'll go back to my husband, I'll get a job. Then, if I decide to get a divorce later, I'll be in a better position. I'll go to work to keep me occupied."*
Dr. H: *"How about the children?"*
P: *"I'll be home with them more than I am now—I'd be home every night."*
(Indefinite leave of absence)

In a conversation with one of the Bay Area researchers prior to the second discharge conference we learn that Mrs. Sand has "learned the system"—that she must, in order to be discharged, convince the psychiatrists that she is getting along with her husband and is willing to go home and be a housewife. Dr. H's first question is, indeed, about an argument she had with her husband. She assures the psychiatrist that she has become more "realistic"—a contemporary analyst would say about her gendered place in society—and is given an indefinite leave of absence. However, she was subsequently returned to the hospital by her husband (on the grounds that she had had an affair with another man) and once again had to seek discharge at a conference.

Mrs. Peggy Sand's Third Discharge Conference, 6/17/59

Dr. H agreed to "discharge her, and give a certificate of competence." He then went on, addressing his remarks to the rest of the staff, that there was considerable argument about whether she was psychoneurotic. He then went on, addressing his remarks to the rest of the staff, that there was considerable disagreement as to whether or not Mrs. Sand was psychotic, but it was felt that she could best be classified as schizophrenic reaction, chronic, undifferentiated. Dr. H then commented that this may have been a diagnosis of convenience. I asked her what the discharge will mean to her. . . ."I don't see how it will affect my life one way or another. If you can't lick them, join them." I asked her if she is referring to her marriage and she said, "I suppose so." I asked her what she thought the future of her marriage would be. "I can't say, for the next 12 years at least I expect to stay where I am." I asked why 12 years. "By that time the girls will be pretty well grown—and I'll be older and more set in my ways—too old to change, if I'm not too old already."

By the time of the third discharge conference Mrs. Sand had concluded that "if you can't lick them, join them," referring both to her mental patient and wife statuses in 1950s/early 1960s society. Follow-up research indicated that Peggy Sand was, indeed, still married to Floyd Sand twelve years after these hospitalization events. Dr. H's comment that her schizophrenic diagnosis "may have been a diagnosis of convenience" indicates that at least some of the psychiatrists at Napa may have been aware of the blending of gendered marital and psychiatric troubles, and gendered marital and psychiatric social control, that characterized mental hospitalization in America in the late 1950s and early 1960s.

Analyzing Interview Transcripts

This ethnographic depiction of psychiatric decision making in the late 1950s is echoed by the interview material transcribed for the Bay Area study. Discussions of psychiatric symptomatology and diagnosis are mixed with questions and concerns about gender role—whether the woman patient is getting along with her husband, doing her housework, taking care of her children, getting a job (pink-collar), or thinking about divorce. One patient, Joyce Noon, when asked why she had been readmitted to Napa, said:

> Every time you ask me that you have to ask him [husband] because I don't know what he's doing…[he] doesn't feel secure unless I'm under some authority…as long *as I'm his wife he can do with me as he pleases*.…I cannot fight him…he will not let me work and he put me under these authorities.

These same themes were taken up by Shirley Arlen in one of the interviews done while she was hospitalized.

> "I just don't see how *they could go ahead and stick me under his thumb like that*—for that's what it amounts to." I asked her if this was something she thought they deliberately tried to do. "I don't know—I wouldn't like to say that—at the same time, that's what it all amounts to." I asked her if she feels now that *she is pretty much under her husband's control*. "Yeah." (More so than when you went into the hospital?) "More so—yes." (In just what ways?) "Because whenever he takes a darn good notion—he can take me right back there—or call and have me picked up—although he may not be able to keep me there." (Do you think he would do this?)

"I wouldn't be surprised if he did." (What kind of circumstances might cause him to do that?) "I think the minute I went and filed for divorce, that's exactly what he'll do." (Just what are you going to do with the situation?) She stared ahead reflectively and then answered, "I'll probably just go on like I did before. What else is there to do? *He doesn't want me to go to work."* (Why doesn't he?) *"He says he doesn't want me to have to work—besides which I belong here with the kids."*

Since the Bay Area study combined interview with ethnographic methods, many of the analyses written into the transcripts by the original researchers depended on both methods. In the following analysis by Warren of the original interviewer's notes, "indefinite leave" refers to the unconditional release from the hospital but with the indefinite possibility of the husband re-signing the expatient back into the hospital. After a few failed discharge conferences, the Napa patients were, like Peggy Sand, more prepared for what was to come. Kate White, who had earlier told the interviewer that she had finally "learned what to say," was successful in her attempts to be discharged once she declared that her marital relationship was improved and that hospitalization had helped her:

> Dr. B then asked, "Do you think your hospitalization has helped you any?"
> Mrs. White: *"It sure has."*
> "How do you and your husband get along now?"
> *"Wonderful." "Better." "We sure do."* (indefinite leave, 4/1/59) (Warren 1987, 106; italics added)

Note that both the fieldnotes and the interview transcripts illuminate the intersection of gendered marital and psychiatric social control in the late 1950s, but with different lenses. In the fieldnote extract, the observer recorded decision-making occasions during which the psychiatrists used marital as well as medical frameworks for questioning patients and discussing cases. In the interview transcripts, the respondents' own interpretative accounts of what happened to them during these decision-making events are illustrated. Joyce Noon, Kate White, and the other women were clearly aware that they were "under the thumb" of their husbands, who could take them back to the hospital at any time (as could wives whose husbands had earlier been committed). They knew that they were consigned by culture, hospital, and husband to the social place of women in the 1950s: dependent, responsible for housework and childcare, working in pink-collar jobs only if "allowed" to, and with divorce an unlikely future option (see Warren 1987).

The analysis of interview transcripts should be done keeping in mind that the respondent is not simply a vessel of answers to be poured out by the interviewer (Gubrium and Holstein 1995); rather, the knowledge gained from interview data is knowledge based on questioning and answering, talking and listening, between a sociologist (or more than one) with personal interests and agendas and a respondent (or more than one) with his or her own. Interview-based knowledge involves not only members' understandings of the social world they are being asked about, but also the time and place of the interview and the interaction and talk between the participants. The relative weight of respondents' meaning and social situation varies with the interview topic: the impact of hospitalization on the Bay Area was generally so great that they talked about it incessantly no matter what the situation—until discharge.

After discharge, the social situation of the interview often took on a different character. One of the adaptations made to ex-patienthood by some Bay Area women was trying to leave the past behind and forget the Napa experience. The research design of the study, however, called for repeated interviews not only during, but also after, hospitalization. Those women who sought to distance their discharged "new selves" from the mental patient "old selves" expressed reluctance, in several ways, to be interviewed about their mental hospital experiences after discharge, and some of the husbands were equally reluctant to "dwell on the past." The following original researcher's fieldnote and interview transcript segments demonstrate some of these ways, from the direct to the indirect:

> [in the interviewer's first telephone conversation after discharge] Eve Low said she should forget the past, continuing to see me would serve as a constant reminder of the past, and even if we did not talk about the past I would still remind her of it anyway, just by my presence.

> Rose Price: "I need people to stay out of my troubles for a while—get the house fixed up—do my own plans."
> Mary Yale: "It makes me uncomfortable...you write down everything I say."
> Ann Rand: "Anything is preferable to this...you keep asking a lot of questions. Things I want to forget about."

> June Mark tells me [the interviewer] that she cannot fully participate in the research simply because the research in itself signifies the stigma of deviance that she is struggling to avoid..."I don't like being a guinea pig...you keep asking a lot of questions...things I want to forget about....It's not normal, my talking to you....It's just that I'm reminded I'm a patient. If you're a patient, you're always a patient."

> Kate White's husband [a year after her release]: "I'm getting a little more reluctant to talk about it. I don't know if it's just that I'm more reluctant to talk about things, or that there's nothing to talk about."

> Mr. Oren asked me if I wanted to join them for dinner, and was rather insistent about this despite my repeated declining. He later invited

> me to drop over to his place some afternoon, bring [along] a broad, and just let my hair down and enjoy myself....I was emphasizing the fact that this was my job, probably in the hope of getting him to accept the situation as such and not redefine it.

This last quote, by a male interviewer, illustrates one strategy used by the interviewees to avoid reminders of the past. Warren (1987, 260–261) called this strategy redefining the interview situation as a social one. A second example of social redefinition comes from an interview with Ann Rand:

> She repeated that she would only see the interviewer again if she would have her over to her house. While the interviewer was evasive, Ann said, "Then I suppose you still see me as a patient. To me you are either a friend or some kind of authority, now which is it? The way I see it, you either see me as a friend or a patient."

Another strategy, which Warren called *role reversal* (1987, 261), involved the wife or husband taking control of the interview situation by asking questions, introducing topics, or making psychoanalytic interpretations of the interviewer. The following examples of attempted role reversal (which the interviewers fought, as they did social redefinition) are from interview transcripts:

> Ann Rand [at the beginning of the interview]
> "What have you been doing?" (both laugh). As we sat down Ann said something to me like, "Well, what's been happening?"
> Donna Urey [to interviewer] "You look slimmer and trimmer—you've let your fingernails grow out, haven't you?"
> Jack Oren: "I think that you're a kid that missed happiness somewhere along the line." He then started speculating about my past life and thought that something had happened to me, maybe in high school, to make me feel like that. Mr. Oren first was critical about my interviewing technique, and then started to question me about my life, and so on.

Some of these classifications overlap; Donna Urey's comment about slimness, trimness, and fingernails could be interpreted both as role reversal and as an attempt to make the interview into a social visit.

The post-hospital interview transcripts also indicate that the patients varied in their wish to distance themselves from the interviewer, and thus from their old selves. Some of the women who still felt quite troubled *cast the researcher into the role of therapist or adviser* in the later interviews (Warren 1987, 262). One interviewer recorded that "Irene James anticipated the next interview in one week, then corrected it to two weeks." Shirley Arlen said to the interviewer at their final meeting, "Goodbye, savior" (Warren 1987, 262).

In summary, interview transcripts provide accounts of individuals' interpretations of their social worlds in a particular context: a social and speech event in which questions are asked and answers provided, on topics which may or may not be welcome to the interviewee in the immediate situation. As indicated in Chapter 7, these social and speech events also take place between, and thus may be shaped by, people of a given gender, age, social class, ethnicity, appearance, and so on—all of which may influence what is said in the interview, and thus what appears to be analyzed in the transcript. The interpretive context of documents or images as sources of qualitative data is also significant, but may not be as readily available to the analyzer as the interview context (that is, providing the analyzer and the interviewer are one and the same person!).

Analyzing Documents and Images

In Chapter 8, we provided examples of the use of textual and visual data in qualitative research, including contemporary magazine advertising, the internet, and historical documents. In this section, we use two one-page historical documents, with both texts and images, as an example of how to analyze all these types of texts (see Figures 9.1 and 9.2). We use historical documents rather than contemporary advertisements for our example of textual analysis for two reasons: it is interesting to listen to voices from the past as well as the present, and our publisher does not have to pay money to reproduce materials that are more than a hundred years old.

A Nineteenth Century Electrical Advertisement: Male

Snatched From Death

AND THE GRAVE.

A YOUNG WIFE RESTORED TO HER LOVING HUSBAND AND FRIENDS IN GOOD HEALTH.

Mrs. Hattie H. McGowan.

KEELERSVILLE, Mich., Feb. 1, 1892.

DR. A. OWEN:

Dear Sir I take pleasure in stating that the Owen Electric Belt purchased from you last May has been worth more than all the medicines in the world to me. On the 27th of January, 1890, I was taken with La Grippe and from that to nervous prostration of the stomach and spine, liver complaint, irritation of the lungs and constipation. About this time I went to consult the best doctor in the county for treatment. I stopped at my mother's home on my return, as my prostration was so great that I could not reach my own home which I dearly loved. I was a young married wife of six months and had kept house only four months. My hopes seemed all blasted as I gradually failed under the care and treatment and nursing by my kind and willing husband and mother, one of the best of mothers. I could not get up or be moved, so my husband sold his farm and turned all of his attention to me. Time passed, and I suffered more than tongue can tell. I could eat nothing to speak of, and what I did eat hurt my stomach. At times I seemed better and then I would get worse. I remained in this condition about sixteen months, or up to the time I purchased your Belt. Then I commenced to improve at once, and life has been brighter ever since. My husband has purchased another farm and we commenced to keep house on Thanksgiving Day, and I have done our work with my husband's help ever since. Before I purchased one of your Belts I could hardly stand on my feet. May God bless you, as the Owen Electric Belt was the means of saving my life and giving me health and strength to live and enjoy life with my husband I once more. I cannot say enough for your Belt if I should write half a day. My sudden improvement caused a good deal of excitement, as the doctors and every one around said I would die of consumption. I can eat my three meals every day. If you wish to publish this letter we will answer all correspondents who wish to inquire fully about my case, by sending directed and stamped envelope.

Yours very truly,

MR. EDWIN and HATTIE McGOWAN,

KEELERSVILLE, MIC.

READ THE NEXT LETTER SIX MONTHS LATER.

KEELERSVILLE, Mich., Aug. 21, 1892.

DR. A. OWEN:

Dear Sir—Six months has passed since I wrote my first testimonial letter in praise of your Electric Belt. I cannot say enough for your Belt. I have been improving rapidly since I wrote you the first letter six months ago. Now I am able to do my work, and this week I rode 22 miles to Thunder Knob on the banks of Lake Michigan, camped out over night, and came back the next day over hills and rough roads, 44 miles in all, through the hot sun. I could not have done the same one year ago for the wealth of Michigan. My health has improved so rapidly that others are waking up to the idea that the Owen Electric Belts are the only means by which they can be cured.

I remain as ever your friend,   HATTIE H. McGOWAN.

(TRADE MARK.)

DR. A. OWEN.

Persons making inquiries from the writers of testimonials will please inclose self-addressed, stamped envelope to insure a prompt reply.

OUR ILLUSTRATED CATALOGUE

Contains fullest information, list of diseases, cut of belts and appliances, prices, sworn testimonials and portraits of people who have been cured, etc. Published in English, German, Swedish and Norwegian languages. This valuable catalogue will be sent to any address on receipt of six cents postage.

The Owen Electric Belt and Appliance Co.,

MAIN OFFICE AND ONLY FACTORY:

THE OWEN ELECTRIC BELT BUILDING,

201-211 STATE ST., CHICAGO, ILL.

THE LARGEST ELECTRIC BELT ESTABLISHMENT IN THE WORLD.

MENTION THIS PAPER WHEN WRITING.   (1000-M.)

A Nineteenth Century Electrical Advertisement: Female

The two documents are exactly as Warren found them—two separate loose pages and not very easy to read. Although you, the reader, are less familiar than she with the interpretive context of these documents—after all, Warren does research on nineteenth-century psychiatry and gender—we do not think you will have much difficulty doing a basic analysis of their similarities and differences. We have listed a few in Box 9.4; what else do you find?

What is most interesting sociologically about these advertisements is their gender differences. The Sanden's advertisement is clearly pitched to male readers: "MEN! WHY ARE YOU WEAK?" since it is women who were supposed to be, in the late nineteenth century, the "weaker sex." In addition, among the many cures promised by the electric belt are specifically sexual ones: "...seminal weaknesses, losses, drains, impotency or lost manhood...." The Owen advertisement is just as clearly directed to women, and probably also their husbands (who would probably control the purse strings and determine whether or not the belt would be purchased). This advertisement does not mention sex, but rather, domesticity. The belt promises a restoration of the woman using it to her social place:

I was a young wife of six months and had *kept house* only four months....[After the treatment] we commenced to keep house on

---

Box 9.4
ANALYZING TWO NINETEENTH-CENTURY ELECTRICAL ADVERTISEMENTS

SIMILARITIES

- They are both advertisements.
- They both advertise electrical belts used medicinally.
- A medical doctor is mentioned in both advertisements.
- Both the advertisements claim the cure of many conditions if you use the device.

Anything else?

SOME GENERAL DIFFERENCES

- The Owen advertisement has a picture of Dr. Owen, while the Sanden's ad does not depict Dr. Sanden.
- The Owen advertisement depicts a patient, while the Sanden's does not.
- The Owen advertisement features personal testimonials (common in contemporary advertising), while the Sanden's does not.
- The Owen advertisement mentions that the catalog may be acquired in Norwegian, Swedish, and German as well as English. (Can you guess why?)

Anything else?

Thanksgiving and *I have done our work with my husband's help ever since.* (italics added)

We can conclude from analyzing these two historical documents that electrical devices were sold directly to consumers via advertisements during the late nineteenth century, and that they were supposed to cure many kinds of ailments. Physician authority and personal testimonials were used to sell these products, as they are today. These two advertisements were highly gendered, selling sexual potency to men, and a return to domestic duties to women and their husbands. They tell us something about medicine, advertising, and gender roles in late nineteenth-century America.

The images displayed in these documents reveal, to the viewer, both the technologies and the visual conventions common in late nineteenth-century print advertising. The images in both illustrations are black-and-white and are drawings rather than photographs. Dr. Sanden's print is elaborate and curly, while the Owen Electric Belt uses a plainer font. Dr. Sanden's advertisement shows the device being sold, while Dr. Owen's shows the people involved in medical treatment. Both advertisements use visually larger and smaller, bolder and nonbolded text to highlight and emphasize aspects of these treatment devices. In Dr. Owen's advertisement, for example, by bolding and setting off the words "Read the next letter six months later," attention is drawn to the claims of the long-term efficacy of his belt.

Dr. Sanden's advertisement displays the technological device it is marketing. The electric belt is full of power and gadgetry, with metal disks shooting out electric rays. The text contrasts the device visually with the large, bold printed words "Weak Men." This contrast tells the reader that if he is a weak man, this powerful belt can make him a strong man. And he will be strong in all areas of the body, from his kidneys to his testicles. In contrast, Dr. Owen's advertisement looks more scientific and sober than Dr. Sanden's. The place of publication may be quite different, although there was no information on where either of these advertisements had been published in the archives where Warren found them. Dr. A. Owen himself is shown with a full beard and a severe countenance, neither of which—at least in our view—would be effective representations of medical competence in today's advertisements. The patient is shown as a normal-looking woman of the late nineteenth century with a modest high collar and upswept hair, someone who could be, and has been with Dr. Owen's belt, restored from emotional and physical "prostration" to mental health and domestic functioning.

If you were to write a paper about the gendered advertising of electrical medical devices in the nineteenth century, you would do some background research into the area as you do for any paper topic in qualitative—or for that matter quantitative—social research, as well as develop your analytic points into a fully developed analytic description. You would do the same kind of background research if you wrote a paper on contemporary gendered advertising. If, for example, you were to write a paper on the images of girls and women in *Seventeen* magazine advertisements in the early 2000s, you would want to find out how advertisements and copy were related to one another during that time period: did the editors, for example, sell advertising space first and then fit the copy to what was being advertised, or the reverse? (See if you can find this out.) Part of the interpretive background of documents is what has gone into their construction; the other part is the reflection of the cultural context of these documents.

And that is what the analysis of qualitative data is all about: listening to and interpreting the voices and representations of others, from past or present, culturally. The analysis of fieldnotes is both similar and different: in them we may listen to and interpret the voices of others in the present, but we can also observe action and interaction. Our analysis of these is through the lens of our own interpretations—not idiosyncratic lenses, but lenses shaped through learning sociological and other (perhaps cultural studies, feminist, or activist) perspectives. Our next step is bringing these disparate themes and voices together into a fully conceptualized analysis.

Linking Themes into Analytic Descriptions

Up until now, we have been discussing and showing how researchers identify themes, codes, or patterns in their data. This is commonly where some scholars fall prey to Lofland's charge of "analytic interruptus," because they stop at this point. At this point, you have lists or compilations of examples of themes, and now you need to make sense of what you have, conceptually or theoretically. Some qualitative researchers link their analysis to concepts derived from the literature (e.g., Goffman and Foucault in Kivett and Warren's [2002] study), while others, such as Jack Katz (2001, 2002) and Michael Burawoy (1991), seek to move from analytic description to a more elaborated theoretical model. Either way,

> In essence, the ethnographer's task is to filter through the myriad of relationships that make up our social worlds and show how they work together in ways that make sense to those who enact them. We accomplish this goal by using our specialized ethnographic skills to help our readers experience the unfamiliar in terms that make it familiar and vice versa. In essence, we try to impose a little order on what could quite easily seem like chaos. (Vail 2001, 720)

In order to move from lists of data excerpts to creating order out of chaos, much remains to be done to develop a fully conceptualized analytic description, including making connections and interpreting and validating the data.

Making Connections

At this point, you have identified your themes and subthemes and collected examples of each into separate piles or documents. Now you need to decide how each of the themes connects the others. This is the time to begin making connections and mapping how your various data elements fit together into a whole and comprehensive representation of your research. Some sociologists use visual diagrams, process flow charts, or organizational structure charts. Others have drawn maps of their settings to identify where various types of interactions occur—how they are spatially clustered. Most often, we find ourselves using the tried-and-true format of an outline. Recall the discussion of colored pencil coding of the Bay Area study. Using an outline format, the ECT part of the analytic description of treatment is below.

Perspectives on Electroshock

1. The medical model of ECT (from interviews with and observations of physicians)
2. The everyday social control uses of ECT (from interviews with and observations of nurses)
3. The meaning of ECT to the woman patient (from interviews with hospitalized women in the 1950s and 1960s)
   a. as punishment
   b. as treatment
      i. the purpose of which is memory loss
      ii. confusion over whether to remember (psychoanalysis) or forget (ECT)
   c. the context of forgetting
      i. forgetting troubles
      ii. forgetting domestic tasks
      iii. forgetting husbands or children
4. ECT in the family context
   a. as a threat by the husband after discharge
   b. memory loss and marital strategies
      i. reminding the expatient of things she has forgotten
      ii. not reminding her
      iii. "reminding" her of things that never happened

This outline could be used for the development of a chapter or article on psychiatric treatments at Napa in the 1950s and 1960s, although it would probably change throughout the process of writing and rewriting drafts. As you write and rewrite outlines, think about how your themes and subthemes are ordered. There are three basic principles of ordering:

1. Random, like a shopping list (I need oranges, cat food, and toilet paper)
2. Temporal, ordered by time as in narrative history
3. Analytic, makes connections based on logic (and is actually quite tricky)

If your study is based on fieldnotes or interview transcripts, you will be using analytic ordering.

Analytic ordering requires that you make the connections between your themes or categories by some logical progression. One analytic strategy is to progress from the most general to the most specific points. In the discussion of electroshock from *Madwives*, you might begin with the most general theme (the gender and marital roles of the 1950s and 1960s), then link this discussion to the subtheme of psychiatric uses of electroshock to reinforce gender roles in that era. Armed with your linked analysis of women and electroshock, you would proceed to analyze the more specific or microlevel ethnographic and interview data on the meaning of treatment to these women and their husbands. These microlevel data, too, should be ordered analytically rather than randomly. Try this exercise: identify whether the above outline for "perspectives on electroshock" is random, analytic, or some combination. Then try reordering it to become more analytic.

As you begin to make your connections among the data themes and patterns, the relationship between analysis and interpretation is at this point reflexive, with the quotes leading to the analytic themes or categories, and the analytic categories used to illustrate the analysis. For you to have identified an analytic theme as important, you should have multiple examples of data to use illustratively. Since you have grouped each example together in your separate documents or piles, as we discussed above, you can easily choose which quotes appear most appropriate. Examples of quotes that led to the development of the category, and that would also be used to illustrate the category, could also be identified at this point. For example:

ECT for women as forgetting troubles (outline 3ci)

Shirley Arlen (interview transcript): "I think the shock treatments are supposed to make you forget—when you do break down or whatever it is you do to get in here—I mean you're pretty sick and I think shock treatment is to make you forget a lot of things that got you sick and the way you felt and everything like that—I mean it succeeded with me—I can't remember a lot of things—and a lot of people try—try to remember—but I'd rather not. There's some things I'd like to but I think it was for the best that I can't remember a lot of things."

ECT for women as forgetting husbands or children (outline 3ciii) and as a marital strategy of not reminding (outline 4bii)

Rita Vick (interview transcript): "I forgot all my children [she names the six of which she had lost custody]. Well, Sunday I was going through my album and I seen these children, and I asked my husband, 'who are these children? They look so familiar. They ring a bell but I don't know who they are.' So he lied to me and told me they were the children of some friends of ours. So I accepted it and I believed it. I said, 'oh.' So I looked at some more pictures and he left the room and went to his mother who was in the other room. And he told her that he lied to me so I wouldn't worry....And I was relaxed. I wasn't thinking about those children or missing them. I understand why he did it but it made me angry when I found out. I kept looking at pictures and then I found a piece of paper, which explained all my children. I got very angry...I started yelling...after he explained I accepted it and forgave him. But now I remember those children all these worries are back."

Once you have developed your initial understanding of the story your data have to tell, you will be able to create your diagram or outline or other visual display of the links between various elements of the story. This chart or outline should illustrate your understanding of the data and is unlikely to ever be used in your final manuscript. Rather, it can assist you as a road map or a tool for the next stage of your analysis—developing your interpretation of the data.

DEVELOPING INTERPRETATIONS

After you have made the initial connections between your analytic themes, you need to develop these themes and connections further and begin to illustrate them with data examples. In the excerpt below from their paper on loss of the remembered self in individuals with Alzheimer's disease, Karner and Bobbit-Zeher (2006) develop and illustrate their analytic description of Alzheimer's caregiving by relatives.

By representing a self that existed in the distant past temporally, caregivers invoke memories of who their relative was previously, before providing examples of their current Alzheimer's state. As Emily White explained: "My mother has been, up to age 92, very independent. A person that had good judgment, was very alert, was always bright...and now to see this, that she is deteriorating, it hurts me. Then she turns on me...with verbal things, then, oh my, it does hurt."

The desire to maintain the memory of the old self is important to the caregivers. They recall biographical fragments (good judgment, very alert, always bright) to signify that this person was once a fully developed, interacting, adult self. It is the storied self (Vittoria 1998) with which the caregiver begins before addressing the current, troubling circumstances. In part, the storied self appears also to answer the unspoken question of why the caregiver would remain active in this relationship. The ill person's self reflects relationally on the caregiver's sense of self as well. As her mother acts in unpleasant and at times verbally abusive ways, Emily White invokes the memory of the mother she knew before Alzheimer's disease. In doing so, she can clearly communicate the painful contrast between the familiar mother and the unfamiliar mother with dementia.

As Alzheimer's disease progresses, the diminishment of the afflicted person becomes more pronounced. "She would take things," Dorothy Lewis, a daughter-in-law recalled, "then she didn't know whose they were, and she would claim sometimes that they were after her husband, and her husband had been dead for years." This erasure of the familiar self is often manifested in behaviors that the previous, known self would never have engaged in. "It got progressively worse, to the point where she might mess in the middle of the floor and then wrap it up like a present," said Wanda Karp, daughter-in-law. These behaviors are often embarrassing to the caregivers. "She flirts with men specifically sometimes and that is kind of embarrassing," Amy Davis offers as an example of how her mother has changed. Marion Kelly also told the interviewer in whispered tones, "It isn't very nice to talk about, [but] he did spit on the floor and I tried to get him to quit that...that would bother me." (Karner and Bobbit-Zeher 2006, 556)

This excerpt exemplifies the fact that data do not speak for themselves but are represented within a researcher-organized framework—here the quotes are organized around the interpretation of loss of a remembered self. Though the quotes are illustrative of this loss of the known self, Karner and Bobbit-Zeher (2006) do not merely label or name it as such but rather rely on symbolic interactionist theories of self for their interpretation. Second, it also shows the exploration of both *emic* and *etic* meanings. Emic interpretations are understood and communicated by the respondent. In the Karner and Bobbit-Zeher example, caregiver comments about behavior changes ("she would take things") and their emotional responses ("it does hurt" and "that is kind of embarrassing") illustrate emic meanings. Etic interpretations are the researchers' understandings, combining the emic meanings with concepts and concerns in the discipline. Karner and Bobbit-Zeher interpret these caregiver comments etically, in the context of symbolic interactionist theories of the self and its transformation.

Some qualitative methodologists refer to the initial articulation of etic interpretations as "memoing." *Memos* are conceptual notes that tie together various data excerpts into a coherent and cohesive assemblage. They are a key aspect of sense-making used by the social analyst. Whether you write your interpretations as separate memos or weave them throughout your thematic quotes, your analysis is not complete without these linkages and connections made as apparent as possible. Writing these clear descriptions of how you, the researcher, are thinking about the data is a final component of analysis that can then be useful in constructing the final document. Memoing is also a process by which you will become more aware of how you are thinking about your data. It is an insightful, interpretive exercise that allows you to make your assumptions and understandings obvious to yourself as well as to your future readers. However, before you begin drafting your manuscript, there is still the step of deciding whether your interpretation and analytic description is a valid one supported by the data.

Validating Analysis

As we saw in Chapter 1, quantitative sociologists seek to establish generalizable knowledge, which is knowledge that can be generalized from the people studied to the entire population of similar people. As a very rough example, if you want to know how rural black Mississippi males will vote in the next election, you select a random sample of such males and then generalize your results to the entire population of black rural Mississippi males. While positivist sociologists are on firmer ground with generalizability than they are with causation, qualitative sociologists do not seek to establish generalizable knowledge. We, who do ethnographic, interview, document, or visual research, know that our conclusions—our analytic descriptions—are specific only to the population that we studied, and perhaps even to the time and process of our involvement.

Where qualitative sociologists have the edge is with *validity*: in its simplest definition, the relationship between the data—setting, people, documents, images— and the conclusions arrived at by the sociologist about those data. There are many more technical definitions of validity in general methods texts, but this one will suffice for our purposes here. Clearly, studying settings, interactions, and individuals firsthand (the empirical world) provides the researcher with at least the possibility of coming to valid conclusions about them. The more remote methods such as large-scale surveys are at a far greater distance from this empirical world than are qualitative methods. Although such methods are ideal for studying, say, voting behavior, they are less than ideal for studying the meaning of that voting behavior to the people doing the voting.

You know that your data have been gathered in an experience-near fashion, and that you are quite familiar with your setting, respondents, or other data, but how do you know that your interpretation is valid? How do you know that you haven't "discovered" in your data only what you wanted to see? What can you do to verify or confirm your analytic description? How can you be sure that your interpretation is actually supported by your data? This is the final task of your analysis. We suggest three routes to validation: evaluating the data, reframing the analysis, and seeking external verification.

An initial test of qualitative validity is to *evaluate your data* as to their appropriateness to the analytic interpretation you proposed. It is important to have the appropriate data: if your analysis is about employers' assessments of subordinates' morale, it should be composed of interviews with employers rather than employee perceptions of management. Or might a study of morale be better accomplished by field research than by interview? Is morale a matter of accounts, or behavior and interaction, or both? Think about these questions, and perhaps discuss your responses in class. What do you think?

Your data need to be conceptually and logically appropriate to your research questions, your choice of methods, and your analysis. Your data also need to be comprehensive. For example, if you noticed a specific hand gesture being used frequently in your setting during your last observation, but hadn't really paid attention to hand gestures prior to that, then your data would be incomplete for an interpretation of the use of hand gestures in that community, and you might want to go back into the field for a while. So, this is the first check of your analysis: do you have the right kind of data, in sufficient quantity and quality, to make the claims you are suggesting?

Second, you should consider the *goodness of fit* of your analysis by reframing it in alternative ways, researching the data to support or refute these new interpretations. One common way to do this is by *negative case testing* (Denzin 1989b). You have already compiled lists of the examples of specific themes in your data. Now go back and see if there are examples of countering themes or patterns. If a negative case is found, you need to rework your analysis to account for this occurrence as well. By searching the data to disprove your analysis, you can reframe your interpretation, making it all the more robust. Another, similar test is called the *null hypothesis trick* (Becker 1998). In this process, you assume that no relationships or patterns exist in your data; in quantitative terms the null hypothesis refers to the proposition that the two variables of interest are not related. You, the qualitative researcher, using this "trick," then return to your data looking for evidence of such a relationship and connection. Always remember, however, that qualitative is not quantitative research, and more than one interpretation of the data may fit.

A third way to validate qualitative interpretation is to seek *external validation* from the research subjects, colleagues, instructors, or other data (triangulation). One approach is to offer your interpretation back to the research subjects for confirmation. Liebow (1993) had the homeless women and shelter staff where he had been a participant observer read and make comments on his analysis. He included their alternative interpretations as footnotes in his final manuscript. Sarah Gatson and Amanda Zweerink (2004) made their data available to the online community they studied, for discussion and comments that helped them frame their final analysis. Stacey (1998) also used this approach in her study of two extended Silicon Valley families and included their comments in her appendixes. If your goal, as we've mentioned before, is to understand the meaning of the life world of your subjects, then asking them if you have it correct is one way to verify your approach.

However, external validation is not always appropriate. Bloor (2001, 394) reminds us "all validating techniques are social products, constituted through particular and variable methodological processes." Indeed, drawing from his own research, Bloor offers examples of member validation experiences where respondents were uninterested in providing feedback (they only read the field-note excerpts that they were featured in), anxious about others' perceptions (they provided interpretive feedback based on their funding agency's criteria), and unconvinced by analyses that went well beyond their own understanding (that is, it did not contain the psychodynamic concepts that were the basis of their daily practices).

Another source of external validation is to have other sociologists read your materials to evaluate the strength of your analysis, or, if you can afford it, an external consultant (Angrosino 2007). Qualitative researchers working alone rarely use this strategy, but it is commonplace in classrooms and in team research. Karner and Warren both read their students' fieldnotes and interview transcripts to advise them on the "fit" of their analyses. Karner has also worked in applied team research where fieldnotes and interview transcripts were discussed and reviewed by fellow team members during the development of the analytic interpretations. In an interview study of community service providers, Lisa Cox Hall conducted the interviews and Karner developed the initial analysis (Karner and Hall 2002). Karner and Hall then discussed the data and analysis with other team members who were involved with different aspects of the same funded project. Similarly, when Karner and Dobbs interviewed nursing home staff persons, they both reviewed the data and sought feedback from other team members to further refine the analysis (Karner et al. 1998). In this study, however, they also compared the qualitative findings to quantitative data collected in the same nursing homes as part of another study. Thus, in this example, Karner and her colleagues both validated their analysis externally with their team members and through triangulation with survey data.

Triangulation of data may also be used to establish external validity. In triangulation, fieldnote data may be used to corroborate interview data, or other data sources can be used along with fieldnotes or interview transcripts to corroborate events or accounts. Among these other data sources are, for example, newspaper accounts of events claimed by respondents, or the contents of garbage cans in relation to claims of not drinking alcohol. In *Spitting Image*, Lembcke (2000) sought out mass media documentation to support the "myth of the spit upon Vietnam veteran." Though there were many informal accounts of such events, Lembcke could not find a single image or media report of the claimed "spitting," and concluded that the myth could not be substantiated as historical fact and more likely had been politically motivated propaganda.

Quantitative sociologists are concerned not only with various kinds of validity but also with reliability (see Chapter 1). In qualitative sociology, the key reliability question is: would any qualitative sociologist examining the texts or images that constitute the data, and attempting to answer similar research questions, develop (roughly) the same analytic description? From a quantitative standpoint, the answer would be no, because qualitative analysis is interpretive, with members' meanings examined through a particular analytic lens and located in a specific interaction bounded by time and space. However, if you are a qualitative researcher, the answer might be yes, or it might be no. In their work on assisted living, Williams and Warren (2008, 2009) both identified, independently, the main themes: "a home is not home," and "fear of the nursing home." A researcher interested in race and ethnicity, analyzing the same *Madwives* (1987) data as Warren, might have focused on the numerous accounts of white women psychiatric patients in the 1950s interacting with African-American male staff persons. Warren, however, made the decision to focus on gender, and to exclude race, in her analysis.

Analysis is a multistep and multilayered process occurring in a particular time and place, done by an individual or team with various applied or theoretical interests, and subject to the readers' assessment of its validity. Developing a thorough and compelling analysis proceeds by working back and forth between what has been typed or scanned into the computer and what has been printed out for reading, rereading, and classification, whether with colored pencils or some more elaborate technology. We have demonstrated in this chapter how to develop bits and pieces of analysis from qualitative materials, as well as how to develop an analytic description from elements of qualitative text. In the next chapter, we follow the analytic process with that of writing class papers, articles, or books.

Suggestions for Further Reading

Becker, Howard. 1998. *Tricks of the Trade: How to Think About Your Research While You're Doing It*. Chicago: University of Chicago Press.

Gibbs, Graham R. 2002. *Qualitative Data Analysis: Explorations With NVivo*. New York: McGraw-Hill.

Lewins, Ann, and Christina Silver. 2007. *Using Software for Qualitative Data Analysis: A Step-by-Step Guide*. London: Sage Publications.

Riessman, Catherine Kohler. 2008. *Narrative Methods for the Human Sciences*. Thousand Oaks, CA: Sage Publications.

Chapter 10

Writing Well

$\mathbf{A}$fter you have completed the fieldwork or other data collection and worked through your analysis, it is time to begin writing your paper, article, or book. Researchers sometimes see the writing phase as a separate and final step in completing a project. However, for qualitative researchers, the process of writing—rather than just the final phase—is an integral part of understanding the "story" of the data. In this chapter, we consider the writing process in general, and the research paper as one outcome of qualitative research. We present the elements of the qualitative research paper from title to references, and stress the need for editing and rewriting of manuscripts.

Crafting a qualitative manuscript is a process through which the writer clarifies how data and concepts fit together. This process is much like putting together a puzzle. You may try ordering the "puzzle pieces" in an initial pattern, but through additional writing, organizing, and contemplating, you may find several ways of placing the "pieces" together. For a paper or article you need only one primary thematic focus with subthemes. You can often write several papers from one set of qualitative data, so you don't have to try to use everything in one manuscript! In this chapter, we discuss writing qualitative sociology research well. We focus, first, on the general process and practice of writing, before turning our attention to the specific issues related to a qualitative research paper.

You have a responsibility to represent your subjects and your fieldwork experience in a thorough and accurate manner. This does not mean that your writing has to be sympathetic to your subjects, but rather that you will present an account of their life worlds that reflects their lived experience to the best of your ability. A simplistic overview does not do justice to the individuals whose lives you have shared and observed. How we write frames the representation of our respondent's life world. As Rosanna Hertz (2006, 541) reminds us, "the teller is a key tool of story telling" in qualitative research. Our role as author has both ethical and political implications; and as qualitative researchers, our most important task is to construct a representation that is faithful to the lived experience of those we study. This goal—a thorough and compelling representation of the individuals and community that you have studied—should guide your writing. Denzin and Lincoln (2007, 500) refer to this process as "the interpretive practice of making sense" of your data.

How we write and what we write—the writing decisions we make—are influenced by our own experiences and disciplinary perspectives, and these choices are also embedded within broader truth claims and power relations. How we write shapes "the forms of knowledge we are able to construct, including the kinds of theories and understandings we have the potential to develop" (Rhoads 2003, 241). Moreover, the manner of our description can have political implications for those we study. Accounts of the lives of marginalized, powerless, or deviant peoples can be used to support or refute various political interventions (Emerson 2001, 314–15). Writing qualitative research well means being attentive to how our representations (and their attendant knowledge claims) reflect upon those we study and the broader social and political contexts within which they may be read.

Writing Well

Writing qualitative research well has two aspects. The first is correct English grammar, spelling, punctuation, paragraphing, and organization; principles you have learned in composition classes should not be forgotten as you write in other areas of the college curriculum. The second requirement is attention to the particular discipline, genre, or type of writing.

Anyone who has attempted to write something for an audience beyond themselves knows that writing well is much more than just putting words on a page. Writing is, indeed, the physical act of typing into the computer or working with pen and paper, but it is also the cognitive process by which the writer decides what ideas to convey and how best to communicate them. It is those decisions about *what* and *how* to write that make writing a complex, creative practice. In this section, we will focus on the physicality of writing— *when* and *where* to write—before turning our attention, in the second part of this chapter, to a discussion of *how to write* for a sociology audience and the various decisions that good writers must make.

Time

The first aspect of the practice of writing is to set aside enough time to do it. (See Box 10.1.) Many students have attempted to write a paper in one all-night session. This is rarely a successful approach to writing well, regardless of the topic; in writing qualitative research, it almost guarantees an inadequate final product. Allowing a significant amount of time for the writing process is crucial for contemplating, refining, and rethinking the representation you are crafting. Many scholars find that writing up their research takes as long as the data collection or analysis. Although time spent writing is loosely correlated to the amount of data one is working with, more data also equals the need for more writing time.

Box 10.1
PREPARING TO WRITE

Step One: Allow a reasonable amount of time

Qualitative research papers cannot be written in one all-night session. Time is required to craft an appropriate representation of your subjects' life worlds and your efforts in the field. Your first responsibility in writing up your research is to do justice to the individuals you are seeking to understand and represent. This cannot be accomplished without adequate time.

Step Two: Identify your writing process

Once you understand the factors that facilitate productive writing sessions for you—time of day, creature comforts, organizational strategies—you can consciously identify when, where, and how the time you spend writing can be most productive. Some people write best in the morning; others at night. Some people need quiet; others like music or background noise. Learning about your process—what works best for you—will help you make the most of the time you have. (Identifying your personal writing process does not, however, negate the need for step one—a reasonable amount of time—and step five—begin!)

Step Three: Organize your materials

Before getting ready to write you will have coded and analyzed your fieldnotes, transcripts, and other data. Organizing your materials to begin the writing phase is yet another opportunity to reframe and refine your perspective of the data. You have to decide what data to report first, which components of the story follow your introduction, and how to integrate your analysis within the representation.

continued

Box 10.1 *continued*

You will be paying attention to logic and clarity as well as accuracy. At this point you should make an outline of your paper. Additionally, you will need to have the literature and citations you plan to refer to close by. The more organized you are as you begin to write, the less time will be spent in interruptions to find quotes, books, or other seemingly productive distractions from the task at hand.

Step Four: Plan your logistics

Be reasonable here and plan on a process that is not too cumbersome but that will save you from common mishaps. We assume that you will be using a personal computer for your paper. So, first plan a backup procedure for your computer work. Save your writing in more than one place (electronic and hard copies) and consider printing out what you write at each session—this is a further backup procedure that also can help with your editing phase.

Second, think about compiling your reference section as you write. You might type the citations in a separate document as you cite a source. This can save you lots of time and aggravation in trying to identify your references after the fact.

Third, plan your writing schedule. For example, you may plan to work on the methods section this week and subsections of your findings over the next four weeks. Work backwards from your deadline and plan enough time for each component of your research paper.

Step Five: Begin

The twin traps that hinder writers the most are the perceived need for inspiration, and perfectionism. Waiting for inspiration to strike may sound like a reasonable excuse for procrastinating, but it seldom strikes without beginning the process of writing. You will already have your materials organized and a writing schedule thought out. This will allow you to begin with some of the instrumental aspects of writing: the literature overview or the methods section. By beginning to work with your data and thoughts, you are more likely to become inspired. Insight most often comes through familiarity with the material and practicing the craft of writing. The old adage of 10 percent inspiration and 90 percent perspiration is very appropriate here.

Perfectionism can leave a writer rewriting the same sentence or paragraph over and over. After an inordinate amount of time, the writer may have a nearly perfect sentence and little else. Remember that editing is essential for good writing, and that editing what you have written is much easier than beginning with the blank page. In this early phase, your goal should be to "put it on paper" knowing that you will continue to refine and craft your writing after you have a draft with which to work.

Writing well takes time. There are no shortcuts. Writing, as we have come to understand the process, is really another way of knowing (Rhoads 2003)—an extension of the analysis, as you continue to "work with" your data to code and identify themes, prioritize concepts, and determine how concepts are connected. Writing in a clear and logical manner requires a clear understanding of the data. Confusing or convoluted writing often comes from a misunderstanding of the data and their context. Most scholars who practice qualitative writing stress the need for adequate time to be allowed for the maturation of the writer's understanding. Writing, Richardson and St. Pierre suggest, is a "method of inquiry." Through the act of writing, new insights and awareness come to be known. Using her own process for an example, Elizabeth Adams St. Pierre finds

> I wrote my way into particular spaces I could not have occupied by sorting [or coding]....I made accidental and fortuitous connections I could not foresee or control....As I wrote, I watched word after word appear on my computer screen—ideas, theories, I had not thought before I wrote them. Sometimes I wrote something so marvelous it startled me. I doubt I could have thought such a thought by thinking alone. (Richardson and St. Pierre 2007, 970)

Writing a first qualitative draft reminds us of the adage that you don't really know something until you try to teach it—in this case, you may not really understand your data until you try to communicate a faithful representation.

INDIVIDUAL WRITING PROCESSES

The second lesson about writing well is the importance of identifying your own process for writing productively. In the classic text *Writing for Social Scientists* (1986), Howard Becker describes the various preparatory rituals that writers may engage in—all those behaviors that one does seemingly to avoid writing, Becker says, may in some cases be part of the process of getting ready to write. Like the story of Ernest Hemingway ritually sharpening twenty pencils before beginning his writing sessions, many people have practices, like cleaning their office or collecting and ordering reference materials in a specific manner, that enable them to begin writing. Becker advises social scientists to acknowledge these practices as part of identifying their own preparation processes, and to plan time for them rather than assuming that they are ways of avoiding writing.

Also, most of us have times of the day that we are more productive than others. (See Boxes 10.2 and 10.3.) Some people like to write in the evenings when it is quiet and they are less likely to be interrupted. Other people carve out times during the day to work. If you can identify when you are most productive, scheduling your writing time accordingly will allow you to make the most of the time you do have. Generally, you can identify your productive time through trial and error—and perhaps with other commitments in your life. When Karner was in graduate school, she found her best time to think and write occurred when she woke at three in the morning. This gave her

---

Box 10.2

FOR EXAMPLE: WARREN'S WRITING PROCESS

I have written qualitative sociological articles and books for more than thirty years, first at the University of Southern California, then at the University of Kansas, and after retirement in a house on the bay in Coronado, California. I learned to write directly onto the computer during the 1980s at USC, replacing my earlier yellow lined pad and typewriter technology. I still work on an earlier form of Word than most of my colleagues—I am at version 6, whereas some of them are up to 11. I'd be back in DOS if it were possible.

At USC and KU I preferred to work in my office rather than at home, despite the eternal interruptions. Now, my "office" is a blue sofa facing out to the blue water of San Diego bay, and my "desk" is my lap with my ancient (four years!!) laptop computer. The materials I am working with are in files in this computer, and in folders in another room: this book, a paperback edition of *Pushbutton Psychiatry: A Cultural History of Electroshock in America* with Timothy Kneeland (Left Coast Press), and various papers on assisted living, together with bits and pieces of new endeavors in e-marketing and advertising copy writing. As a retiree, I work whenever I want to—when the sky is cloudier than usual and the sun less bright, or when deadlines loom.

The setting is different but the tasks of writing are the same. I prefer to have a few hours of uninterrupted writing, but as a consequence of years of practice I can still be a "ten minute" writer if necessary. I no longer use outlines as much as I should, but I do start with writing and rewriting the introduction so that I have some idea where I am going. But I also find that writing the conclusion to an article often leads me to rewriting the introduction—saying to myself, "so this is where this piece was really going"!

For an article or chapter I generally start with a short first draft of about 20–25 pages. Then I rewrite at least twice and usually more, adding and refining concepts, reordering, and selecting quotes from fieldnotes, interviews, cultural artifacts, or historical documents. Next, I impose on several colleagues to read my draft (I do the same for them) before I take the step of submitting the article to a journal. I rewrite according to their comments with a triage strategy: yes, I agree I should change that, no, I don't think I should do that (and why I shouldn't), and the most difficult category, the middle one—maybe, maybe not. Then...off to the journal or book publisher!

approximately three solid hours of work time before her children awoke and the responsibilities of the day enveloped her. However, now that her children are grown, Karner still prefers to work in the mornings, though she no longer rises quite so early to do so.

In addition to the time of day that may work well for you, think also about the creature comforts that will help you stay on task. Just as with

---

Box 10.3
FOR EXAMPLE: KARNER'S WRITING PROCESS

I have written in many different environments and with a variety of coauthors over the years. I have found what works for me through trial and error and mostly from needing to be productive in places and at times that were a real challenge to my personal style. Mostly, I've found that I enjoy writing in my office at home. In my home office, I have long worktables to organize my materials on and an extremely comfy desk chair. I learned long ago that if I was not physically comfortable, it was harder to stay on task.

My worktables are antique yellow pine doors that I have covered with glass tops and to which I have attached legs. These tables suit my need for a pleasant aesthetic environment, as well as my visual organizing style. I organize my data and literature, visually, on my tables (and in larger projects I sometimes spread it out on the floor as well). I stack hard copies of the materials together for each section of my writing and then physically organize the literature and data, within each section, in the order I plan to write about it.

Mornings are the most productive writing time for me. I usually review what I wrote the day before over my morning tea and then move to the computer to tackle the current day's project. I write in two- to three-hour blocks interspersed with short breaks to eat or walk my dog or visit the gym. When I am writing, I like to clear my calendar (as much as possible) so that the writing process is my central task and focus for that time period. (Yes, I am primarily a *sporadic, secluded writer* though I aspire to being more of a *consistent, everyday writer*.) Though in the real world this is seldom possible, it is my preference.

When I am beginning a new project, I start with the instrumental writing tasks first. I usually write the methods section first, then the findings and results. I usually have a rough outline of my literature overview before I write my findings, but I do not begin to draft the literature section until after I have "written through" my data and analysis. After drafting these three sections, I work on the introduction and conclusion somewhat concurrently. When I have a draft of all the components, I begin editing and refining the work. The abstract is the very last thing I write. Throughout the writing process, I maintain a separate file so I can compile my references as I use them. I also make backup copies rather compulsively; I save to hard disk and save backup copies to a separate external drive at the end of each writing session.

interviewing, physical comfort allows individuals to continue what they are doing longer. If you are hungry, tired, or uncomfortable at a desk that is too high or on a chair that is too hard, you are not likely to continue writing. Part of planning your productivity is providing for as much of your comfort as possible. Will you need snacks close by? Are you able to be more focused at your home computer—or will you have multiple distractions? Are you more likely to work well at a table in the library? As you will see in the examples of our work processes that we offer in Boxes 10.2 and 10.3, we have different approaches to the craft of writing—yet we have each identified our own process. We offer our examples to help you think about the various aspects of identifying your own process to enable you to be as productive as possible.

After you have identified a good time and place for your writing, you might give some thought to your approach to writing in general. Writing approaches can, for the most part, be divided into three patterns: the all-night adrenalin writer, the consistent everyday writer, and the sporadic writer. We've already discussed the inadequacies of the all-night adrenalin approach for writing faithful and ethical representations of qualitative research. If that has been your pattern in the past, we urge you to consider either of the other two approaches, at least for your qualitative work.

The consistent, everyday approach is perhaps the most disciplined pattern for writing. Scholars who use this process carve out time to write on a regular basis and proceed to write a small section or subsection of their project each day. This is often the most fruitful pattern of writing, as those who write regularly are always moving forward on their projects no matter what other obligations they may have. Professional writers often recommend this steady, ongoing approach as well. As you experiment with various processes and come to understand your own better, this is an approach to strive to emulate both for its discipline and steady rate of productivity.

The sporadic approach is perhaps the more common pattern among academic writers, who often attempt to accomplish their writing between semesters and over summer breaks. These writers generally put a lot of thought into conceptualizing and organizing their data and literature prior to beginning to write. When they write, they set aside specific amounts of time to focus on their writing to the exclusion of other tasks. They may isolate themselves away from colleagues and family during these writing periods, and emerge only after completion of their initial draft.

As students, your time and thus your approach will be somewhat constrained both by your instructor's requirements and the semester or quarter system of your school. The consistent, everyday approach may be your only real option to writing well for your course. If so, you can be assured that you are engaging in a productive and successful approach that is used by many, and aspired to by many others, not only in the social sciences but in other disciplines as well.

Organizing Your Data

Prior to beginning to write your research paper or report, you need to organize your materials for the writing process. You may feel "buried under an increasing mountain of fieldnotes, transcripts, newspaper clippings, and audio tapes" (Fontana and Frey 2008, 140); it is from this mountain that you face the challenging task of making sense of what you have learned. And the first step is to organize. Think about how you understand materials and organize other aspects of your life. Are you a visual organizer like Karner (see Box 10.3)? Or do you like a neat desktop with materials filed electronically (ready for cut and paste into your document) or in nicely labeled file folders or in tabbed notebooks for quick reference? Think about what kind of system is likely to work well with the way you think and work.

In organizing your materials to write, keep two things in mind: one, you need a system by which you can find and retrieve images and text from the data to illustrate your analysis, and two, you need something manageable so that you don't waste all your writing time chasing down details. How you choose to organize should address both concerns. One approach is to construct a thorough outline of the document you plan to write, including notations of where the quotes and materials you wish to put in the various sections are located. This outline can then be used as the guide for writing the various sections and fitting them together. One caution about this process is that it assumes that the analysis is complete prior to the writing, which may not be an accurate assumption given the reflexive quality of qualitative research.

Another approach (favored by Karner) is to physically organize the materials. You can identify the quotes and illustrations from the data that you plan on incorporating into your writing and excerpt them into a separate document—you might create a separate document of each subtheme for manageability (as we suggested in Chapter 9). Be sure to include notation labels with each excerpt as to where it came from (for example, *Gary: Interview one, page 6* or *Park observation, 12-03-08, page 5*). At this point, a working outline for the paper can be developed. We see this as a flexible road map for the process of writing. As an author, a working outline gives you an overview of how all your data and conceptual components relate to each other.

Over the years, we have heard many interesting stories of how our colleagues have fashioned their outlines with moveable parts, allowing for a flexible writing process interspersed with further refinement and contemplation. Karner's favorite story is the graduate student who taped section notes to the sliding glass doors in her apartment. She organized them conceptually and began to work on a specific section. At the end of each session, she would draw the curtains closed. At the beginning of her next working session, she would open the curtains and view her conceptual organization with fresh eyes. In light (literally!) of what she had written the previous day, she would then rearrange her section notes and continue her writing. Others have used grease boards or poster boards with Post-It notes to allow them to organize their thoughts both visually and physically in a very flexible manner.

This is also a good time to plan the logistics of writing. By this, we are referring to the process by which you back up your writing and compile your reference section. These are instrumental details of writing that can cause anguish if not addressed initially. We recommend that you back up everything in a regular and systematic manner. As we discussed earlier in terms of your data, you should back up what you write every day. Many a deadline has been missed due to computer crashes and files lost in cyberspace. Since these events only seem to happen when you haven't backed up your work, it is wise to do so often. Equally aggravating and time consuming is trying to construct your reference section after you have completed the manuscript. We recommend that you initiate a process to record the works you cite and use while you are writing. You can open a separate document and enter citations as they are used, as we both do. Or you may enter all the works you've used at the end of your writing session. Either way, it will alleviate the need to identify works long after you've returned the book or journal to the library. Make sure you also record the page numbers of any quotations you include from the literature.

Writing that first sentence signifies that you have begun the process of representing your subjects' life worlds and communicating your research experience. This is a daunting task to be sure, but it is also something that you have been doing all along if you've followed our advice. You have been writing conceptual notes to yourself, you may have been keeping an analytic journal, and you've written organization notes as you have developed your writing outline (whether thorough or flexible and moveable). These notes can serve as the beginning of the writing process—the fitting of the puzzle pieces together. You have already organized the relevant literature and the illustrative excerpts from your data; now your task is to join all the pieces together in one well-written and crafted document.

At this point, we offer you two cautions from experience: don't wait for inspiration, and don't expect perfection in your first draft. Waiting for inspiration before beginning to write is a common excuse for procrastination. Inspiration and insight most often occur when you are actively engaged in writing; seldom does it occur out of the blue. We recommend beginning with the methods section, as this should be a relatively straightforward and temporally ordered account of the work you have done and how and why you did it. You might begin as though you were telling a friend or a colleague about your project. What did you set out to do? What challenges did you face and how did you overcome them? How did you approach the various methodological and analytical decisions that you had to make? What impact did these decisions have on the research? Beginning your writing with the methods section is a good reminder of all the work that you have done as well as giving you an instrumental place to begin your representation.

The answer to perfectionism is later editing (see below). Many writers get caught up in constructing perfect sentences or paragraphs; rather than continuing to write, they proceed to rewrite small sections hoping to achieve perfection. Perhaps some people can do this, but we have yet to write the perfect sentence—especially not in our first drafts. Remember that everything you write can be edited later. Initially, you just need to put the words on paper that convey your ideas. Once you have written a full draft and know what the document in its entirety will look like, only then can you effectively edit and seek to refine and perfect your words and phrases. Remember that qualitative work is emergent, and that the writing process is iterative. Seeking perfection too early in the writing process can inhibit much of the insight that comes only through reflection and working with the materials.

Writing the Qualitative Research Paper

The end point of qualitative research is often a paper written for a class, a journal article, or a chapter in an edited book, sometimes a book-length scholarly monograph, thesis, or dissertation. Experimental social scientists may write plays or memoirs (see, for example, Richardson 2007). Applied qualitative researchers may complete program or other evaluation reports for the government or for granting agencies. And the researcher may also have to present work orally as well as (or instead of) in writing. Whichever format you are working toward, the basic, guiding principles are similar: pay attention to the audience for your work, and make sure that your work follows a coherent and complete outline.

One early writing decision is what style guide you are going to use. Style guides provide the format for headings and subheadings, capitalization, citations (in text or in footnote or endnote), and references. If you are writing something for submission to a journal or for inclusion as a book chapter, you should check the style requirements of the journal or publisher. If you write a paper for a class, the audience for your work is your instructor, who will provide you with requirements for your paper in terms of length, reference format, and other elements. For example, in undergraduate sociology classes using qualitative methods we both require papers of approximately 18–20 pages for undergraduates, 30–35 for graduate students. For both, we expect them to use a consistent and recognized format, such as the American Sociological Association Style Guide, http://www.asanet.org/apap/quickstyle.html, or the Chicago style of referencing used in this textbook.

The audiences for published qualitative researchers' work are likely to be fellow scholars, working on the editorial boards of journals or putting together edited books. The content of journals and edited books varies according to the theoretical and methodological principles espoused by the editors, from positivist, quantitative applied journals and readers to social constructionist qualitative ones. Obviously, for the purposes of this chapter, our examples come from audiences attuned to qualitative, social constructionist work. Within this general framework, as we saw in Chapter 1, there are a variety of perspectives, including symbolic interactionism, and the work of Goffman on everyday life. If you want to present or publish your work among those who have these qualitative and conceptual interests, you will not only use qualitative methods in your research, but also various conceptual frameworks from the social constructionist literature.

The paper you write using your qualitative data will not only cite and use conceptual frameworks from the social constructionist literature, but will also include anything substantive that has been written on the topic by sociologists and perhaps others. It will also follow certain conventions, such as a balance of (say) 60% analytic text and 40% illustrative description. Although your instructor may or may not require this, sociologists who write articles and books as part of their professional work generally write a number of drafts prior to the finished draft to be submitted for publication.

JOURNAL PUBLICATION

You should be aware of the process a paper goes through to be published in a journal. The first step is submission of the paper to the journal's editor, following the guidelines stated at the beginning of each issue of the journal. The editor typically requires the submission of three to five hard copies and perhaps an electronic version, and some journals also ask for a fee of ten dollars or more for processing the submission (other journals ask for a processing fee after the article is accepted for publication). The editor then asks three to five experts to read the paper and judge its suitability for publication. These reviewers may be members of the journal's editorial board (listed toward the front of the journal), or other scholars known to the editor for their expertise in the topic, theory, or methods of the paper.

The reviewers make recommendations to the editor as to whether the paper should be rejected, accepted with major or minor changes, or returned to the author for revision and possible resubmission. They provide detailed suggestions for the author, including recommendations for changes in writing style, methods or conceptualization, and the inclusion of prior scholarly work on the topic that might have been overlooked. The journal editor then writes a letter to the author indicating whether or not the article has been accepted for publication, and summarizing the most important suggested revisions. The comments of the reviewers are generally included, anonymously, in the materials sent to the author. The author then revises and resubmits the paper for publication, at which point the editor may accept the paper or send it back to the reviewers for another look. This process may take several months, and the entire process from submission to publication may take more than a year.

Elements of the Qualitative Research Paper

Qualitative research papers generally include the following components: title, author's name and affiliation, abstract, introduction, literature review, methods, findings and results, conclusions, and references. (See Box 10.4.) We discuss each of these sections in the order it would appear in a published work, though that is seldom the order in which the sections are written. Barnes and her colleagues (2003) suggest that writing is more like a "spiral" than a linear process, whereby the writer takes ideas from the literature and incorporates, modifies, or adapts them into the execution of the research and writing.

The general guide to writing order that we offer is to begin with your flexible outline or overview. Then draft the methods section—a straightforward account of what you have done. Follow this with a draft introduction so that you know, roughly, where you are going, and perhaps the literature section. Write your analysis, including your illustrative data excerpts. Then write the conclusion and return to polish the introduction and literature review to make sure that the conclusion addresses the issues raised in these sections. At this point you will want to edit the entire manuscript for cohesion, accuracy, and consistency. Again, we recommend that you compile your reference section as you refer to others' works so the references will be complete when you have finished writing. The last thing you will work on will be the abstract. Finally, the manuscript title may be tentatively held throughout the writing process and adopted or changed at its conclusion.

TITLE

There are two main approaches to title selection in qualitative research. In titling their work, some researchers begin with a compelling or vivid phrase followed by a more descriptive subtitle. Warren's 1996 paper demonstrates this two-part approach—"Older Women, Younger Men: Self and Stigma in Age-Discrepant Relationships." The first phrase, "Older Women, Younger Men," is meant to capture the potential readers' interest so they will take the time to read the paper. The subtitle "Self and Stigma in Age-Discrepant

Box 10.4
QUALITATIVE RESEARCH PAPER COMPONENTS

What to write first?

Begin with the **Methods** section
Outline or draft the **Literature Review**
Write the **Findings and Results**
Craft the **Conclusions** and **Introduction** concurrently
Polish the Literature Review to lead to Findings and Results
Compile the **References,** endnotes or footnotes
Write the **Abstract**
Select a vivid and informative **Title**

How is the paper organized?

Title
Abstract
Introduction
Literature Review
Methods
Findings and Results
Conclusions
References

Relationships" locates the paper within the sociological concepts of interest (self, stigma) and the study sample (age-discrepant relationships). You can see this same pattern in the selection of sociology titles below:

Tell Them Who I Am: The Lives of Homeless Women
Dancing at Armageddon: Survivalism and Chaos in Modern Times
Making Grey Gold: Narratives of Nursing Home Care
Slim's Table: Race, Respectability and Masculinity
Losing Selves: Dementia Care as Disruption and Transformation
If Only Time Healed All Wounds: Post Traumatic Stress Disorder in Older Men
Gendered Transitions: Mexican Experience of Immigration
Hard Hats: The Work World of Construction Workers
Medicalizing Masculinity: Post Traumatic Stress Disorder in Vietnam Veterans

Other researchers select a single descriptive title that signals only the conceptual focus of the manuscript to the reader. For example, Karner and Hall's 2002 paper is entitled "Successful Strategies for Serving Diverse

Populations." The reader can tell that the paper is about strategies of providing services to multicultural communities. In making decisions about how to title your work, it is important to keep in mind the disciplinary conventions and expectations of your audience. Warren's "Older Women, Younger Men" title was intended for a qualitative sociology audience and was published in *Clinical Sociology Review*. The Karner and Hall manuscript, in contrast, was published as a book chapter intended for an audience of community service practitioners.

Author's Name and Affiliation

In publications, Tracy Xavia Karner uses her full middle name and Carol A. B. Warren uses middle initials. The use of middle names has always been rare in the United States, whereas using middle initials in published work seems to be less popular than it was a decade or so ago. In other countries, however, social science researchers often use only initials to identify themselves, as in "A. E. Smith." Women researchers have to decide, if they marry (or for that matter divorce and remarry), whether they want to keep and use their maiden name or change it for publication purposes. There has been some speculation that articles submitted for publication using only initials or male-sounding first names are more likely to be accepted than clearly female names. No matter which form of name the author chooses to use, this section also commonly includes academic level and affiliation—for example, "Associate Professor, Department of Sociology, Columbia University," together with an address and an email or phone method of contact.

Abstract

Although the abstract is printed at the beginning of the article, after the title and author, it is generally written after the article has been completed. Abstracts enable the editor of the journal (and potential readers) to determine what the article is about, substantively, conceptually, and methodologically. The number of words allowed for the abstract is determined by the editor, and is generally between 150 and 250. It is a challenge to compress the essence of a study into these few lines but it is also a useful exercise; if an abstract can be written only with great difficulty, it is probably because the paper is unclear and unfocused, its point or points lost somewhere in the text. The abstract serves as a concise overview of what will be found in the manuscript that follows. It should include the central conceptual focus of the work, the theoretical approach used, the methods employed (sample, data collection, and analysis), and the key findings. If applicable and space permitting, the author may include any implications for practice or policy that the research findings offer.

In the following example, Karas and Karner (in 161 words) outline their topic and its relevance (diabetes as sixth leading cause of death in the United States), their theoretical approach (Arthur Frank's ideal body-types), the method of data collection (interviews) with their sample (two practitioners and eight individuals with diabetes), the key finding (persons with diabetes tended to be most closely associated with the "disciplined body-type" and pursued high levels of bodily control and predictability), and the practice implications (more effective treatment and better practitioner-patient relationships).

> Diabetes is the sixth leading cause of death from disease, shortens the average lifespan by up to 15 years, and is the main cause of new blindness, kidney failure, and amputations in the United States. In this study, interviews were conducted with two practitioners and eight individuals with diabetes to discover which embodiment choices and ideal body types were most frequently expressed. Developed by Arthur Frank (1995), the ideal body-type provides a framework for better understanding the behavior and needs of ill persons. Interviewed persons with diabetes tended to be most closely associated with the "disciplined body-type" and pursued high levels of bodily control and predictability. Frank offers a prescriptive, idealized type, the communicative body, as an ethical ideal for bodies living with illness. This framework is evaluated for its heuristic value in providing insight into the behaviors, needs, and struggles of persons with diabetes, as well as providing a means to promote more effective treatment options and better practitioner-patient relationships. (Karas and Karner 2005, 1086)

INTRODUCTION

The first sentence and the first paragraph of a qualitative research paper are very important, because it is there that the reader should be able to discern the analytic descriptive topic of the paper, and how it will be developed. In the first paragraph from our paper "The Dangerous Listener: Unforeseen Perils in Intensive Interviewing," for example, we let the reader know that our focus is the potential dangers of social science research to participants. Since our intended audience is other sociologists and social scientists, we hoped this beginning would hold their attention.

> Human subjects legislation over the past ten years has framed social science research, like the biomedical, as potentially dangerous. What such legislation frames as dangerous is the interview or questionnaire topic, or the way questions are posed, particularly for vulnerable respondents. What we propose is that in the intensive interview, the act of listening,

thus the listener her- or himself, may become perceived as dangerous. The conditions under which this danger arises are those in which a past, suppressed or forgotten self emerges in the interview, and becomes associated with the listener. We suggest that mental patienthood, and the events and relationships that preceded and led to it, may be one such set of circumstances. (Karner and Warren 1995, 80)

Following the first sentence, we go on to distinguish our analysis of potential danger from those other dangers that human subjects regulations are meant to address. The remainder of the first paragraph develops our analysis of the ways in which being interviewed invokes past (damaged or spoiled) selves— like mental patienthood—that represent a threat to the interviewee's current presentation of self.

The author should also reaffirm, in the introductory paragraphs, why this work is important and relevant to other researchers. Clinton Sanders (2003) accomplishes this in the first paragraph of his paper "Actions Speak Louder Than Words: Close Relationships Between Humans and Nonhuman Animals."

Relationships, which are composed of routine and patterned interactions, are central to the symbolic interactionist view of social life. Relationships range from those that are instrumental, emotionally uninvolving, and typically of short duration to those that are intrinsically rewarding and long-term and in which participants have considerable emotional stake. Conventionally, interactionists and other analysts of social life have seen the interdependence, commitment, and emotionality of close relationships as existing within, and sustained by, the symbolic exchanges of humans. I maintain that this characterization of close relationships is overly restrictive. It excludes from consideration a class of affiliations that are commonplace, imbued with emotion, and central to the shaping of the identities and selves of those involved. Traditionally, conventional sociologists (e.g., Perrow 2000, 473) have ignored or denigrated relationships between people and their companion animals. However, the intense, involving, and routine interactions forming these relations are worthy of serious attention and have the potential of adding significantly to the sociology of intimate exchanges. (Sanders 2003, 405–6)

Sanders tells his readers that even though relationships are a central research focus of sociologists and especially interactionists, these scholars have excluded a significant and commonplace relationship (between humans and animals) from serious investigation. In his last sentence, Sanders assures his readers that their time will be well spent by considering his work and the insights it brings to bear on the sociology of intimate exchanges. In addition to his analytic themes, Sanders discusses who will (or should) be interested—sociologists and interactionists—in reading the manuscript.

The introductory section of a paper sets the tone of the work and gives readers a good idea of what awaits them in the rest of the paper. A common mistake that novice writers make is in not previewing their analysis. It is important to tell the reader what you are going to say, why it is important, and to whom the information will be most useful (the expected audience). It is also useful to offer a summary at the end of each paper section, with a transition to the next section. The introductory section of a paper may vary in length from a couple of paragraphs to a couple of pages. However, it should conclude with a strong statement of the value of the research and its broader relevance. See how Sanders returns to the key points of his opening paragraph in more direct and vivid manner in the final paragraph of his introduction:

> Identity, personhood, empathy, love, mindedness, culture, and other key issues are of considerable interest to interactionists and are of central relevance for the sociology of close relationships. The central point of this article is that these key issues may be fruitfully explored if we turn serious and appreciative attention to the human-animal bond and the social exchanges that both define and result from this unique form of sociation. The task requires that we move beyond the analytic restraints imposed by the presumption that shared symbols are the sole foundation for "real" intimate relationships and "authentic" interactions. (Sanders 2003, 407)

Providing readers with these summary sections continually remind them of your purpose in writing this representation. They help guide the reader through your work.

LITERATURE REVIEW

After the introductory paragraphs, the literature review situates the study in the substantive literature on the topic, and the conceptual literature that will be used to frame the topic. Like the introduction, this section may be drafted early on or just outlined and then written after completing the findings and results portion. The literature review is a key part of the manuscript, because it sets your analysis in the context of the relevant and up-to-date published work. The purpose of discussing the literature is to present your work as the next logical step for research in this area.

For the beginning researcher, the literature review can seem as daunting as entering the field. The traditional source of academic literature is the campus library, where you can find journals and books relevant to the topic you have chosen to frame your analysis. There are also a number of online databases with academic journals, as well as several search engines (such as http://

scholar.google.com) available for your use. Some of these electronic resources will let you download the entire article in Acrobat PDF format, while others offer only the abstract and full citation. Some citation compilation software can download the full citation into your reference file automatically.

We suggest that spending some time in your campus libraries getting familiar with their resources might be your best way to begin, especially if you are doing ethnographic, interview, document, or historical research. Most university libraries offer tours and tutorials (some online) about the opportunities for doing research in their facility that can be quite useful. Taking the time to consult with a reference librarian can provide insights, as they are experts at accessing information. If your research is internet- or visual-based, you might want to begin with some of the online resources discussed in Chapter 8.

Once you are familiar with your library and internet resources, you will be able to choose the method that works for your topic. There is a lot of social science writing that may or may not be germane to your topic and the argument you are constructing in your paper. In the example (Box 10.5) below, Warren had to identify appropriate topics or search terms for her review of the literature—demographics on marital patterns, age-discrepancy in marital relationships, gender inequities in marriage, media images and cultural norms regarding age and relationships, stigma, neutralization techniques, and relevant clinical practices. Warren read and evaluated many more articles than she eventually included, and a number of which she did not include at all. In reviewing the literature on a topic, you are doing just that—reviewing a wide body of literature to familiarize yourself with the various debates, key theories, and broader trends that your colleagues have explored. From this review, you select the articles and books that best fit your data and the analytic theme you are developing.

You need to demonstrate an awareness of the key theories and debates as you write the literature section of your paper, so it is important to include work that is central to your analysis. For example, it is unlikely that a paper dealing with social stigma would ever be accepted by a journal (or your instructor, perhaps) without referring to the work of Erving Goffman, arguably the most significant sociologist to write on the topic. A paper that did not refer to Goffman's writings would be seen as uninformed. So, as you read, if a specific name or study comes up in a number of the articles you are reading—you will need to familiarize yourself with that author or research. In many cases, the reference section of a relevant article will lead you to other pertinent books and articles.

As you read all the articles your search identifies, you should also assess the quality of the work. How did they design their study? What methods did they use? Were the methods appropriate (and ethical)? How do their results relate to your findings? Many authors conclude their articles with a discussion of how their work could be improved or extended, and these comments can be helpful to you in evaluating the work. Moreover, you will want to refer to current work rather than older work (unless it is a core study or theorist such as Erving Goffman). Work done within the previous ten years is usually considered timely. Once you have identified, read, and evaluated the relevant literature, it is time to begin to organize and synthesize it.

The review of the literature should be ordered analytically (see Chapter 9) rather than author by author. A listing such as "Jones says....; then Smith found....; later Johnson elaborated" is not only boring to read, but it does not give the reader any clues as to why the materials are even being presented and what the relevance of the various research publications are to the current project. The literature review should discuss any debates or controversies related to the topic, and any limitations of previous research that the author's project will be addressing. The literature review section then concludes with a strong restatement of the central research questions (or goals) of the current project. Box 10.5 presents the literature for Warren's "Older Women, Younger Men" paper. A reverse outline of this literature review—a handy device for assessing the ordering of written work—indicates that she arranges the substantive literature in the following way:

1. Age discrepancy in relationships
   a. contemporary demographic patterns of marriage, divorce, and age discrepancy.
   b. historical inequality between the genders in marriage, in general and in relation to age-discrepant marriage.
   c. contemporary media discussions of older women and younger men.
   d. attitude studies demonstrating unfavorable views of age-discrepant relationships, especially those involving older women and younger men.

Warren then uses the attitude studies to make the transition into the conceptual frame:

2. Stigma
   e. stigma and its impact on the self (using Goffman, 1961).
   f. techniques of neutralization (citing the sociological literature on this topic) used to counteract the stigma of age discrepancy and its impact on the self.
   g. the relationship of the general cultural themes of stigma to clinical practice.

Note that Warren concludes with the issue of clinical practice that she had previously introduced in the last paragraph of her literature review. Warren did this not only because she published the paper in a clinical

Box 10.5
LITERATURE REVIEW SECTION FROM "OLDER WOMEN, YOUNGER MEN: SELF AND STIGMA IN AGE-DISCREPANT RELATIONSHIPS"

Studies of contemporary demographic patterns indicate that marital age discrepancy is related to gender, divorce, remarriage, and lifespan. A study of marriage in England and Wales showed that the tendency to marry a younger person peaks for both sexes at 30 to 34 years old, and falls to its lowest point at 50 to 54. Unmarried people in their 50s are more likely to marry someone younger (Bytheway 1981), although there are many more unmarried women than men at this age and upward. Remarriages are more likely than first marriages to involve an age discrepancy (Veevers 1984); women who were married previously are more likely to marry younger men who are marrying for the first time, and vice versa (Presser 1975).

Age-discrepant intimate relationships are part of Western history, and have had different historical meanings over time (Banner 1992). What has remained fairly constant is the institutionalized power relation between the genders which fosters resource inequalities between men and women, and which, at its worst, frames women as men's resources. Throughout Western history, women have been traded in marriage by fathers and brothers, to cement aristocratic alliances, to end wars, or settle disputes (Banner 1992). A woman's dowry or bride-price, lineage, virginity, appearance, and age were all bargaining chips in the marriage market; older women (even widows) were sometimes "married off" to younger men who could not obtain better bargains.

The development in the eighteenth century of notions of choice in marriage based on romantic love (an idea that was superimposed on, rather than a replacement for, earlier patterns), precipitated some changes in older women's romantic options. Since romantic love was, and is, viewed as the property of youth, older women were seen as even more undesirable than when they only had to bring a higher bride-price. With the twentieth century development of competitive dating, a process which located all the power of choice normatively with men rather than women, older women faced an interesting situation. Rhetorically, they were free to love a man of any age. Realistically, women's choices were made within a structural context that virtually mandated men's choice of a younger woman.

Contemporary media discussions of older women and younger men insist that romance and marriage between older women and younger men are on the increase, both statistically and normatively (Houston 1989). These discussions focus neither on psychodynamic nor cultural areas of possible difficulty, but, rather, seek to justify and celebrate these relationships. A letter to Dear Abby, and Dear Abby's response, exemplify media treatments:

> Q: I am a 43-year-old woman, divorced, no children, have an excellent job, and am secure in my position. Fourteen months ago, a bright 31-year-old man came to work here in another department. The last thing I had in mind

Box 10.5 *continued*

was a serious relationship with this kid, but you guessed it. It happened. I fell in love with him. He didn't pursue me. I invited him out first. We discovered we had so much in common we couldn't wait to see each other again. We're still "in the closet" about our relationship, but we can't keep it under wraps much longer....I'm embarrassed—almost ashamed—and terribly concerned about what people will think about "us." He's more in charge and mature about this than I am....Am I crazy? Can this work? Meanwhile we are sneaking about like a couple of thieves. Help me!...

A: Quit sneaking around and don't worry about what people will think. Can it work? Yes, if you both want it. Please read the new book *Loving a Younger Man* by Victoria Houston....It's written by a woman who once walked in your shoes. She resolutely reaffirms my advice: "Forget the numbers, and follow your heart." (*Los Angeles Times* Nov. 7, 1987, p. 3)

Although statistics on changes in rates of younger women/older men marriage over time are not easily obtainable (at least in published form), there is no doubt that the mass media have publicized the idea of increasing, and increasingly legitimate, intimacy between older women and younger men. And it is also possible that the increasing ability of women to earn high salaries and develop their own resources enable some women to operate in the dating and marriage market much as men once did. However, while cultural and normative changes may indeed be occurring, intimate relationships between older women and younger men remain stigmatized.

In attitude studies (Derenski and Landsburg 1981; Cowen 1984; Hartnett, Rosen, and Shumate 1981) both adults and adolescents viewed age-discrepant relationships unfavorably, especially where the discrepancy was large, and saw the older woman/younger man type as more suspect and less promising than the older man/younger woman type. There were almost no gender or age differences between male and female respondents in their stigmatization of age-discrepant relationships.

Much has been written, following Goffman (1961), on stigma and its impact on the self. Goffman (1961) defines stigma as an elusive intersection of culturally disvalued attributes and identities with particular audiences and with the generalized other. He identifies three types of stigma: moral stigma, based on engagement in disapproved behaviors; "tribal" stigma, or racial difference; and physical stigma, based on anomalies of the physical self. The knowledge that one is stigmatized leads to an attempt to change the self in the culturally desirable direction, or to techniques that neutralize the stigma.

Techniques of neutralization are those ways in which the stigmatized seek to bridge, verbally, the gap between cultural expectations and their violation. While accounts are features of everyday disjunctures of conduct (Mills 1959; Lyman and Scott 1970), techniques of neutralization are directed toward the justification of stigmatizing behaviors or statuses such as juvenile delinquency

continued

> **Box 10.5 *continued***
>
> (Sykes and Matza 1959) or mental patienthood (Goffman 1961; Warren and Messinger 1988).
>
> A theory of stigma in age-discrepant relationships can illuminate the clinical interpretation of those relationships. Problems that are brought to marriage counselors not only have psychodynamic elements (Singer-Magdoff 1988) but also reflect general themes in the culture. These themes are neutralized during the idealizing phase of the marriage; once marital trouble is experienced and defined, they emerge as clinical problems. I propose that people in age-discrepant marriages neutralize stigma through the denial and refocusing techniques described below, protecting their relationship from the implications of stigma. By contrast, I expect that people who seek counseling for what they perceive as marital trouble redefine cultural stigma as legitimate, and seek to change themselves.
>
> (Warren 1996, 63–65)

sociology journal, but also because it is at the point of separation that one or both members of the couples stop seeking to neutralize the stigma and reveal the ways in which they share it. In her final two sentences, Warren offers the reader an idea of what she proposes to demonstrate in the pages that follow:

> I propose that people in age-discrepant marriages neutralize stigma through the denial and refocusing techniques described below, protecting their relationship from the implications of stigma. By contrast, I expect that people who seek counseling for what they perceive as marital trouble redefine cultural stigma as legitimate, and seek to change themselves. (Warren 1996, 65)

Methods

The first thing to be said about the methods section is that it should be called "METHODS"; don't use "METHODOLOGY," since this word means the study of methods. Often, methods is the first section written, and it should give a complete accounting of the research process—what was done and how and why. The methods section of a qualitative research paper typically discusses the research design or research questions; the method(s) used, the setting, population, documents, or images; data collection, data analysis, and any special problems or issues raised by the methods. Some researchers add a paragraph or two on ethical dilemmas and challenges raised in doing the study in this section.

In general, the methods section should contain enough detailed information for a reader to be able to evaluate the analysis and conclusions. For example, stating that the data consisted of twenty intensive interviews is not enough. Rather, a reader will need to know if you interviewed respondents once in a casual setting or multiple times over the course of the research. Additionally, readers want to know how the data were recorded—did you write your fieldnotes in the field or immediately after, or was there some delay? Were your interviews audio or video recorded and thoroughly transcribed? In order to evaluate and understand the data you will be presenting in your analysis, the reader needs to have a pretty detailed idea about how your research has been accomplished.

In Karner's (1995) article on "Medicalizing Masculinities: Post Traumatic Stress Disorder in Vietnam Veterans" she described the following: setting, interview sample, images or documents and how they were selected; data collection procedures, including challenges that had to be overcome and decisions that had to be made; and how the analysis was accomplished:

> Using the techniques of naturalistic inquiry—specifically participant observation and intensive interviewing of veterans on a Vietnam unit of a VA Medical Center in a large midwestern city—I was able to find men steeped in a therapeutic process of retelling. Tracing their childhood recollections of family, religion, and community through basic training, their military experience in Vietnam, and the years that followed, I analyzed the veterans' stories with attention to how their strategies may have shifted and evolved over the years. Since the social context of meaning was an integral aspect of the study, it was important to find a single consistent environment within which to interact with the veterans. An initial intensive participant observation phase served as interpretive backdrop for the rest of the study by allowing me to familiarize myself with the therapeutic milieu. Subsequently, I continued my unit participation and observation throughout my entire time in the field, although my primary focus shifted toward the interviews.
>
> After the initial immersion process, I began lengthy intensive interviews with the newly admitted veterans. These interviews provided a conceptual interplay with the observations of the social context. The webs of significance from the observations and interviews were approached from several different viewpoints. The veteran interviews allowed me to make comparisons between the men as well as to consider the discourse of the environment. At the end of my time in the field, I also interviewed staff members for approximately an hour each, which illuminated the differences between the intention and the reception of program goals.

Veteran autobiographies afforded representational documents written early in treatment permitting another life story for contrast to the narratives expressed publicly on the unit and privately in the interviews. Thus I sought interpretations of the process of reconstructing Vietnam in the setting as well as by the individual.

The data that form the basis of this study are drawn from these intensive interviews (see Karner 1994). In the Midwest during the spring of 1991, one half of the inpatient population—15 veterans—were interviewed one to four times each, and were observed in a variety of hospital settings. In addition, I interviewed hospital staff, sat in on staff meetings, and had access to autobiographies written by the veterans as they entered the hospital. During the study, all the patients were Vietnam veterans and one was also a Gulf War veteran. All but one of the men interviewed were white, one was African American. The veterans ranged in age from 38 to 47 years and all were from the midwestern states. (Karner 1995, 33–34)

Following this overview, Karner provides a table of her interview sample demographics and a narrative description of the site of her research, the PTSD unit of a Veteran's Administration hospital. A reader is able to judge the variety of data sources Karner was able to access (participant observation, interviews with veterans, veteran autobiographies, interviews with staff members), why this site was selected (unique opportunity to study therapeutic retelling in a gendered—all male—setting) and how the interviewees were chosen (new admissions), who was interviewed (all staff members and half the inpatient population), and the time frame of the data collection (spring 1991). In referencing her previous work (Karner 1994), she lets the reader know that this paper is part of a larger project where the research design was more thoroughly described and discussed.

The methods section of a qualitative paper often does not address generalizability or reliability because the methods are not designed to be generalized to larger populations or replicated by other researchers. Qualitative researchers are, however, concerned with the validity of the data and analysis—whether or not the text provides answers for questions such as these: How do you know what you say you know? What support can you offer for your analysis? As we saw in Chapter 9, some qualitative researchers use external audits or "member tests" to assess the validity of their analyses, or comments from other researchers. At the point of writing, the author has to decide how much of the information they have compiled about validity they will include in the methods section.

Although the principles we have outlined suggest a fairly lengthy methods section, the extensiveness of methodological discussion varies by the journal editor's policies and the type of article. *Clinical Sociology Review* prefers relatively short methodological discussion, so that in our "Dangerous Listener" article, the methods section was very brief:

> Our data are two sets of intensive interviews, one with female mental patients-to-expatients in the 1950s in California (see Warren 1987), and one with Vietnam veterans on a trauma ward at a Veterans Administration hospital (see Karner 1994). In the first study, referred to as the "Bay Area" study, seventeen women were interviewed at intervals ranging from one week to three months for a period of thirty-six months between 1958 and 1961 (see Sampson, Messinger, and Towne 1964). In the second, in the Midwest in the 1990s, fifteen men were interviewed one to four times each, and were observed in a variety of hospital settings by Karner. In addition, Karner interviewed hospital staff, and had access to autobiographies written by the veterans as they entered the hospital. (Karner and Warren 1995, 81)

Methodological articles such as "The Dangerous Listener" often emerge from doing a series of substantive studies and thinking about methodological issues that are common to, or differ among, these studies. Methodological articles may be written about aspects of interview, ethnographic, or other qualitative research. In "The Social Relations of Intensive Interviewing" Harkess and Warren (1993) wrote about interviews as social encounters, and the variations that occur depending upon the kind of prior association between interviewer and respondent, from stranger to intimate. In another methodological article, "Writing the Other, Inscribing the Self," several student coauthors and Warren (2000) used fieldnotes from a variety of settings, including a gay bar, a Hispanic health care association, and a group home for delinquent boys, to explore ethnographic writing. They analyzed the ways in which fieldnotes are designed to communicate the interactions and meanings of the Other in the setting, and the ways in which they also communicate (if read by another) aspects of the self of the writer. Because the focus of such papers as "The Dangerous Listener," "The Social Relations of Intensive Interviews," and "Writing the Other" is methodological, the formal methods section is often abbreviated.

ANALYSIS, REPRESENTATION, AND ILLUSTRATION

The analysis is the conceptual heart of the paper. This section should not, however, be given a first level subheading such as "Analysis" or, as in quantitative research, "Findings" and "Results." Your analysis section subhead may reiterate part of the title of the paper: for example, "The Dangerous Listener." In this—the longest section of the paper—the writer develops the main theme and subthemes.

In writing qualitative sociology well, the author is presented with a number of decisions that must be made about how to best present the data. The actual details and complexities of representing qualitative research are "handled only upon putting ideas into words on paper" (Emerson 2001, 311). The decisions we make about how to represent our data in a paper or book include representation—voice and genre—and illustration—how to use quotes or visual material as illustrations of analytic points made. In her classic text on writing strategies in sociology, Laurel Richardson (1990) demonstrates how different modes of writing (research paper, magazine article, academic book, popular book) highlight various aspects, constructing different analyses of the topic at hand.

Interpretive or sense-making decisions are contemplated by the author throughout the research process. Interpretation guides the overarching framework for organizing the text. Whatever understanding of the data that the researcher arrives at—how the "puzzle pieces are put together"—constitutes the frame of interpretation within which other decisions about how to "write the data" will be made. What aspects are considered important to the story or understanding and will be included? Which elements will not be told? Maines (1998, 388) reminds us that writing is also "a way of not knowing" the components that remain absent from our interpretation. The goal of writing qualitative research well, from our perspective, is to provide a compelling interpretation of the data that provides a faithful representation of the lives of those studied. Representation of the data (see Chapter 1) is a key component of "telling the story." Whose voice or narrative will be at the center of your account?

> Deciding how to present voices and lives is a continuous problem for qualitative writers. Because we use the voices and experiences of the people we study, both for their own sake and as evidence of our credibility, we are constantly making writerly decisions about who gets to say what and how often in the text, and who the narrator talks about, how and how often. (Richardson 1990, 39)

How will you represent the individuals that you've studied? Will you tell the research story through your experience? These questions about representations have been asked and answered in various ways, for the past three decades in sociology (see, for example, Gusfield 1976; Clifford and Marcus 1986; Van Maanen 1988; Richardson 1990; Rhoads 2003; Richardson 2007). Among the options are analytic-descriptions, narrative unfolding, and sociobiography.

The most traditional approach to writing qualitative research is analytic description, used in all the Karner, Warren, and Karner and Warren studies we refer to in this text, and the one most often used to teach qualitative methods writing. With this approach, the main theme and its subthemes are developed from ethnographic, interview, visual, or documentary data; these same data are then used, reflexively, to illustrate the analysis descriptively. One of two rhetorical devices is used in the analytic-descriptive approach to representing the data: the typology or the continuum. A typology classifies the data into categories and offers a discussion of each. There are examples of typologies throughout this book, including the discussion of references under "Endnotes and References," above. A continuum, on the other hand, arrays the data along some kind of imaginary line, for example Goffman's (1961) discussion of the "moral career of the mental patient" as prepatient, patient, and expatient.

In his classic study *Making Grey Gold*, Diamond (1992) employed the strategy of narrative unfolding, as did Mitchell (2002) in his work *Dancing at Armageddon*. They locate themselves at the center of the narrative and invite the reader to share their experience by describing their understandings and interactions in the field, and by telling a story that has a beginning, middle, and end. Geertz (1988, 78) calls this first-person, biographical form of writing "I-witnessing." I-witnessing highlights the "ethnographer's inner life and social experiences in the field as a personal story" (Emerson 2001, 307). In another variation of I-witnessing, Krieger (1991) borrows the term "quest form" from Heilbrun's *Writing a Woman's Life*. In the quest form, writers "chronicle a problem of inquiry using their personal dilemmas and research experiences as the central interest of their account" (Krieger 1991, 51). Much like with autoethnography (see, for example, Ellis 2007, discussed in Chapter 1), the writer is on a quest to understand some aspect of his or her own biography by studying others with similar experiences.

Another approach to representation is to place the individuals studied at the center of the account. In *Writing Strategies*, one of the most comprehensive discussions of variations in scholarly writing of qualitative data to date, Laurel Richardson (1990) discusses two options for this: individual sociobiographies or the collective story. In individual sociobiographies, each person's story is presented and analyzed separately, a format generally associated more with literature than sociology, but used by some qualitative sociologists (Richardson 1990, 2007). The collective story, which seeks to understand the individual's experiences within a coherent social context, is more commonly used in sociology. The collective story uses an analytical chronology—that is, the common elements to each individual's story are used to frame the collaborative, joint accounting. The weaving of individual voices together to tell a collective story can be a powerful mode of representation (see for example Duneier 2000; Venkatesh 2008).

Whatever genre or style of analysis you use, you will have to decide the number and length of quotes to use illustratively from your fieldnotes, interviews, or documents—and what images, if you have them. There are variations of opinion on what constitutes enough of this illustrative material.

Esterberg (2002, 213) says there are "no magic numbers" and that support should meet the "believability" test. That is, you should include enough examples for your analysis to be believable, but not so much that your reader will be bored. On the other hand, Berg (2004, 284) offers a rule of three as a guide and states that every assertion in the analysis should be backed up by a minimum of three examples.

There are also different ways of presenting your illustrative material. Emerson et al. (1995, 179–80) suggest two strategies for quoting: excerpt and integrative. Using an excerpt strategy, quotes from fieldnotes, interviews or documents or selected visual images are presented as indented quotations and set off from other text. With an integrative strategy, briefer sections of data are inserted within the surrounding text and identified with quotation marks. Often, both approaches are used within a single paper and it is up to the writer to decide how to best make use of their data as evidence.

Conclusion

The conclusion or discussion—or both—is the final narrative section of a qualitative research paper, and its length can vary from a few paragraphs to a few pages. In this section, it is important to return to the major conceptual, theoretical, or applied issues discussed at the beginning of the paper and restate what has been learned or can be concluded. The conclusion should include an overview of any new insights the research has offered and how it contributes to (or advances) sociological knowledge. Any limitations of the current research should be addressed, as well as suggestions for future research (if relevant). If there are any practice or policy implications that can be derived from the research, they should be specified in this section as well, especially in applied work.

For our example of a conclusion (see Box 10.6), we return to Warren's 1996 paper. Notice how she returns to the themes discussed in the introduction (see Box 10.5): the mother/son psychodynamics of these age-discrepant relationships; the embodiment of social stigma, with the wife worrying about her appearance and whether she looks like or is acting like her husband's mother; the husband privately lamenting the loss of children and the loss of his own age cohort. Warren notes that these themes tend to be verbalized only after separation or divorce, because during the marriage the focus is on techniques of neutralization that attempt to deny the stigma and shore up the sense of belonging together. As Warren's example illustrates, there should be some symmetry between the introduction and conclusions—as one frames the upcoming discussion and the other concludes it.

Box 10.6

CONCLUSION SECTION FROM *"OLDER WOMEN, YOUNGER MEN: SELF AND STIGMA IN AGE-DISCREPANT RELATIONSHIPS"*

The uneven psychodynamic, cultural, structural, and gendered set of relations between older men and younger women arises from the context of contemporary Western marriage, and from stigma—the public and private distrust of intimacy between older women and younger men. When older women and younger men are embarking on what they perceive as viable marriages, they protect the sense of self and other in the relationship by neutralization techniques. When older women and younger men enter the clinical setting, or contemplate divorce, the stigma of age discrepancy may be affirmed rather than denied or neutralized.

The central feature of stigma for the women in these marriages is the visual: the appearance of an older woman with a younger man. For the men, it is the cohort: exile from one's proper age group and place in history. But the lurking fear, for both, is the relation between child and parent: the playing out in the marriage of a mother and a son, and the absence of a mutual child within the marriage.

What, given a theory of stigma, can clinicians expect from older women and younger men? Once couples decide that they are experiencing troubles and seek help, the mutual and individual neutralization of stigma may give way to a redefinition of stigma as legitimate rather than illegitimate. The husband may reconnect with cultural themes related to fathering children, and to the definition of involvement with older women as related to being mothered. He may take up the woman's theme of visual differentiation, and begin to find his wife's appearance problematic. He will reconnect with his cohort.

The wife may, in turn, take up the theme of the cohort self, re-finding her own place in an age cohort with its more sedate musical expression. She will approach the youth-reviving techniques of our culture with renewed tenacity, blaming her own aging for the breakdown of the marriage. Perhaps she will come to define herself as having sought to mother this younger man. The psychodynamic principles of suppression, repression, and the Oedipal-parental origins of current problems will be pressed into service by spouses as well as clinicians to replace techniques of neutralization.

This is the prediction of stigma theory to a clinical setting; it is borne out by our interview with Keith, the divorced man, and contact with him and his ex-wife throughout their marriage and divorce. His post-divorce comments indicate a marital history of neutralization followed by a separation-linked reinterpretation:

> She was seeking a bearded entity to father more children. I didn't know that was her agenda, so I was kind of agenda-ized by her without my knowing it clearly....The negative thing for me was the rush to have children....Another

continued

Box 10.6 *continued*

negative thing was just the complications inherent, she was married twice before, she had a stepdaughter, a son, and a daughter, none of which I particularly wanted, then she had two daughters from the second marriage that I was very close to....

I: Was this sort of an attraction for you that she had some of the things you didn't have?

K: Oh yes. In part some of the difficulty now is that since we've been separated I'm sort of growing up all over again....I think consciously and to a larger extent unconsciously, I had an instant family to walk into. I didn't have to make those decisions. I had to catch up real quickly. It was illusory in some ways, but I kind of caught up real quickly SES wise....I was an overnight success....But it was in a pretty illusionary sense.

Thus, in the waning or aftermath of an age-discrepant marriage, the real becomes illusory, and the illusory real. What seemed, during the days of idealization, to be the cultural illusion of stigma now becomes the suppressed reality. What seemed to be the reality of a good relationship now becomes illusory. This process, of course, occurs in the wake of any relational breakdown. It is the content, not the structure of the redefinitions, which will vary with age discrepancy and other marital patterns. And it is this content that is shaped by the interaction of psychodynamic with the cultural images of ideal marriages, and of stigmatized ones.

(Warren 1996, 83–85)

Endnotes and References

The first endnote (or perhaps footnote, depending upon what the journal or book publisher requires) is often used to thank organizations and people who were helpful in carrying out the research presented in the paper. If the research is published in a book format, the acknowledgements generally go in a separate section at the beginning of the book (as you will note in this text), before the preface. The remaining endnotes consist of comments, asides, or addenda to the main points made in the text. Scholarly articles or books almost always have footnotes or endnotes, although a few do not (Kneeland and Warren 2008).

References in qualitative sociology publications are generally of three types, the first two of which correspond to the sections of the review of the literature discussed above: (1) substantive references dealing with the topic of the article; (2) theoretical, conceptual, or applied references situating the article in a particular qualitative sociology tradition; and (3) methodological references linking the study to others in the same tradition. In general, all works that are quoted, paraphrased, or referred to should be properly cited and included in the reference section. Most universities and colleges have a statement of academic honesty that outlines what practices constitute plagiarism and should be avoided. We recommend that you get a copy of your school's statement and familiarize yourself with the issues.

Editing and Rewriting

After completing a first draft of your text, it is time to begin editing. Editing and rewriting, as we have mentioned before, are fundamental to writing well. In the process of writing, you are crafting communication—attempting to share your insights and perspective in a way that others will understand. As you reread what you have written, ask yourself: Is the writing clear and does it make sense? Does your argument seem logical? Does each sentence follow logically and easily from the sentence before and lead naturally to the sentence that follows? Then read through each sentence again, and delete any nonessential words. Each word and sentence that remains in your final version should be necessary to communicate your ideas. Continue to reread, refine, and reflect. Remember, writing well takes time, patience, perseverance, and practice.

For classroom purposes, your instructor may require only one, finished draft of a paper, or perhaps two drafts. But if you, as an undergraduate or graduate student, want to publish your work, you will generally have to write one, two, three, or even more versions. Qualitative researchers commonly circulate their work to colleagues prior to publication submission; this is a good way to get informal feedback and editing assistance. The paper you submit to a journal should be polished, free of typographical or other errors, and already have been read and edited by at least two or three other people working in the fields. Polishing is especially important if you have to pay an up-front submission fee that many journals now charge to offset publishing and reviewing costs. If you are serious about publication, your instructor will often be willing to help you even after the semester is over—Karner and Warren have, over the years, both helped students to publish class materials successfully. A successful publication is, of course, more likely if you are a graduate student, but it is certainly possible for undergraduates to, at least, present a finished paper at a regional profession meeting such as the Central States Communication Association, the Pacific Sociological Association, the Mid-South Educational Research Association, or the Central States Anthropology Association.

Throughout this arduous editing and rewriting process it is important not to lose your desire (Denzin 1994). Denzin describes desire as the interest that keeps both the writer *writing* and the reader *reading*. Though not often discussed in the context of academic writing, the pleasure of the text (to borrow Barthes's phrase) is a key aspect of whether research gets finished (as many papers, theses, and dissertations do not) and whether the writing is read or gathers dust on library shelves. Part of writing qualitative research well is crafting an engaging, compelling account that is vital as well as carefully edited and rewritten. Vital texts engage readers intellectually; they are not boring to write, or to read.

Whether the article you write is substantive or methodological, or you venture to write a monograph or book, the important thing is to write well, and to write well for your instructor or other audience. As we indicated at the beginning of this chapter, the organization, grammar, spelling, and even appearance of your paper are important. Equally important is your analytic description, using both your analysis of the data and, illustratively, parts of the data themselves. This analytic description should be at least somewhat original and novel, not just reflecting analyses that have been published elsewhere. And it should be set within both a thorough and up-to-date substantive literature review, and a relevant social constructionist conceptual framework. Then you will have a good, publishable work of qualitative research—and, always remember, an ethical one. As we mentioned at the beginning of this chapter, written and published qualitative work also has ethical and political implications for a variety of individuals and groups—those who are written about as well as those who do the reading.

In writing your paper, you have reached the end of your first stage in the discovery of qualitative methods. For some of you, this will be your last as well as your first step. For others, it will be the beginning of something you love and want to do for the rest of your life. Either way, we wish you luck in your future work, and hope you have enjoyed the discoveries you have made about yourself and others in doing qualitative research.

Suggestions for Further Reading

Becker, Howard S. 1986. *Writing for Social Scientists*. Chicago: University of Chicago Press.

Rhoads, Richard A. 2003. "Traversing the Great Divide: Writing the Self into Qualitative Research and Narrative." In *Studies in Symbolic Interaction*, vol. 26, ed. N. K. Denzin, 235–259. Oxford: JAI Press.

Richardson, Laurel. 1990. *Writing Strategies: Reaching Diverse Audiences*. Newbury Park, CA: Sage.

Van Maanen, John. 1988. *Tales of the Field: On Writing Ethnography*. Chicago: University of Chicago Press.

References

Abell, Jackie, Abigail Locke, Susan Condor, Stephen Gibson, and Clifford Stevenson. 2006. "Trying Similarity, Doing Difference: The Role of Interviewer Disclosure in Interview Talk with Young People." *Qualitative Research* 6 (2): 221–244.

Adams, Jane, and D. Gordon. 2006. "Confederate Lane: Class, Race, and Ethnicity in the Mississippi Delta." *American Ethnologist* 33(2): 288–309.

Adams, Laura L. 1999. "The Mascot Researcher: Identity, Power and Knowledge in Fieldwork." *Journal of Contemporary Ethnography* 28: 331–363.

Adler, Patricia A. 1985. *Wheeling and Dealing: An Ethnography of an Upper-Level Drug Dealing and Smuggling Community.* New York: Columbia University Press.

Adler, Patricia A., and Peter Adler. 1987. *Membership Roles in Field Research.* Newbury Park, CA: Sage Publications.

——. 2002. "The Reluctant Respondent." In *Handbook of Research Interviewing: Context and Method,* ed. Jaber F. Gubrium and James A. Holstein, 515–535. Thousand Oaks, CA: Sage Publications.

Agustin, Laura Maria. 2007. "Fast Money in the Margins": Migrants in the Sex Industry. In *Livelihoods at the Margins: Surviving the Cities,* ed. James Staples, 145–162. Walnut Creek, CA: Left Coast Press.

Altheide, David L., and John M. Johnson. 1994. "Criteria for Assessing Interpretive Validity in Qualitative Research." In *Handbook of Qualitative Research,* ed. Norman K. Denzin and Yvonna S. Lincoln, 485–99. Thousand Oaks, CA: Sage Publications.

Ammerman, Nancy T. 1987. *Bible Believers: Fundamentalists in the Modern World*. Rutgers, NJ: Rutgers University Press.

Anderson, Elijah. 1990. *Streetwise: Race, Class and Change in an Urban Community*. Chicago: University of Chicago Press.

——. 1999. *Code of the Street*. New York: W. W. Norton.

——. 2004. "Urban Ethnography." In *Workshop on the Scientific Foundations of Qualitative Research*, ed. Charles C. Ragin, Joane Nagel, and Patricia White, 33–37. Arlington, VA: National Science Foundation.

Angrosino, Michael V. 2007. *Naturalistic Observation*. Walnut Creek, CA: Left Coast Press.

Arendell, Terry. 1997. "Reflections on the Researcher-Researched Relationship: A Woman Interviewing Men." *Qualitative Sociology* 20: 341–368.

Arksey, Hilary, and Peter Knight. 1999. *Interviewing for Social Scientists: An Introductory Resource With Examples*. Thousand Oaks, CA: Sage Publications.

Armstrong, David. 1986. "The Invention of Infant Mortality." *Sociology of Health and Illness* 8: 211–232.

——. 1993. "Public Health Spaces and the Fabrication of Identity." *Sociology* 27: 393–410.

——. 2002. *A New History of Identity: A Sociology of Medical Knowledge*. Basingstoke, UK: Palgrave.

——. 2006. "Embodiment and Ethics: Constructing Medicine's Two Bodies." *Sociology of Health & Illness* 28 (6): 866–881.

Atkinson, Paul, and Sara Delamont. 2005. "Analytic Perspectives." In *The SAGE Handbook of Qualitative Research*, ed. Norman K. Denzin and Yvonna S. Lincoln, 821–840. Thousand Oaks, CA: SAGE Publications.

Atkinson, Robert. 2002. "The Life Story Interview." In *Handbook of Research Interviewing: Context and Method*, ed. Jaber F. Gubrium and James A. Holstein, 121–140. Thousand Oaks, CA: Sage Publications.

Bailey, Carol. 1995. *A Guide to Field Research*. Thousand Oaks, CA: Pine Forge Press.

Ball, Michael. 2005. "Working with Images in Daily Life and Police Practice." *Qualitative Research* 5(4): 499–521.

Banks, Marcus. 2001. *Visual Methods in Social Research*. London: Sage Publications.

——. 2008. *Using Visual Data in Qualitative Research*. London: Sage Publications.

Barber, Bernard. 1976. "The Ethics of Experimentation With Human Subjects." *Scientific American* 243(2): 25–31.

Barnes, Vivienne, Deanne Lynn Clouder, Jackie Pritchard, Christina Hughes, and Judy Purkis. 2003. "Deconstructing Dissemination: Dissemination as Qualitative Research." *Qualitative Research* 3(2): 147–164.

Bateson, Gregory, and Margaret Mead. 1942. *Balinese Character: A Photographic Analysis*. New York: New York Academy of Sciences.

Becker, Howard S. 1986. *Writing for Social Scientists*. Chicago: University of Chicago Press.

——. 1995. "Visual Sociology, Documentary Photography, and Photojournalism: It's (Almost) All a Matter of Context." *Visual Sociology* 10 (1–2): 5–14.

——. 1998. *Tricks of the Trade: How to Think About Your Research While You're Doing It.* Chicago: University of Chicago Press.

——. 2002. "Studying the New Media." *Qualitative Sociology* 25 (Fall): 337–343.

Becker, Howard S., and Robert R. Faulkner. 2008. "Studying Something You Are Part Of: The View from the Bandstand." *Ethnologie Française* XXXVIII: 15–21.

Behar, Ruth. 2003. "Ethnography and the Book That Was Lost." *Ethnography* 4 (1): 15–39.

Berg, Bruce L. 2004. *Qualitative Research Methods for the Social Sciences.* Boston: Allyn & Bacon.

Biella, Peter, Napoleon Chanon, and Gary Seaman. 1997. *Yanamamo Interactive: The Ax Fight* [CD-ROM]. New York: Harcourt Brace.

Bloor, Michael. 2001. "Techniques of Validation in Qualitative Research: A Critical Commentary." In *Contemporary Field Research*, 2nd ed., ed. Robert M. Emerson, 383–395. Prospect Heights, IL: Waveland Press.

Blumer, Herbert. 1969. *Symbolic Interaction: Perspective and Method.* Berkeley: University of California Press.

Boelen, W. A. Marianne. 1992. "Street Corner Society: Cornerville Revisited." *Journal of Contemporary Ethnography* 21: 11–51.

Bordo, Susan. 1999. *The Male Body: A New Look at Men in Public and in Private.* New York: Farrar, Straus, and Giroux.

——. 2003. *Unbearable Weight: Feminism, Western Culture, and the Body.* Berkeley: University of California Press.

Boyd, Danah M. 2002. "Faceted Id/entity: Managing Representation in a Digital World." Masters thesis, School of Architecture and Planning, Massachusetts Institute of Technology.

Brajuha, Mario, and Lyle Hallowell. 1986. "Legal Intrusions and the Politics of Fieldwork." *Urban Life* 14: 454–478.

Briggs, Charles L. 2002. "Interviewing, Power/Knowledge, and Social Inequality." In *Handbook of Interview Research*, ed. Jaber F. Gubrium and James A. Holstein, 911–922. Thousand Oaks, CA: Sage Publications.

Browne, Joy. 1976. "Fieldwork for Fun and Profit." In *The Research Experience*, ed. M. P. Gordon, 77–84. Itasca, IL: F. E. Peacock.

Brumberg, Joan J. 1997. *The Body Project: An Intimate History of American Girls.* New York: Random House.

Bryant, Clifton. 1999. "Gratuitous Sex in Field Research: 'Carnal Lagniappe,' or 'Inappropriate Behavior.'" *Deviant Behavior* 20 (4): 325–329.

Bulmer, Martin. 1984. *The Chicago School of Sociology: Institutionalization, Diversity, and the Rise of Sociological Research.* Chicago: University of Chicago Press.

Burawoy, Michael. 1991. *Ethnography Unbound: Power and Resistance in the Modern Metropolis.* Berkeley and Los Angeles: University of California Press.

Carson, Barbara A. 2001. "Creating Grassroots Change Through Service Learning." In *Applying Sociology: Making a Better World*, ed. William Du Bois and R. Dean Wright, 193–200. Needham Heights, MA: Allyn & Bacon.

Cavan, Sherri. 1966. *Liquor License: An Ethnography of Bar Behavior*. Chicago: Aldine.

Chalfen, Richard. 1974. "Akeret's Photoanalysis." *Studies in the Anthropology of Visual Communication* 1 (1): 57–60.

Chalfen, Richard, and Michael Rich. 2007. "Combining the Applied, the Visual and the Medical: Patients Teaching Physicians with Visual Narratives." In *Visual Interventions: Applied Visual Anthropology*, ed. Sarah Pink, 53–70. New York & Oxford: Berghahn Books.

Clifford, James. 1986. "On Ethnography Allegory." In *Writing Culture: The Poetics and Politics of Ethnography*, ed. James Clifford and George E. Marcus, 98–121. Berkeley: University of California Press.

Clifford, James, and George E. Marcus, eds. 1986. *Writing Culture: The Poetics and Politics of Ethnography*. Berkeley: University of California Press.

Clough, Patricia Ticineto. 2000. *Autoaffection: Unconscious Thought in the Age of Technology*. Minneapolis: University of Minnesota Press.

Cockcroft, Tom. 2005. "Using Oral History to Investigate Police Culture." *Qualitative Research* 5 (3): 365–384.

Cohen, Kris R. 2005. "What Does the Photoblog Want?" *Media Culture Society* 2005; 27 (6): 883–901.

Collier, John. 1967. *Visual Anthropology: Photography as a Research Method*. New York: Holt, Rinehart, & Winston.

Conticini, Alessandro. 2007. "Children on the Streets of Dhaka and Their Coping Strategies." In *Livelihoods at the Margins: Surviving the City*, ed. James Staples, 75–100. Walnut Creek, CA: Left Coast Press.

Cooley, Charles H. 1922. *Human Nature and the Social Order*. New York: Scribner.

Coontz, Stephanie. 2000. *The Way We Never Were: American Families and the Nostalgia Trap*, NY: Basic Books.

Crapanzano, Vincent. 1985. *Waiting: The Whites of South Africa*. New York: Random House.

Crowder, Jerome. 2007. "Aymara Migrants in El Alto, Bolivia: A Photographic Essay." In *Ethnic Landscapes in a Global World* (R. Hutchison and J. Krase, editors), 181–195. Oxford, UK: Elsevier Ltd.

Crowley, Jocelyn Elise. 2007. "Friend or Foe? Self-Expansion, Stigmatized Groups, and Researcher-Participant Relationship." *Journal of Contemporary Ethnography* 36 (6): 603–630.

Damico, Sandra B. 1985. "Two Worlds of a School: Differences in the Photographs of Black and White Adolescents." *The Urban Review* 17: 210–222.

Daniels, Arlene K. 1967. "The Low-Caste Stranger in Social Research." In *Ethics, Politics, and Social Research*, ed. Gideon Sjoberg, 267–296. Cambridge, MA: Schenkman.

Davies, Julia. 2007. "Display, Identity and the Everyday: Self-Presentation Through Online Image Sharing." *Discourse: Studies in the Cultural Politics of Education* 28 (4): 549–564.

De Andrade, Lelia Lomba. 2000. "Negotiating from the Inside: Constructing Racial and Ethnic Identity in Qualitative Research." *Journal of Contemporary Ethnography* 29 (3): 268–290.

Denzin, Norman K. 1989a. *Interpretive Biography.* Newbury Park, CA: Sage Publications.

——. 1989b. *The Research Act.* Englewood Cliffs, NJ: Prentice Hall.

——. 1994. "The Art and Politics of Interpretation." In *Handbook of Qualitative Research,* ed. Norman K. Denzin and Yvonna S. Lincoln, 500–515. Thousand Oaks, CA: Sage Publications.

——. 2003a. *Performance Ethnography: Critical Pedagogy and the Politics of Culture.* Thousand Oaks, CA: Sage Publications.

——. 2003b. "The Call to Performance." *Symbolic Interaction* 26 (1): 187–207.

——. 2003c. "Reading and Writing Performance." *Qualitative Research.* 3 (2): 243–268.

Denzin, Norman K., and Michael D. Giardina, eds. 2007. *Ethical Futures in Qualitative Research: Decolonizing the Politics of Knowledge.* Walnut Creek, CA: Left Coast Press.

Denzin, Norman K., and Michael D. Giardina. 2007. "Introduction: Ethical Futures in Qualitative Research." In *Ethical Futures in Qualitative Research: Decolonizing the Politics of Knowledge,* ed. Norman K. Denzin and Michael D. Giardina, 9–43. Walnut Creek, CA: Left Coast Press.

Denzin, Norman K., and Yvonna S. Lincoln. 2007. *The SAGE Handbook of Qualitative Research.* Thousand Oaks, CA: SAGE Publications.

DeSantis, Grace. 1980. "Interviewing as Social Interaction." *Qualitative Sociology* 2: 72–98.

DeVault, Marjorie L., and Liza McCoy. 2002. "Institutional Ethnography: Using Interviews to Investigate Ruling Relations." In *Handbook of Interview Research,* ed. Jaber F. Gubrium and James A. Holstein, 751–775. Thousand Oaks, CA: Sage Publications.

Diamond, Timothy. 1992. *Making Grey Gold: Narratives of Nursing Home Care.* Chicago: University of Chicago Press.

Dick, Hilary Parsons. 2006. "What to Do with 'I Don't Know': Elicitation in Ethnographic and Survey Interviewing." *Qualitative Sociology* 29 (1): 87–102.

Doucet, Andrea. 2008. "'From Her Side of the Gossamer Wall(s)': Reflexivity and Relational Knowing." *Qualitative Sociology* 31: 73–87.

Douglas, Jack D. 1985. *Creative Interviewing.* Beverly Hills, CA: Sage Publications.

Duneier, Mitchell. 1994. *Slim's Table: Race, Respectability and Masculinity.* Chicago: University of Chicago Press.

——. 1999. *Sidewalk.* New York: Farrar, Straus, and Giroux.

——. 2001. "On the Evolution of *Sidewalk.*" In *Contemporary Field Research,* 2nd ed., ed. Robert M. Emerson, 167–187. Waveland Heights, IL: Waveland Press.

Duneier, Mitchell. 1994. 2002. "What Kind of Combat Sport is Sociology?" *The American Journal of Sociology* 107 (May): 1551–1576.

Easterday, Lois, Diana Papademas, Laura Schorr, and Catherine Valentine. 1977. "The Making of the Female Researcher: Role Problems in Field Work." *Urban Life* 6: 333–348.

Ebaugh, Helen Rose Fuchs. 1977. *Out of the Cloister: A Study of Organizational Dilemmas.* Austin: University of Texas Press.

Elliott, Carl. 2000. "A New Way to Be Mad." *Atlantic Monthly* (December): 73–84.

Ellis, Carolyn. 1995a. "Emotional and Ethical Quagmires in Returning to the Field." *Journal of Contemporary Ethnography* 24: 68–98.

——. 1995b. *Final Negotiations: A Story of Love, Loss, and Chronic Illness.* Philadelphia: Temple University Press.

——. 2007. "'I Just Want to Tell MY Story': Mentoring Students about Relational Ethics in Writing about Intimate Others." In *Ethical Futures in Qualitative Research: Decolonizing the Politics of Knowledge*, ed. Norman K. Denzin and Michael D. Giardina, 209–228. Walnut Creek, CA: Left Coast Press.

Ellis, Carolyn, and Arthur P. Bochner. 1996. *Composing Ethnography: Alternative Forms of Qualitative Writing.* Walnut Creek, CA: Alta Mira Press.

——. 2000. "Autoethnography, Personal Narrative, Reflexivity: Researcher as Subject." In *Handbook of Qualitative Research*, 2nd ed., ed. Norman K. Denzin and Yvonna S. Lincoln, 733–768. Thousand Oaks, CA: Sage Publications.

Emerson, Robert M. 1989. "Tenability and Troubles: The Construction of Accommodative Relations by Psychiatric Emergency Teams." In *Perspectives on Social Problems: A Research Annual*, vol. 1., ed. Gale Miller and James A. Holstein, 215–237. Greenwich, CT: JAI Press.

——. 2001a. "Fieldwork Practice: Issues in Participant Observation." In *Contemporary Field Research*, 2nd ed., ed. Robert M. Emerson, 113–151. Prospect Heights, IL: Waveland Press.

——. 2001b. "The Face of Contemporary Ethnography." In *Contemporary Field Research*, 2nd ed., ed. Robert M. Emerson, 27–53. Prospect Heights, IL: Waveland Press.

——. 2001c. "Preface." In *Contemporary Field Research*, 2nd ed., ed. Robert M. Emerson, vii–xi. Prospect Heights, IL: Waveland Press.

——. 2001d. "Producing Ethnographies: Theory, Evidence, and Representation." In *Contemporary Field Research*, 2nd ed., ed. Robert M. Emerson, 281–316. Prospect Heights, IL: Waveland Press.

——. 2001e. "Introduction: The Development of Ethnographic Field Research." In *Contemporary Field Research*, 2nd ed., ed. Robert M. Emerson, 1–26. Prospect Heights, IL: Waveland Press.

Emerson, Robert M., Rachel I. Fretz, and Linda L. Shaw. 1995. *Writing Ethnographic Fieldnotes.* Chicago: University of Chicago Press.

Emerson, Robert M., and Melvin Pollner. 1976. "Dirty Work Designations: Their Features and Consequences in a Psychiatric Setting." *Social Problems* 23: 243–255.

——. 2001. "Constructing Participant/Observation Relations." In *Contemporary Field Research*, 2nd ed., ed. Robert M. Emerson, 239–259. Prospect Heights, IL: Waveland Press.

Erikson, Ken, and Donald Stull. 1998. *Doing Team Ethnography: Warnings and Advice*. Thousand Oaks, CA: Sage Publications.

Esterberg, Kristin. 1997. *Lesbian and Bisexual Identities: Constructing Communities, Constructing Selves*. Philadelphia: Temple University Press.

——. 2002. *Qualitative Methods in Social Research*. Boston: McGraw-Hill.

Fantasia, Rick. 1988. *Cultures of Solidarity: Consciousness, Action, and Contemporary American Workers*. Berkeley: University of California Press.

Faulkner, Susan. 2007. "Real Reality TV: Using Documentary-Style Videos to Place Real People at the Center of the Design Process." *Intel Technology Journal* 11 (Feb. 15): 1–9.

Felstead, Alan, Nick Jewson and Sally Walters. 2004. "Images, Interviews and Interpretations: Making Connections in Visual Research," Studies in Qualitative Methodology, Vol.7: 105–121. Amsterdam: Elsevier Ltd.

Fine, Gary A., 1993. "10 Lies of Ethnography: Moral Dilemmas in Fieldwork." *Journal of Contemporary Ethnography* 22: 267–294.

——. ed. 1995. *A Second Chicago School? The Development of a Postwar American Sociology*. Chicago: University of Chicago Press.

——. 1996. *Kitchens: The Culture of Restaurant Work*. Berkeley: University of California Press.

Fontana, Andrea, and Anastasia H. Prokos. 2007. *The Interview: From Formal to Postmodern*. Walnut Creek, CA: Left Coast Press.

Fontana, Andrea and James Frey. 2008, "The Interview: From Neutral Stance to Political Involvement" pps. 115–160 in *Collecting and Interpreting Qualitative Materials*, eds. Norman Denzin and Yvonna Lincoln, Thousand Oaks, CA: SAGE Publications.

Forrest, Burke. 1986. "Apprentice-Participation: Methodology and the Study of Subjective Reality." *Urban Life* 14 (January): 431–453.

Foucault, Michel. 1977. *Discipline and Punish: The Birth of the Prison*. New York: Pantheon Books.

Frankel, Mark S., and Sanyin Siang. 1999. *Ethical and Legal Aspects of Human Subjects Research on the Internet*. Washington, DC: American Association for the Advancement of Science.

Friedman, Judith. 2003. "How Visual Artifacts Preserve the Past." Paper presented to the International Visual Sociological Association meetings, Southampton, England. July.

Ganguly, Keya. 1992. "Migrant Identities: Personal Memory and the Construction of Selfhood." *Cultural Studies* 6 (1): 27–50.

Gardner, Carol Brooks. 1995. *Passing By: Gender and Public Harassment*. Berkeley: University of California Press.

Gatson, Sarah N., and Amanda Zweerink. 2004. "Ethnography Online: 'Natives' Practicing and Inscribing Community." *Qualitative Research* 4 (2): 179–200.

Geertz, Clifford. [1973] 2000. *Interpretation of Cultures.* New York: Basic Books.

——. 1976. "From the Native's Point of View: On the Nature of Anthropological Understanding." In *Meaning in Anthropology*, ed. Keith H. Basso and Henry A. Selby, 221–237. Albuquerque, NM: University of New Mexico Press.

——. [1983] 2000. *Local Knowledge.* New York: Basic Books.

——. 1988. *Works and Lives: The Anthropologist as Author.* Stanford, CA: Stanford University Press.

——. 2001. "Thick Description: Toward an Interpretive Theory of Culture." In *Contemporary Field Research*, ed. Robert M. Emerson, 55–75. Prospect Heights, IL: Waveland Press.

Godel, Margaret. 2007. "Images of Stillbirth: Memory, Mourning and Memorial." *Visual Studies* 22 (3): 253–269.

Goffman, Erving. 1959. *The Presentation of Self in Everyday Life.* Garden City, NY: Doubleday.

——. 1961. *Asylums: Essays on the Social Situation of Patients and Other Inmates.* Garden City, NY: Doubleday.

——. 1963a. *Behavior in Public Places: Notes on the Social Organization of Gatherings.* New York: Free Press of Glencoe.

——. 1963b. *Stigma: Notes on the Management of Spoiled Identity.* Englewood Cliffs, NJ.: Prentice-Hall.

——. 1967. *Interaction Ritual: Essays on Face-to-Face Behavior.* Garden City, NY: Anchor Books.

——. 1979. *Gender Advertisements.* Boston: Harvard University Press.

Gold, Steven J. 2004. "Using Photography in Studies of Immigrant Communities." *American Behavior Scientist* 47(12): 1551–1572.

Goode, Erich. 1999. "Sex With Informants as Deviant Behavior: An Account and Commentary." *Deviant Behavior* 20: 301–324.

——. 2002. "Sexual Involvement and Social Research in a Fat Civil Rights Organization." *Qualitative Sociology* 25 (4) (Winter): 501–534.

Gordon, David F. 1987. "Getting Close by Staying Distant: Fieldwork with Proselytizing Groups." *Qualitative Sociology* 10 (Fall): 267–287.

Gould, Emily. 2008. "Exposed." *New York Times Magazine.* May 25, p. 32ff.

Grady, John. 2007. "Advertising Images as Social Indicators: Depictions of Blacks in *LIFE* Magazine, 1936–2000." *Visual Studies* 22(3): 211–239.

Greenblat, Cathy S. 2003. "Tales of the Asilo." Paper presented to the International Visual Sociological Association meetings, Southampton, England. July.

——. 2004. *Alive with Alzheimer's.* Chicago and London: University of Chicago Press.

Greenspan, Henry. 1992. "Lives as Texts: Symptoms as Modes of Recounting in the Life Histories of Holocaust Survivors" pps. 145–64 in Storied Lives (George Rosenwald and Richard Ochberg, editors). New Haven and New York: Yale University Press.

Gubrium, Jaber F. 1975. *Living and Dying at Murray Manor.* New York: St. Martins.

Gubrium, Jaber F., and James A. Holstein. 1995. *The Active Interview.* Thousand Oaks, CA: Sage Publications.

———. 1997. *The New Language of Qualitative Method.* New York: Oxford University Press.

Gubrium, Jaber F., and James A. Holstein. 2002. "From the Individual Interview to the Interview Society." In *Handbook of Research Interviewing: Context and Method,* ed. Jaber F. Gubrium and James A. Holstein, 3–32. Thousand Oaks, CA: Sage Publications.

———. 2003. Postmodern Interviewing. Thousand Oaks, CA: Sage Publications.

Gusfield, Joseph R. 1976. "The Literary Rhetoric of Science: Comedy and Pathos in Drinking Driver Research." *American Sociological Review* 41: 16–34.

Hackney, Jennifer. 1996. "Stairway to Heaven: Religious Expressions in an Overeaters Anonymous Group." Paper presented to the American Sociological Association meeting, New York.

Halbert, Shawn C. 2003. "Rhythm and Reminiscence: Popular Music, Nostalgia, and the Storied Self." Senior thesis, University of Houston.

Hall, Lisa Cox. 2008. "Special Methodological Issues with Older Women in a Qualitative Breast Cancer Study." Paper presented to the 79th Annual Meeting of the Pacific Sociological Association, Portland, OR, April 10–13.

Harkess, Shirley, and Carol Warren. 1993. "The Social Relations of Intensive Interviewing: Constellations of Strangeness and Science." *Sociological Methods and Research* 21 (3): 317–339.

Harkness, Geoffrey. 2003. "Living on the Fringe: How Pawn Shops Keep Poor People Poor." Master's thesis, University of Kansas.

Harper, Douglas. 1982. *Good Company.* Chicago: University of Chicago Press.

———. 1992. *Working Knowledge: Skill and Community in a Small Shop.* Berkeley, CA: University of California Press.

———. 1994. "On the Authority of the Image: Visual Methods at the Crossroads." In *The Handbook of Qualitative Research,* ed. Norman K. Denzin and Yvonna S. Lincoln, 403–412. Thousand Oaks, CA: Sage Publications.

———. 2001. *Changing Works: Visions of a Lost Agriculture.* Chicago: University of Chicago Press.

———. 2002. "Reimagining Visual Methods: Galileo to Necromancer." In *Handbook of Qualitative Research,* 2nd ed., ed. Norman K. Denzin and Yvonna S. Lincoln, 717–732. Thousand Oaks, CA: Sage Publications.

———. 2005. "What's New Visually?" In *The SAGE Handbook of Qualitative Research,* ed. Norman K. Denzin and Yvonna S. Lincoln, 747–762. Thousand Oaks, CA: SAGE Publications.

Heap, Chad. 2003. "The City as a Sexual Laboratory: The Queer Heritage of the Chicago School." *Qualitative Sociology* 26 (Winter): 457–487.

Heffernan, Virginia. 2008. "Narrow Minded." *New York Times Magazine.* May 25, p. 16–17.

Hertz, Rosanna. 2006. "Stories as Evidence." *Qualitative Sociology* 29: 539–543.

Herzog, Hanna. 2005. "On Home Turf: Interview Location and Its Social Meaning." *Qualitative Sociology* 28 (1): 25–47.

Hessler, Richard M., Jane Downing, Cathleen Beltz, Angela Pelliccio, Mark Powell, and Whitley Vale. 2003. "Qualitative Research on Adolescent Risk Using E-Mail: A Methodological Assessment." *Qualitative Sociology* 26 (Spring): 111–124.

Hine, Christine M. 2000. *Virtual Ethnography.* London: Sage.

Hollander, Jocelyn A. 2004. "The Social Context of Focus Groups." *Journal of Contemporary Ethnography* 33 (5): 602–637.

Holman Jones, Stacey. 2005 "Autoethnography: Making the Personal Political" In *The SAGE Handbook of Qualitative Research,* ed. Norman K. Denzin and Yvonna S. Lincoln, 763–791. Thousand Oaks, CA: SAGE Publications.

Holstein, James A. 1987. "Mental Illness Assumptions in Civil Commitment Proceedings." *Journal of Contemporary Ethnography* 16: 147–175.

Holstein, James A., and Jaber F. Gubrium. 1995. *The Active Interview.* Thousand Oaks, CA: Sage Publications.

Hopper, Columbus B., and Johnny Moore. 1990. "Women in Outlaw Motorcycle Gangs." *Journal of Contemporary Ethnography* 18 (January): 363–387.

Humphreys, Laud. 1970. *Tea Room Trade: Impersonal Sex in Public Places.* Chicago: Aldine.

Hunt, Jennifer. 1984. "The Development of Rapport Through the Negotiation of Gender in Field Work Among Police." *Human Organization* 43: 283–296.

Indigenous Language Institute. 2001. Tribal Language Field Survey Project Reports. Unpublished reports of the Indigenous Language Institute, Santa Fe, New Mexico.

Irving, Leslie. 1999. *Codependent Forever More: The Invention of Self in a Twelve Step Group.* Chicago: University of Chicago Press.

Jack-Roller, The, and Jon Snodgrass. 1982. *The Jack-Roller at Seventy.* Lexington, MA: Lexington Books.

Jackson, Janet E. 1990. "I Am a Fieldnote: Fieldnotes as a Symbol of Professional Identity." In *Fieldnotes: The Making of Anthropology,* ed. R. Sanjek, 3–33. Ithaca, NY: Cornell University Press.

Johnson, John M. 1975. *Doing Field Research.* New York: Macmillan Publishing Co.

Johnson, John. 1983. "Trust and Personal Involvement in Fieldwork." In *Contemporary Field Research,* ed. R. M. Emerson, 203–215. Prospect Heights, IL: Waveland Press.

Johnson, Richard. 2002. "The Sale Barn." PhD diss., University of Kansas.

Jones, James H. 1993. *Bad Blood: The Tuskegee Syphilis Experiment.* New York: The Free Press.

Joos, Kristin E., and K. L. Broad. 2007. "Coming Out of the Family Closet: Stories of Adult Women with LGBTQ Parent(s)." *Qualitative Sociology* 30: 275–295.

Jules-Rosette, Bennetta. 1975. *Vision and Realities: Aspects of Ritual and Conversion in an African Church.* Ithaca, NY: Cornell University Press.

Karas, Jennifer, and Tracy Xavia Karner. 2005. "Understanding the Diabetic Body-Self." *Qualitative Health Research* 15(8): 1086–1104.

Karner, Tracy Xavia. 1991. "Ideology and Nationalism: The Finnish Move to Independence, 1809–1918." *Ethnic and Racial Studies* 14 (2): 152–169.

——. 1994. "Masculinity, Trauma, and Identity: Life Narratives of Vietnam Veterans with Post Traumatic Stress Disorder." PhD diss., University of Kansas.

——. 1995. "Medicalizing Masculinity: Post Traumatic Stress Disorder in Vietnam Veterans." *masculinities* 3 (4): 23–65.

——. 1998a. "Professional Caring: Homecare Workers as Fictive-Kin." *Journal of Aging Studies* 12 (1): 69–82.

——. 1998b. "Retelling Selves through Visual Narratives: The Reciprocity of Culture and Identity." In *Communication and Cognition*, ed. Michael S. Ball, 3 (2/3): 145–60.

——. 1999. "Demonstrated Lessons: Case Management Strategies for Serving Ethnically Diverse Families." *Geriatric Care Management Journal* 9 (2): 9–12.

——. 2001. "Caring for an Aging Society: Cohort Values and Eldercare Services." *Journal of Aging and Social Policy* 13 (1): 15–36.

——. 2008. "Changing Lens: An Autoethnographic Account of Seeing and Knowing." *Selection of Articles from the Second International Conference of Qualitative Research*, Guanajuato: University of Guanajuato, Mexico.

Karner, Tracy Xavia, and Donna Bobbit-Zeher. 2006. "Losing Selves: Dementia Care as Disruption and Transformation." *Symbolic Interaction* 28 (4): 549–570.

Karner, Tracy Xavia, and Lisa Cox Hall. 2002. "Successful Strategies for Serving Diverse Populations." In *A New Look at Community Respite Programs: Utilization, Satisfaction, and Development*, ed. R. Montgomery, 107–132. Binghamton, NY: Haworth Press.

Karner, Tracy Xavia, Rhonda Montgomery, Debra Dobbs, and Cara Wittmaier. 1998. "Increasing Staff Satisfaction: The Impact of Special Care Units and Family Involvement." *Journal of Gerontological Nursing* 24 (2): 39–44.

Karner, Tracy Xavia, and Carol A. B. Warren. 1995. "The Dangerous Listener: Unforeseen Perils in Intensive Interviewing." *The Clinical Sociology Review* 13: 80–105.

Katz, Jack. 1972. *Experimentation with Human Beings*. New York: Russell Sage.

——. 1999. *How Emotions Work*. Chicago: University of Chicago Press.

——. 2001. "From How to Why: On Luminous Description and Causal Inference in Ethnography, Part 1." *Ethnography* 2 (4): 443–473.

——. 2002. "From How to Why: On Luminous Description and Causal Inference in Ethnography, Part 2." *Ethnography* 3 (1): 63–90.

Kaul, Adam R. 2004. "At Work in the Field: Problems and Opportunities Associated with Employment During Fieldwork." *Anthropology Matters Journal* 6, 1–4.

Kemmis, Stephen, and Robin McTaggart. 2000. "Participatory Action Research." In *Handbook of Qualitative Research*, 2nd ed., ed. Norman K. Denzin and Yvonna S. Lincoln, 567–606. Thousand Oaks, CA: Sage Publications.

Kilbourne, Jean. 2000. *Can't Buy Me Love: How Advertising Changes the Way We Think and Feel*. Carmichael, CA: Touchstone Books.

Kivett, Doug, and Carol A. B. Warren. 2002. "Social Control in a Group Home for Delinquent Boys." *Journal of Contemporary Sociology* 31 (Summer): 3–32.

Kleinman, Sherryl, and Martha A. Copp. 1993. *Emotions and Fieldwork.* Thousand Oaks, CA: Sage Publications.

Kneeland, Timothy, and Carol A. B. Warren. 2008. *Pushbutton Psychiatry: A Cultural History of Electroshock in America.* Walnut Creek, CA: Left Coast Press.

Knowles, Caroline. 2006. "Seeing Race Through the Lens." *Ethnic and Racial Studies* 29 (3): 512–529.

Kondo, Dorrine K. 2001. "How the Problem of Crafting Selves Emerged." In *Contemporary Field Research,* 2nd ed., ed. Robert M. Emerson, 188–202. Prospect Heights, IL: Waveland Press.

Kosloski, Karl, Rhonda Montgomery, and Tracy Xavia Karner. 1999. "Differences in the Perceived Need for Assistive Services by Culturally Diverse Caregivers of Dementia Patients." *Journal of Applied Gerontology* (July): 239–256.

Krase, Jerry. 2002. "Park Slope, Brooklyn: In the Aftermath of the Destruction of the World Trade Center." Fall 2001 and Spring 2002 (Photoessay). http://www. brooklynsoc.org/WTC/KraseWTC/index.shtml.

——. 2004. "Visualizing Ethnic Vernacular Landscapes." In *Race and Ethnicity in New York City,* vol. 7, ed. J. Krase and R. Hutchison, 2–24 . Oxford, UK: Elsevier Ltd.

Krieger, Susan. 1983. *The Mirror Dance: Identity in a Women's Community.* Philadelphia: Temple University Press.

——. 1991. *Social Science and the Self: Personal Essays on an Art Form.* New Brunswick, NJ: Rutgers University Press.

Kuhn, Annette. 2007. "Photography and Cultural Memory: A Methodological Exploration" *Visual Studies,* 22(3): 283–292.

Kumin, Beatrice. 2007. *Expedition Brasilien.* Bern, Switzerland: Benteli Verlag.

Kusenbach, Margarethe. 2003. "Street-Phenomenology: The Go-Along as Ethnographic Research Tool." *Ethnography* 4 (3): 455–485.

Kvale, Steinar. 1996. *InterViews: An Introduction to Qualitative Research Interviewing.* Thousand Oaks, CA: Sage Publications.

Lembcke, Jerry. 2000. *The Spitting Image: Myth, Memory, and the Legacy of Vietnam.* New York: New York University Press.

Leo, Richard A. 1995. "Trial and Tribulations: Courts, Ethnography, and the Need for an Evidentiary Privilege for Academic Researchers." *The American Sociologist* 26: 113–134.

Leo, Richard A. 2001. "No Trials but Tribulations: Courts, Ethnography, and the Need for an Evidentiary Privilege for Academic Researchers." In *Contemporary Field Research,* 2nd ed., ed. Robert M. Emerson, 260–279. Prospect Heights, IL: Waveland Press.

Leopold, Robert. 2008. "Guide to Anthropological Fieldnotes and Manuscripts in Archival Repositories." www.nmnh.si.edu/naaa/other-archives.htm.

Levi, Ken. 1981. "Becoming a Hit Man: Neutralization in a Very Deviant Career." *Urban Life* 10 (April): 47–63.

Lewins, Ann, and Christina Silver. 2006. "Choosing a CAQDAS Package: A Working Paper." http://caqdas.soc.surrey.ac.uh/.

——. 2007. *Using Software for Qualitative Data Analysis: A Step-by-Step Guide.* London: Sage Publications.

Lidz, Charles W., Alan Meisel, Eviatar Zerubavel, Mary Carter, Regina M. Sestak, and Loren H. Roth. 1984. *Informed Consent: A Study of Decisionmaking in Psychiatry.* New York: The Guilford Press.

Liebow, Elliott. 1967. *Tally's Corner: A Study of Negro Streetcorner Men.* Boston: Little Brown.

——. 1993. *Tell Them Who I Am: The Lives of Homeless Women.* New York: Penguin.

Littrell, W. Boyd. 1979. *Bureaucratic Justice: Police, Prosecutors, and Plea Bargaining.* Beverly Hills, CA: Sage Publications.

Lofland, John. 1966. *Doomsday Cult.* Englewood Cliffs, NJ: Prentice-Hall.

——. 1970. "Interactionist Imagery and Analytic Interruptus." In *Human Nature and Collective Behavior: Papers in Honor of Herbert Blumer,* ed. T. Shibutani, 35–45. New Brunswick, NJ: Transaction Books.

Lofland, John, and Lyn Lofland. 1995. *Analyzing Social Settings: A Guide to Qualitative Observations and Analysis.* Belmont, CA: Wadsworth.

Lofland, Lyn. 1973. *A World of Strangers.* New York: Basic Books.

——. 1998. *The Public Realm.* New York: Aldine de Gruyter.

Loseke, Donileen. 1992. *The Battered Woman and Shelters.* Albany, NY: SUNY Press.

Lovejoy, Tracey and Nelle Steele. 2007. "Engaging our Audience through Photo Stories," pps. 295–313 in Visual Interventions: Applied Visual Anthropology, ed. Sarah Pink, New York: Berghahn Books.

Lyman, Karen. 1993. *Day In, Day Out with Alzheimer's.* Philadelphia: Temple University Press.

Maines, Douglas R. 1998. "Review of Fields of Play: Constructing an Academic Life." *Social Forces* 77 (1): 388–390.

Mann, Chris, and Fiona Stewart. 2002. "Internet Interviewing." In *Handbook of Interview Research,* ed. Jaber F. Gubrium and James A. Holstein, 603–628. Thousand Oaks, CA: Sage Publications.

Marcus, George E. 1986. "Ethnography in the Modern World System." In *Writing Culture: The Poetics and Politics of Ethnography,* ed. James Clifford and George E. Marcus, 165–193. Berkeley: University of California Press.

Margolis, Eric. 1988. "Mining Photographs: Unearthing the Meanings of Historical Photos." *Radical History Review* 40: 32–48.

——. 1994. "Video Ethnography." *Jump Cut* 39: 122–131.

——. 2000. "Class Pictures: Representations of Race, Gender, and Ability in a Century of School Photography." *Educational Policy Analysis Archives* 8 (31) online, *http://epaa.asu.edu/epaa/v8n31.*

Margolis, Eric. 1988. 2001. *The Hidden Curriculum in Higher Education.* New York: Routledge Falmer.

Markham, Annette N. 2005. "The Methods, Politics, and Ethics of Representation in Online Ethnography." In *The SAGE Handbook of Qualitative Research,* ed. Norman K. Denzin and Yvonna S. Lincoln, 793–819 . Thousand Oaks, CA: SAGE Publications.

Mauthner, Natasha S., and Andrea Doucet. 2003. "Reflexive Accounts and Accounts of Reflexivity in Qualitative Data Analysis." *Sociology* 37 (3): 413–431.

McCracken, Grant. 1988. *The Long Interview.* Thousand Oaks, CA: Sage Publications.

Mead, George H. 1934. *Mind, Self, and Society.* Chicago: University of Chicago Press.

Messinger, Sheldon L. and Carol A.B. Warren, "The Homosexual Self and the Organization of Experience" p 196–206 in *The Existential Self in Society* ed. Joseph A. Kotarba and Andrea Fontana, University of Chicago Press, 1984.

Milgram, Stanley. 1963. "Behavioral Study of Obedience." *Journal of Abnormal and Social Psychology* 67: 371–378.

Millard, Jennifer E., and Peter R. Grant. 2006. "The Stereotypes of Black and White Women in Fashion Magazine Photographs: The Pose of the Model and the Impression She Creates" *Sex Roles* 54: 659–673.

Miller, Gale, and James Holstein. 1996. *Dispute Domains and Welfare Claims.* Greenwich, CT: JAI Press.

Milligan, Megan. 2003. "The House Told Me: Historic Preservation and Dwelling as Social Actor." Paper presented at the Annual American Sociological Association meetings, Atlanta, GA. August.

Mitchell, Richard G., Jr. 2002. *Dancing at Armageddon: Survivalism and Chaos in Modern Times.* Chicago: University of Chicago Press.

Montgomery, Rhonda, Karl Kosloski, and Tracy Xavia Karner. 1996. "Integrating Support Services for Alzheimer's Families in Managed Care Systems." HRSA-Bureau of Primary Health Care.

Montgomery, Rhonda, Tracy Xavia Karner, and Karl Kosloski. 2003. "Analyzing the Success of a National Demonstration to Create State Responsibility for Long Term Care." *Journal of Aging and Social Policy* 14 (3–4): 119–139.

Montgomery, Rhonda, Tracy Xavia Karner, Karl Kosloski, and Jay Schaefer. 2002. "Initial Findings from the Evaluation of the Alzheimer's Disease Demonstration Grant to States Program." *Home Health Care Quarterly* 21 (3–4): 5–32. Reprinted in *A New Look at Community Respite Programs: Utilization, Satisfaction, and Development,* ed. R. Montgomery. Binghamton, NY: Haworth Press, 2002.

Moore, Ryan. 2007. "Friends Don't Let Friends Listen to Corporate Rock: Punk as a Field of Cultural Production." *Journal of Contemporary Ethnography* 36 (4): 438–474.

Morgan, David. 2002. "Focus Group Interviewing." In *Handbook of Interview Research,* ed. Jaber F. Gubrium and James A. Holstein, 141–159. Thousand Oaks, CA: Sage Publications.

Morse, Janice M. 2006. "The Politics of Evidence." In *Qualitative Inquiry and the Conservative Challenge*, ed. Norman K. Denzin and Michael D. Giardina, 79–92. Walnut Creek, CA: Left Coast Press.

Murray, P. 1997. "Using Virtual Focus Groups in Qualitative Health Research." *Qualitative Health Research* 7(4): 542–549.

Nairn, Karen, Jenny Munro, and Anne B. Smith. 2005. "A Counter-Narrative of a 'Failed' Interview." *Qualitative Research* 5 (2): 221–244.

Naples, Nancy A. 1996. "A Feminist Revisiting of the Insider/Outsider Debate: The 'Outsider Phenomenon' in Rural Iowa." *Qualitative Sociology* 19 (1): 83–106.

Narayan, Kirin, and Kenneth M. George. 2002. "Personal and Folk Narratives as Cultural Representations." In *Handbook of Research Interviewing: Context and Method*, ed. Jaber F. Gubrium and James A. Holstein, 815–832. Thousand Oaks, CA: Sage Publications.

Nee, Victor. 2004. "A Place for Hybrid Methodologies." In *Workshop on the Scientific Foundations of Qualitative Research*, ed. Charles C. Ragin, Joane Nagel, and Patricia White, 101–104. Arlington, VA: National Science Foundation.

Newton, Esther. 1972. *Mother Camp: Female Impersonators in America*. Englewood Cliffs, NJ: Prentice-Hall.

Noblit, George W., and Janie M. Burcart. 1975. "Ethics, Powerless Peoples, and Methodologies for the Study of Trouble." *Humboldt Journal of Social Relations* 2 (2): 20–25.

Nugent, Stephen, 2007. *Scoping the Amazon: Image, Icon, Ethnography*. Walnut Creek, CA: Left Coast Press.

Obbo, Christine. 1990. "Adventures With Fieldnotes." In *Fieldnotes: The Makings of Anthropology*, ed. Roger Sanjek, 290–302. Ithaca, NY: Cornell University Press.

O'Connell Davidson, Julia, and Derek Layder. 1994. *Methods, Sex and Madness*. London: Routledge.

Palmer, Vivian. 1928. *Field Studies in Sociology: A Student's Manual*. Chicago: University of Chicago Press.

Park, Julie, and A. Echo Zeanah. 2005. "An Evaluation of Voice Recognition Software for Use in Interview-Based Research: A Research Note." *Qualitative Research* 5 (2): 245–251.

Paterniti, Debora A. 2003. "Claiming an Identity in a Nursing Home." In *Ways of Aging*, ed. Jaber Gubrium and James Holstein, 58–74. Oxford: Blackwell Publishing.

Perks, Robert, and Alistair Thomson. 2004. *The Oral History Reader*. London and New York: Routledge.

Perrow, Charles. 2000. "An organizational analysis of organizational theory" *Contemporary Sociology*; Vol. 29, pp. 469–476.

Personal Narratives Group. 1989. *Interpreting Women's Lives: Feminist Theory and Personal Narratives*. Bloomington and Indianapolis: Indiana University Press.

Peshkin, Alan. 1984. "Odd Man Out: The Participant Observer in an Absolutist Setting." *Sociology of Education* 57: 254–264.

Peter, Lizette, 2003. *A Naturalistic Study of the Cherokee Language Immerson Preschool Project.* PhD diss., University of Kansas.

Pink, Sarah. 2006. *The Future of Visual Anthropology: Engaging the Senses.* Oxon, England: Routledge Press.

——. 2007. "Walking with Video." *Visual Studies* 22 (3): 240–252.

Platt, Jennifer. 2002. "The History of the Interview." In *Handbook of Interview Research,* ed. Jaber F. Gubrium and James A. Holstein, 33–54. Thousand Oaks, CA: Sage Publications.

Poland, Blake D. 2002. "Transcription Quality." In *Handbook of Interview Research,* ed. Jaber F. Gubrium and James A. Holstein, 629–650. Thousand Oaks, CA: Sage Publications.

Prosser, Jon. 1998. "The Status of Image Based Research." In *Image Based Research: A Sourcebook for Qualitative Researchers,* ed. Jon Prosser, 97–110. London: Falmer Press.

Prosser, Jon, and Dona Schwartz. 1998. "Photographs Within the Sociological Research Process." In *Image Based Research: A Sourcebook for Qualitative Researchers,* ed. Jon Prosser, 115–129. London: Falmer Press.

Punch, Maurice. 1994. "Politics and Ethics in Qualitative Research." In *The Handbook of Qualitative Research,* ed. Norman K. Denzin and Yvonna S. Lincoln, 83–97. Thousand Oaks, CA: Sage Publications.

Radley, Alan, and Diane Taylor. 2003. "Images of Recovery: A Photo-Elicitation Study on the Hospital Ward." *Qualitative Health Research* 13 (1): 77–99.

Rae, Ruth. 2003. "Visual Images of Meaning: Photographic Explorations of Homes and Gardens." Paper presented to the International Visual Sociological Association meetings, Southampton, England. July.

Ragin, Charles C., Joane Nagel, and Patricia White. 2004. *Workshop on the Scientific Foundations of Qualitative Research.* Arlington, VA: National Science Foundation.

Reinharz, Shulamit, and Susan E. Chase. 2002. "Interviewing Women." In *Handbook of Interview Research,* ed. Jaber F. Gubrium and James A. Holstein, 221–238. Thousand Oaks, CA: Sage Publications.

Reiss, Albert J. 1979. "Governmental Regulation of Scientific Inquiry: Some Paradoxical Consequences." In *Deviance and Decency: The Ethics of Research with Human Subjects,* ed. Carl B. Klockars and Finbarr W. O'Connor, 61–95. Beverly Hills, CA: Sage Publications.

Rhoads, Richard A. 2003. "Traversing the Great Divide: Writing the Self Into Qualitative Research and Narrative." In *Studies in Symbolic Interaction* 26, ed. Norman K. Denzin, 235–259. Oxford: JAI Press.

Rich, Michael and Jennifer Patashnick. 2002. "Narrative Research with Audiovisual Data: Video Intervention / Prevention Assessment (VIA) and NVivo," *International Journal of Social Research Methodology* 5(3): 245–261.

Richardson, Laurel. 1985. *The New Other Woman: Contemporary Single Women in Affairs with Married Men.* New York: Free Press.

——. 1990. *Writing Strategies: Reaching Diverse Audiences.* Newbury Park, CA: Sage Publications.

——. 1994. "Writing: A Method of Inquiry." In *Handbook of Qualitative Research*, ed. Norman K. Denzin and Yvonna S. Lincoln, 516–529. Thousand Oaks, CA: Sage Publications.

— —. 2007. *Last Writes: A Daybook for a Dying Friend.* Walnut Creek, CA: Left Coast Press.

Richardson, Laurel, and Elizabeth Adams St. Pierre. 2007. "Writing: A Method of Inquiry." In *The SAGE Handbook of Qualitative Research*, ed. Norman K. Denzin and Yvonna S. Lincoln, 959–978. Thousand Oaks, CA: SAGE Publications.

Riemer, Jeffrey W. 1979. *Hard Hats: The Work World of Construction Workers.* Beverly Hills: Sage Publications.

Riessman, Catherine K. 1992. "Making Sense of Marital Violence: One Woman's Narrative." In *Storied Lives*, ed. George Rosenwald and Richard Ochberg, 231–249. New Haven and New York: Yale University Press.

Riessman, Catherine Kohler. 2008. *Narrative Methods for the Human Sciences.* Thousand Oaks, CA: Sage Publications.

Robbins, Thomas, Dick Anthony, and Thomas E. Curtis. 1973. "The Limits of Symbolic Realism: Problems of Empathetic Field Observation in a Sectarian Context." *Journal for the Scientific Study of Religion* 12: 259–271.

Robinson, Christine. 2008. *The Web: Social Control in a Lesbian Community.* Lanham, MD: University Press of America.

Robson, Kate, and M. Robson. 1999. "Your Place or Mine? Ethics, the Researcher and the Internet." In *Ethical Dilemmas in Qualitative Research*, ed. T. Welland and L. Pugsley, 94–107. Aldershot: Ashgate.

Rochford, E. Burke. 1985. *Hare Krishna in America.* New Brunswick, NJ: Rutgers University Press.

Rogers-Dillon, Robin H. 2005. "Hierarchical Qualitative Research Teams: Refining the Methodology." *Qualitative Research* 5 (4): 437–454.

Rosenwald, George C., and Richard L. Ochberg. 1992. "Introduction: Life Stories, Cultural Politics, and Self Understanding." In *Storied Lives*, ed. George Rosenwald and Richard Ochberg, 1–18. New Haven and New York: Yale University Press.

Roth, Julius A. 1966. "Hired Hand Research." *The American Sociologist* 1: 190–196.

Rubin, Irene, and Herbert J. Rubin. 1995. *Qualitative Interviewing: The Art of Hearing Data.* Thousand Oaks, CA: Sage Publications.

——. 2004. *Qualitative Interviewing: The Art of Hearing Data.* Thousand Oaks, CA: Sage Publications.

Rubin, Lillian B. 1976. *Worlds of Pain: Life in the Working-Class Family.* New York: Basic Books.

Russell, Lisa. 2005. "It's a Question of Trust: Balancing the Relationship Between Students and Teachers in Ethnographic Fieldwork." *Qualitative Research* 5 (2): 181–199.

Sanchez-Jankowski, Martin. 1990. *Islands in the Street: Gangs in American Urban Society.* Berkeley: University of California Press.

Sanders, Clinton R. 1998. "Animal Passions: The Emotional Experience of Doing Ethnography in Animal-Human Interaction Settings." In *Doing Ethnographic Research: Fieldwork Settings*, ed. S. Grills, 184–198. Thousand Oaks, CA: Sage Publications.

——. 2003. "Actions Speak Louder Than Words: Close Relationships Between Humans and Nonhuman Animals." *Symbolic Interaction* 26 (3): 405–426.

Sanjek, Roger. 1990. "Fire, Loss, and the Sorcerer's Apprentice." In *Fieldnotes: The Makings of Anthropology*, ed. R. Sanjek, 34–44. Ithaca, NY: Cornell University Press.

Scarce, Rik. 1994. "(No) Trial (but) Tribulation: When Courts and Ethnography Conflict." *Journal of Contemporary Ethnography* 23: 123–149.

Shaw, Clifford R. 1966. *The Jack-Roller: A Delinquent Boy's Own Story*, 2nd ed. Chicago: University of Chicago Press.

Shields, Carolyn. 2003. "Giving Voice to Students: Using the Internet for Data Collection." *Qualitative Research* 3 (3): 397–414.

Shoemaker, Helen J. 1991. "Self-Construction in a Small Group Setting: Journal Narratives." *Small Group Research* 22 (3): 339–359.

Shuy, Roger. 2002. "In-Person Versus Telephone Interviewing." In *Handbook of Interview Research*, ed. Jaber F. Gubrium and James A. Holstein, 537–556. Thousand Oaks, CA: Sage Publications.

Simmel, Georg. 1950. *The Sociology of Georg Simmel*, ed. and trans. K. H. Wolff. New York: Free Press.

Sinding, Christina, and Jane Aronson. 2003. "Exposing Failures, Unsettling Accommodations: Tensions in Interview Practice." *Qualitative Research* 3 (1): 95–117.

Smith, Dorothy E. 1987. *The Everyday World as Problematic*. Toronto: University of Toronto Press.

Smith, Richard C. 2002. "Analytic Strategies for Oral History Interviews." In *Handbook of Research Interviewing: Context and Method*, ed. Jaber F. Gubrium and James A. Holstein, 711–732. Thousand Oaks, CA: Sage.

Smith, R. Tyson. 2008. "Pain in the Act: The Meanings of Pain Among Professional Wrestlers." *Qualitative Sociology* 31 (June): 129–148.

Sniezek, Tamara. 2002. "On Wedding and Becoming a Couple." Paper presented at a Conference on Fieldwork in Contemporary Society, UCLA, May 16–17.

Snow, A. Lynn., Tracy Xavia Karner, Mark E. Kunik, and Cornelia Beck. 2007. "Nursing Home Staff Explanatory Models of Pain for Persons with Severe Dementia." Presented at the Gerontological Society of America meetings, San Francisco, CA. , November.

Spradley, James P. 1979. *The Ethnographic Interview*. New York: Holt, Rinehart, and Winston.

Spradley, James P., and Brenda J. Mann. 1975. *The Cocktail Waitress: Woman's Work in a Man's World*. New York: Alfred A. Knopf.

Stacey, Judith. 1998. *Brave New Families: Stories of Domestic Upheaval in Late-Twentieth-Century America*. Berkeley: University of California Press.

Staggenborg, Suzanne. 1988. "'Hired Hand Research' Revisited." *The American Sociologist* 19 (3): 260–269.

Stewart, Kate, and Matthew Williams. 2005. "Researching Online Populations: The Use of Online Focus Groups for Social Research." *Qualitative Research* 5 (4): 395–416.

Sudnow, David. 1967. *Passing On.* Englewood Cliffs, NJ: Prentice-Hall.

Taylor, Stephen J. 1987. "Observing Abuse: Professional Ethics and Personal Morality in Field Research." *Qualitative Sociology* 10 (Fall): 288–302.

——. 1991. "'Leaving the Field' Research, Relationships, and Responsibilities." In *Experiencing Fieldwork: An Inside View of Qualitative Research*, ed. William B. Shaffir and Robert A. Stebbins, 238–247. Newbury Park, CA: Sage Publications.

Thomas, William I., and Florian Znaniecki. 1958. *The Polish Peasant in Europe and America (1918–1920).* New York: Dover Publications.

Thompson, Paul. 1988. *The Voice of the Past.* Oxford University Press.

Thorne, Barrie. 1971. "Resisting the Draft: An Ethnography of the Draft Resistance Movement." PhD diss., Brandeis Univ.

——. 1980. "'You Still Takin' Notes?' Fieldwork and Problems of Informed Consent." *Social Problems* 27: 284–297.

——. 1983. "Political Activist as Participant Observer: Conflicts of Commitment in a Study of the Draft Resistance Movement of the 1960s." In *Contemporary Field Research*, ed. Robert M. Emerson, 216–234. Prospect Heights, IL: Waveland Press.

Trousdale, William B. 2007. *Military High Schools in America.* Walnut Creek, CA: Left Coast Press.

Vail, D. Angus. 2001. "Researching from Afar: Distance, Ethnography, and Testing the Edge." *Journal of Contemporary Ethnography* 30 (6): 704–725.

——. 2002. "On Presenting the Tattooed Self." Paper presented at a Conference on Fieldwork in Contemporary Society, UCLA, May 16–17.

van der Kolk, Bessel A. 1988. "Trauma in Men: Effects on Family Life," pps. 170–87 in *Abuse and Victimization Across the Life Span* (Martha B. Straus, editor). Baltimore and London: Johns Hopkins University Press.

Van Maanen, John. 1983. "The Moral Fix: On the Ethics of Fieldwork." In *Contemporary Field Research*, ed. R. M. Emerson, 269–287. Boston: Little, Brown.

——. 1988. *Tales of the Field: On Writing Ethnography.* Chicago: University of Chicago Press.

Vaughan, Diane. 1990. *Uncoupling: Turning Points in Intimate Relationships.* New York: Vintage.

Venkatesh, Sudhir. 2006. *Off the Books: The Underground Economy of the Urban Poor.* Cambridge, MA: Harvard University Press.

——. 2008. *Gang Leader for a Day: A Rogue Sociologist Takes to the Streets.* New York, NY: Penguin Press.

Wacquant, Loic. 2002. "Scrutinizing the Street: Poverty, Morality, and the Pitfalls of Urban Ethnography." *The American Journal of Sociology* 107 (May): 1468–1532.

Wacquant, Loic. 2004. *Body and Soul: Notebooks of an Apprentice Boxer.* New York: Oxford University Press.

Wakeford, Nina, and Kris Cohen. 2003. "Photoblogging: Digital Photography and Sociology as Strange Chronicles." Paper presented to the International Visual Sociological Association meetings, Southampton, England. July.

Wang, Caroline, and Mary Ann Burris. 1994. "Empowerment Through Photovoice: Portraits of Participation." *Health Education Quarterly* 21 (2): 171–186.

Wang, Caroline, Mary Ann Burris, and Yanping P. Xiang. 1996. "Chinese Village Women as Visual Anthropologists: A Participatory Approach to Reaching Policymakers." *Social Science and Medicine* 42 (10): 1391–1400.

Warren, Carol A. B. 1972. *Identity and Community in the Gay World.* New York: Wiley-Interscience.

———. 1982. *The Court of Last Resort: Mental Illness and the Law.* Chicago: University of Chicago Press.

———. 1983. "The Politics of Trouble in an Adolescent Psychiatric Hospital." *Urban Life* 12: 327–348.

———. 1987. *Madwives: Schizophrenic Women in the 1950s.* Rutgers, NJ: Rutgers University Press.

———. 1996. "Older Women, Younger Men: Self and Stigma in Age-Discrepant Relationships." *Clinical Sociology Review* (Fall): 62–86.

———. 1998. "Aging and Identity in Premodern Times." *Research on Aging* 20 (January): 11–35.

———. 2000. "Writing the Other, Inscribing the Self." *Qualitative Sociology* 23: 183–199.

———. 2001. "Gender and Fieldwork Relations." In *Contemporary Field Research*, 2nd ed., ed. Robert M. Emerson, 203–223. Prospect Heights, IL: Waveland Press.

———. 2002. "Qualitative Interviewing." In *Handbook of Interview Research: Context and Method*, ed. Jaber F. Gubrium and James A. Holstein, 83–101. Thousand Oaks, CA: Sage Publications.

———. 2003. "Sex and Gender in the 1970s." *Qualitative Sociology* 26 (Winter): 499–513.

Warren, Carol A.B. , Tori Barnes-Brus, Heather Burgess, Lori Wiebold-Lippisch, with Jennifer Hackney, Geoffrey Harkness, Vickie Kennedy, Robert Dingwall, Paul C. Rosenblatt, Ann Ryen, and Roger Shuy, 2003. "After the Interview" *Qualitative Sociology* 26 (Spring): 93–110

Warren, Carol A. B., and Jennifer K. Hackney. 2000. *Gender Issues in Ethnography*, 2nd ed. Thousand Oaks, CA: Sage Publications.

Warren, Carol A. B., and Tracy X. Karner. 1990. "Permissions and the Social Context." *The American Sociologist* (Summer): 116–135.

Warren, Carol A. B., and Kristine N. Williams. 2008. "Interviewing Elderly Residents in Assisted Living." *Qualitative Sociology* 31: 407–424.

Watson, Cate. 2006. "Unreliable Narrators? 'Inconsistency' (and Some Consistency) in Interviews." *Qualitative Research* 6 (3): 367–384.

Wax, Rosalie H. 1979. "Gender and Age in Fieldwork and Fieldwork Education: No Good Thing Is Done by Any Man Alone." *Social Problems* 26: 509–522.

——. 1983. "The Ambiguities of Fieldwork." In *Contemporary Field Research*, ed. Robert M. Emerson, 191–202. Prospect Heights, IL: Waveland Press.

Weiss, Robert S. 1994. *Learning from Strangers: The Art and Method of Qualitative Interview Studies*. New York: Free Press.

Weitzman, Eben A. 2004. "Advancing the Scientific Basis of Qualitative Research." In *Workshop on the Scientific Foundations of Qualitative Research*, ed. Charles C. Ragin, Joane Nagel, and Patricia White, 145–147. Arlington, VA: National Science Foundation.

White, Shirley. 2003. *Participatory Video: Images That Transform and Empower*. Thousand Oaks, CA: Sage Publications.

Whyte, William F. 1943. *Street Corner Society*. Chicago: University of Chicago Press.

——. 1984. *Learning from the Field: A Guide from Experience*. Newbury Park, CA: Sage Publications.

——. 1992. "In Defense of Street Corner Society." *Journal of Contemporary Ethnography* 21: 5–68.

Williams, Kristine N., and Carol A. B. Warren. 2008. "Assisted Living and the Aging Trajectory." *Journal of Women and Aging* 20: 309–327

——. 2009. "Communication in Assisted Living." *Journal of Aging Studies* 23: 24–36.

Williams, Terry, Eloise Dunlap, Bruce D. Johnson, and Ansley Hamid. 1992. "Personal Safety in Dangerous Places." *Journal of Contemporary Ethnography* 21 (3) (Oct.): 343–374.

Wilson, Anita. 2007. "Impossible Images." Paper presented to the Third Annual Congress of Qualitative Inquiry, Urbana-Champaign, May 2–5.

Windance Twine, France. 2006. "Visual ethnography and racial theory: Family photographs as archives of interracial intimacies," *Ethnic and Racial Studies* Vol. 29 No. 3 May 2006 pp. 487–511

Winlow, Simon, Dick Hobbs, Stuart Lister, and Philip Hadfield. 2001. "Get Ready to Duck: Bouncers and the Realities of Ethnographic Research on Violent Groups." *British Journal of Criminology* 41: 536–548.

Wirth-Cauchon, Janet. 2000. *Women and Borderline Personality Disorder: Symptoms and Stories*. New Brunswick, NJ: Rutgers University Press.

Worth, Sol, and John Adair. 1972. *Through Navajo Eyes: Explorations in Film Communication and Anthropology*. Bloomington: Indiana University Press.

Wright, R. Dean. 2001. "Tramp Training: Constructing a Service Learning Program in Homeless Intervention." In *Applying Sociology: Making a Better World*, ed. William Du Bois and R. Dean Wright, 201–212. Needham Heights, MA: Allyn & Bacon.

Young, Pauline. 1935. *Interviewing in Social Work*. New York: McGraw-Hill.

Zafirau, Stephen. 2008. "Reputation Work in Selling Film and Television: Life in the Hollywood Talent Industry. *Qualitative Sociology* 31 (June): 99–127.

Zhan, Heying. 2000. "The Inverted Pyramid: Familial Eldercare in China." PhD diss., Univ. of Kansas.

Ziller, Robert C. 1990. *Photographing the Self: Methods for Personal Orientations.* Newbury Park, CA: Sage Publications.

Zink. 2003. http://www.ahrp.org/infomail/0303/09.php

Zinn, Maxine Baca. 1979. "Insider Field Research in Minority Communities." *Social Problems* 27 (2): 159–166.

Zola, Irving K. 1982. *Missing Pieces: A Chronicle of Living With Disability.* Philadelphia: Temple University Press.

Index

Abell, Jackie, 162
Abstract, in qualitative research paper, xiii, 260–261
Action research, 17–19
Adair, John, 196
Adams, Jane, 45
Adams, Laura L., 88, 89
Adler, Patricia A., 65, 68, 92, 97, 103, 104, 105, 154
Adler, Peter, 65, 68, 97, 103, 104, 105, 154
Advertisements, magazine, xiii, 30, 179–181, 185
    as data sources, 178–179
    nineteenth-century electrical, 235, 236
Affiliation, in qualitative research paper, 260
Agustin, Laura Maria, 17, 105
All-night adrenalin approach, 248, 253
Altheide, David L., 8
American Anthropological Association (AAA)
    ethical guidelines, 50
American Sociological Association (ASA)
    code of ethics, 33, 50
    complaint to, 34
Ammerman, Nancy T., 65
Analysis, qualitative, 215
    analytic description, 218–221
    connections, 238–240
    documents, 233–236
    field notes, 226–229, 230
    images, 236–237
    interpretation, 240–242
    interview transcripts, 229–233
    logistics of, 221
    open coding, 218–220

process, 216–218
research paper, 271, 273–274
software, types of, 222, 223, 224
technology of, 221–226
themes, 237–238
validation, 242–245
Anderson, Elijah, 10, 15, 86
Anderson, Nels, 108
Angrosino, Michael V., 8, 57, 66, 91, 105, 115, 244
Anorexia, 209
Anorexia nervosa, 209
Anthony, Dick, 98
Anthropology, 11, 12
    still photography, 187–188
Applied research, 16–17
Arendell, Terry, 142, 173
Arksey, Hilary, 128
Armstrong, David, 184
Aronson, Jane, 157, 165
Atkinson, Paul, 226
Atkinson, Robert, 29
Author's name, in qualitative research paper, 260
Autoethnography, 20–24

Bacon, Francis, 186
Bailey, Carol, 127, 128
Ball, Michael, 201
Banks, Marcus, 188, 203
Barber, Bernard, 39
Barnes, Vivienne, 258
Bateson, Gregory, 117, 187
Bay Area study, 138, 156, 174, 229, 230, 231

301

CPSIA information can be obtained at www.ICGtesting.com
Printed in the USA
BVOW050504260911

272057BV00003B/1/P